D1522285

LORD BUTE: ESSAYS IN RE-INTERPRETATION

LORD BUTE

Essays in Re-interpretation

EDITED BY KARL W. SCHWEIZER

LEICESTER UNIVERSITY PRESS
1988

First published in 1988 by Leicester University Press

Copyright © Leicester University Press 1988

Designed by Douglas Martin
Filmset in 10 on 12 point Baskerville No. 2
Printed and bound in Great Britain by Billing and Sons, Worcester

British Library Cataloguing in Publication Data

Lord Bute : essays in re-interpretation.
1. Bute, John Stuart, *Earl of* —
Biographies
I. Schweizer, Karl W.
941.07′3′0924   DA506.B/

ISBN 0-7185-1261-8

Frontispiece: John Stuart, 3rd earl of Bute
Painting by Sir Joshua Reynolds, (National Portrait Gallery)

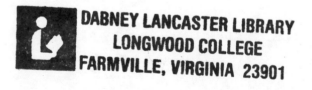

Contents

Acknowledgments

The editor's first obligation is to the Marquess of Bute for allowing ready and generous access to the manuscripts in his possession and for his interest and encouragement over a number of years. I would also like to pay tribute to the memory of Miss Catherine Armet, late archivist at Mount Stuart, whose kindness and generous help to scholars will long be remembered. Special thanks are due to my contributors for their hard work and co-operation and various friends and correspondents for assistance and advice. I am likewise indebted to the Social Sciences and Humanities Research Council of Canada, to Bishop's University for providing sabbatical leave which permitted the completion of this volume, and to the Department of History, Queen's University, Kingston, for providing a stimulating environment in which to work. I am grateful to Mrs K. Hermer and Mrs J. Doherty for their skilful typing. Last, but not least, I wish to thank my wife for her help at every stage.

KWS

Abbreviations

AECP	Archives du Ministère des Affaires Étrangères Correspondance Politique
AUL	Aberdeen University Library
BL	British Library
DNB	*Dictionary of National Biography*
DZA	Deutches Zentral Archiv Merseburg
EHR	*English Historical Review*
EUL	Edinburgh University Library
GUA	Glasgow University Archives
GUL	Glasgow University Library
Hist J	*Historical Journal*
NLS	National Library of Scotland
NRAS	National Register of Archives (Scotland)
PRO	Public Record Office
RCSL	Royal College of Surgeons' Library
SPF	State Papers Foreign
SRO	Scottish Record Office
TRHS	*Transactions of the Royal Historical Society*

Manuscript sources

Locations of manuscript sources mentioned in the volume are listed below to avoid the necessity of repeating them at each citation in the notes.

Atholl MSS	Blair Atholl Castle, Perthshire
Bedford MSS	Bedford Estate Office
Bute MSS	Mount Stuart, Isle of Bute
Caldwell MSS	National Library of Scotland, Edinburgh
Cardiff MSS	Mount Stuart, Isle of Bute
Chatsworth MSS (or Devonshire MSS)	Chatsworth House, Derbyshire
Clerk of Penicuik MSS	Scottish Record Office, Edinburgh
Dowdeswell MSS	William Clements Library, Ann Arbor, Michigan
Egerton MSS	British Library, London
Ellis Correspondence	Linnean Society, London
Fettercairn MSS	National Library of Scotland, Edinburgh
Fox MSS	British Library, London
Gordon MSS	Aberdeen University Library
Grantham MSS	Bedfordshire Record Office
Grenville MSS	Henry E. Huntington Library, San Marino, California
Hardwicke MSS	British Library, London
D.B. Horn MSS	Edinburgh University Library
Hume MSS	Royal Society of Edinburgh Library
Knight MSS	Aberdeen University Library
Liverpool MSS	British Library, London
Loudon MSS	Mount Stuart, Isle of Bute
Mackenzie of Delvine MSS	National Library of Scotland, Edinburgh
Minto MSS	National Library of Scotland, Edinburgh
Murray MSS	Glasgow University Library
Newcastle (Clumber) MSS	Nottingham University Library
Newcastle MSS	British Library, London
Newdegate MSS	Warwickshire Record Office

Portland MSS	Nottingham University Library
Rockingham MSS	Sheffield Public Library
Saltoun Papers	National Library of Scotland, Edinburgh
Scott of Harden MSS	Scottish Record Office, Edinburgh
Seafield MSS	Scottish Record Office, Edinburgh
David Skene MSS	Aberdeen University Library
Stanley MSS	Hampshire Record Office
Townshend MSS	William L. Clements Library, Ann Arbor, Michigan
John Walker MSS	Glasgow University Library
Wentworth Woodhouse MSS	Sheffield Public Library
Weston MSS	Lewis Walpole Library, Farmington, Connecticut

Notes on contributors

Peter Douglas Brown was educated at Harrow and Balliol College, Oxford, and is a Fellow of the Royal Historical Society. Author of *The Chathamites* (1967), *William Pitt: Earl of Chatham*(1978), and co-editor of *The Devonshire Diary* (1982), he is presently working on a new life of George Grenville.

John L. Bullion is Associate Professor of History at the University of Missouri, Columbia. He has published *George Grenville and the Genesis of the Stamp Act 1763–1765*, and numerous articles in scholarly journals including *Albion* and the *Mary and William Quarterly*.

Roger L. Emerson is Professor of History at the University of Western Ontario. Author of many articles, his most recent publications were on the Philosophical Society of Edinburgh, and he is currently preparing a book-length study of patronage in the Scottish universities from 1690 to 1800.

David Philip Miller is Senior Lecturer in History and Philosophy of Science at the University of New South Wales, Australia. A native of Yorkshire, he was trained at the universities of Manchester and Pennsylvania. He has written a number of papers on the social history of British science and is currently working on a history of the Royal Society of London and other institutions from 1750 to 1830.

Alexander Murdoch received his Ph.D. from the University of Edinburgh in 1978. He is currently based in Edinburgh as researcher for the North Carolina Colonial Records Project. He is the author of *The People Above: Politics and Administration in Mid-Eighteenth-Century Scotland* (1980) and has contributed essays and reviews to various scholarly publications.

Frank O'Gorman studied at the University of Leeds and Corpus Christi College, Cambridge, and is now Senior Lecturer in the Department of History, University of Manchester. His numerous publications include *The Whig Party and the French Revolution* (1967), *Edmund Burke: his Political Philosophy* (1973), *The Rise of Party in England* (1975), *The Emergence of the British Two-Party System 1760–1832* (1982) and the *Ideology of British Conservatism 1780–1980* (1986).

Marie Peters teaches at the University of Canterbury, New Zealand. She has published *Pitt and Popularity: The Patriot Minister and London Opinion during the Seven Years War* (1980), as well as articles on the ideological origins of English radicalism in the eighteenth century, and English political propaganda from 1755 to 1765.

Karl Schweizer received his Ph.D. at the University of Cambridge where he studied under the late Professor Sir Herbert Butterfield. He is co-editor of *The Devonshire Diary* (1982), and has published *François de Callières: The Art of Diplomacy* (1983), *England, Prussia and the Seven Years War* (1987), *Essays in European History in Honour of Ragnhild Hatton* (1985), contributions to *The Modern Encyclopedia of Russian and Soviet History* and many articles on British diplomatic themes.He is currently writing a biography of Count C. B. Münnich.

Richard Sher is a Ph.D. graduate of Yale University and presently Associate Dean at the New Jersey Institute of Technology. He is the author of *Church and University in the Scottish Enlightenment: The Moderate Literati of Edinburgh* (1985), contributor to *New Perspectives on the Politics and Culture of Early Modern Scotland*, and has published articles on the Scottish Enlightenment and political patronage in the eighteenth century.

Introduction
Lord Bute: interpreted in history
Karl W. Schweizer

Few British politicians have been so poorly served by historians as John Stuart, 3rd Earl of Bute (1713–92), Scottish representative peer, political adviser to George III, Secretary of State (1761–2) and Head of the Treasury from May 1762 to April 1763, the first Scotsman ever to attain this eminent position. Despite his importance, there are still no satisfactory biographies[1] (in marked contrast to such contemporaries as Newcastle, Pitt and, most recently, George Grenville),[2] no full-scale studies of his ministerial career,[3] nor have his intellectual contributions – as promoter of literature, science and the fine arts – received the appreciation they deserve.[4] Even the references to Bute in most general histories are invariably brief and usually hostile,[5] their authors obviously relying on contemporary views – the majority of which were not impartial assessments but rather reflections of political prejudice or personal dislike. As a result, Bute to this day remains a shadowy, ambiguous figure, his government dismissed as an unredeemed failure, himself remembered primarily as the most unpopular, indeed hated, minister of his time.

Certainly Bute's swift success, allied to his nationality – Scotsmen then being much disliked in England[6] – earned him relentless public abuse rarely matched for intensity:[7] popular hostility which had its political counterpart in his proscription (after 1763) by the nation's political leaders[8] and concurrent censure by opposition writers – polemicists like John Almon, Horace Walpole and Burke,[9] all united in bitter condemnation of Bute's alleged responsibility for the divisions in politics following the accession of George III. Thus in Almon's *History of the Late Minority*, and elsewhere in the opposition literature of the period,[10] Bute is depicted in uniformly negative, almost stereotyped terms, as an ambitious yet mediocre man, 'a favourite without talents',[11] whose position and status were solely dependent upon royal support, corruption[12] and the attempted expansion of monarchical power by unconstitutional means.[13] 'To the gratification of his [Bute's] ambitious views', wrote Almon

> is to be attributed all the divisions and distractions into which this unhappy kingdom has been plunged since his present Majesty's advent to

the Crown. ... He made certain of meeting with the cordial affection of the Jacobites; and ... he was certain of having the support of that other infatuated set of men called Tories; these with a great part of the Scots ... formed his troop. The slavish and arbitrary doctrines, which they had imbibed with their milk they hoped to see soon established as the law of the land.[14]

From these (and similar) allegations developed what John Brewer has called the 'Whig case' against Bute[15] – a comprehensive recital of Bute's supposed political sins – commonly invoked in the 1760s and 1770s to explain the nation's political difficulties and even the aggressive policies which culminated in the disastrous American war.[16] For the parliamentary opposition each crisis, each new setback represented evidence confirming their belief in a conspiracy, conceived by Bute and supported by the King, to create a system of government 'designed to vaunt prerogative, unbalance the constitution and subvert liberty in the Old World and the New'.[17] Only this system, it was maintained, could explain the political upheavals under George III and the autocratic treatment of the colonists that led to the loss of America.

Although, constitutionally speaking, the Whig critique added important dimensions to contemporary political debate,[18] on a rhetorical level it was also propaganda posing as historical truth: the portrayal of Bute's character and actions in the most iniquitous terms in order to justify and legitimize opposition to government and the Court.[19] As such, it represents a distorting mirror in which Bute's historical reputation came to be adversely and enduringly reflected. Indeed, how far 'Whig' polemics set the guidelines for historical scholarship of the time, is illustrated by the work of William Belsham, whose *Memoirs of the Reign of George III* (published in 1795) summarily dismisses Bute 'as a nobleman haughty in his manners, contracted in his capacity, despotic in his sentiments and mysterious in his conduct'.[20] Also, the fact that largely identical assessments are featured in the writings of many other contemporary or near contemporary historians, among them Charles Coote, Edward Holt and Robert Huish,[21] suggests their dependence on the same hostile tradition, established by Whig propagandists in the early decades of George III's rule but, as Herbert Butterfield has shown,[22] kept in currency well into the nineteenth century.

More impartial, typifying a distinctively moderate interpretation of political events, was John Adolphus who, in 1802, published his *History of England* extending from 1760 to 1783, a mainly sympathetic account of George III's earlier years, which set the tone for similar supportive or 'Tory' commentary throughout much of the Victorian period. Utilizing hitherto unprinted sources, including Bute's own papers, Adolphus agreed that Bute and the King had sought to alter the character of English government, but only, he argued, to free royal authority from aristocratic domination ('a plan well conceived and necessary') and only through the 'moderate assertion of royal prerogatives'[23] – through legitimate and entirely constitutional techniques. Adolphus's sympathy for Court policies also carried over to Bute, whom he absolves from all charges of conspiracy, subversion or corruption and credits with personal virtues – honesty, loyalty, dedication – but not the attributes that make an effective politician.

> He [Bute] was not connected either by blood or familiar intercourse with the leading families in England; he was not versed in the arts of popularity or used to the struggles of parliamentary opposition; and his manners were cold, reserved and unconciliating. Prejudices were easily exerted against him as a native of Scotland.[24]

Ultimately Bute's well-intentioned efforts proved unsuccessful, partly because of his political failings, but equally because of the selfish irresponsibility of the opposition organized against him. London in the 1760s had shown a 'factious and overbearing resistance to the exertions of government'; while the 'licentiousness of the press ... became unbounded and disgraceful to the nation'. This party spirit, so Adolphus argued, had produced highly biased and unfair judgments of Bute's administration, for 'such were the effects of a constant and acrimonious opposition that not only the prudence of his measures but the purity of his intentions were doubted'.[25] Obviously, the interpretation of the validity (or otherwise) of royal ideals and actions during the 1760s had direct ramifications for historical perceptions of Bute: the more George III's conduct appeared justified, even praiseworthy, the greater the likelihood that Bute would also be viewed in a favourable or at least more balanced perspective. Adolphus was the first to illustrate this tendency towards fairer treatment of both the King and Bute, sustained and refined by a succeeding generation of Tory writers and historians including Robert Bisset,[26] Nathaniel Wraxall who considered Bute 'irreproachable in private character' and 'by no means deficient in abilities',[27] Lord Brougham[28] and, above all, Lord Mahon, whose influential *History of England in the Eighteenth Century* appeared in 1844. The latter defended George III as the opponent of 'oligarchical abuses', and Bute, too, emerges in a rather positive light, praised for his intellect, moral principles and attention to duty – as a man of undoubted potential, 'unfairly maligned in a licentious press imbued with party prejudice and faction'.[29] Yet, like Adolphus and Bisset, Mahon feels that Bute lacked the political experience, not to mention temperament, to cope with the problems he had to face, especially in time of stress and war.

Despite such measured attempts at rehabilitation, personally and politically biased accounts of Bute, reminiscent of earlier opposition propaganda, still appeared at intervals. Restricted at first to relatively popular or anecdotal works, these attacks were intensified – made more persuasive and adaptable to serious scholarship – by the publication in the 1830s and 1840s (on a hitherto unprecedented scale) of political memoirs and letters such as the *Chatham Correspondence,* the *Rockingham Memoirs,* the *Grenville Correspondence* and the recollections of Horace Walpole.[30] This new material proved prejudicial to Bute, precisely because so much of it embodied the views of his enemies and competitors – hostile opinions once more becoming the basis for expositions of Bute as the enemy of liberty and the constitution.[31]

Contributing to this process were the changing conditions of British political life resulting from the triumph of parliamentary government. By the 1860s new constitutional conventions had developed and 'the spirit of the constitution' had changed in important ways. These developments in turn influenced English historiography at a critical point: they henceforth led historians to equate the political practices of the eighteenth century with those of the nineteenth – to imagine that, prior to 1760, there had flourished a regularly established system of 'responsible government' which Bute (through George III) had schemed to overthrow. This meant that once again historical judgment of Bute was defined by the attitude of political writers towards the constitutional controversies of George III's early reign – attitudes now reflecting not the standards of Bute's own day but those of a later and quite different age. It also meant that the old Whig charges against Bute – the party attacks revived in the newly published sources – were gradually transmuted into 'a form of academic orthodoxy'[32] in which fact and legend, myth and reality, became intricately conflated.

Thus in their characterization of Bute, nineteenth-century Whig historians were content for the most part with sweeping condemnations, making virtually no attempt to assess his career and significance on the basis of serious documentary research. Once more, therefore, Bute appeared in the role of villain – in politics depicted as a shallow intriguer, the evil influence behind the throne – in private life as a vain, affected man full of intellectual aspirations, grandiose ideas beyond his capacity to execute. 'He was a man of some literary and artistic taste', wrote W.E. Lecky, 'but of very limited talents, entirely inexperienced in public business, arrogant, reserved, and unpopular in his temper, and with extreme views of the legitimate powers of royalty'.[33] This

harsh verdict, set forth earlier by Thomas Erskine May,[34] received
strong endorsement from both J.W. Fortescue[35] and A. Ballantyne,[36] is
clearly expressed by George O. Trevelyan in his work on Charles
James Fox[37] and repeated by such Whig scholars as the Rev. William
Hunt,[38] J.R. Green[39] and Goldwin Smith.[40]

Indeed, for all its fallacies and contrivances, the Whig conception of
Bute was long to endure, whether in general histories, biographies of
leading political figures[41] or in specialist works on diplomatic and
colonial themes like those of Julian Corbett, Kate Hotblack and Richard
Lodge.[42]

Possibly the sole exception were the writings of A. von Ruville, a
German historian, who not only defended Bute's foreign – specifically
Prussian – policy on the basis of new archival evidence,[43] but, for the
first time, advanced the opinion that Bute was a diligent and, within
limits, able minister whose dedicated commitment to British national
interests had been unduly ignored. Unfortunately, von Ruville's
immediate impact on the historical community was negligible: his
conclusions went generally unrecognized by contemporaries and were
incorporated into the mainstream of scholarship only at a later date.

It was above all with the advances of the Namier school during the
1940s and 1950s that the grosser distortions of Whig historiography
were eradicated by new scholarly standards and a revised interpretation of Georgian politics, a counter system to that of May, Lecky and
others, firmly established. Herbert Butterfield's valuable survey, *George
III and the Historians*, makes it unnecessary to elaborate on this transformation except to note that much of the Namierite research did not
centre on Bute directly; neither did it modify the by then conventionally negative image of Bute in important respects. Certainly in Namier's
England in the Age of the American Revolution the most melodramatic
feature of the Whig tradition regarding Bute – his representation as the
aspiring agent of royal absolutism – is effectively swept away. Yet, the
equally damaging charges of incompetence, ignorance and failure,
reiterated by Whig partisans from John Almon to Lecky and Hunt,
were accepted without question. It was Namier, in fact (evidently
building on Lord Shelburne, a notoriously biased source), who represented what has become the conventional picture of Bute: an
honourable but timorous, unimaginative man, well educated yet hope-
lessly deficient in political abilities and sense: totally 'unfit for a place of
responsibility', to quote Namier himself.[44]

Can such judgment be sustained? No doubt a major contribution of
the Namier school to English political history has been the massiveness
of its research: detailed and penetrative, but preoccupied essentially

(too much so according to some critics)[45] with structural analysis and collective biography to the neglect of statesmanship, Cabinet politics, and political/ideological controversy – all areas in which Bute was active or influential. This has led to an underestimation of Bute's role in national affairs and consequently has fostered judgments less favourable than a more comprehensive re-evaluation in a wider context would suggest.

Illuminating here is the field of foreign policy – one of the leading topics of political activity and debate at the time – yet an area the Namierites, engrossed by factional intrigues, have seriously ignored.[46] Though diplomatic history, in general, has proved academically unfashionable for many years, British scholarship since the 1960s has experienced a steady revival of interest in eighteenth-century diplomacy, with studies illuminating the complex factors determining policy decisions,[47] the military/naval dimensions of diplomatic action,[48] as well as the contributions of diplomats and ministers,[49] Bute included. From this work it seems clear that, contrary to common belief, Bute was a conscientious,[50] talented (if not inspired) Secretary of State quite capable of pursuing coherent policies with intelligence and resolution.[51]

Not a politician by nature or choice (only out of duty to the king),[52] Bute rapidly gained in self-confidence once in office, winning both the regard and respect of his subordinates, especially the veteran Under-Secretary Edward Weston,[53] with whose collaboration he greatly increased the operational efficiency of the Northern Department.[54] Moreover, Bute made a good impression on the foreign representatives in London (usually shrewd and well informed), as industrious, perceptive and competent (his austere manner notwithstanding)[55] – qualities considerably higher than his historical reputation suggests.[56] This conclusion is reinforced by the editor's essay in this volume re-examining the crucial peace negotiations of 1761, where the Cabinet primacy traditionally ascribed to Pitt appears unfounded, while Bute's overall importance and political effectiveness are correspondingly enhanced. These findings serve to underline a current revisionist trend, one that acknowledges Pitt's leadership abilities but questions his alleged supreme direction of the war effort, predominance over vital government departments and putative domination of his ministerial colleagues – the 'heroic' view of Pitt given classic expression in the writings of Julian Corbett and Basil Williams.[57] A number of works over the last three decades – particularly the recent monograph on the Seven Years war by Richard Middleton[58] – have gradually dispelled the myth of Pitt 'the absolute war minister' and, at last, given hitherto lesser figures – Newcastle, Ligonier and Anson – their historical due.

Bute also has benefited from this revisionist trend to the extent that his diplomatic programme – especially the policy towards Russia and Prussia (Britain's wartime ally) between 1761 and 1763 – has received sympathetic reinterpretation. Expanding upon the earlier writings of von Ruville, Walter Dorn and Frank Spencer,[59] a series of recent studies have not only vindicated Bute from the charges of treachery which a generation of German historians (misled by the biased memoirs of Frederick the Great) had levelled against him;[60] more importantly, they have reassessed Bute's diplomacy within a broader interpretative framework: with reference to inherited problems, the interplay of domestic and external pressures, the exigencies of intra-alliance politics and in relation to new configurations throughout the international system as a whole towards the close of the Seven Years War and after. This research, combining evidence from European and British archives, has led scholars to conclude that the negative aura surrounding Bute's foreign policy owed less to faulty statesmanship than to domestic difficulties, fiscal restraints, new international tensions, alliance complications, and above all, the gradual eastward shift of the European system which seriously diminished Britain's continental influence, thereby precluding any innovative or brilliant diplomatic strokes.[61] Seen in this light, Bute's diplomacy – despite some misjudgments – was fundamentally effective in difficult circumstances: adapted to domestic political requirements, economic capability, and international dynamics, its overall objectives were achieved. During his brief career, it has been pointed out, Bute was faced with formidable tasks: the conduct and winding-up of world-wide military operations, the settling of relations with Prussia, the consolidation of Britain's imperial achievements and at least three parliamentary crises; however, he prevailed, resigning in 1763 certain of having 'served my loved sovereign to the best of my power and promoted as far as I was able the glory, honour and happiness of my country.'[62] Indeed, many historians would now agree that what Bute himself considered his major achievement – the Peace of Paris with France – was in fact an honourable, advantageous settlement, rich compensation for Britain's global victories and eloquent testimony to Bute's concern for British imperial security.[63] There is, furthermore, increasing recognition that on many issues, diplomatic questions in particular, Bute merely brought to successful completion policies initiated earlier, between 1758 and 1760, by the Newcastle–Pitt coalition. This indicates that the contrasts between Bute's administration and that of his immediate predecessors, certainly in foreign affairs, were less drastic than usually assumed – an important conclusion with wide implications for Bute's historical status.

Clearly, the avenues opened by British diplomatic historians demonstrate the need for an up-to-date reassessment of Bute, incorporating current scholarship as well as giving special emphasis to those aspects of his role in government and society neglected in the past or still subject to controversy and debate. The essays collected in this volume are intended as a contribution to this reassessment. They each contrast in scale and approach, but they have as their common focus the aim to place Bute in better historical perspective by dispelling lingering distortions or myths and by re-evaluating his diverse achievements on the basis of fresh reflection and research.

Supporting evidence of Bute's political capacity is provided in the first two chapters. With impressive documentation, Dr Bullion demonstrates how astutely Bute managed to harmonize diplomatic and fiscal goals with military provisions for American post-war security in the deliberations preceding the Peace of Paris. He also shows that Bute's cogent arguments in favour of a speedy peace (although vigorously resisted in some quarters) convinced the vast majority of Parliament and key policy-makers during the 1760s, thus giving Bute intellectual influence extending beyond his ministry, ultimately even to men who were his political opponents and their colonial policies as well. Dr Bullion's generally positive verdict on Bute's statesmanship is endorsed in Chapter 2, which argues that Bute more than Pitt was the decisive force in the 1761 negotiations with France, and was indeed able to devise and implement a coherent political strategy.

Long the corner-stone of Whig polemics, the 'myth' of Bute's secret influence is examined and its long-term impact assessed by Dr O'Gorman in Chapter 3, while Chapter 4 exonerates Bute from the still prevailing indictment, dating back to John Almon and Walpole, of having attempted to destroy Pitt's political reputation through violent press attacks following the latter's resignation in October 1761.

Usefully amplifying John Brewer's work on ideology and political culture, Marie Peters' contribution enhances our understanding of Bute's importance for eighteenth-century constitutional development by showing how his ascendancy precipitated a public debate about the foundations of political power, the factors that legitimized the enjoyment of power in high office, which would persist throughout much of George III's reign. The evidence she presents not only illuminates the function of the popular press – the pamphlets, newspapers and broadsheets – in the articulation of constitutional ideas, but demonstrates how the debate of 1761–2 produced substantial confrontation between competing constitutional theories, the so-called 'royalist' and populist views, thereby reviving party contention and ideologically strengthening the arguments underlying the Whig opposition to Bute.

Bute's firm reliance on the power of the Crown, so widely noticed by contemporaries, is closely illustrated in Alexander Murdoch's essay on the management of Scotland after the death of Argyll in April 1761. While acknowledging Bute's responsible concern for vital aspects of Scottish national life, and for the Argathelian interest which he inherited, Dr Murdoch questions Bute's method of governing Scotland via a separate minister, accountable to the King alone, when so much Scottish patronage passed through offices which the Scottish minister did not control. The minister in question was James Stuart Mackenzie, Bute's younger brother, an honest, hard-working but insensitive man, wholly unsuited for a political post requiring diplomacy and tact. In Dr Murdoch's opinion, Mackenzie's difficult personality and ambiguous position caused no problem while Bute was in office, but swiftly led to policy disputes under George Grenville who, resenting Mackenzie's initiatives in Scottish affairs and close relationship with the King, compelled his resignation in 1765.

Besides his part in public affairs, Bute also had a key role in the intellectual life of his day, a subject explored in the next three chapters. Since a major distinguishing characteristic of the Scottish Enlightenment was its basis in the academic institutions of the country, Bute's discriminating support of higher education in Scotland, as Dr Emerson demonstrates, represented a notable contribution to Scottish culture and was of vital importance in making Glasgow, and especially Edinburgh, leading centres of cultural innovation. Significant also in the advancement of learning was the patronage of literature and the arts by enlightened men of wealth, an enterprise in which Bute proved outstandingly active, his beneficiaries including (among others) Samuel Johnson, Thomas Sheridan, Allan Ramsay the painter, Robert Adam the architect, Robertson the historian and the playwright John Home. Here, Dr Sher's detailed case study of Bute's relationship with Home explores new ground by discussing the complex factors, political, personal, ideological, in addition to the criterion of merit, which influenced Bute's patronage decisions, yielding insights relevant to the wider phenomenon of literary patronage at this time. Dr Miller's paper restores Bute to his rightful place in the history of science, both as gifted botanical scholar and collector and as patron of eminent scientists instrumental in enlarging the quality of botanical teaching and research. The final essay, by Mr Peter D. Brown, investigating Bute's varied activities in retirement, fills some crucial gaps and greatly enhances our knowledge of what has been probably the most obscure phase of the Earl's life.

Perhaps the most important conclusion to emerge from these essays
is that Bute's abilities, influence and, hence, intrinsic historical importance, were greater than scholars, contemporary and of later ages,
affected by partisan judgments, have realized. Admittedly, Bute does
not rank as a giant of British statesmanship nor (unlike Pitt) was he a
natural politician, being temperamentally ill suited to the rigours of a
political career. Also, as royal favourite, without established political
connections or pedigree, Bute was anathema to the Whig political elite,
which created misunderstandings and uncertainties greatly inimical to
political progress and success. A shy, withdrawn man, Bute entered
public office out of duty, not out of ambition, and yet, once committed, he proved competent and conscientious in adverse conditions:
his political decisions were often sound, though regarded with scepticism or fear,[64] his contributions to British foreign and imperial policy,
in a highly critical phase, were significant, while his patronage of
artistic, literary and academic merit was an enduring achievement,
according to Dr Emerson, possibly his most important legacy.

NOTES

1. Two biographical accounts exist: J.
Lovat-Fraser, *John Stuart, Earl of Bute*
(1912), a lively but cursory and
undocumented introduction; and the
lightweight sketch by Alice Coats, *Lord
Bute: An Illustrated Life* (1975). These
should be supplemented by the entry
on Bute in the *DNB* and the perceptive
contribution by John Brewer in
Herbert van Thal (ed.), *The Prime
Ministers* (1974), 105–13. Useful
information on family matters may be
found in E. Stuart Wortley (ed.), *A
Prime Minister and his Son. From the
Correspondence of the 3rd Earl of Bute and
of the Lt. General the Hon. Sir Charles
Stuart* (1925). Vital also are Romney
Sedgwick, *Letters from George III to Lord
Bute 1756–66* (1939), the introduction
of which discusses the relationship
between the King and Bute; James L.
McKelvey, *George III and Lord Bute: The
Leicester House Years* (Durham,
NC, 1973).
2. See the following recent studies: Peter
D. Brown, *William Pitt, Earl of
Chatham: The Great Commoner* (1978);

Reed Browning, *The Duke of Newcastle*
(New Haven, CT, 1975); Phillip
Lawson, *George Grenville: A Political Life*
(1985).
3. Different aspects of his political career
have been examined in Sir Lewis
Namier, *England in the Age of the
American Revolution* (2nd edn, 1963);
John Brewer, *Party Ideology and Popular
Politics at the accession of George III*
(1976); *idem*, 'The misfortunes of Lord
Bute: a case study in eighteenth
century political argument and public
opinion', *Historical Journal*, XVI (1973),
113–43; *idem*, 'The faces of Lord Bute:
a visual contribution to Anglo-
American political ideology',
Perspectives in American History, VI
(1972), 95–116; Richard Pares, *George
III and the Politicians* (1953), ch. IV;
Marie Peters, *Pitt and Popularity: The
Patriot Minister and London Opinion during
the Seven Years War* (1980), chs. VII and
VIII; John Bullion, *A Great and
Necessary Measure: George Grenville and
the genesis of the Stamp Act 1763–1765*
(Columbia, SC, 1982), chs. I and II.

For Bute's diplomatic activities see the sources cited in n.60 below.

4. A beginning, no more, has been made in Coats, *op. cit.*, 37–47, and in the articles by Jeremy Cater, 'The making of Principal Robertson in 1762: politics and the University of Edinburgh in the second half of the eighteenth century', *Scottish Historical Rev.*, XLIX (1970), 60–84; and James L. McKelvey, 'William Robertson and Lord Bute', *Studies in Scottish Literature*, VI no. 4 (April 1969), 238–47.

5. J. Steven Watson, *The Reign of George III, 1760–1815* (1960), 69–72, 79–82; R.K. Webb, *Modern England: From the 18th Century to the Present* (1968), 73–6; William Willcox and Walter Arnstein, *The Age of Aristocracy* (Toronto, 1983), 134–6, 140–2.

6. On anti-Scottish feeling in English society during the eighteenth century see Brewer, 'The misfortunes of Lord Bute', 19–22; Karl W. Schweizer, 'Lord Bute and anti-Scottish feeling in 18th century English political propaganda', *Proceedings of the Eighth and Ninth Colloquia on Scottish Studies*, ed. Alexander Brodie (Guelph, Ont., 1974), 23–33; Robert Rea, *The English Press in Politics, 1760–1774* (Lincoln, Nebr., 1963), 25–6; N.T. Phillipson and R. Mitchison (eds), *Scotland in the Age of Improvement* (1970), 238–40.

7. For detailed accounts see Brewer, 'The misfortunes of Lord Bute', 3–22; Peters, *Pitt and Popularity*, 241–64. Dorothy George, *English Political Caricature to 1792: A Study of Opinion and Propaganda* (1959), 119–22; 133–8; Frederick Stephens, *Catalogue of Prints and Drawings in the British Museum* (1883), IV, lxxii–lxxx.

8. Brewer, *Party Ideology and Popular Politics*, 83–8; Ninetta S. Jucker (ed.), *The Jenkinson Papers 1760–1766* (1949), 393–400; Fitzmaurice, *Life of Shelburne* (2nd edn, 1912), I, 202–4. Cf. Cumberland to Newcastle, July 1765, BL Add. MSS 32968, f. 381; Newcastle to Portland, 1 July 1765, BL Add. MSS 32967, f. 187; Rockingham to Scarbrough, 20 Nov. 1766,

Rockingham MSS, 1–703; Rockingham to Dowdeswell, 9 Sept. 1767, Rockingham MSS, 1–857; Newcastle to Lord Frederick Cavendish, 25 Sept. 1767, BL Add. MSS 32985, f. 215.

9. John Almon, *The History of the Late Minority. Exhibiting the Conduct, Principles and Views of that Party during the Years 1762, 1763, 1764 and 1765* (1766); idem, *Memoirs of John Almon: Bookseller of Piccadilly* (1790); idem, *Biographical Literary and Political Anecdotes, of Several of the Most Eminent Persons of the Present Age* (1797), I; Horace Walpole, *Memoirs of the Reign of King George the Third*, ed. Denis Le Marchant (1845), I; Edmund Burke, *Thoughts on the Cause of the Present Discontents* (1770).

10. Cf. John Almon, *A Review of Lord Bute's Administration* (1763); idem, *A Letter from a Member of the Opposition to Lord Bute* (1763); idem, *Le Montagnard Parvenu; or the New Highland Adventurer in England* (1763); idem, *The Favourite: with a Dedication to my Lord Bute* (1765); John Butler, *An Address to the Cocoa Tree. From a Whig* (1762); [Kearsley], *Political Disquisitions Proper for Public Consideration in the Present State of Affairs* (1763); idem, *The Principles of the late changes impartially examined* (1766); idem, *The Political Register* (1769); idem, *A Letter to Lord Bute* (1771).

11. Walpole, *op. cit.*, I, 5.

12. Almon, *Biographical, Literary and Political Anecdotes*, II, 8.

13. Cf. Almon, *A Review of Lord Bute's Administration*, 76; idem, *Observations on Public Liberty* (1769), 15–16; idem, *A Letter from a Member of the Opposition to Lord Bute*, 13–17, 35–8.

14. Almon, *History of the Late Minority*, 10–27.

15. Brewer, 'The misfortunes of Bute', 23–43.

16. 'It must not be forgot', wrote Almon, 'that the Earl of Bute's system of government, which had been continued by other hands, and although it has sometimes been interrupted, yet it has always revived, has been the true source and cause of

all the disturbances at home, and disgraces abroad, which have distinguished the present reign' (*Biographical, Literary and Political Anecdotes*, I, 3–4). Cf. [Charles Lloyd], *A Critical Review of the New Administration* (1765), 19–25; *idem, The Political Detection; or the Treachery and Tyranny of Administration, Both at Home and Abroad, Displayed in a Series of Letters* (1770), 68–9; *idem, The Phaenomenon; or Northern Comet; Proving that all the evils and Misfortunes that have befallen this Kingdom from the close of the last glorious war to the present ruinous and disgraceful period originated in one sole individual and identical person* (1780).

17. Brewer, 'The faces of Lord Bute', 98.

18. Particularly by clarifying and redefining vital constitutional conventions such as the notion of 'ministerial responsibility'. This has been discussed at length in Brewer, *Party Ideology and Popular Politics*, ch. 7. See also the observations in Richard Pares, *King George III and the Politicians* (1953), 93–4, 131–40; and Herbert Butterfield, 'Some reflections on the early years of George III's reign', *J. British Studies*, IV, 2 (1965), 78–101.

19. This was recognized by some government apologists at the time: see *London Magazine*, XXXII (1763), 24–6; *A Letter to a Noble Member of the Club in Albemarle Street from John Wilkes, at Paris* (1764); *A Letter from a Gentleman in Town to his friend in the Country occasioned by a late Resignation* (1763), 6–9. 'Will those noble Dukes', asked one author, 'deny that they ever tried to represent the influence of Lord Bute as dangerous to the public safety with every circumstance of exaggeration which their Party have been able to invent?' (*The Anatomy of a Late Negotiation* (1763), 14). Cf. H.T. Dickinson, *Liberty and Property: Political Ideology in Eighteenth-Century Britain* (1977), 206; Frank O'Gorman, *The Rise of Party in England: The Rockingham Whigs 1760–82* (1975), ch. I.

20. William Belsham, *Memoirs of the Reign of George III to the Session of Parliament ending A.D. 1793* (1795), I, 7.

21. Charles Coote, *History of England* (1802); Edward Holt, *The Public and Domestic Life of His Late Most Gracious Majesty, George the Third* (1820); Robert Huish, *Memoirs of the Reign of George the Third* (1821).

22. Herbert Butterfield, *George III and the Historians* (1957), 69–75.

23. John Adolphus, *History of England from the Accession of George the Third to the Conclusion of Peace in the Year One Thousand Seven Hundred and Eighty Three* (1802), I, 14–15.

24. *Ibid.*, I, 15.

25. *Ibid.*, I, 127–8, 131, 360–1.

26. Robert Bissett, *The History of the Reign of George III to the Termination of the Late War* (1803), I, 258: 'It would, perhaps, be difficult to show that there was any other statesman at that time but Mr. Pitt (except Mr. Fox was a supporter of the existing administration) in point of genius much elevated above Lord Bute.'

27. Sir Nathaniel Wraxall, *Historical Memoirs of My Own Time* (1815), 321–2.

28. Lord Brougham, *Historical Sketches of Statesmen who Flourished in the Time of George III* (1855), I.

29. Lord Mahon, *History of England from the Peace of Utrecht to the Peace of Versailles* (1844), IV, 312–16.

30. W. Stanhope and J.H. Pringle (eds), *The Correspondence of William Pitt Earl of Chatham* (4 vols, 1838–40); Albemarle, *Memoirs of the Marquis of Rockingham and his Friends* (2 vols, 1852); Lord John Russell (ed.), *The Correspondence of John, Fourth Duke of Bedford* (3 vols, 1842–6).

31. 'It must I think be admitted that Lord Bute was the immediate instrument, whatever might be the remote causes, of bringing the constitution of this Country into great jeopardy.' R.J. Phillimore (ed.), *Memoirs and Correspondence of George, Lord Lyttleton 1734–1773* (1845), I, 629. Cf. Butterfield, *George III and the Historians*, 97–107.

32. Butterfield, *ibid.*, 151.

33. W.E.H. Lecky, *A History of England in the Eighteenth Century* (1883), III, 12.

34. Thomas Erskine May, *Constitutional History* (1861).
35. J.W. Fortescue, *A History of the British Army* (2nd edn, 1910), III, 544.
36. A. Ballantyne, *Lord Cartaret: A Political Biography* (1887), 355–6.
37. George O. Trevelyan, *The Early History of Charles James Fox* (1880), 95–8.
38. W. Hunt, *The Political History of England* (1905), X, 5–6: 'He [Bute] was a fine showy man, vain of his handsome person, theatrical in his manners, pompous, slow and sententious in his speech ... He had literary and scientific tastes and a good deal of superficial knowledge. His abilities were small.'
39. J.R. Green, *A Short History of the English People* (1903), IV, 1671–2.
40. Goldwin Smith, *The United Kingdom: A Political History* (1890), 198.
41. Cf. Basil Williams, *The Life of William Pitt, Earl of Chatham* (2 vols, 1913); P.C. Yorke, *The Life and Correspondence of Philip Yorke, Earl of Hardwicke* (3 vols, 1913); Lord Fitzmaurice, *Life of William, Earl of Shelburne* (2nd edn, 2 vols, 1912); F. Harrison, *Chatham* (1905); W. Riker, *Henry Fox, First Lord Holland* (2 vols, 1911); W.D. Green, *William Pitt, Earl of Chatham* (1900), 164.
42. Richard Lodge, *Great Britain and Prussia in the Eighteenth Century* (1923); Julian Corbett, *England in the Seven Years' War* (2 vols, 1918); Kate Hotblack, *Chatham's Colonial Policy* (1917).
43. Albert von Ruville, *Die Auflösung des preussisch-englischen Bündnisses vom Jahre 1762* (Berlin, 1892); cf. *idem*, *William Pitt und Graf Bute* (Berlin, 1895).
44. Sir Lewis Namier, *England in the Age of the American Revolution* (2nd edn, 1963), 134. See also J. Plumb, *Chatham* (1965), 82–3; P.J. White, *A short History of England* (1967), 73; and J. Brooke, *King George III* (1972), 47–8, for essentially similar judgments.
45. Butterfield, *George III and the Historians*, 208–15; cf. H.T. Dickinson, 'Party, principle and public opinion in eighteenth century politics', *History*, VI (1976), 231–7. H. Mansfield, 'Sir

Lewis Namier again considered', *J. British Studies*, III, no. 2 (1964), 109–19.
46. As Hamish Scott, 'British foreign policy in the age of the American Revolution', *International History Rev.*, VI (1984), 114, has rightly observed: 'The Namierite preoccupation with political intrigue led to the neglect of larger questions of policy, foreign as well as domestic. When, two decades ago, Sir Herbert Butterfield reviewed British diplomacy after the Seven Years War, the only substantial work available to him was Dr. F. Spencer's edition of the Sandwich correspondence which was the sole study of British foreign policy sponsored by Namier.'
47. See among other accounts, D.B. Horn, *Great Britain and Europe in the Eighteenth Century* (1969); Frank Spencer (ed.), *The Fourth Earl of Sandwich, Diplomatic Correspondence 1763–1765* (1961); Michael Roberts, *Splendid Isolation 1763–1780* (1970); Sir Herbert Butterfield, 'British foreign policy 1762–5', *Historical Journal*, VI (1963), 131–40; Paul Langford, *The Eighteenth Century, 1688–1815* (1976); H.L. Dunthorne, 'The alliance of the maritime powers 1721–40' (Ph.D. thesis, University of London, 1978); Jeremy Black, *British Foreign Policy in the Age of Walpole* (1985); and the relevant essays in R. Hatton and M.S. Anderson (eds), *Diplomatic History: Essays in Memory of David Bayne Horn* (1970).
48. Ragnhild Hatton, *War and Peace 1680–1720* (1969); S. Baxter (ed.), *England's Rise to Greatness 1660–1783* (1983); Nicholas Tracy, 'British assessments of French and Spanish naval reconstruction 1763–1778', *Mariner's Mirror*, LXI (1975), 73–85; *idem*, 'The gunboat diplomacy of the government of George Grenville 1764–5', *Hist J.*, XVII (1974), 711–31; *idem*, 'The Royal Navy as an instrument in British foreign relations 1763–75' (Ph.D. thesis, University of Southampton, 1972); Michael Roberts, *British Diplomacy and*

Swedish Politics 1758–1773 (1980); Karl W. Schweizer, 'The Seven Years War: a system perspective', in *The Origins of War in Early Modern Europe*, ed. J. Black (1986), 242–60. Jeremy Black, 'The British navy and British foreign policy in the first half of the eighteenth century', in *Essays in European History in Honour of Ragnhild Hatton*, eds Karl W. Schweizer and Jeremy Black (Studies in History and Politics, 1985), IV, 137–55. See also Jeremy Black, 'British foreign policy in the 18th century: a survey', *J. British Studies*, XXVI (Jan. 87), 26–53.

49. P.F. Doran, 'Andrew Mitchell and Anglo-Prussian diplomatic relations during the Seven Years War' (Ph.D. thesis, University of London, 1972); Michael Roberts, 'Macartney in Russia' (*English Historical Review*, Supplement, VII, 1974); G. Rice, 'The diplomatic career of the Fourth Earl of Rochford, 1749–68' (Ph.D. thesis, University of Kent, 1973); H.M. Scott, 'Anglo-Austrian relations after the Seven Years War: Lord Stormont in Vienna 1763–1772' (Ph.D. thesis, University of London, 1977); Karl W. Schweizer, 'Scotsmen and the British Diplomatic Service, 1714–1789'; *Scottish Tradition* (1977–8), VII–VIII (1977–8), 115–36.

50. As the Duke of Newcastle recorded with some surprise, 'My Lord Bute, will do all his business at the office and be there every morning at nine', Memorandum, 21 March 1761, BL Add. MSS 32920, f. 381.

51. Karl W. Schweizer, 'Lord Bute, William Pitt and Frederick the Great: the origin, development and dissolution of the Anglo-Prussian Alliance 1756–63' (Ph.D. thesis, University of Cambridge, 1976), 186–90.

52. As Bute wrote shortly after his appointment: 'I don't know that I have in any light changed for the better. I have given up peace and quiet for hurry and vexation, my own time (of all things to me the most precious) to eternal occupation; however, the consciousness of faithfully discharging my Duty will support me in the execution of it.' (Bute to Lincoln, 6 April 1761, Newcastle (Clumber) MSS 3.871). Cf. Bute to George III, 24 March 1761, BL Add. MSS 36797, fos 47–50; Bute to Lord Henley, 26 Dec. 1761, Bute MSS 730.

53. On Edward Weston, see L. Scott, 'Under-Secretaries of State 1755–1775' (MA thesis, University of Manchester, 1950). A short but useful resumé of Weston's tenures of office may be found in J.C. Sainty, *Officials of the Secretaries of State, 1660–1782* (1973), 115. For an index of Weston's papers still in private hands, see Karl W. Schweizer, 'A handlist to the additional Weston papers', *Bull. Institute of Historical Research*, LI (1978), 123, 99–102. Other papers are located in the Egerton MSS (2683–94), and BL Add. MSS 6808–09, 6823, 6831, 38201–5.

54. Schweizer, 'Lord Bute, William Pitt and Frederick the Great', 188–9; L. Scott, *op. cit.*, 22–5; Weston to Mitchell, 31 March 1761, BL Add. MSS 6823 f. 121.

55. In a letter dated 4 Nov. 1760, Lord Bute was described by the Dutch minister Hop as 'a man of merit, sense and application moderation and very polite … He is a Scotsman and therefore whether as a minister or only conductor of court matters will meet with great jealousy from the English nobility' (bundle marked 'Odd. Papers', Bute MSS). Cf. Galitzin to Kauderbach, 31 March 1761, PRO 107/91 (intercept); Knyphausen to Frederick II, 20 March 1761, DZA, Rep. 96.33.E. fos. 126–7.

56. This conclusion is supported by current work on the parliamentary session of 1762 which indicates that, again contrary to the hitherto accepted view, Bute was a proficient public speaker. See Karl W. Schweizer, 'The Bedford Motion and House of Lords debate, 5 Feb. 1762',

Parliamentary History, V (1986), 107–23.

57. H. Scott, Review of R. Middleton, *The Bells of Victory*, in *International History Review* (1986), 639–40.

58. Richard Middleton, *The Bells of Victory: The Pitt–Newcastle Ministry and the Conduct of the Seven Years War 1757–1762* (1985); *idem*, 'Pitt, Anson and the Admiralty, 1756–1761', *History*, LV (1970), 189–90; Kent Hackmann, 'William Pitt and the generals: three case studies in the Seven Years War', *Albion*, III (1971), 128–37; Eric McDermott, 'The elder Pitt and his admirals and generals', *Military Affairs*, XX (1956), 65–8; E. Frazer, 'The Pitt–Newcastle coalition and the conduct of the Seven Years War' (D.Phil. thesis, University of Oxford, 1976).

59. Von Ruville, *Die Auflösung des preussisch-englischen Bündnisses, passim*; W.L. Dorn, 'Frederick the Great and Lord Bute', *Journal of Modern History*, I (1929), 529–60; F. Spencer, 'The Anglo-Prussian breach of 1762: an historical revision', *History*, XLI (Feb. 1956), 100–12.

60. For complete details, see the following articles: Karl W. Schweizer, 'The non-renewal of the Anglo-Prussian subsidy treaty 1761–1762: a historical revision', *Canadian Journal of History*, XIII no. 3 (1978), 384–96; *idem*; 'Bute, Newcastle, Prussia and the Hague overtures: a reexamination', *Albion*, VIII, no. 1 (1977), 72–97; Karl W.

Schweizer with Carol Leonard, 'Britain, Prussia, Russia and the Galitzin letter: a reassessment', *Hist J.*, XXVI, no. 3 (1983), 531–56; Karl W. Schweizer, 'Britain, Prussia and the Prussian territories on the Rhine 1762–63', in *Essays in Honour of Ragnhild Hatton*, ed. Schweizer and Black, 103–14.

61. See Schweizer, 'Lord Bute, William Pitt and Frederick the Great', 219–425, and the articles cited in n.60; *cf.* Spencer, *The Sandwich Diplomatic Correspondence*, 17–25. See also R. Hatton, 'Frederick the Great and the House of Hanover', in *Friedrich der Grosse in seiner Zeit*, ed. O. Hauser (Cologne, 1987), 151–64.

62. Bute to General Townshend, 8 Apr. 1763, BL Add. MSS 36797, f. 43.

63. L.H. Gipson, *The Great War for Empire, the Culmination 1760–3* (New York, 1954), 299–311; Langford, *op. cit.*; 150–1; Ronald Hyam, 'Imperial interests and the Peace of Paris (1763)', in Ronald Hyam and Ged Martin, *Reappraisals in British Imperial History* (Toronto, 1975), 22–43; John Brewer, 'Lord Bute', in *The Prime Ministers*, ed. van Thal, 109–10.

64. Hence Bute's frequent complaint of being 'censured for things I cannot prevent or accomplish and deprived of the merit, even of the little good I may be able to do' (Bute to Lord Henley, 26 Dec. 1761, Bute MSS 730). Cf Bute to Gilbert Elliot [March 1762], NLS, Minto MSS 132/72.

1

Securing the peace:
Lord Bute, the plan for the army, and
the origins of the American Revolution

John L. Bullion

When the Earl of Shelburne praised the preliminary treaty of peace in the House of Lords on 9 December 1762, he emphasized that 'the security of the British colonies in North America was the first cause of the war'. That security, he boasted, 'has been wisely attended to in the negotiations for peace.' Removing the French from Canada and the Spanish from Florida would improve commerce, increase navigation and naval power, and 'of millions more consequence than all our other conquests, ... insures to Great Britain the pleasing hopes of a solid and lasting peace.'[1] Were these hopes realistic? Shelburne and other spokesmen for the Bute administration tried to convince their audiences that they were. But Lord Bute and his colleagues were keenly aware that success in this war did not guarantee security in the present or in the future. That security would depend upon planning wisely for the army after the war. As Bute later remarked, 'I hope this peace will be [as] permanent as it is great, but certainly a respectable force kept up will not lessen its duration.'[2]

The King took the responsibility for drafting the plan for that respectable force upon himself. He began in early September 1762, two months before the signing of the preliminaries.[3] Throughout the process he and Bute had 'two things principally in view: security and economy', which they felt 'ought certainly to go together.'[4] Economy they defined without difficulty: it meant keeping the expenses of the army in 1763 from exceeding the cost of the army in 1749, the first year of peace after the War of the Austrian Succession.[5] Though no papers describing why they settled on this definition have yet been found, their reasoning may be safely inferred from a number of sources. As an official at the War Office observed, in planning for the post-war army, it was necessary to begin by 'follow[ing] some Rule', and 'it seemed the most natural' to start with a knowledge of the numbers and cost of the military in 1749.[6] The fiscal and political advantages of reducing the army's expenses to that level were obvious. Doing so would enable the ministry to devote more of the government's resources to restoring its financial strength, which the King, Bute, and the consensus of political opinion agreed had been seriously weakened by a long and expensive war.[7] Moreover, the ministers would not have to justify spending more on the army in 1763 than in 1749 to a sceptical House of Commons that would certainly be economy-minded.[8] Security, however, could not be defined so quickly and precisely. That definition involved both analysis of military problems Britain faced in the past, and predictions of the sorts of problem she would confront in the future. In particular, it included assessments of where Britain would be vulnerable in the years ahead, and of the capacity and will of the nation's enemies to take advantage of any opportunities. Once these decisions were made, it involved planning the practical details of the size, establishment, and disposition of the post-war army. While working on these details, the King and Bute had to be careful not to go over the cost of the army in 1749, so security and economy would indeed 'go together'.[9] George III and his 'dearest friend' planned for Britain's security conscientiously and boldly, departing from precedent as they did so. They knew that the consequences of their efforts could be momentous, either for good or bad.

As events transpired, the consequences of their plan for the American army were unexpected. Efforts to keep the cost of the army below the 1749 level by taxing colonists for the support of the regulars stationed there precipitated the imperial crisis of 1765–6, and ultimately helped bring about the American Revolution. It is fair to say that that revolution began with the plan formulated by the King and Bute, and approved by the ministry and Parliament. What that plan was, and the considerations that inspired it, are the subjects of this essay.

To the King and Bute, it was obvious that Britain had to station a large force of regulars in America. As early as September, *The Briton* warned that 'considerable supplies of men' would be necessary 'to maintain all the countries and islands which we have wrested from the enemy'.[10] The only question was, how large should that force be? The Duke of Newcastle was confident on 23 December that the ministry meant to station 12,000 regulars in America.[11] Whether his information was accurate or not is unknown, since no evidence confirming it has yet been discovered. The King's plan, which was ready on 27 December, called for 10,542 officers and men in the New World. These troops were to be organized into 21 battalions.[12] This number of battalions discloses that King George intended that these units would have many fewer enlisted men than was usual in a peacetime establishment, but would retain an unusually large number of officers. 'Small corps with a great many officers' was the way Welbore Ellis, the Secretary at War, later depicted the American establishment, and his statement accurately described this aspect of the King's plan.[13]

George did not indicate on this plan how he wanted to finance the 21 battalions. Indeed, he did not estimate their cost on it. Before the Cabinet met on 28 December to consider the plan, someone (probably Ellis) estimated the expense of the American army at £225,159 per year. When Bute and his colleagues in principle approved stationing 21 battalions in the colonies, they decided that this expense would be borne by Great Britain in 1763.[14] If they went on to discuss the future financing of this force on 28 December, no record of their considerations has so far surfaced. Still, one needed only to glance at the total expense of the army in 1749 and in 1763 to realize that a larger American army, if paid for by Britain, meant that the cost of the entire army in 1763 would be higher than in 1749.[15] This violated the King and Bute's principle of economy. Thus it is not surprising that whenever the King and his ministers began discussing the future financing of the force in America, they determined that colonists should pay for the troops defending them in 1764 and thereafter. That revenue, they further decided, would be raised by parliamentary taxation. For a time, they evidently were optimistic that they could levy a tax on colonists that would support the army in 1763. In early February, George sent Bute a note, enclosing a comparison he had devised between the army's size and cost in 1749 and its projected size and cost in 1763. That comparison did not include troops in the colonies. 'I have not put down the 10,000 in America', he explained, 'as [it is] proposed that being no expense to Great Britain.' The postponement of that scheme did not weaken their determination to tax the colonists in 1764, and lower the cost of the army that year to below the level of 1749.[16]

Why did the King and his ministers believe a large army organized in 'small corps with a great many officers' was necessary in the colonies? 'As to the 10,000 in America,' George observed to Bute, 'that is become necessary from our successes.'[17] Though he did not elaborate on this flat statement, his meaning is clear. In part, the King was alluding to problems identified by one of Bute's hired hacks months earlier. *The Briton* had noted 'the extent of our conquests in North America, ... peopled by new subjects, indisposed to our dominion from national as well as religious aversion, and surrounded by innumerable nations of fierce Indians, whom it will be absolutely necessary to over-awe and restrain by a chain of strong forts and garrisons', then predicted that these circumstances called for 'considerable supplies of men'.[18] When Ellis justified the number of troops for America to the House of Commons on 4 March 1763, he referred to the same considerations. He pointed out that Britain had acquired '90,000 Canadians ... besides Indians' as new subjects. Then he observed that 'French missionar[ies had] interwove politics with religion' in Canada, and 'combined their prejudices', with the result that the new subjects were 'not familiaris'd to civil government unsupported by arms'.[19] In order to preserve British authority against the possibility or the reality of internal disturbance, the government of Canada would need the support of a considerable force of regulars. Moreover, these problems of internal government had grave implications for the external security of all British colonies in America. Disaffection in Canada, and troubled Indian relations, would be serious enough in times of the profoundest peace. During periods of international tension or actual war, the connections the *habitants* and Indians had with European enemies could be disastrous for Britain. Apparently the ministers thought that the best solution to these related problems of internal and external security was peopling the conquered territories with Britons and Anglo-Americans, for the King asked Parliament to 'consider of such methods in the settlement of our new acquisitions as shall effectually tend to the security of those countries.'[20] Until this could be effected, a large army would be necessary in the New World.

The size of that army was only one of its strengths. From the viewpoint of the King and his ministers, its establishment was equally important. The extent of territory in Canada, and the isolation of the conquered islands from other British possessions required creating and garrisoning many small posts. 'No post can be without a commissioned officer,' Ellis pointed out, 'nor with one only.' 'From this, a greater number of officers are clearly necessary', and this necessity justified an establishment of 'small corps with a great many officers'.[21] Even more significant, however, was the advantage such an establishment promised to hold when war broke out again. The King and Bute were convinced that keeping a large number of battalions, with 'a great many officers', on active duty meant that the army in the colonies could expand rapidly and quickly. Rather than trying to activate regiments and staff them with officers from the half-pay list during a national emergency, the government could simply recruit more enlisted men. As Ellis put it, 'you will have the bottom of an army easily ... augmented' in the colonies. The difference between this army and the force in America in 1749 was dramatic. 'Then you had only four battalions in

America. Now you will have the foundations of a great army there.'[22] That army would be prepared for the next war. It would need to be, according to the King. 'The reason for keeping so many nominal corps,' he reminded Bute, 'is that an army may be formed on any new war'. 'If we don't take the precaution,' George predicted, 'I will venture to affirm whenever a new war breaks out we shall run great risk of losing the great advantages we are at this hour to be blessed with by this great, noble, and perfect definitive treaty.'[23]

The King's words aptly summarize the reason why he and the ministers decided to station a large force in America. They believed new possessions were vulnerable to French and Spanish aggression, especially at the beginning of war. Britain therefore had to prepare to defend them. Although later colonists – and much later, historians as well – argued that the regulars were also in America to help enforce imperial regulations in the older colonies, there are no indications that George III, or Bute, or the other ministers contemplated using them for this purpose during 1762–3.[24] Instead, considerations of military security dictated their presence in those numbers with that establishment. Furthermore, the government made that decision before late February 1763, when London learned about 'the royal edict of France in a Gazette. They are to have 23,000 men, half in their [West Indian] islands, half on board their fleet, to serve alternatively.' Such 'a great force' obviously threatened British possessions in the Caribbean, and heightened concern about relations with Canadians and Indians. As Ellis told the House, this French military presence was 'a sufficient reason for our keeping a great force in America'.[25] It also confirmed the Bute administration's suspicions about French intentions for the future and concern about the enemy's power. Clearly, now, the ministry had not erred by preparing to meet France's challenge to British security in the New World with an army than was larger, better able to expand rapidly and efficiently, and, after 1763, less expensive than the force in America in 1749.

The plan for the American army was not the only effort the government made to be ready to defend the new possessions at the beginning of the next war. The King's plan for the establishment of regiments to be stationed in Britain followed the same principles as that for those in America.[26] The purpose of that establishment was the same as well. 'You could not increase your army when war came suddenly so conveniently by [creating] new corps – more speedy, more effectual this way', Ellis explained to the House. And, just as he observed about the American army, the Secretary at War emphasized, 'Without exceeding the cost of 1749 [for troops in Britain], you will have an army more ready, more convenient, etc.'[27] The major reason why the King and Bute were eager to take advantage of what they supposed to be the willingness of the Irish parliament to pay for 6,000 more troops in Ireland, organized into 15 battalions of infantry, was their conviction that these units, once expanded, could be of crucial importance in helping defend the new possessions in time of war.[28] Like the regulars in the colonies, these battalions would be no expense to Britain. Indeed, by employing officers who otherwise would be on half pay, they would reduce the cost of the British establishment.[29] Thus in this case, too, the nation would have the benefit of an army that was larger and readier to expand for less money than in 1749.

During their planning for the peacetime army, the government did not neglect 'that part of our force in which our safety is most immediately concerned'. The First Lord of the Admiralty, George Grenville, had been interested in improving the recruitment of experienced seamen into the navy since the 1750s.[30] As the end of the war approached, he recalled the 'constant complaint that as soon as the peace is concluded the government of Great Britain has no longer given any attention necessary for maintaining that peace by keeping the kingdom in as respectable a situation as is consistent with that economy which is always desirable and which is now indispensable'. To remedy this complaint, he began thinking about employing some of the seamen the navy would discharge during peace in ships to be rented by the customs service, for use in patrols against smuggling. Such a measure would improve Britain's revenues and commerce. When the next war began, these seamen would be readily available for service in the fleet. By neglecting to take measures such as this in the past, 'we have laboured under very great disadvantages whenever we have been obliged to enter into a new war, and we have been at an immense expense before we get together and put into action that national strength which is necessary for our own defense and the annoyance of our enemies.' In previous wars, Britain had been fortunate that enemies gave her the time to augment her forces. In the future, the First Lord implied, she might not be so lucky.[31]

Grenville's reasoning on the necessity for preparing to expand the navy's manpower swiftly and efficiently obviously duplicated the thoughts of the King and Bute on the army. That it was attractive to them is not surprising. On 1 December, after informing the House that the administration planned to keep more seamen on active duty than after the previous war, Grenville disclosed that it was also contemplating making 'provisions for the disbanded [seamen]' and for officers who would otherwise be on half pay 'by employing ... [them] against smuggling etc.'. The plan he settled on called for 2,060 officers and men in 60 vessels, to be stationed off the coasts of Great Britain and Ireland. For reasons that remain unknown, the administration did not act on the plan. Still, Grenville's work may have been the initial inspiration for its decision to improve the enforcement of customs laws by increased use of the navy's ships as water patrols.[32]

From this record of thought and action on the army and navy, it is clear that the King and Bute firmly rejected the course of following the example of earlier monarchs and ministers at the beginning of peace. Obviously, their determination was grounded in part on their conviction that the new circumstances of defending an enlarged empire, one which now included recent enemies, demanded new policies. Yet what is illuminated even more vividly by a consideration of their plans during 1762–3 is their awareness of the transitory nature of peace, and of the formidable power and inveterate hostility of France. That awareness inspired them to commit themselves and the administration to preparing militarily for the beginning of the next war at the end of the present one. What caused them to be so sensible of a French threat to peace? And which considerations persuaded them to try to meet that threat with their plan for the army? In answering these questions, a knowledge of the reactions of other politicians to the post-war situation and to the plan is useful. Comparing their ideas with those of the King and Bute reveals not only the differences between them, but also some illuminating similarities.

The Tories had been staunch supporters of George III since the early days of his reign, and of the ministry during the parliamentary debates over the preliminaries. Still, they balked at supporting the plan for the army. Part of their reaction was due to their traditional opposition to large standing armies and to anything that promised to increase the crown's influence, such as keeping large numbers of officers on active duty. 'To keep up ... so large a number of corps in time of peace ... which may soon be raised to their old complement', Sir John Phillips told Bute, was unconstitutional. Sir John also noted that he and many other Tories thought there was no military justification for so large a force 'now, when so large a body of well-trained militia are in the kingdom, ready and able to defend it against the attacks of any power whatever,' and at the beginning of 'such a peace that is likely to continue'. 'Let not the first measure taken after obtaining a safe and honorable peace be to demand a large standing army, unnecessary for his majesty's and the kingdom's safety', he pleaded, before proceeding to threaten that the Tories would oppose the plan in the House.[33]

Tory reasoning impressed neither George III nor Bute. The King thought their analysis of the military situation was entirely founded on their political and military prejudices, not on any assessment of present realities. The militia did not lessen the need for a large regular army, he protested to Bute, no doubt recalling that militia units had not faced regular soldiers during the last war and could not be sent out of England. Their presence and numbers did, however, make any Tory fears of an absolute monarchy patently ridiculous. If the government yielded to Tory 'passion', he angrily wrote Bute, ''tis not worthwhile to consider two minutes what is to be done.'[34] Tory political power, however, could not be shrugged off. Ultimately the ministers gave up their hope of adding 6,000 troops to the Irish establishment, gaining in return Tory support for the rest of the plan. Since this apparent concession to the Tories was due at least as much to opposition in Dublin, it may well have been an artful manoeuvre that got Tory support for the British and American establishments in return for a change the administration had to make anyway.[35] The loss of these troops displeased the King and Bute, for they did not share the Tories' optimism that a smaller regular army would be sufficient to maintain the security of Britain and the empire.[36]

The Duke of Newcastle and his allies and supporters had opposed the ministry since the opening of the parliamentary session. Unsurprisingly, they opposed the plan for the army. To them, it obviously increased the influence of the King and his favourite.[37] Equally important, they believed it was the wrong way to secure the nation in the future. They did not deny that the French would pose a threat to peace in the future. As H.B. Legge, former Chancellor of the Exchequer, noted in the House, the continuation of the Bourbon alliance between France and Spain, the retention by France of a share in the Newfoundland fisheries, and the restoration of French sugar islands would 'in a short time furnish them with the means of maintaining another war.' Britain was not so fortunate. Her acquisitions would require improving for many years before they added to the nation's power and wealth. Before that time was up, 'we shall have this dance to go over again with [a debt of] 140 millions upon our backs.'[38] But the way to prepare for that day was not by enlarging the military. Instead, the government should follow France's example, reduce the army to below the strength of 1749, and concentrate on improving revenues. Preparation for the next war should be devoted to fiscal retrenchment and reform, not military enlargement.[39]

In contrast, William Pitt, who opposed the government during the debate on the preliminaries, felt that the ministry's plan was the right idea but not carried far enough. He favoured keeping more officers and men on active duty, and increasing the number of troops in Britain and America. Pitt professed he 'was for economy, but in great matters, not a starving, penurious economy in little offices that amounted to nothing material and only rendered the promoters ridiculous.' In so far as military preparedness was concerned, 'in so early a peace, the nation ought to show itself on a respectable footing'. 'The peace was inadequate, precarious, and hollow; ... it would soon be broke; ... [and] whenever France broke with you, she would do it without giving notice.'[40] The major reasons why Pitt regarded the peace as 'an armed truce only' were the same as those Legge mentioned when he predicted France would soon be able to fight again: the Bourbon alliance, the fisheries, and the French sugar islands.[41]

Comparing the King and Bute's views with those of Pitt and Newcastle is more difficult than with the Tories' opinions. Pitt and Newcastle's followers in the House announced they would not vote against the army estimates, so there was no cause for a ministerial rebuttal on 4 March. Moreover, because the ministers were determined to defend the peace treaty against the criticism of Pitt and Newcastle, they portrayed it in public in glowing terms. When he sought to persuade, Bute did not hesitate to 'be bold enough to affirm that this country has not made so great, so safe, and so permanent a peace (for so it promises) as this, for some hundred years past.'[42] In private, he and his colleagues were satisfied that by their conviction 'we had obtained the highest conditions that could be got'.[43] The difference is a telling one. The King and Bute were genuinely proud of the treaty, they honestly regarded it as 'great, noble, and perfect', but pride did not blind them to the reality that it did not attain everything they had wished for.[44] How it fell short of their desires, and their assessment of the significance of those shortcomings, are revealed by their opinions during the peace negotiations of 1761–2.

The King and Bute had agreed with Pitt in June 1761 that excluding the French from the Newfoundland fisheries would be 'a vast thing for us'.[45] Such a stroke would bring considerable commercial advantages to Britain, while denying any profits from the trade to France. Of even greater significance, it would 'incapacitate them from being any longer a naval power', and thus secure Britain and her possessions from attack.[46] Unlike Pitt, the King and Bute did not want to make exclusion a *sine qua non* for peace. They did not think the fisheries were worth

prolonging the war over. It was, however, worth a try, particularly as
an opening gambit. 'As the Fishery, which was proposed to be left to
France, would be a ruined Fishery', Bute told the Cabinet on 25 June
1761, 'it was possible that they might give it up now'. The moderates in
the Cabinet, Newcastle and his allies, were less sanguine. They did not
quarrel about the benefits Britain would gain from excluding the
French from Newfoundland; they opposed making the proposal because they were sure France would never agree to it, and a good chance
for peace might be lost.[47] Events immediately bore out their prediction,
and ultimately their fear. The French not only refused to give up all of
the Newfoundland fisheries, but they insisted on the right to continue
fishing in the Gulf of St Lawrence, and the cession of a suitable *abri*
there for their fishing fleet to shelter and to dry the catch, as well as
demanding a place on the coast of Newfoundland to dry cod caught in
those waters. The Cabinet countered by proposing that the French get
a share of the fishing off Newfoundland, plus a drying station on that
island, on condition the fortifications at Dunkirk be destroyed. Bute
agreed reluctantly. He did so 'because all the Council thought it was
right', but he bluntly told Newcastle 'that he regretted that concession
[of the right to dry fish] more than anything else.'[48] His hopes of
Britain's dominating the cod commerce and seriously weakening, if not
destroying, France's naval power were clearly fading. What followed
utterly extinguished them.

In early August, the enemy's counter-proposals arrived in London,
and the Cabinet discovered that France still insisted on part of the St
Lawrence fishery and an *abri* in the Gulf, preferably Cape Breton or St
John's. Bute's immediate response was to consider this 'as a declaration of war'. Significantly, Newcastle 'thought it was very bad but
hoped Lord Bute would not however lose sight of Peace': the first sign
of a crisis within the Cabinet fully as grave as the one in the negotiations.[49] Initially, Bute sided with Pitt, and argued for a flat rejection of
the French ultimatum. Newcastle, the Earl of Hardwicke, and the
Duke of Bedford urged acceptance of the demands in principle in the
interest of making peace, then limiting the damage by refusing to grant
Cape Breton or St John's as the *abri*. By a majority of one, Pitt and Bute
prevailed in the first vote. At this point, as the Duke of Devonshire
observed to Bute, 'our situation at home appeared to me as serious as
that abroad'. 'I feared', he continued, 'we should break to pieces', and
the moderates leave the ministry. The King and Bute fully appreciated
the implications of such a withdrawal. Aware this would leave them
dependent on Pitt, and thus shackled to his policy of continuing the war
until French power was crushed; fearful that Britain's finances might

collapse before this occurred; believing that diplomacy rather than *force majeure* was the best way to end the war, and cognizant that they must have the moderates' support to pursue negotiations, the two men yielded on the St Lawrence fishery and on an *abri*.[50] The realism of their decision did not blind them to what had been lost, however. Even as he conceded, Bute could not help reminding the Cabinet that he had favoured excluding the French from the entire fisheries, and that now 'he could not ... but consider the favourite object the Fisheries as in a great measure by their means given up'.[51] He clearly believed that, during the next peace, France would again enjoy the commercial and military advantages she had reaped before from the fisheries.

Bute also believed that Britain had not demanded adequate compensation for her concessions on the fisheries. On 26 June, he had declared that 'the King would not consent to leaving to France the Right of fishing given them by the Treaty of Utrecht without receiving some great Compensation in return', and hinted that the prize should be Guadeloupe.[52] This met with no positive response from the Cabinet, either at that time or later. When the Cabinet decided to agree to let France dry fish on Newfoundland in exchange for the demilitarization of Dunkirk, Bute asked Bedford how they could 'advise the king to sit down satisfied with a barren country [Canada], not equal in value to the duchies of Lorraine and Barr, and yet an acquisition invidious from its vast extent, while the French have restored to them the very essence of the whole?' Instead, he went on, why not keep 'something that will bring in a clear, certain, additional revenue, to enable [posterity] to pay the interest of the enormous debt we have, by this most expensive war, laid upon them?'[53] During the first debates on France's ultimatum in August, Bute was against granting France an *abri* 'unless we insisted on Guadeloupe instead of [the fishery].'[54] Since no one agreed to that, he argued against further concessions on the fishery on these grounds: 'that we ought after our successes to reap some advantage from the war, that we have given up *Sugar Islands* ... which brought a revenue of £4 or £500,000 to France, and had only a long barren tract of country that did not produce £40,000 p.a.; that therefore if we had not the Fishery we really got nothing.'[55] This argument was as unsuccessful as his use of the King's name in June. After he and the King accepted the moderates' position, their only solace was Bute's *cri de coeur* on 19 August.

> He was by no means convinced that we had not gone much too far in our concessions, that his conscience told him, that we had; and that he was averse to every step that had been taken towards conceding to the French any share in the Fisheries; or if this was to be conceded that we ...

demand some great compensation in return and particularly the Island of
Guadeloupe etc.; and that in giving up his opinions on this head he had
only submitted to the Majority.[56]

This outburst, and Bute's other comments during the negotiations of
1761, are interesting. His criticism of the concessions on the fisheries,
his estimate of the value of Canada without a virtual monopoly of that
commerce, and his appreciation of the comparatively much greater
worth of Guadeloupe, are indistinguishable from the charges his opponents levelled at the peace during 1762–3. His assessment in 1761 of the
significance of these terms for France's economic and military power in
the future was identical as well. It is clear that Bute had hoped and
tried to achieve in 1761 what they claimed the treaty failed to accomplish. His principal goal had been to gain complete military security for
Britain's American possessions, plus a virtual monopoly of a lucrative
commerce, by ending entirely or restricting sharply French participation in the fisheries. If the French would not agree to that, he wanted
Guadeloupe in return for the fisheries, which would amount to British
domination of the even more lucrative sugar trade, and provide the
means for a faster restoration of the nation's finances. He got neither of
his wishes. Moreover, his analysis of the reasons why he got neither
convinced him that he had to change his priorities to conform with the
reality of Britain's and his own situation.

During the negotiations of 1761, Bute learned that the French would
not 'hold ... out their throats to be cut'.[57] The enemy would fight on
rather than make a concession that would ruin France's navy and
ensure the military security of British possessions in the New World.
The question had become whether Britain should continue the war in
the hope that more victories would compel France to give in on this
point. Bute had never shared Pitt's facile confidence in Britain's fiscal
strength, and thus had never regarded another year of war with the
same equanimity. Moreover, important members of the Cabinet did
not believe British arms were capable of accomplishing that end, and
regarded attempting it as very likely ruinous. No matter how reluctantly he had done it, Bute had cast his lot with these men. When he
did so, he effectively gave up the hopes he had had when the negotiations began. None of the moderates believed Britain should demand
Guadeloupe as compensation for the fisheries. All of them explained
the 'reason why France has not made peace' by noting 'if these concessions [the Cabinet made on the fisheries] had been sooner made it
would have [been] better'. The first British proposals caused the
French to look for assistance from Spain, and, having been granted it,
to raise their demands. To make peace, Britain would have to be more

reasonable in her demands. The French would respond favourably if convinced their antagonists wished for peace, without having to have it, and offered moderate terms.[58] France's obduracy over the fisheries, his own convictions about the advisability of concluding peace soon, and his political allies' opinions on what a reasonable peace was and how it could be obtained, made Bute change his goals. Never again after 19 August 1761 did he express any regret about Britain's failure either to keep most of the fisheries, or to get Guadeloupe instead of them. He accepted the reality that he could not ask for either of these and hope to end the war. Thus when Bute made his secret attempts during the period from November 1761 to January 1762 to renew negotiations with France, he encouraged his Sardinian go-betweens to intimate 'that as there was no great seeming difference between us when the negotiation broke off, it might be easily accommodated if France was disposed to peace.' Pleased by the Duc de Choiseul's reply to this, and convinced Choiseul genuinely desired peace in 1762, he responded by indicating 'we should be ready to treat on the same terms' as the last two ultimatums exchanged in 1761.[59]

This meant that from the beginning of the negotiations of 1762, Bute recognized that although Britain would retain Canada, the future security of her North American colonies would not be completely assured, because she could not exclude the French from 'the nursery of seamen', the fisheries. He also was aware that since he had no support within his own government for keeping Guadeloupe, France would enjoy again the considerable benefits of the sugar trade, with the consequence that both her navy and her revenues would be restored more quickly than would otherwise have been the case. He quickly had to acknowledge another reality as well. With the entrance of Spain into the war in January 1762, adjusting what had seemed in 1761 to be minor differences between Britain and France became much more difficult. France now had an ally, one which had not been weakened by six years of fighting. Britain now had an additional drain on her human and fiscal resources, which the war had already seriously depleted. Bute could expect that the French would be more optimistic at the very time that mounting expenses would make a speedy peace all the more necessary for Britain.

To deal with this situation, Bute and his colleagues decided to strike a telling blow against Spain in the Caribbean by conquering Havana, while sending troops to assist against any attack on Portugal. The loss of Havana, the ministers reasoned, would make Spain amenable to ending the war quickly.[60] In order to relieve the fiscal strain of another year of fighting and a new foe, the Cabinet also looked for ways of reducing expenses in Germany. Ultimately, Bute did not act on the advice many pressed on him, to withdraw British troops from western Germany. Still, the fact that he seriously contemplated a measure that was fraught with logistical difficulties, and might conceivably expose Britain itself to invasion, reveals the depth of his concern about the nation's finances.[61] That concern heightened his determination to make an honourable peace in 1762.

What was an honourable peace as far as the New World was concerned? Bute defined it first to the Cabinet in late April, then in a letter to Bedford on 1 May. Britain would restore Martinique and Guadeloupe, with Marie Galante, to France. The neutral islands and the Grenadines would be British. On the North American continent, 'to prevent future disputes', the Mississippi River would be the boundary between the two nations' possessions. Thus the French would part with nothing in America they had a legal claim to, 'and we secure in perpetuity our Northern conquests, from all future chicane.'[62] This last point deserves elaboration, because it discloses what Bute aimed at after recognizing that the concessions on the fisheries and in the Caribbean would prevent both the establishment of complete military security for North America and the monopoly of a lucrative commerce. The French had, in his opinion, a well-deserved reputation for chicanery, the use of legalistic artifices to claim what was not rightly theirs, thereby prolonging or initiating conflicts. The Mississippi would be a precise and unmistakable boundary, offering no opportunity for this favourite tactic of the enemy's.[63] Remove this potential *casus belli*, and one could expect that the chances for a longer peace would be increased. Put another way, the possibility of any renewal of a military struggle with a renascent France in the near future would be lessened.

How could the French be induced to accept an honourable peace? To Bute, the success of diplomatic efforts would depend on recognizing France's determination to maintain her pre-war position in the West Indies, and being reasonable about demands in that area. Thus he warned the Cabinet in late April that the French would never agree to the cession of Guadeloupe or Louisiana in return for the restoration of Martinique. To prevent the breakdown of negotiations and the continuation of the war, it would be necessary to restore the two islands in exchange for the four neutral islands and the Grenadines.[64] Privately, Bute was willing to go further than that. In June, he secretly offered to give up Santa Lucia, the most important of the neutral islands. He was ignorant neither of the 'worth of St Lucia compared with the three others', nor of the consequences of that cession.[65] The French wanted Santa Lucia because it was vital to them commercially and militarily.

When their demand became known to members of the Cabinet, George Grenville strenuously objected to it. Yielding that island, he argued, meant the French would be in a better military and economic position in the West Indies than before the war. They would dominate the sugar trade, and engross most of its wealth. That trade would improve their merchant navy, and train and employ seamen who would man their fleet in wartime. The fine harbour and windward position of Santa Lucia would give their navy the strategic advantage during war, and pose a continual and grave threat to the security of the British islands. Grenville formally notified the King of his dissent, and the reasons for it.[66] Bute did not dispute Santa Lucia's value. In his mind, however, that value was outweighed by two considerations. The first was the risk Britain would run by continuing the war to try to retain it. As the King noted, if the fighting went on, 'in a year or two from being brought to a state of beggary we shall be forced to sue for peace', and the ministers would be responsible for 'having drawn this nation into the shameful situation of setting down with what it may be permitted to keep by the French'.[67] The second was the risk of a quickly renewed conflict even if Britain did succeed in keeping Santa Lucia. In terms reminiscent of his explanation of the rationale for making the Mississippi River the boundary in America, Bute explained to Bedford and the French the cession of the island by observing it was done 'not only with a view to cut off all other present matters in dispute between us ... but chiefly to render the peace stable and permanent: to remove everything likely to produce animosities thereafter.'[68] He assumed, as Devonshire did, that if France did not get Santa Lucia, she would not rest until she regained it.[69] Restoring it would certainly speed the end of the war, and probably lengthen the peace. Ultimately, he persuaded his colleagues to agree to its return.

Bute stuck with this strategy for the remainder of the negotiations. He was ready to make concessions to Spain's vital interests in the Caribbean, even going so far as to argue in the Cabinet in favour of returning Havana without seeking an equivalent. When his colleagues insisted that the nation must have some compensation for that important conquest, he persuaded them to leave the Spanish with the choice of ceding Florida or Puerto Rico. This enabled Spain to preserve her West Indian possessions intact. In exchange for this moderation, he insisted on keeping the boundary between Canada and Louisiana as precise as possible, on an unequivocal statement of the right to cut logwood in Spanish possessions in Central America, and on as clear a demarcation and as wide a separation as possible between British and French fishing areas.[70] As had been his intent in returning Santa Lucia, his motive was removing what would otherwise obviously be causes of dispute in the future. To critics such as George Grenville, the economic and military effects of Bute's concessions 'undermine[d] the strategic advantage gained over France during the war.'[71] But to the King and Bute, and ultimately to other members of the Cabinet as well, trying to achieve the degree of strategic advantage and security that Grenville wished for would be an unmitigated disaster. As one of Bute's defenders pointedly asked: 'Is there any reason to believe that France is reduced so low as to surrender at Discretion? to give up everything but France itself? to give up its existence as a Trading State and a Maritime Power?' The answer was clear: there was no justification for such 'a precarious, nay, an improbable, Supposition'. Even assuming the government could raise 'the immense Sums required for another Year ... there is no certainty, no Likelihood of compelling France to submit to Terms better for us than now offered, by another Campaign, and another after that'. What was certain was 'if the War continues, our Distress is near at hand'. That distress would be felt for years, too, for 'France supports the Expense of this War with an immediate and cruel Taxation; we borrow immense sums, the Burden of which we shall feel hereafter.'[72] This reasoning led to an inescapable conclusion. The administration had to make an honourable peace, one which gained Canada, parts of the fisheries, and some West Indian islands while removing as soon as possible potential causes for a quick renewal of conflict. The preliminary articles of peace, signed by Bedford and approved by the King in November 1762, fulfilled these criteria to the satisfaction of Bute and his colleagues. They 'had obtained', Bute told Henry Fox, Paymaster of the Forces, 'the highest conditions that could be got'.[73]

Those conditions were not, of course, what Bute and the King had hoped for in 1761. In the future, Britain would still have to deal with a powerful France, and her old antagonist would be restoring her full naval and commercial strength through the fishery and the sugar trade. France would also have important military advantages in the Caribbean, particularly the strategically important island of Santa Lucia. The course of the negotiations of 1761–2 had impressed the value of these concessions on George and his 'dearest friend'. Indeed, they had conceded them only because of the dynamics of the Cabinet's internal politics in 1761 and their sense of Britain's overriding need for an honourable (but not wholly triumphant) peace in 1762. Their awareness that France had the means at hand to restore her strength quickly strongly influenced their planning for the peace.

So did their assessment of France's intentions for the peace. If the French did not intend to renew the struggle as soon as they were able, the ministry could rest easier about her return to full power. The King and Bute did not, however, feel that Britain could safely rely on France's goodwill in the years ahead. The concessions the government had made in the interests of a 'stable and permanent' peace had not been founded upon the expectation that they would mitigate or remove entirely French hostility in the future. Bute only voiced that hope publicly, to the French or to politicians whose support he hoped to gain for the preliminaries. In private, it is clear that he made those concessions to facilitate the conclusion of the present war, and to guard against French 'chicane'. The fact that he believed it was necessary to prevent chicanery from the very beginning of the peace reveals that he had no confidence whatsoever in any remission of France's hostility toward Britain. Had he ever had any such faith, it would have been removed by the twists and turns of negotiations during September and October 1762. In the same letter in which he held out the hope of a stable and permanent peace to the French, Bute complained to Bedford about 'all the French evasions' that were 'obstacles to the peace', and told him to warn them that any departure from articles already agreed upon would mean the continuation of the war.[74] Bute was proceeding according to the same rule he had formulated in 1761: the French invariably reacted to signs of weakness by raising their demands.[75] There are no indications that he stopped following that rule after the preliminary articles were signed, even though they guarded against the aggressive use of chicanery by the enemy. 'A respectable force', he told Phillips, 'will not lessen [the peace's] duration.'[76] Indeed, he expected such a force would lengthen it, by serving as visible proof of Britain's strength and determination.

One other consideration probably strengthened Bute's resolve to maintain a respectable force from the very beginning of peace. Soon after the conclusion of the preliminaries, he discovered that he could not assume that, in the immediate future at least, France's fiscal problems would be as serious as Britain's. During the war, he had never been as sure as Pitt that France's finances were in a perilous condition. To help in planning for the peace, in November 1762 he had Charles Jenkinson write to Richard Neville in Paris, asking him to procure as soon as possible 'as exact accounts as possible of the present state of the French finances.' Neville replied on 1 December that the public credit of France was in good condition. The government did not contemplate laying any new taxes, and would not have even if the war had continued, and did not intend borrowing any more money. He also noted that the Comptroller-General had told him that France 'had one advantage of us in respect to finance which must at least bring on our ruin first.' That was, 'their expenses in war never exceeded their revenue above one-fourth, whereas we were constantly obliged to borrow three-fourths, or very near.' Neville hoped this information 'may facilitate the loans we must want in England.' His letter arrived in London as the King, Bute, and other ministers were concentrating on planning for the future. It was received there as 'some very useful intelligence'.[77] There was, therefore, good reason for Bute, who tended toward a dark view of fiscal affairs anyway, to be apprehensive that France was in better fiscal condition than Britain. Together with the reasons he had for believing that France, though defeated and weakened, had the means at hand to restore her power in a relatively short time, and the will to keep testing Britain's strength and resolve, this was an additional cause for concern for Britain's security in the future. Moreover, this news not only indicated that Britain should maintain a large peacetime force, but also revealed that she should look for external sources of revenue to help pay for it, in order to lighten her fiscal burdens, and improve her fiscal situation *vis-à-vis* France. There are no hints that Bute had revised in 1762 the pessimistic estimate of the immediate value of Canada to Britain's commerce and revenue he made in 1761. Nor did he anticipate that the nation's acquisitions in the West Indies would provide much help soon.[78] This meant that the revenue would have to come from the older colonies.

It is not surprising, therefore, that Bute and the King believed that the security of Britain's new possessions depended upon stationing a large force which could be easily expanded in America. In the future, Britain would still confront a powerful enemy, one which was rapidly renewing its strength through the fisheries and the West Indies trade. That enemy would also enjoy important military advantages in the Caribbean, particularly the strategically important island of Santa Lucia. Finally, France would continue to look for opportunities to defeat Britain, and would try to take advantage of any weaknesses. Given these circumstances, if Bute and his colleagues had ever considered reducing the army to 1749 levels, as both the Tories and the Newcastle Whigs thought advisable, they would have instantly rejected it. Such a plan would leave Britain's new possessions far too vulnerable to a powerful, vengeful France.

It is also not surprising that Bute and George III would conclude that the safety of Britain depended as well upon keeping military expenses at the level of 1749, or below. Britain's fiscal condition, especially considered in comparison with France's, demanded the strictest economy. Pitt might scorn certain measures of economy; Bute and the King did not believe the nation could afford to follow his advice. They also believed that economy could not be achieved without finding new sources of revenue, from outside Britain, and that this revenue would not be found immediately from the new possessions. Raising revenue in the older colonies was as necessary to security as a large army. Thus the origins of the American Revolution may be found in the imperatives of imperial security, as perceived by George III and Lord Bute.

NOTES

1. Quoted in R.B. Morris (ed.), *The American Revolution, 1763–1783: A Bicentennial Collection* (Columbia, SC, 1970), 13–14.
2. Bute to Sir John Phillips, 23 Feb. 1763, BL Add. MSS 36797, f. 34.
3. George III to Bute, 13 Sept. 1762(?), in R. Sedgwick (ed.), *Letters from George III to Lord Bute, 1756–1766* (1939), 135.
4. Bute to Phillips, 23 Feb. 1763, BL Add. MSS 32797, f. 34.
5. George III to Bute, 13 Sept. 1762(?), in Sedgwick, *op. cit.*, 135. For further examples of this definition of economy, see J.L. Bullion, ' "The ten thousand in America": more light on the decision on the American army, 1762–1763', *William and Mary Q.*, 3rd ser., XLIII (1986), 646–57.
6. 'A representation designed to shew what were the Forces kept up in the year 1749, and upon what Establishment: The Reduction necessary to be made in the present Forces to bring them to the same Numbers and Establishment, and what will then be the Charge of the Half Pay at the Conclusion of the War', October 1762, Charles Townshend MSS, 299/3/16.
7. For the King and Bute's concern about Britain's financial strength, see George III to Bute, 26 July 1762, in Sedgwick, *op. cit.*, 126.
8. The ministry's estimate of the mood of the House is in the King's speech, 25

Nov. 1762, *Journals of the House of Commons*, XXIX, 354.
9. It is instructive to compare the King and Bute's understanding of the relationship between security and economy with the one expressed in 1767 by Charles Jenkinson, who had been Bute's private secretary in 1762 and privy to the plans made then for the post-war army. Jenkinson observed in 1767: 'The two great ends of security and economy may seem at first view to combat each other, but it is our duty to reconcile them. Security must have the first place. Without this the whole may be lost, the whole at least is in danger. Economy can save a part only. The first therefore must be obtained, but in obtaining we should apply every principle of economy to render the burden as light as possible, and when once obtained there we should stop' (Jenkinson, 'naval argument', Jan.–Feb. 1767, BL Add. MSS 38336, f. 361). In contrast to this view – which was informed by Jenkinson's knowledge in 1767 that military costs could not safely be reduced below those of 1749 – the King and Bute were determined to make security and economy equal priorities, and planned accordingly.
10. *The Briton*, 25 Sept. 1762.
11. The Duke of Newcastle to the Duke of Devonshire, 23 December 1762, BL Add. MSS 32945, f. 335.

12. Enclosure in Richard Rigby to the Duke of Bedford, 27 December 1762, Bedford MSS, XLVI, nos 218, 224. Henry Fox identified this as 'his majesty's plan' in his letter to Bute, 30 Dec. 1762, Bute MSS, Fox Correspondence.

13. Charles Jenkinson, notes, 4 March 1763, R.C. Simmons and P.D.G. Thomas (eds), *Proceedings and Debates of the British Parliaments Respecting North America* (1982), I, 440.

14. 'State showing the number of land forces proposed to be kept for the service of the year 1763' [early Jan. 1763], Charles Townshend MSS, 299/3/15. Fox told Bute he had sent Townshend these estimates; see Fox to Bute, 5 Jan. 1763, Bute MSS, Fox Correspondence.

15. Compare 'State showing the number of land forces proposed to be kept for the service of the year 1763' with 16 Dec. 1748, *Journals of the House of Commons*, XXV, 671–2.

16. George III to Bute, [early Feb. 1763], Bute MSS, Correspondence with George III, no. 414. This letter may be approximately dated by its reference to 10,000 troops in America. In early February, the ministry decided to reduce the number of battalions to be stationed there from 21 to 20. See Bullion, *op. cit.*

17. George III to Bute, [c.17 Feb. 1763], Bute MSS, Correspondence with George III, no. 274. For a discussion of the significance of this letter, see Bullion, *op. cit.*

18. *The Briton*, 25 Sept. 1762.

19. Gilbert Elliot, notes, 4 March 1763, in Bullion, *op. cit.*

20. The King's speech, 25 Nov. 1762, *Journals of the House of Commons*, XXIX, 354.

21. Sir Roger Newdigate, notes, 4 March 1763, and Jenkinson, notes, 4 March 1763, in Simmons and Thomas, *op. cit.*, I, 440.

22. Newdigate, notes, 4 March 1763, in *ibid.* To my knowledge, no historian has previously called attention to this aspect of the plan for America. Yet

Ellis publicly and the King privately stressed the importance of the speed and efficiency with which 'nominal corps' could expand. George III to Bute, [c.17 Feb. 1763], Bute MSS, Correspondence with George III, no. 274.

23. *Ibid.*

24. See Bullion, *op. cit.*

25. Newdigate, notes and Jenkinson, notes, 4 March 1763, in Simmons and Thomas, *op. cit.*, I, 440.

26. George III to Bute, 13 September 1762(?), in Sedgwick, *op. cit.*, 135; enclosure in Rigby to Bedford, 27 Dec. 1762, Bedford MSS, XLVI, no. 224; and 'State showing the number of land forces proposed to be kept for the service of the year 1763', [early January 1763], Charles Townshend MSS, 299/3/15.

27. Newdigate, notes, 4 March 1763, Newdegate MSS B. 2543/11.

28. George III to Bute, [c.17 Feb. 1763], Bute MSS, Correspondence with George III, no. 274. For a discussion of the background of the attempt to station more troops in Ireland, see J. Shy, *Toward Lexington: The Role of the British Army in the Coming of the American Revolution* (Princeton, NJ, 1965), 73–8.

29. Bute to Phillips, 23 Feb. 1763, BL Add. MSS 36797, f. 34.

30. S.F. Gradish, 'Wages and manning: the Navy Act of 1758', *EHR*, XCIII (1978), 63–5.

31. [George Grenville], 'Some thoughts upon a plan for the useful employment of a body of seamen in the king's pay in time of peace and for the suppression of the dangerous and infamous practice of smuggling' [Oct. 1762], BL Add. MSS 57834, fos 109–10.

32. See Sir James West to Newcastle, 1 Dec. 1762, BL Add. MSS 32945, f. 233, for Grenville's speech, in which the First Lord announced the government would keep 16,000 officers and men, including 4,000 marines, on the peace establishment. For the navy establishment in 1750s, see 18 February 1750/1, *Journals of the House of Commons*, XXVI, 45. For the plan, see

'Proposals ...', December 1762,
George Grenville MSS, STG18–(30);
for the government's ultimate action,
see 24 March 1763, *Journals of the House
of Commons*, XXIX, 609.

33. Phillips to Bute, 17 Feb. 1763, Bute
MSS, 11/34/1–4.

34. George III to Bute, [*c.*17 Feb. 1763],
Bute MSS, Correspondence with
George III, no. 274.

35. When the King learned that Bute
'seems to doubt whether the Irish will
agree to pay the additional 6000', he
immediately suggested an alternative
plan for reduction that did not include
the 15 battalions. George III to Bute, 5
Feb. 1763, Bute MSS, Correspondence
with George III, no. 195. This letter
bears out the suspicion voiced in Shy,
op. cit., 76.

36. Bute to Phillips, 23 Feb. 1763, BL
Add. MSS 36797, f. 34.

37. H.B. Legge to Newcastle, 26 Feb.
1763, and Newcastle to the Earl of
Hardwicke, 3 March 1763, BL Add.
MSS 32947, fos 98, 163–4.

38. Legge's speech, 10 Dec. 1762, in
Simmons and Thomas, *op. cit.*, I, 426.

39. Legge's speech, 4 March 1763, in
Newdigate, notes, Newdegate MSS B.
2543/11; and Elliot, notes, NLS MS
11036, f. 47.

40. West to Newcastle, 4 March 1763, BL
Add. MSS 32947, fos 265–6.

41. Pitt's speeches, 4 March 1763 and 9
Dec. 1762, in Simmons and Thomas,
op. cit., I, 441, 419–22.

42. Bute to the Marquis of Granby, 5 Nov.
1762, BL Add. MSS 38200, f. 93.

43. Bute to Fox, 30 Nov. 1762, BL Add.
MSS 51379, f. 118.

44. George III to Bute, [*c.*17 Feb. 1763],
Bute MSS, Correspondence with
George III, no. 274.

45. Newcastle to Devonshire, 28 June 1761,
BL Add. MSS 32924, f. 314. The best
analysis of the negotiations during the
summer of 1761 is Karl W. Schweizer,
'William Pitt, Lord Bute, and the peace
negotiations with France, May–
September 1761', *Albion*, XIII (1981),
262–75, reprinted with some additions
as Chapter 2 of this volume. For a

lengthy description, see Z.E. Rashed,
The Peace of Paris 1763 (1951), 56–114.

46. Bedford to the Earl of Gower, 27 June
1761, PRO 30/29/1/14. fos 527–8.

47. 25 June 1761, Jenkinson, notes on
cabinet meetings, June–Sept. 1761,BL
Add. MSS 38336, fos 237–8. These
notes are based on conversations
Jenkinson had with Bute, and thus
constitute the Earl's record of the
meetings, and the most complete
account of his statements at them.
Jenkinson used these notes while he
was working on an answer to the
French *mémoire* on the negotiations of
1761. That answer was never
published, because Bute feared it
might hinder his secret contacts with
the French during November 1761–
January 1762, see Rashed; *op. cit.*, 112–
14. For notes on cabinet meetings by
an influential colleague of Bute's, see
the Duke of Devonshire's diary, in
P.D. Brown and Karl W. Schweizer
(eds), *The Devonshire Diary: William
Cavendish, 4th Duke of Devonshire;
Memoranda on State of Affairs, 1759–1762*
(1982), 99–120.

48. 15 July 1761, Jenkinson notes, BL
Add. MSS 38336, f. 249.

49. 6 August 1761, Jenkinson notes, BL
Add. MSS 38336, f. 253.

50. See Schweizer, *op. cit.*, 272–3; and Karl
W. Schweizer, 'The cabinet crisis of
August 1761: unpublished letters from
the Bute and Bedford manuscripts',
Bull. Institute for Historical Research, LIX
(1986), 225–9. The quotation is from
14 August 1761, Brown and Schweizer,
op. cit., 110.

51. 19 August 1761, Jenkinson notes,
BL Add. MSS 38336, f. 264.

52. 26 June 1761, Jenkinson notes, BL
Add. MSS 38336, fos 241–2.

53. Bute to Bedford, 12 July 1761, in Lord
John Russell (ed.), *Correspondence of
John, Fourth Duke of Bedford, Selected from
the Originals at Woburn Abbey* (1846),
III, 32.

54. 13 Aug. 1761, Jenkinson notes, BL
Add. MSS 38336, f. 254.

55. 14 Aug. 1761, Brown and Schweizer,
op. cit., 109.

56. 19 Aug. 1761, Jenkinson notes, BL Add. MSS 38336, fos 265–6.
57. The phrase in quotations is the Earl of Gower's, in a letter to Bedford, 3 July 1761, Bedford MSS, XLIV, no. 90.
58. 15 Sept. 1761, Brown and Schweizer, *op. cit.*, 123–5.
59. 8 Jan. 1762, *ibid.*, 155. For an account of these negotiations through the Sardinian envoys in London and Paris, see Rashed, *op. cit.*, 113–22.
60. 6 Jan. 1762, Brown and Schweizer, *op. cit.*, 154. For a full discussion of the benefits to be gained by taking Havana, see Henry Ellis to the Earl of Egremont, 16 January 1762, PRO 30/47/14/1, fos 240–5. An account of the planning may be found in R. Middleton, *The Bells of Victory: the Pitt–Newcastle ministry and the Conduct of the Seven Years' War, 1757–1762* (1985), 205.
61. This struggle over the war in Germany may be followed in Brown and Schweizer, *op. cit.*, 154–70; and in the King's letters to Bute from January to May 1762 in Sedgwick, *op. cit.*, 78–101. George's willingness to remove British troops from Germany is a sure sign that Bute seriously considered a withdrawal. For another indication, see Jenkinson to George Grenville, 13 April 1762, in W.J. Smith (ed.), *The Grenville Papers: being the correspondence of Richard Grenville Earl Temple, K.G., and the Right Hon. George Grenville, their friends and contemporaries* (1852–3), I, 440.
62. Bute to Bedford, 1 May 1762, in Russell, *op. cit.*, III, 76.
63. For the contemporary definition of 'chicane', see the *Oxford English Dictionary*. France's reputation as a 'chicaning power' was proverbial at the time. See Bedford to Bute, 4 May 1762, in Russell, *op. cit.*, III, 77.
64. Bute to Bedford, 1 May 1762, in Russell, *op. cit.*, 76.
65. For the secret concession of Santa Lucia, see Rashed, *op. cit.*, 149–50; for the awareness of the value of that island, see Grenville's notes on cabinet meetings, 18 March 1762, George Grenville MSS, STG 17–(43). There is a modern transcription of these notes in BL Add. MSS 57834, fos 59–62.
66. See Grenville, notes on the French statement, July 1762, George Grenville MSS, STG17–(35); Edward Weston to Grenville, July 1762, *ibid.*, STG 17–(37); and George III to Bute, July 1762, Bute MSS, Correspondence with George III, no. 188.
67. George III to Bute, 26 July 1762, Sedgwick, *op. cit.*, 126.
68. Bute to Bedford, 28 Sept. 1762, BL Add. MSS 36797, f. 12. See also Bute to Fox, 26 Oct. 1762, *ibid.*, fos 14–15.
69. Devonshire to Newcastle, 25 August 1762, BL Add. MSS 32942, fos 9–10.
70. Rashed, *op. cit.*, 179–80.
71. Phillip Lawson, *George Grenville: A Political Life* (1984), 136.
72. [Edward Richardson], *A letter to a gentleman in the City*, St James Chronicle, 7–9 September 1762. For a brief account of the success of this essay, more generally known as 'the Wandsworth letter', see John Brewer, *Party Ideology and Popular Politics at the Accession of George III* (1976), 223; for responses to it by Bute's enemies, see *St James Chronicle*, 11–14 September 1762, and *North Briton*, XV.
73. Bute to Fox, 30 Nov. 1762, BL Add. MSS 51379, f. 118.
74. Bute to Bedford, 28 Sept. 1762, BL Add. MSS 36797, f. 12. For a contrary argument, that Bute hoped to end French hostility toward Britain, see R. Hyam, 'Imperial interests and the Peace of Paris (1763)', in R. Hyam and G. Martin, *Reappraisals in British Imperial History* (1975), 34–5; for a convincing rebuttal of Hyam's interpretation, see R.W. Tucker and D.C. Hendrickson, *The Fall of the First British Empire: Origins of the War of American Independence* (Baltimore, MD, 1982), 40–1.
75. Bute to Bedford, 12 July 1761, in Russell, *op. cit.*, III, 32–3.
76. Bute to Phillips, 23 Feb. 1763, BL Add. MSS 36797, f. 34.
77. Jenkinson to Richard Neville, 14 Nov. 1762, and Neville to Jenkinson, 2 Dec. 1762, PRO 30/50/48, fos 45–6, 73. The

judgment on the usefulness of Neville's intelligence is in Jenkinson to Neville, 22 July 1763, PRO 30/50/52, f. 59. Neville was Bedford's secretary when the latter was negotiating peace in Paris.

78. In his speech to Parliament on 25 November 1762, *Journals of the House of Commons*, XXIX, 354, the King emphasized the necessity of improving the new acquisitions. Though the speech understandably emphasized their potential for future improvement, such an argument implicitly recognized that these additions to the empire would not be much present help to the nation.

2

Lord Bute, William Pitt, and the peace negotiations with France, April–September 1761

Karl W. Schweizer

The failure of the Anglo-French peace negotiations of 1761 – the so-called Stanley–Bussy talks – is usually ascribed to two principal causes: British intransigence over the Canadian fisheries and, closely related, the deficiency of William Pitt's diplomacy: the fact that he lacked both the technique and personality for successful negotiation.[1] British historians in particular have tended to assess the course and failure of the negotiations with exclusive reference to the policies of the elder Pitt, a tendency symbolic of the dominance that Pitt supposedly exercised over national affairs at this time. The picture they present is that of a domineering, almost dictatorial figure, subduing Cabinet opposition to his extreme demands with the same harsh tactics he employed against defeated France.[2] Though more recent works on the Seven Years War have questioned and significantly curtailed Pitt's 'directing role' – certainly in administrative and strategic matters[3] his alleged diplomatic pre-eminence throughout the critical summer of 1761 has remained undisputed. In the words of Kate Hotblack (taking a view which is still current), 'until his resignation in October, Pitt dominated the peace negotiations as he had dominated the war.'[4] The present essay seeks to question this interpretation by showing that Pitt, eminent political figure though he was, did not singly control the Cabinet and its decisions but worked more in collaboration with his co-ministers, especially Lord Bute, his then fellow Secretary,[5] whose role in decision-making and hence impact on policy was greater than traditionally realized. Indeed, if any single factor proved decisive for the deliberations with France, it was their association – long in materializing, uneasy in practice and brief in duration. While Bute supported Pitt, the latter managed to prevail against his opponents in Council and Britain's policy remained firm; when, early in August of 1761, Bute shifted support to the moderates, those favouring last-minute concessions on the fisheries, Pitt swiftly lost ground and resigned shortly afterwards. At the same time, there is evidence that ultimately peace miscarried, not so much due to poor statesmanship, to anything done or left undone, or even the contentious fisheries question, but as a result of extraneous developments: England's continuing victories on land and sea which set a limit to concession and, certainly in the eyes of Pitt and Bute, necessitated a strong stand; and the prospect of a French alliance with Spain. Thus, precisely when Britain expected terms and advantages commensurate with her success, France gained new strength and confidence, correspondingly becoming less desperate for peace, especially if such peace involved the surrender of vital national interests.[6]

The immediate context for Bute's *rapprochement* with Pitt was the political situation, specifically the alignment of ministerial forces and personalities at the accession of George III. At centre, dating from 1757, stood the Whig coalition led by Newcastle and William Pitt – an administration of unprecedented efficiency which maintained relative domestic stability while assuring the vigorous pursuit of global war.[7] Their respective roles within this coalition, as has recently been shown,[8] remained fairly constant as the war progressed: Pitt supplied the administration with popularity and success, giving Newcastle a secure background against which he could devote his energy to Treasury affairs and above all to the disposal of patronage.[9] No less vital was Newcastle's function as liaison between the King and Cabinet. Secure in George II's confidence, he was able to press Pitt's periodic demands on the King, leaving Pitt free to pursue his imperial schemes. Thus it was not his but Newcastle's strength – royal favour and a majority in the Commons – which helped Pitt to carry his policies in the Cabinet; while his own implicit weakness often enabled him to evade personal responsibility for controversial measures.[10] This, in turn, did much to reinforce the image of independence, virtue and patriotism, key elements in the 'patriot role', cultivated and exploited by Pitt to sustain his credit and popularity with the nation at large.[11] With the advent of a new King, however, and the resultant reconfiguration of politics, such an arrangement was no longer feasible. Admittedly, Newcastle still controlled Parliament and Pitt had his popular support, but it was the Earl of Bute, close friend and former tutor of George III, who now monopolized royal favour. A new political equation was clearly necessary. The ideal solution, as diagnosed by Devonshire (the Lord Chamberlain)[12] was union between the factors – Newcastle, Pitt and Bute – who presently dominated the political scene; alternatively, since Newcastle would inevitably gravitate towards Court,[13] agreement between Pitt and Bute – reminiscent of the

Leicester House days – might avert political confusion and strife. Ministerial discord, however, compounded of old grievances and new fears, momentarily ruled out such an *entente* and for nearly five months Bute was forced to drift, manoeuvring uneasily in a world of political makeshifts, all the while trying to renew his former friendship with Pitt.[14]

While a true reconciliation was highly unlikely, neither Pitt nor Bute being compatible in character or personality, political exigency and lack of any other course finally provided the impetus for at least a temporary partnership, one to hold the administration together and make possible joint action and co-operation.[15] Moreover, uncertain though Pitt and Bute were with each other, they had identical views (initially) on the major policy issue of 1761: the peace negotiations with France which had begun in April of that year. By then Pitt's co-Secretary, and so able to use his connection with the King officially,[16] Bute acknowledged the need for peace, on political as much as financial grounds, but, like Pitt, he wanted a settlement commensurate with Britain's world-wide victories, a treaty that would satisfy national interests and thereby enhance the prestige of both the government and the new King.[17] If there was a difference between them it was not in principle but approach: where Pitt was prepared to enforce peace through continued, even intensified operations,[18] Bute, by contrast, sought more reliance on compromise and conciliation;[19] diplomacy not *force majeure* was his ideal. Representing the moderate or pacifist position was Newcastle, supported by Hardwicke, Granville, Devonshire and, above all, the Duke of Bedford, probably the most outspoken advocate of peace, partly from magnanimity, partly because he feared the prospect of a European combination against Britain if victory was pushed too far. As he told Bute:

> Let us do as we would be done by, the most golden rule ... always to be observed ... We have too much already – more than we know what to do with; and I very much fear that if we retain the greatest part of our conquests out of Europe we shall be in danger of overcolonising and undoing ourselves by them as the Spaniards have done.[20]

Though undoubtedly in sympathy with Pitt, Bute, faced by two extreme possibilities – escalated warfare or precipitate peace – could not, consistent with his aims, endorse either wholeheartedly. In order to maintain Cabinet solidarity, while seeking honourable but also realistic terms, Bute had to hold a careful balance, sometimes restraining Pitt,[21] at other times toughening the attitude of the pacifists.[22] His near success in this necessarily delicate enterprise reveals a grasp of issues, a degree of political potential, even a touch of statesmanship that has never been acknowledged.

On the French side, negotiations were conducted by Louis XV's principal minister, Étienne-François, Duc de Choiseul, soldier, courtier, administrator and, by consensus, one of the best diplomatists of his age.[23] While evidently sincere in his desire for peace,[24] France no longer having the resources to challenge, much less reverse, British colonial supremacy, Choiseul had from the outset played an intricate if not dangerous diplomatic game. Aware of his weak bargaining position, the French minister was determined to have a safeguard, a reassurance – namely, alliance with Spain – in case Britain refused to meet the limit of his concessions and war continued. What resulted were dual negations: those held at London, whose avowed object was peace, and those pursued with Spain – seeking Spanish participation in the war – which culminated in the famous Third Family Compact signed on 15 August 1761.[25] More than anything, Choiseul's strategem turned on developments within the British Cabinet: so long as the ministers were inclined to compromise and peace seemed assured, union with Spain was not of immediate concern; as expectations of peace faded, however, the value of the Spanish alliance correspondingly increased.[26] The real difficulty was timing: chosing the proper moment to abandon conciliation and actually close with Spain.

Choiseul's first concrete proposals were dispatched on 17 June. He proposed an exchange of Minorca (France's sole conquest) for Guadeloupe, Marie Galante and Goree; England was to retain the whole of Canada, with the exception of Cape Breton, which would be restored to France but kept unfortified. As expected, he also demanded continued participation in the Newfoundland fisheries (granted by the Treaty of Utrecht) in return for which France agreed to restore all conquests in Germany, including Wesel, Guelders and Cleves, provinces belonging to Prussia, Britain's wartime ally.[27] No mention was made of Belle Île or the demilitarization of Dunkirk, another potentially contentious issue. Like Pitt, Choiseul placed supreme importance on the fisheries,[28] both realizing not only the commercial value of the industry – the French share alone being worth about £500,000 per annum[29] – but, even more, their strategic significance. According to mercantilist theory, the fisheries were a 'nursery for seamen'[30] and thus an essential component of naval power, or in France's case, naval reconstruction. The cod trade of peace provided the naval complements of war.

Choiseul's proposals arrived in London on 21 June and three days later a Cabinet Council convened to consider them. While all the ministers agreed to reject the French claim for Cape Breton[31] – Canada was to be surrendered in its entirety – struggle came over the question of the fisheries. Pitt (seconded by Temple) demanded exclusive British control and proposed to break off negotiations immediately if Choiseul failed to comply.[32] Newcastle, Bedford, Hardwicke and Granville all took the other side, the latter rightly arguing that France would never consent to part with such a valuable industry, and that to enforce its surrender could only provoke the hostility of Spain and other as yet neutral maritime powers.[33] Newcastle supported him, asserting that it was unwise to put the chance of a good peace at risk. Bedford also stressed that while the Cabinet argued over the fisheries the position in Germany might collapse. Bute's view was more in harmony with Pitt's: he acknowledged the value of the fisheries but argued against cutting short the negotiations, convinced that patience and sustained firmness would untimately induce Choiseul to give way.[34] In the end, after further arguments for and against, the Council adopted the sensible *via media* suggested by Bute: namely, that Britain try to obtain sole possession without, however, making this a necessary condition of peace.[35]

Embodied in an official 'Counter-Project', the Cabinet's decision was dispatched by Pitt to Stanley on 26 June. In somewhat harsh terms,[36] Pitt's letter not only rejected the French demand for Cape Breton, but made French access to the Newfoundland fisheries dependent upon further concessions – such as the complete demolition of the Dunkirk fortifications; Guadeloupe and Marie Galante would be restored only if the territories of Britain's German allies – Prussia included – were evacuated. France was also to cede Senegal and Goree and to restore Minorca.

According to most historians,[37] this was the turning point in the negotiations, prompting Choiseul to take the irrevocable step and unite with Spain. If so – and the evidence seems conclusive – it is clear in retrospect that Choiseul misread developments and acted too soon. After all, London's response had sprung from the reasonable assumption – encouraged by the British envoy in France[38] – that Choiseul's proposals were preliminaries, an opening move in diplomatic chess; that 'if we reject one proposition', as Bute told Bedford, 'the French will try another and by negotiation peace may at last be made.'[39] Better than Pitt, Bute realized that a lasting settlement invariably takes the form of adjustment and compromise – a compromise he hoped to reach through bargaining and diplomacy. But here he received no co-operation from Choiseul who, having no sooner examined the British memorandum, prematurely despaired of peace and immediately consolidated relations with Austria and Spain.[40] This action appears all the more precipitate when we remember that there were other points in dispute, even in the fisheries themselves. Choiseul wanted a share in the St Lawrence fisheries, in addition to rights in Newfoundland, and an *abri* – or station on the mainland for shelter. Bute's formula had only covered the limited fishing rights, and so far certainly the Cabinet was almost unanimous in refusing the other two demands – which were equally essential in Choiseul's eyes. Continued effort on both sides was needed for agreement on these and other outstanding questions, but this meant time – something Choiseul did not have, pressured as he was by his allies – one actual, Austria, one potential, Spain. Sure of victory, Austria wanted no part of peace,[41] while Spain, anxious for an alliance, engaged to support French interests and take part in the war, if Britain proved inflexible and the peace talks collapsed. Obviously, and in the long run the decisive factor, even Britain's minimum conditions seemed too exacting so long as France still had the resources and the prospect of a new ally with which to fight another campaign and possibly improve her bargaining strength.

The ominous change in Choiseul's attitude made itself felt at once. During the next interview with Stanley, he not only retracted his earlier offer to evacuate the Prussian territories[42] (besides reiterating his demand for Cape Breton and a share in the Newfoundland fisheries) but, on 13 July, forwarded two private *mémoires* which reached London at the worst moment – just after the news of further British victories (at Pondicherry and Dominica), thus inevitably hardening the Cabinet's view on peace.[43] The first enumerated Spain's long-standing grievances[44] against Britain and advised that these be resolved within the context of the current negotiations;[45] the other declared that Austria would agree to a separate Anglo-French treaty only provided the Prussian provinces captured by France were retained and neither France nor England lend assistance of any sort to their respective allies in Germany.[46] What might have been foreseen in fact happened: this time all the ministers, not only Bute and Pitt, declared the French proposals 'totally inadmissable',[47] and during a lengthy Cabinet session on 21 July unanimously voted to reject them. At a second meeting on 24 July, Choiseul's other proposals were discussed. Again Council agreed to a firm reply, some members reluctantly, though later criticized the style ('haughty and dictatorial' according to Hardwicke) employed by Pitt, without receiving much sympathy either from Bute or the King.[48] Most of the French demands were decisively rejected: the right to fish in the Gulf of St Lawrence and restoration of Cape Breton were again refused; access to the Newfoundland fisheries would not be granted unless France agreed to demolish the fortifications at

Dunkirk. Belle Île was offered as an equivalent to Minorca, the neutral islands would be divided equally, but Senegal and Goree were to remain under British control.[49] Both in form and substance, this crucial ultimatum, contrary to accepted interpretation, was the work of Pitt *and* Bute: left to themselves, Newcastle and friends would probably have been more accommodating, certainly less severe in tone and manner. With the two Secretaries of State acting together, however, the moderates in Council gave way and the British ultimatum, haughty style and all, remained unchanged.

Upon receiving this reply on 29 July, Choiseul decided definitely to continue the war, and while managing to protract the talks until September, far from being sincere, was merely temporizing until the preparations of France and her new ally were complete.[50] This double game required no little care and skill, for in order to prevent a collapse of the talks before his other plans had matured, Choiseul had to offer terms sufficiently exacting to prevent them being accepted; yet also conciliatory enough to keep negotiations alive.

In London, the decisive turn in the deliberations came towards the middle of August – following receipt of Choiseul's counter-ultimatum of 5 August, which reaffirmed the union of interest between France and Spain, and once more demanded fishing privileges in the St Lawrence together with a suitable *abri* – preferably Cape Breton or St John.[51] During two stormy Cabinet sessions, on 13 and 14 August, Pitt encountered mounting opposition over his staunch refusal to soften the wording of his draft reply to the latest French communiqué. In the end, his dispatch, indignantly rejecting Choiseul's ultimatum, was approved by a slender majority, but such was the bitterness engendered that Bedford, still the warmest advocate of peace, refused to attend any further meetings and there were signs that others – notably Newcastle and Devonshire – might follow his example.[52]

With a political crisis impending, the Duke of Devonshire, influential and widely respected, now set out as mediator attempting to draw the various factions together. He conferred with the King, who insisted that the fisheries question be further explored,[53] wrote letters to Newcastle and Bedford,[54] convincing the latter to return to Council and, most important, approached Lord Bute, whose abiding connection with Pitt had thus far been a major hindrance to the pacifists in the Cabinet. By now Bute was of two minds: still anxious for a profitable peace, but worried by the growing divisions in Council. Also, though not wishing to dissent from Pitt, he was no longer confident – given recent events – that the forceful approach until now endorsed by Pitt and himself would ultimately bring the French to compliance.[55]

Consequently he proved receptive to Devonshire's arguments in favour of concession, agreeing in the end to yield on the St Lawrence fisheries, ostensibly to preserve ministerial unity. 'That whatever his opinion,' as he told Devonshire,

> When he saw so many Lords of great consequence and character, of opinion to relax upon the point of the fishery, so far as they thought consistent with the honour of the Nation he should so far as he could in conscience and for the sake of unanimity give up his opinion; that he had done it on the point of the Newfoundland Fisheries and that he should be inclined to do it in this instance.[56]

The effect of Bute's decision was immediate. A formal reply to the last French ultimatum had to be framed and the Cabinet met during the week of 19–24 August – with Bedford present – to settle Britain's final offer. At these meetings, isolated, with none but Temple to support him, Pitt unwillingly gave way to majority opinion and the policy of concession, advocated for so long by Bedford and Newcastle, unanimously carried the day. The right to fish in the Gulf of St Lawrence was now granted together with the island of St Pierre. As a further gesture, the fortifications of Dunkirk were to conform to the less stringent provisions of the Treaty of Aix-la-Chapelle. The British insistence that the Prussian territories be restored unconditionally, remained unchanged.[57]

Unfortunately, as is well known, Choiseul could not accept these new, more lenient terms, for he was already too deeply committed to Spain, the Family Compact having been signed on 15 August. As a result, he sent another temporizing *mémoire* – rejecting in part Britain's offer and demanding additional advantages – which ultimately decided the Cabinet that Stanley must be recalled and the negotiations broken off.[58] About the actual details of the new Family Compact, Pitt probably knew little or nothing, though by the beginning of September its existence had been established.[59] But on the basis of suggestive evidence – certain intercepted dispatches in particular[60] (not to mention Choiseul's intervention on Spain's behalf) – Pitt shrewdly surmised that the two Bourbon powers were in accord, and that hostilities with Spain were inevitable.[61] It was this conjecture, joined with his low opinion of Spanish strength, which prompted his famous 'advice in writing' (dated 18 September 1761), the proposal to recall Lord Bristol at once from Madrid and launch a pre-emptive strike before the Spanish treasure fleet from America could make port.[62] There, however, he encountered staunch opposition from both Cabinet and the King, who felt (rightly) that a *casus belli* did not yet exist and that further diplomatic effort should precede any recourse to arms.[63] To take the offensive now and so enlarge – needlessly perhaps – the scope of military/naval operations before Spain's intentions were really clear, seemed morally and politically indefensible. In effect, the Cabinet favoured precautionary measures over hostile ones: strong reinforcements for the West Indies, additional squadrons in the Mediterranean, and new instructions for Lord Bristol to demand immediate explanation and reassurance from Spain.[64] Disregarding Bute's repeated attempts to dissuade him, Pitt persisted in his views on 'preventative war' and after attending one final but inconclusive Cabinet meeting on 2 October, resigned his Seals three days later.[65]

In conclusion, the traditional picture of Pitt dominating a Cabinet of compliant nonentities requires extensive modification when re-examined in the light of wider documentary evidence. Often difficult, usually outspoken, Pitt still invariably submitted in the end to the collective opinion of the Cabinet Council.[66] Had Pitt truly dominated his colleagues, the peace talks, no doubt, would have ended much sooner. Only when convinced that the Franco-Spanish compact was a *fait accompli* could he no longer conform, and having his advice rejected, he consequently resigned. Equally, the negotiations show no departure from accepted Cabinet practice: critical decisions were based upon collective discussion not imposed by any one member, however popular or influential, though voting patterns frequently depended on the prevailing coalition of internal political forces.

The events of these months also indicate that Pitt was not the best negotiator – lacking the ability to compromise, and the suppleness required in diplomacy. But arguably, given the larger issues at stake, these deficiencies had little if any bearing on the outcome of the talks. Significantly, Choiseul did not complain of Pitt's 'dictatorial tone' until mid-August, when he had decided to unite with Spain, but was eager to attribute his actions to the intransigence of Pitt and the British government. Even Stanley, who likewise considered Pitt's diplomatic methods too harsh, was hardly objective, being primarily concerned to justify his own dealings with Choiseul.

The same evidence which restricts Pitt's pre-eminence, brings into new prominence Lord Bute whose role (partly because of his standing with the King) was equally or possibly even more decisive throughout this period. Far from merely following Pitt's initiatives, Bute took an active part throughout: collaborating constantly with Pitt and others on the major policy issues,[67] participating prominently in all the Cabinet discussions and on more than one occasion formulating the recommendations which after Cabinet approval were submitted to the King.[68] From the first, Bute pursued consistent objectives:

to moderate Pitt, to maintain Cabinet unity, and to devise reasonable but also honourable terms. Had it not been for Choiseul's precipitate involvement with Spain, he might well have succeeded in time.

To argue, as does Richard Pares, that if Bute had agreed in June to what he yielded later, the Family Compact might never have materialized is to ignore one fundamental fact: when Pitt and Bute first refused the fisheries, it was in the wake of new British victories and on the legitimate premise that, anxious for peace, France would eventually concede the point. They did not know that, anticipating Spanish aid, Choiseul had a limit of concessions beyond which he would not go and that peace was only possible if this limit coincided with what the British government was willing to accept. To guard against all contingencies, Choiseul held simultaneous negotiations for war and peace; in the event, the former were to prove fatal to the latter.

NOTES

This essay is an amended version of an earlier paper published in *Albion*, XIII (1981), 262–75 and I am indebted to Dr M. Moore for permission to reprint it in this volume.

Research for this paper was made possible by a grant from the Social Sciences and Humanities Research Council of Canada and from Bishop's University Research Fund. For permission to consult and cite their manuscripts, I wish to thank the following: The British Library; the Public Records Office; the Central Library, Cardiff; the Marquis of Bute, Mount Stuart; His Grace the Duke of Devonshire (Chatsworth MSS); the Trustees of the Bedford Estate (Bedford MSS); the Hampshire Record Office (Stanley MSS); the Archives du Ministère des Affaires Étrangères; and the Deutsches Zentral Archiv Merseburg.

1. The most detailed accounts of the deliberations are: B. Williams, *The Life of William Pitt, Earl of Chatham* (1913), II, 80–102; P.C. Yorke, *The Life and Correspondence of Philip Yorke, Earl of Hardwicke* (1913), III, 268–72, 280–3; H.V. Temperley, 'The Peace of Paris', in *Cambridge History of the British Empire* (1929), ch. XVII; J.S. Corbett, *England in the Seven Years War* (1907). 328–50; K. Hotblack, 'The Peace of Paris', *TRHS*, II (1908), 248–53; L.H. Gipson, *The British Empire Before the American Revolution VIII, The Great War for Empire: the Culmination, 1760–1763* (New York, 1954), 207–27; W.L. Dorn, *Competition for Empire 1740–1763* (1940), 370–84; R. Waddington, *La Guerre de Sept Ans* (Paris, 1911), IV, 500–603; Z.E. Rashed, *The Peace of Paris* (1951). Important primary materials may be found in F. Thackeray, *A History of the Right Honourable William Pitt, Earl of Chatham* (2 vols, 1827); *Mémoire historique sur la negotiation de la France et de l'Angletere depuis le 26 mars 1761 jusqu'au 20 septembre de la même année avec les pièces justificatives* (New York, reprint 1966).

2. French scholars equally have tended to criticize Pitt's imperious ways, W.L. Grant calling him 'le dictateur de la politique britannique' in 'La mission de M. de Bussy a Londre en 1761,' *Revue d'histoire diplomatique*, XX (1901), 351. Compare this with the views of Waddington, *op. cit.*, 600–1: 'A notre avis c'est bien à Pitt qu'incombe la responsabilité de l'échec. Comme conditions de paix il etait bien

déterminé à n'accorder que celles qui imposent au vaincu la loi du vainqueur.' Similarly see A. Bourguet, 'Le Duc de Choiseul et l'Angleterre, la mission de Monsieur de Bussy a Londres', *Revue historique*, LXXI, 1–32; *idem, Le Duc de Choiseul et l'alliance Espagnole* (Paris, 1906); P. Muret, *La Prépondérance anglaise, 1715–1763* (Paris, 1942), 532.

3. Kent Hackmann, 'William Pitt and the generals: three case studies in the Seven Years War', *Albion*, III (1971), 128–37; Eric McDermott, 'The elder Pitt and his admirals and generals', *Military Affairs*, XX (1956), 65–6; Richard Middleton, 'Pitt, Anson and the Admiralty, 1756–1761', *History*, LV (1970), 189–98; *idem, The Bells of Victory: The Pitt–Newcastle Ministry and the Conduct of the Seven Years War 1757–1762* (1985).

4. Hotblack, *op. cit.*, 248; E. Eyck, *Pitt vs. Fox, Father and Son, 1735–1806* (1950), 99–100; Stanley Ayling, *The Elder Pitt*, 288; H.T. Dickinson, 'The Duke of Newcastle', in *The Prime Ministers*, ed. Herbert van Thal (1974), 87–90; R. Browning, *The Duke of Newcastle* (New Haven, CT, 1975), 279.

5. Though Bute was one of the most complex, if not controversial figures in eighteenth-century politics, he has been unduly neglected by historians. The only biographies, C.A. Lovat-Frazer's *John Stuart, 3rd Earl of Bute* (1912) and Alice Coats, *Lord Bute: An Illustrated Life* (1975), are incomplete, superficial and based solely on secondary sources. Other aspects of Bute's career have been examined with varying degrees of scrutiny by Sir Lewis Namier, *England in the Age of the American Revolution* (2nd edn, 1961); J.L. McKelvey, *Lord Bute and George III: The Leicester House Years*, (1973); and R. Sedgwick (ed.) *Letters From George III to Lord Bute 1756–66*, (1939). For the wider significance of his career see J. Brewer, *Party ideology and Popular Politics at the Accession of George III* (1976); *idem*, 'The misfortunes of Lord Bute: a case study of 18th century political argument and public

opinion,' *Hist J*, XVI, no. 1 (1973), 113–43. On Bute's diplomatic activity see Karl W. Schweizer, 'Bute, Newcastle, Prussia and the Hague Overtures: a re-examination', *Albion*, I (1977), 72–98; *idem*, 'The non-renewal of the Anglo-Prussian Subsidy Treaty 1761–1762: a historical revision', *Canadian J. of History*, XIII (1978), 383–98: *idem*, with C. Leonard, 'Britain, Prussia, Russia and the Galitzin Letter: a reassessment', *Hist J*, XXVI, no. 3 (1983), 531–56; *idem*, 'Lord Bute the Bedford Motion and House of Lords debate, 5 Feb. 1762', *Parliamentary History*, V (1986), 107–23; and 'Britain, Prussia and the Prussian territories on the Rhine 1762–1763', *Essays in European History in Honour of R. Hatton*, ed. K.W. Schweizer and J. Black (1985), 103–14.

6. As Bedford prophetically wrote on 9 May 1761: 'I fear the rock we may split upon will be the demanding of terms which to oversanguine minds our successes may seem to entitle us to, but which will be inadmissable by France even was she reduced much lower than she really is' (letter to Newcastle, BL Add. MSS 32922, f. 451).

7. For complete details see D. Marshall, *18th Century England* (New York, 1966), 285–321; P.D. Brown, *William Pitt, Earl of Chatham* (1978), 148–213; Namier, *op. cit., passim*.

8. E. Fraser, 'The Pitt–Newcastle coalition and the conduct of the Seven Years War 1757–1760' (D.Phil. thesis, University of Oxford, 1976). Cf. Middleton, *The Bells of Victory*, chs I–IV.

9. See: Browning, *Newcastle*, 145f; *idem*, 'The Duke of Newcastle and the financial management of the Seven Years War in Germany', *J. Society of Army Historical Research*, XLIX (1971), 20–35; *idem*, 'The Duke of Newcastle and the financing of the Seven Years War', *J. Economic History*, XXXI (1971), 344–77.

10. As Fraser, *op. cit.*, observed: 'Again and again Pitt cleverly exploited the weakness of his own position in the

government while retaining Tory support by disclaiming any responsibility for the control of the Commons and retaining an apparently independent attitude. He took advantage also of Newcastle's favour in the closet as a means of forcing disagreeable policies on the King, and frequently continued to put the blame on Newcastle for decisions unpopular with his own supporters but which were in reality of his own devising.' This view parallels closely that of R. Pares, *War and Trade in the West Indies, 1739–1763* (1963), 570, who considered Pitt 'an exceedingly artful demagogue', always ready to take credit for anything popular but 'equally ready to shirk responsibility for things which were not.'

11. On the nature, function and importance of the patriot stereotype see: Brewer, *Party Ideology and Popular Politics*, 96–111; and Marie Peters, *Pitt and Popularity: The Patriot Minister and London Opinion during the Seven Years War* (1980), 63–5, 265–70.

12. See P.D. Brown and K.W. Schweizer (eds), *The Devonshire Diary: William Cavendish, 4th Duke of Devonshire; Memoranda on State of Affairs, 1759–1762* (1982), Nov. 1760; 23 Jan. 1761; 9 Feb. 1761; 25 Feb. 1761.

13. *Ibid.*, 31 Oct. 1760.

14. For Bute's attempts at reconciliation after the death of George II, see Namier, *op. cit.*, 120f; 'An account given by Mr. (Thomas Walpole) of what passed with Mr. Pitt, 13 November 1762', BL Add. MSS 32945, fos. 1–2, Hardwicke to Newcastle, 29 Oct. 1760, BL Add. MSS 32913, fos. 426–9.

15. Gilbert Elliot to Bute, 25 March 1761, Bute MSS no. 161. Newcastle to Mansfield, 18 March 1761, BL Add. MSS 32920, f. 295. Symmer to A. Mitchell, 17 March 1761, BL Add. MSS 6839, fos. 215–18.

16. For the intensive intrigues and negotiations leading to Bute's appointment as Secretary of State, see Namier, *op. cit.*, 156–70; Brown, *op. cit.*,

221–30. The relevant documents are in BL Add. MSS 32917–20; Brown and Schweizer, *op. cit.*, entries from January to March 1761.

17. As he wrote to Bedford on 12 July, at a crisis point in the talks: 'Your Grace cannot wish for peace more sincerely than I do, but let that peace prove in some measure answerable to the conquests we have made. I join with you in wishing heartily for a peace – a peace such as the bulk of the nation have a right to expect from such a triumphant war' (Bedford MSS, XLIV, no. 8, f. 110). Cf. J. Russell (ed.), *The Correspondence of John, 4th Duke of Bedford* (1846), III, 31–3.

18. 'My conversation with Mr. Pitt, 10 April, 1761', BL Add. MSS 32931, fos. 381–2; Brown and Schweizer, *op. cit.*, 9, 10, Apr. 1761. For Pitt's minimum terms which included all of Canada, Cape Breton, the islands, harbours and particularly exclusive fishing rights, see Newcastle to Hardwicke, 17 Apr. 1761, BL Add. MSS 32922, fos. 19–22.

19. Bute to Bedford, 12 July 1761, Russell, *op. cit.*, III, 34.

20. Bedford to Bute, 9 July 1761. Bute MSS 478.Cf. Newcastle to Devonshire, 2 April 1761, BL Add. MSS 32921, fos. 271–3; Newcastle to Hardwicke, 14 May 1761, BL Add. MSS 32923, fos. 63–71; Hardwicke to Newcastle, 16 May 1761, *ibid.*, fos. 123–8, Brown and Schweizer, *op. cit.*, 13 May 1761, 30 June, 11 July 1761, Rigby to Bedford, 22 April 1761 and Bedford to Bute, 13 June, 1761, Russell, *op. cit.*, III, 6–7, 14–17, 22–9; Lady E. Waldegrave to J. Calcraft, 28 June 1761, PRO 30/8/86, f. 308, cf. R. Hyam and G. Martin, *Reappraisals in British Imperial History* (Toronto, 1975), 26–8; Pares, *op. cit.*, 576–8.

21. Thus Newcastle observed to Devonshire in a letter of 18 June, after the talks were well under way: 'As to public affairs, I mean the negotiation for peace, he [Bute] has done

admirably well and with success. I found on Monday morning, Mr. Pitt in a very right way of thinking, I own contrary to my expectations. Lord Bute has had a good deal of conversation with him' (BL Add. MSS 32934, fos. 157–9). See also the interesting observations in Knyphausen to Frederick, 19 May 1761, DZA, Rep. 96. 33. E, 243–4.

22. Jenkinson to Grenville, 21 July 1761, in W.J. Smith (ed.), *The Grenville Papers* (1852), I, 376; Hardwicke to Newcastle, 16 May 1761, BL Add. MSS 32923, f. 125; Newcastle to Devonshire, 5 Aug. 1761, BL Add. MSS 32926, f. 187.

23. On Choiseul, see Roger H. Soltau, *The Duke de Choiseul* (1908); Bourguet, *Le Duc de Choiseul et l'alliance Espagnole, passim*; and, for his earlier years, the masterly boigraphy by Rohan Butler, *Choiseul: Father and Son 1719–1754* (1980). Almost without exception, secondary studies concentrate exclusively on Choiseul's activities after the Seven Years War (see the bibliography in: H.M. Scott, 'The importance of Bourbon naval reconstruction to the strategy of Choiseul after the Seven Years War', *International History Rev.* (1979), 17–35.

24. As is clearly shown by his detailed instructions to Bussy, 18 May 1761: *Recueil des Instructions* (Paris, 1965), III, 372–85. See also 'Mémoire sur la manière de procéder à la paix,' 6 Jan. 1761, AECP 281, f. 47.

25. For the history of the complex deliberations leading to the Treaty, see A. Soulange-Bodin, *La Diplomatie de Louis XV et le Pacte de Famille* (Paris, 1894); F. Rousseau, *Règne de Charles III d'Espagne, 1759–1788* (Paris, 1907), I; and the historiographical account by D. Ozanam, 'Les Origines du Troisième Pacte de Famille', *Revue d'histoire diplomatique*, LXXV (1961) 307–40.

26. Choiseul to Ossun, 3 February 1761. AECP, Espagne, 531, fos. 126–8. Soulange-Bodin, *op. cit.*, 242–3; J.

Calmette (ed.), *Memoires du Duc de Choiseul* (Paris, 1904), 386–7.

27. French memorial enclosed in Stanley to Pitt 18 June 1761, PRO SPF 78/251; Thackeray, *op. cit.*, I, 539–543. For a full account of Prussia's interest and role in these negotiations, see K.W. Schweizer, 'Frederick the Great, William Pitt and Lord Bute: Anglo-Prussian relations 1756–1763' (Ph.D. thesis, University of Cambridge, 1976), 212–21.

28. His excellency, Stanley observed on 18 June, 'will struggle hard for the Fisheries and had rather part with almost anything else.' Choiseul promised that Cape Breton would not be fortified, and since the Dutch, among other nations, had a share in the fisheries, 'them being excluded would be a disgrace and an inconvenience which the Country could not bear' (Stanley to Pitt, 18 June 1761, PRO SPF 78/251); cf. Yorke, *Hardwicke*, III, 269; Thackeray, *op. cit.*, II, 574. On the fisheries the standard works are R.G. Lounsbury, *The British Fishery at Newfoundland, 1634–1763* (1934); R.F. Grant, *The Canadian Atlantic Fisheries* (1934); M. Bronkhorst, *La pèche à la morue* (Paris, 1927).

29. For complete statistics, see BL Add. MSS 35913, DLXV, fos. 75–92. Hotblack, *op. cit.*, 265–6; PRO. 30/8/85 (Chatham MSS), fos. 365–6.

30. K. Hotblack, *op. cit.*, 265.

31. Even Bedford was opposed for fear such a concession might revive French naval power in that area: Bedford to Newcastle, 10 Aug. 1761, BL Add. MSS 32926, fos. 358–9.

32. Newcastle to Devonshire, 28 June 1761, BL Add. MSS 32934, fos. 312–13.

33. *Ibid.*, fos. 313–14. Cf. Bedford to Gower, 27 June 1761. PRO 30/29/14, fos. 526–8, I, 371–3.

34. Newcastle to Devonshire, 28 June 1761, BL Add. MSS 32923, fos. 318–19.

35. *Ibid.*

36. Criticizing the style of Pitt's letter,

Newcastle observed to Devonshire: 'I wish, we had not put too many *sine qua non* and that the letter had been wrote with more seeming confidence ...' (BL Add. MSS 32924, f. 32). For the British memorandum of 26 June, see Thackeray, *William Pitt*, II, 546–7; Pitt to Stanley, 26 June 1761, Stanley MSS, 10M55/127 no. 26.

37. Pares, *op. cit.*, 577–8; Rashed, *op. cit.*, 85–6; Yorke, *Hardwicke*, III, 269, 270–71; Grant, *op. cit.*, 362–3; Williams, *William Pitt*, II, 93–4.

38. Stanley to Pitt, 18 June 1761. Thackeray, *op. cit.*, I, 542. 'I do by no means conclude that these terms are the best that can be made with France, they are her first offer.' Obviously, Middleton has completely misinterpreted this phase of the negotiations: see *The Bells of Victory*, 188–190.

39. Bute to Bedford, 12 July, 1761, in Russell, *op. cit.*, III, 34; cf. Hardwicke to Newcastle, 23 June 1761, BL Add. MSS 32934, f. 221.

40. Waddington, *op. cit.*, IV, 600–61; Rashed, *op. cit.*, 85–6.

41. A. von Arneth, *Geschichte Marie Theresia's* (Vienna, 1875), VI, 268–80. Cf. Count of Choiseul to Duc de Choiseul, 15 February 1761, AE CP, Autriche 281, fos, 256–8.

42. Stanley to Pitt, 12 July 1761, PRO SPF 78/251.

43. Memo, 29 July 1761, BL Add. MSS 32926, fos. 47–49; Jenkinson to Grenville, 21 and 25 July 1761, in Smith, *op. cit.*, I, 376–7, 378–9, Knyphausen to Frederick II, 23 July 1761, DZA, Rep. 96.33, fos. 26–29.

44. These were Britain's illegal capture of Spanish merchant vessels, Spain's claim to the Newfoundland fisheries, and Britain's encroachments on the coast of Honduras.

45. Thackeray, *op. cit.*, II, 552–3.

46. *Ibid.*, II, 553–4. See also: Kaunitz to Starhemberg, 18 July 1761; von Arneth, *op. cit.*, VI, 269–70.

47. Memo, 24 July 1761, BL Add. MSS 32925, f. 251; Pitt to Bussy, 24 July 1761, PRO 30/8/85, f. 201.

48. Newcastle to Devonshire, 2 August 1761, BL Add. MSS 32926, fos. 187–93. Devonshire to Newcastle, 9 August, 1761, Chatsworth MSS 260/329.

49. Pitt to Stanley, 29 July 1761, PRO SPF 78/251.

50. Cf. Choiseul to Havrincourt, 30 July 1761 (intercept), BL Add. MSS 32926, f.67; Choiseul to Ossun, 30 July 1761, Bourguet, *l'Alliance Espagnole*, 225; AECP Espagne 533, fos. 176–8.

51. Thackeray, *op. cit.*, II, 566–9.

52. Brown and Schweizer, *op. cit.*, 13 and 14 Aug. 1761; Hardwicke to Royston, 15 Aug. 1761, BL Add. MSS 35352, fos. 183–4; Pitt to Bussy, 16 Aug. 1761, in Thackeray, *op. cit.*, II, 589–91; Bedford to Devonshire, 17 Aug. 1761, Chatsworth MSS 286/8.

53. Russell, *op. cit.*, III, 36–9; Devonshire to Bute, 18 Aug, 1761, Bute MSS no. 584.

54. Devonshire to Newcastle, 21 Aug. 1761, BL Add. MSS 32927, fos. 154–5; Devonshire to Bedford, 16 Aug. 1761, Bedford MSS 44, f. 128; Devonshire to Bedford, 18 August 1761, Russell, *op. cit.*, III, 41–2; Bedford to Devonshire, 18 Aug. 1761, Chatsworth MSS 286.9. For Devonshire's role with supporting documents, see K.W. Schweizer, 'The cabinet crisis of August 1761: unpublished letters from the Bute and Bedford Manuscripts', *Bull. Institute of Historical Research*, LIX (1986), 225–9.

55. Brown and Schweizer, *op. cit.*, 18 Aug. 1761.

56. *Ibid.*, 19 Aug. 1761. Hardwicke to Royston, 22 Aug. 1761, BL Add. MSS 35352, fos. 188–9.

57. Thackeray, *op. cit.*, II, 591–7.

58. *Ibid.*, 619–23. Stanley, notes on meeting with Choiseul, 2 Sept. 1761, Stanley MSS 10M55/124; Newcastle to Bedford, 13 Sept. 1761, BL Add. MSS 32928, fos. 131–2.

59. Stanley to Pitt (private), 2 September 1761, PRO SPF 78/252.

60. Grimaldi to Fuentes, 31 Aug. 1761, in W.S. Taylor and J.S. Pringle *Chatham Correspondence* (4 vols, 1838–40), II, 139–41.

61. Minute, Cabinet Session, 18

Sept. 1761, BL Add. MSS 35870, fos. 304–5.

62. Smith, *op. cit.*, I, 386–7.

63. Hunt, 'Pitt's retirement from office 1761', *EHR*, XXI (1906), 119–32. Brown and Schweizer, *op. cit.*, 18, 19, 20, 21, 23 Sept. 1761.

64. Minute, 19 Sept. 1761, BL Add. MSS 32928, fos. 248–50; Minute, BL Add. MSS 33000, fos. 271–2; Newcastle to Hardwicke, 20 Sept. 1761, BL Add. MSS 32928, fos. 259–60.

65. Yorke, *op. cit.*, III, 280–1. For the aftermath of this event see K.W. Schweizer, 'Lord Bute and William Pitt's resignation in 1761', *Canadian J. of History*, VIII, no. 2 (1973), 111–25.

66. For examples, see Newcastle to Hardwicke, 14 May 1761, BL Add. MSS 32923, fos. 63–71; Newcastle to Devonshire, 28 June 1761, BL Add. MSS 32924, fos. 313–14; Brown and Schweizer, *op. cit.*, 19 Aug. 1761; Minute, 24 Aug. 1761, BL Add. MSS 35870, f. 301.

67. There are among the Bute MSS numerous draft dispatches and copies of official documents which Pitt submitted regularly for Bute's inspection and comment before they were communicated to the Cabinet. As he wrote in one letter 'Mr. Pitt will be happy to receive Lord Bute's ideas relating to this affair [e.g. the last French communiqué] and to conform the draught entirely to them' (Pitt to Bute, 30 June 1761 no. 472). See also Pitt to Bute, 4, 26, 28 Apr., 31 May, 12 July, and 14 Aug. 1761, Bute MSS nos. 226, 320, 354, 448, 509, 570.

68. From the various records of attendance, Cabinet minutes and other supporting documents in the Newcastle, Hardwicke, Bute, Devonshire and Bedford manuscripts, it is clear that some of the most vital proposals discussed by the Cabinet during these months either originated with Bute or, at times, were modifications he suggested by way of compromise.

3

The myth of Lord Bute's secret influence

Frank O'Gorman

The political convulsions of the early years of the reign of George III have been notoriously difficult to understand and to interpret. For those who lived through them, still more for the men who were the victims of those convulsions, it must have been almost impossible to maintain a sense of rationality as crisis succeeded crisis. The myth of Lord Bute's secret influence was used by men in opposition to successive administrations appointed by George III in the 1760s to give some explanation for their political proscription, to lend some sense of interpretative continuity to a bewildering series of inexplicable developments and to maintain a consistent moral focus upon events as they unravelled. It was in the early 1760s, within the political connection led by Thomas Pelham Holles, First Duke of Newcastle, that the myth was first generated. It was fostered and nurtured within the party of Charles Watson-Wentworth, Second Marquis of Rockingham, after 1765. The Newcastle Whigs had opposed the secret influence of Lord Bute. The Rockingham Whigs opposed the principle as well as the practice of secret influence and advocated party connection as a means of destroying it. In the writings of Edmund Burke,[1] personal grudges and group vendettas against Bute were elevated into a coherent historical account of the early years of the reign of George III. Within a few years, a steady stream of writers, most notably Horace Walpole, had taken Burke's essentially partisan account of the 1760s as their point of departure for the elaboration of a 'Whig interpretation' of the reign of George III and, consequently, for eighteenth-century history in general.[2] The rise and fall of that particular historiographical tradition have been memorably treated by the late Professor Sir Herbert Butterfield.[3] What is still needed, however, is a detailed analysis of the process by which certain individuals and groups involved in the political dramas of the 1760s became addicted to a belief in the myth of Lord Bute's secret influence. The only modern treatment of this phenomenon is the essay 'Myth and reality in eighteenth century British history' by Professor Ian Christie. That essay, however, is

20 years old.[4] The quantity and the quality of scholarship on the
1760s have increased enormously since then.[5] Christie's precise subject,
moreover, was not so much the myth of Lord Bute's secret influence as
'the Rockingham party's concept of the "King's Friends" and the
"double cabinet"', not quite the same thing.[6] These he did not choose
to trace further back than the end of Bute's administration in April
1763. Although such a decision is chronologically impeccable, it may
be argued, *per contra*, that the myth of Lord Bute's secret influence can
only be thoroughly understood by returning to the most formative
years of the reign of George III.

Even before the accession of George III the situation of Lord Bute
had threatened to create confusion, conflict and misunderstanding.
Between 1756 and 1758 Bute and Prince George appear to have assumed that he would take the Treasury in the new reign and employ
Pitt as his Secretary of State. The strength of the Pitt–Newcastle
coalition and the successful prosecution of the Seven Years War, however, dampened their enthusiasm for such extensive changes.[7] The
Prince wrote to Lord Bute on 4 May 1760:

> What I still flatter myself is, that some method may turn of regulating
> affairs, which may still make the Treasury not unpalatable to you; if that
> should not happen, you will for all that be Minister, for all men, will find
> the only method of succeeding in their desires, will be by first acquainting
> you with what they mean to request before they address themselves to me.[8]

Significantly, it was Pitt and his friends rather than the circle around
Newcastle which at this stage manifested the greater degree of hostility
towards the favourite. His refusal to serve under Bute was decisive in
keeping the favourite out of the Cabinet for the first few months of the
reign. He made it clear to Bute that things must go on as before.
Although Bute accepted his own exclusion from the Cabinet, Pitt did
not believe his protestations that he would be content to remain a
private man. 'What could Lord B. mean by declaring that he would be
a private man?', wondered Pitt. 'And shadow'd out, tho' he did not say
it, that he must mean to be *the* Minister behind the curtain'.[9] Pitt
wanted Bute to remain Groom of the Stole, the honorific office which
Bute had accepted on the accession of George III. Nevertheless, Pitt
took Bute's eventual promotion to a Secretaryship of State in March
1761 philosophically. 'He would overlook it and would go on with good
humour, though if my Lord Bute had consulted him he should have
advised him to have stayed where he was'.[10]

At this early stage Newcastle and his friends had few of Pitt's
reservations concerning Bute. They feared his ambition and recognized

his wish to be minister but they doubted his abilities and, if any thing, underestimated the danger to their own positions which he represented.[11] Devonshire epitomized this early, stoical and somewhat fatalistic view of things in his advice to Pitt of 5 November 1760. 'I recommended to him patience; allowances ought to be made for a young King who was entirely in the hands of a Favourite ... We agreed that Bute meant to govern absolutely. However, I recommended strongly that it should be borne with'.[12] There was every reason why it should. Bute could be used by the old Whigs as a useful lever against Pitt. If the influence of Newcastle and his friends were removed and if that of Bute were weakened then the King would be defenceless against Pitt and the Grenvilles, just as his grandfather had been in 1746 and between 1754 and 1757.[13]

It can readily be understood, then, why Newcastle and his friends should react far more favourably than Pitt did to the suggestion that Bute be brought into the Cabinet. As Newcastle put it, Devonshire and Hardwicke warmly agreed to 'bringing my Lord Bute into a ministerial office, and to make Him, who did Every Thing, responsible with the other ministers'.[14] It was he, Newcastle, who, in fact, publicly 'suggested' to the King that Bute be made a Cabinet minister.[15] As he later confessed to Devonshire not a little ruefully: 'In this Reign, I own, I did, in Concert with Your Grace, and My Friends, prefer My Lord Bute to Him [Pitt], & was an Insignificant Instrument to bring My Lord Bute into the Secretary's Office'.[16] In March 1761 there was no open disagreement between the court, on the one hand, and the Newcastle Whigs, on the other, concerning the constitutional legitimacy of Bute's promotion to the Cabinet. Horace Walpole protested that it was 'preposterous' and 'injudicious' but he did not claim that it was in any sense unconstitutional.[17] Although Newcastle himself quickly began to feel neglected by the King in favour of Bute and began to consider his own position, he specifically ruled out a difference of principle between himself and Bute. Even when he contemplated resignation from the ministry it was not because of the unconstitutional nature of Bute's position as favourite. On 13 October 1761, for example, Newcastle assured Bute 'that we were all ready to be his friends, if he would let us; that we wish'd for nothing but to support him'[18] It seems quite astonishing that in little more than a year the myth of Lord Bute's secret influence had almost become the political *raison d'être* of these men.

Within a few months they were beginning to regret their hasty deference towards Bute. For one thing, public opinion was beginning to turn against the Scottish favourite. Already in October 1760 there had

been some indications of the tidal wave of media hostility which was to
engulf Bute in 1762–3. Handbills pointed suggestively at the suspected
relationship between the Scottish favourite and the Princess Dowager.[19]
His promotion to the Cabinet, his endeavours to negotiate a peace
treaty and then, dramatically, in October 1761, the resignation of Pitt
culminated in vigorous pamphlet attacks.[20] For another, Newcastle
had his own worries about Bute, whose plan 'was to get the whole
power and disposition of business, as well as employments, to himself'[21]
Indeed, to some extent it was. The King and Bute would act in concert:
'a little seeming good humour from me and your telling him things
before he hears them from others are the sure maxims to keep him in
order'.[22] Meanwhile, they were preparing to abandon the continental
war, of which Newcastle had always been a staunch advocate, in favour
of a campaign against Spain. The adoption of that policy early in 1762
undermined Newcastle's position. The cancellation of the subsidies
paid to Frederick the Great led him in May to threaten resignation.
The King jumped at the opportunity to oust Newcastle and to install
Bute at the Treasury in his place.[23] Newcastle's world was beginning to
crumble. He began to suspect a deliberate plot on the part of the Court
to humiliate himself and his friends.[24] For the present, however, he
could only wait on events and advise his friends to keep themselves
clear as to any engagements for their future behaviour.[25] To the King
he announced that he felt himself 'at liberty to act as his conscience
shall guide him'.[26] Yet resentment proved a surer guide to conduct
than did conscience. On 7 October he declaimed to Hardwicke about
'the haughtiness and power of an absolute Scotch Minister, ignorant of
business, and unacquainted with the necessary qualifications of an
English Minister'.[27] The dismissal of the Duke of Devonshire from the
Cabinet on 3 November 1762 and, in particular, the high-handed and
provocative manner in which it was done,[28] seemed like the opening
shots in a new and disturbing kind of political warfare. They could only
have been fired by a ministry which 'founded all their hopes upon
corruption'.[29] To do so was not good Whiggism. The patient Kinnoul
was now considering resignation from the Bute administration because
he could 'not act with those, who put the Government upon Measures
that are contrary to those which supported the King's family at the
Head of the Constitution'.[30] But if it was a fight that Bute wanted then
he could have one. Newcastle and his friends decided to engage on the
issue of the peace preliminaries, which came before Parliament on 9
and 10 December 1762. Their objective was 'to deliver this Countrey
[sic] from the sole and arbitrary power of my Lord Bute'.[31]

  The tactic failed. Bute survived the peace debates with considerable

ease[32] and punished the friends of Newcastle for their votes and speeches
by removing them from the offices they retained. This 'massacre of the
Pelhamite innocents', as it came to be called, was irrefutable proof of
the malevolence of Lord Bute. Punishment for those who had actually
spoken and voted against the peace preliminaries was one thing. The
wholesale purge of friends and relatives of such members of the lower
House was quite another. For Newcastle, such a ruthless demonstration of the exercise of power was 'hardly constitutional'.[33] For
Hardwicke, his lifelong friend and *confidant*, however, the 'massacre'
'cannot be called a breach of the Constitution ... tho' undoubtedly the
carrying it to so many persons out of the House is an extension beyond
example in former times'.[34] The 'massacre' did not extend to the
Hardwicke family, however, who were just beginning some complex
trimming manoeuvres in order to save their political futures. Most of
Newcastle's friends took up a position somewhere between these two.
Devonshire welcomed the 'massacre' as further evidence of Bute's
malevolent intentions while Rockingham denounced 'the arbitrary
violence of the Ministers [which] will go hand in hand with their
inhumanity'.[35] One of his friends hoped for 'a true British spirit to rise
up again ... to wrench the reins of Government out of the hands of a
Man whose Ambition is unbounded, and who I believe endeavours to
instill Despotism into the Heart of his Sovereign'.[36] By the end of the
year, then, even the cautious Newcastle Whigs were moving in the
direction of systematic opposition to the ministry of Lord Bute. Furthermore, they were coming to believe in the unconstitutional nature of his
influence.

Yet how could Bute's position as the chosen minister of George III
possibly be unconstitutional? Did he not hold that position through
exercise of the royal prerogative? Everything depended upon the limitations which might be imposed upon the exercise of the royal prerogative of appointing ministers. Was it the case, as Bute's newspaper, *The
Briton*, argued, that 'That appointment is personal to the King and to
the King only'[37] or, as *The Annual Register* argued, on the other hand,
that 'the crown should be directed to the exercise of this public duty by
public motives, and not by private liking and friendship'? How could
these 'private motives' be defined? The *Annual Register* was in no doubt:
'great talents, great and eminent services to the nation, confidence
among the nobility, and influence among the landed and mercantile
interests, were the directions, which the crown ought to observe in the
exercise of its right in nominating officers of state'.[38] The same distinction was made by John Almon, who rejected the argument that a
minister ought to be 'a servant of the crown only' because 'he was a

servant of the nation likewise, and accountable to the people as well as
to the King'. Almon proceeded to argue that Bute lacked any natural
interest in England and possessed, therefore, 'no popularity of character'.Further, 'there is not a single drop of English blood in his genealogy'.
His appointment merely served to revive old party animosities within
England and latent national animosities between the two countries.
Lacking interest and popularity 'thereby he had not the principal thing
necessary towards his stability, *the confidence of the people*'.[39] It was this
which ultimately safeguarded the constitution against tendencies
towards monarchical absolutism. Whiggism was essentially a popular
principle. 'The great object of it is the liberty of the people, for which
monarchy and legislature are established.' Contrasting the behaviour
of Pitt with that of Bute, Almon proceeds:

> A *known* Whig will of course enjoy popularity; he will not flatter the King
> with more *independency,* and prerogative, than he really has;[40] he will
> sooner chuse to retire from court. But such a conduct is not expected from
> a Minister, who has no obligations to the people, who has received from
> them many marks of dislike, and may be supposed to value himself upon
> the firmness with which he despises the voice of the people.[41]

In the end, of course, Bute was not able to ignore the voice of the people[42]
and in April 1763 he withdrew from office, leaving George III to
wrestle with the problems of ministerial instability which had tor-
mented him since his accession. At once, the position of Bute became
more rather than less sinister. As a minister he had, at least, occupied a
responsible situation and his ministerial actions could be subjected to
public scrutiny and even ridicule. Out of office, that could no longer be
the case. So convinced had Bute's opponents and victims become of his
influence over the King and the malevolence of his intentions that they
could not imagine that he would retire from politics.[43] As early as 2
July 1762, Devonshire had written to Newcastle suggesting that it was
'not impossible that Ld. Bute may desire to quit a responsible Employment & take a place about the King's person; in that case, how cou'd
he be trusted'?[44] It was a simple step to reach the conclusion that the
Grenville ministry was 'an experiment to see whether he can govern
this country in this mode, as it was plain he cou'd not long maintain
himself at the Head of the Treasury'. He added, significantly: 'That is
the notion that we must endeavour to propagate and keep alive'.[45]

Although Professor Christie has dismissed the myth of Lord Bute's
secret influence as evidence that the opposition lived in 'a Looking-
Glass world'[46] it was common gossip in ministerial circles that Bute
wrote frequently to the King to advise him on matters of state.[47]
Grenville's wife, reflecting her husband's frustration, resented Bute's

lingering influence with the King. Until June she tended to refer to it as 'that superior influence' but by August Bute had become 'that secret influence'.[48] Some of the more controversial, and allegedly autocratic actions of the new ministry, notably the harsh treatment meeted out to John Wilkes, looked like further evidence that Lord Bute was 'looking on, and directing, behind the curtain'.[49] Indeed, between April and August 1763, there is nothing 'mythical' in the stories of Lord Bute's secret influence. As John Brooke has written: 'The Grenville ministry was intended as a mere façade. Bute was to remain the power behind the throne and final authority would rest with him'.[50] Bute had wanted to retire completely from politics and thus avoid 'the imputation of being a Minister behind the Curtain',[51] but the King had no intention of permitting a quiet retreat for his 'Dear Friend'. He persuaded Bute to give his advice on the King's Speech to Parliament within days of leaving office. Bute decided to quit the scene of his political humiliations and seek rest and repose in Harrogate for a few weeks. The King assumed that on his return Lord Bute would be 'ready once more to enter on the public scene'.[52] He was exactly right. The King was toying with the idea of removing the Grenville ministry and Lord Bute obliged him with a few half-hearted overtures to the opposition.[53] Neither the opposition, nor, of course, the government, can be blamed for thinking that the secret influence of Lord Bute was more reality than myth.

By August 1763 the King and his ministers had come thoroughly to mistrust each other. In early August, Grenville and the two Secretaries of State, Egremont and Halifax, had had enough of Bute's meddling and told the King roundly that if he was not prepared to give them his full confidence then he should send for the opposition.[54] The death of Egremont on 27 August threw the political scene once more into confusion and gave the King his chance. George III now looked to Pitt to save him from George Grenville and salvage some of his 'Independency'.[55] To get him, however, he would have to rely on Bute's good offices. Bute was responsible for getting the negotiations under way and for advising the King on their progress. Lord Bute himself talked with Pitt for three hours on one occasion.[56] He may have been involved in the decision to terminate the negotiations with Pitt.[57] No wonder Newcastle believed that 'Lord Bute is the Sole Minister ... Nobody else does any Thing of Consequence ... His influence is full as great as ever and will continue so'.[58] As for Grenville himself, he insisted that the King promise to 'suffer no secret Influence whatever to prevail against the advice of those to whom he trusted the management of his affairs'. To this George III agreed, promising that 'Lord Bute wished to retire absolutely from all business whatever'.[59]

On this occasion, Bute was as good as his word. 'I protest on the word of a gentleman I know no more of politicks, of the King's, or the Ministers' ideas or measures than I do of the Mogul's Court'.[60] As promised, he withdrew to Luton Hoo on 5 October for the winter but controversy and suspicion would not leave him alone. Rumours occasionally connected Bute with Pitt and the establishment of a new administration. Although there was nothing in them they served to unsettle George Grenville and soured further his relationship with George III.[61] Bute sent one message to Grenville congratulating him on his handling of the Wilkes affair to which Grenville returned a predictably stiff and formal response.[62] On the whole, however, both the King and Bute appear to have conducted themselves properly and with appropriate regard to the undertakings given to Grenville in late August.

Lord Bute, however, did not find the life of a reclusive country squire at all congenial. He returned to London on 19 March 1764 and at once found himself swimming, however diffidently, in political waters. He had some small dealings with Grenville and these led to a renewed acquaintance with the King.[63] They met on several occasions in the spring and summer of 1764 but Bute appears to have lost his stomach for politics and the King made no attempt to unsettle his administration.[64] Nevertheless, ministers thought the worst. They had cultivated their fear and loathing of Bute to such a pitch that his reappearance threatened their sense of political security. Their fear, almost their paranoia, damaged their relationship with the King. As their (now groundless) suspicions rose, so, correspondingly, did the King's detestation of his ministers. It was entirely symbolic of the King's determination to maintain his 'Independency' that he should resist Grenville's attempts to assume control of all domestic patronage. In particular, Grenville found it obnoxious that Scottish patronage should remain in the hands of Bute's brother, James Stuart Mackenzie, the Lord Privy Seal of Scotland. The last year of the Grenville administration consequently became a pitched battle between Grenville and Mackenzie for control of Scottish appointments. At stake in these apparently trivial questions were the crucial issues of ministerial authority and royal 'Independency'. In this battle, it was difficult to believe that Lord Bute might be taking a wholly unconnected part.[65]

These tensions finally destroyed the Grenville ministry in 1765. The King's illness and his subsequent attempt to provide for the succession by passing a Regency Bill proved too much for what was left of his relationship with George Grenville. Grenville inevitably placed the worst possible construction upon the stratagems adopted by the King during the Regency Crisis, suspecting that Lord Bute was behind them.[66] However suspicious the King's actions may have been[67] there is, in fact, little evidence that Bute was behind them. There are *fewer* surviving letters between the King and Bute for this than for other comparable periods in their relationship. Although Jenkinson has a story that Bute and the King were corresponding daily, the King confiding to Bute 'a journal every day of what passed',[68] he also comments that Bute *disapproved* of the King's actions.[69] Grenville was taking no risks. To put an end once and for all to the influence of the favourite, he imposed five humiliating conditions upon the King.[70] One of these, the dismissal of Mackenzie, forced the King to break a solemn promise he had given to Bute's kinsman. This was the last straw for the King. Grenville would have to go. If Pitt would not agree to replace him then the old Whigs, now led by the Marquis of Rockingham, would have to form an administration in his place.

Newcastle and his friends were full of admiration for Grenville. He and his friends 'had done their country a great service and themselves great honor [sic] in having removed my Lord Bute from his Influence in the Closet'.[71] In the event of a ministry formed from among the old Whigs it was vital 'that some effectual means should be taken, to convince the Publick, that neither His Majesty, nor his intended Ministers, should have anything to do with My Lord Bute directly or indirectly, in the conduct of the Administration, and in the management of publick affairs'.[72] This is exactly what they did. On replacing Grenville, their leaders

> were unanimously of opinion that they could not venture to come into any new Administration, except it was agreed that the thought of replacing Mr. Mackenzie should be laid aside; and also, that some of the particular friends of the Earl of Bute should be removed, as a proof to the world that the Earl of Bute should not, either publicly or privately, directly or indirectly, have any concern or influence in public affairs, or in the management or disposition of public employments.[73]

The King, of course, hated the imposition of such conditions but, in the circumstances, had no alternative but to submit to them. He agreed 'That It Is not his Intention, that the Earl of Bute should, either publicly or privately, interfere in the Management of Publick Affairs, either at Home, or Abroad; Or recommend to any Employments either in England, or Scotland'.[74]

There was more to come. Although there was no purge of the friends of Bute who remained in office it was made perfectly clear to the King that the Rockingham Whigs would tolerate no nonsense from them.

Cumberland was able to announce to a meeting of the party leaders on 5 July that:

> His Majesty had given him the strongest assurances that my Lord Bute should not be suffered to interfere in the least degree in any publick business whatever; and that, if those of his friends who might remain in office did not vote with, and, by speaking, support the present administration, His Majesty promised to remove them the next day.[75]

What exactly did the King's promise mean? How far, and in what circumstances might it be extended? Could he be relied upon to keep his word? The early signs seemed quite promising. Evidence of his initial good faith may be found in his instructions to some of Bute's friends to support the Rockingham administration.[76] How far this would be maintained throughout the course of the administration remained to be seen. Newcastle wanted the King to realize that 'whenever there should be the least appearance of my Lord Bute's intermeddling, that we should all then desire His Majesty's leave to resign our employments'.[77] It is, therefore, no small wonder that in view of these impositions George III came to detest the Rockingham administration as bitterly as he had come to detest its predecessor.

For the present, however, there was little he could do but submit to the realities of the situation. Bute offered to keep out of the political limelight during parliamentary sessions. When Bute attempted to retract that promise, the King stood firm. He kept Bute at arm's length and refused to allow him access to his person. Bute wrote in June 1766: 'I have not been at court these 9 months, nor seen HM for this year past, nor know when I shall. Ignorant to the last degree of what is going forward, the papers are my only intelligence'.[78] Yet a few letters appear to have passed between them. In one of them the King begged Bute to 'keep my friends from personal opposition and when they from opinion differ let them be as civil in their expressions as the occasion will permit'.[79] At the start of the parliamentary session in December 1765 the behaviour of Lord Bute and his friends was exemplary in both Houses of Parliament. Hardly a speech was delivered nor a vote cast which was not in support of the Rockingham administration.[80]

On the issue of the repeal of the Stamp Act the behaviour of the friends of Lord Bute was to be very different. The stamp duty had first been mooted during Bute's administration and it had passed through its parliamentary stages with their enthusiastic support and approval.[81] On this issue Rockingham had expected trouble from the very beginning of the ministry.[82] He cannot have been altogether surprised, then, when on the four major divisions in the Commons and on the one major division in the Lords, the friends of Lord Bute voted against the repeal. Two features of these incidents call for comment. On the one hand, King George III was doggedly determined to make his own controversial views on the subject plain and public. He was in favour of modification rather than repeal of the Stamp Act and he was resolutely determined that the world should not confuse his own opinions with those of his ministers on the issue. On two extraordinary occasions[83] the King contrived to convey to the parliamentary and political nation exactly what his own opinions were, whatever the impact upon the stability of his administration.[84] Not at all surprisingly, the ministers thought the worst and bewailed the continuing influence of the Scottish Thane. On the other hand, if this were not enough, the King now refused to discipline the placemen, in spite of his promise to ministers just a few months earlier. Indeed, he now advised Bute that it would be a positive obligation for his friends to vote according to their consciences on the repeal even if that meant voting against the government. 'I think that it is also incumbent on my Dear Friend to act entirely so also'.[85]

At exactly this moment, in what was already a complex and distressing situation, King George III decided to open up a secret negotiation with Lord Bute and his friends. The King was absolutely terrified at the possible consequences of Bute's opposition to the Repeal of the Stamp Act and he wanted desperately to soothe the bitter feelings that were being aroused. The day after Bute had announced his hostility to Repeal he confided in Egmont: *'I think He & his friends are going head long into a Precipice they don't well see'*.[86] To stop them falling into it he opened up lines of communication with Bute through Egmont and Norton. If he had hoped that he might yet be able to bridge the widening chasm of distrust that separated the friends of Bute from the friends of Rockingham he was to be sorely disappointed. By now it was much too late. For one thing, Bute himself was quite uninterested in making friends with the Rockingham ministry. He responded to the King's overtures by vaguely suggesting that the ministry needed to think of 'admitting some persons of the different parties' but he would go no further.[87] For his part, Rockingham was aghast and agitated. After all that had passed, he and his friends could have, and would have, nothing at all to do with secret negotiations with Lord Bute.[88] At this point, this strange and secret little affair came to an end.

While there is no evidence to suggest that the King and Bute were guilty of unconstitutional designs, as the grosser versions of Whig historiography have suggested, their conduct is difficult to defend. Bute's continuing inability to abandon the political stage and the

King's lofty conception of his own opinions – to the detriment of the interests of his own administration – naturally perpetuated enormous suspicion of his own intentions, and of those of Bute. No wonder the Rockinghams attributed their mounting misfortunes to Lord Bute and his friends and, perhaps, began to wonder about the reliability of the King himself. With marvellous irony, however, Lord Bute was now finally severing himself from the royal connection which had taken him to the highest political station in the land. As the Rockingham ministry tottered to its destruction, the King turned in desperation to Bute and his friends.[89] This time Bute did not come to the King's rescue. He announced to the House of Lords that he would never again hold office and he advised the ministry to 'take in men from all parties'.[90] George III now had to look to others to defend his 'Independency'. In the summer of 1766 he turned to William Pitt.

Coming on top of everything else – the shocks and surprises of the regency crisis, the mysterious collapse of the Grenville administration, the sinister revolts against the repeal of the Stamp Act and the steady decline of the Rockingham Whigs in the confidence of the King – this sudden emergence of Pitt, soon to be made Lord Chatham, as an ally of the King could only have one explanation. As the young Lord Hardwicke remarked to Rockingham:

> I presume you know by this time where the source of this sudden resol-ution to send for Mr. Pitt has arisen. I presume from that *quarter* which had, and *will have the real interior* influence and weight, which turned out the last Ministers, and will the present, let the outward instruments and actors change ever so often.[91]

The systematic character of these accusations becomes standard. Chatham 'openly shakes hands with My Lord Bute . . . and He depends upon the Corruption of the Times, and upon the Instability of our own Friends'.[92] The Chatham administration could be depicted not merely as the consequence of Bute's malevolence but as a natural part of a steady campaign to weaken all resistance to him. 'Every day, more and more, Ld. Chatham's Union and dependence upon Ld. Bute will appear & I should hope will occasion Some of our Friends now in Office to reconsider the Propriety of their remaining'.[93] After their resignation, and their replacement by some notable friends of Lord Bute, Rockingham wrote plainly about the long term objectives of his party as 'an *Anti-Bute* and *Anti-Chatham* system'.[94]

These were, of course, hysterical exaggerations. Yet there was just enough justification for them to render them credible. The King's intentions, as he wrote to Bute on 12 July 1766, were

to try through Mr. Pitt to build an Administration on so general a basis as
the times will permit, to see as many of those gentlemen who were contrary to my inclinations remov'd reinstated particularly Mr. Mackenzie,
in short to see you my Dear friend once quit of the unmerited usage you
have so long suffer'd and openly appearing as my private friend.[95]

Bute was no longer willing to play the role of Minister behind the
Curtain in a Chatham administration, nor would Chatham have tol-
erated it. The King was forced to sacrifice his lingering attachment to
Bute on the altar of 'Independency' and Chatham. He had to accept
Chatham's harsh treatment of Bute's friends and his refusal to treat
with them as a party, even though they were a party devoted to the
King's service. Bute was furious at this most significant slight and
wrote angrily to the King declaring that he was done with politics. 'I
have for ever done with this bad public, my heart is half broke and
my health ruined, with the unmerited, barbarous treatment I have
received, the warmest wish remaining is to see you happy, respected
and adored'.[96]

Belief in the secret influence of Lord Bute now began to give way
fairly rapidly to a belief in the corrupt *system* of secret influence which
he had left behind him. 'Is not the present court system', wrote Burke
in 1767, 'built on the ruins of his'?[97] The Rockingham Whigs undertook
the defence of the East India Company in the session of 1767 in the
context of resistance to a conspiratorial and unconstitutional system of
secret influence which threatened the security of chartered rights and
the sanctity of property. The currency of the East Indian issue and, in
particular, the control of the vast amounts of patronage and influence
allegedly involved in the affairs of the East India Company, did much
to consolidate belief in a *system* of secret influence even though Lord
Bute himself was in retirement.[98] This transmutation of myth to theory
may be seen in the negotiations between the political groups in 1767,
negotiations which forced the groups to refine their thinking and define
not only their differences with each other but also their own political
objectives and justifications. The Rockingham Whigs laid out their
principles in the Dowdeswell Memorandum in July 1767. The misfortunes of the old Whigs in the reign of George III 'must be imputed
not to the influence of particular persons but to the prevalence of a
political principle which says that the power of the Crown arises out of
the weakness of the Administration'. To remove it must in future be a
condition of taking office. Indeed, 'there should appear a manly resolution not to maintain the pageantry of Administration an hour after it
is divested of its necessary weight in the Closet, and its necessary power
in other places'.[99] Suspicious of the Court and distrustful of executive

influence, the Rockingham Whigs preferred to maintain their integrity
in opposition. They would be prepared to form an administration only
if they would be permitted to undertake a thoroughgoing elimination of
all traces of secret influence. To guarantee that this should be done they
were prepared to co-operate with other groups but only in an arrangement led, and dominated, by the Rockingham Whigs themselves, and
with Rockingham himself at the Treasury. Rockingham realized in
1767 that the elimination of secret influence could not be undertaken by
his party alone because 'we shall not be sufficiently strong to check the
power we had reason to be attentive to'.[100] The immediate historical
reference point for the Rockingham Whigs was the accession of George
III and the spectacular instances of the operation of secret influence
which had since been witnessed. To these, members of the party
'should constantly look back'.[101] From the systematic operations
of secret influence which had since arisen it was the constitutional
duty of the Rockingham party to rescue the monarchy (from itself, if
necessary), the people and the constitution.[102]

In 1767, then, there emerged a secular and depersonalized version of
the myth of Lord Bute's secret influence. It was at one and the same
time a version of the political history of the reign of George III and an
obligingly appropriate source of partisan commentary upon the events
of the day. At the same time, references to Bute's personal interventions
in politics become significantly less common.[103] In 1768, in fact, he
went to Italy, where he stayed until the following year. Thereafter, they
inevitably became still rarer, though, perhaps understandably, they
did not cease altogether. The general election of 1768 threw up a
number of uncomplimentary references to Bute, a number which was
significantly increased by the uproar caused by the Middlesex election
issue of 1768 and the Petitioning Movement of 1769.[104] Nevertheless,
the Rockingham Whigs had largely ceased to rail at the Scottish
Thane, reserving their bile for the system of secret influence which he
had bequeathed. In the writings of Edmund Burke[105] these resentments
were transformed into a respectable and logically coherent political
theory. Deliberately, and with much consultation, he worked upon the
long-standing prejudices of the old Whigs. In 1769 he wrote of the
plans of the Court 'long pursued, with but too fatal success ... to break
the strength of this kingdom by frittering down the bodies which
compose it, by fomenting bitter and sanguinary animosities, and by
dissolving every tie in social affection and public trust'.[106] A year later
he spelled out the detail and progress of this new Court plan which it
was the historic destiny of the Rockingham Whigs to confront by
grounding their political activities upon a party basis.[107] In so doing,
he once and for all buried the myth of Lord Bute's secret influence.

It may appear somewhat affected that in so much discourse upon this extraordinary party, I should say so little of the Earl of Bute, who is the supposed head of it ... This system has not risen solely from the ambition of Lord Bute, but from the circumstances which favoured it, and from an indifference to the constitution which had been for some time growing among our gentry. We should have been tried with it, if the Earl of Bute had never existed; and it will want neither a contriving head nor active members, when the Earl of Bute exists no longer'.[108]

The myth of the secret influence of Lord Bute had done its work and served its purpose. Although a few rumours continued to circulate and a few prejudices against his family persisted, history had largely done with Lord Bute.[109] For their part, the Rockinghams could now construe any untoward event, a political failure on their part or an instance of high-handedness on the part of government, as a manifestation of secret influence. The existence of a secret cabal of advisers, corrupting the monarchy and subverting the ministry from within, could be blamed for almost anything.[110] The danger to the constitution, in fact, was now greater for, as Burke himself confessed, 'His System is got into firmer and abler hands'.[111]

Lord Bute might have gone but his impact upon the opposition Whigs, and consequently upon the nature of political partisanship in Britain, was to remain. The ideas and the language which Burke used in the *Thoughts* were to have an enduring impact upon what may be termed the mentality of political oppositions until the 1830s. The conviction that conspiracies and cabals existed within the executive, the idea that corruption rendered sound government impossible, the conviction that the executive was secretly subverting the legislature through the use of 'influence', the belief in the existence of a settled plot against the constitution, the cultivation of fear and hatred of government by favourites – these were the staple elements in the mentality of parliamentary oppositions in Britain in the age of Rockingham, Fox and Grey.[112] Whatever justification there may once have been for believing in the secret influence of Lord Bute – and, as we have seen, the fears of the men around Newcastle and Rockingham were far from baseless – there is no doubt that they exaggerated the danger and magnified the threat to the constitution. Why did they do so?

Their disposition to believe in the myth of Lord Bute's secret influence has normally been explained in psychological terms. 'The failure of the Rockinghams to win the lasting confidence of the Commons was far less discreditable if it could be explained by the influence of Bute, acting through a small group of personal followers within the ranks of Administration, and with the connivance of the King

himself'.[113] Failure to attain office could be explained away just
as conveniently in this manner as could failures in office.[114] Secret
influence could be – and usually was – used as a stick with which
to beat any ministry and any measure. Nevertheless, there is much
more to it than that. The repeated intransigence exhibited by Rockingham's supporters on the subjects of Lord Bute and secret influence
injected a dogged consistency of attitude into the politics of opposition. That there were deeply held fears and genuine concerns behind the rhetoric cannot be doubted. There *were* ambiguities in
the formal relationship between the King and his ministers and
George III certainly displayed a lofty and singular view of his own
prerogative rights and freedom of action. Much of the rhetoric employed against Bute and the King was consequently exaggerated
yet it is difficult to see how this could have advanced the interests
of the opposition. How could they possibly have ingratiated themselves at Court when they could scarcely neglect an opportunity
of insulting it? They were solicitous for the safety of the mixed constitution and for the continued independence of the House of Commons
within it. Arguably, their preoccupation with Bute preserved the
Rockingham Whigs from an exclusive concern with their own political interests and drew them into the arena of larger issues of parliamentary concern. Professor Brewer has defended the 'solid constitutional foundation' of those who attacked Bute, namely their defence
of the idea of ministerial responsibility to Parliament, on which
depended 'parliamentary control of the executive and the justification
of political opposition'.[115] As the late Professor Sir Herbert Butterfield
argued 30 years ago: 'In seizing upon the appointment of Bute, the
question of closet influence and the whole problem of the relations
between party, ministry and king, these men would seem to have put
their finger on the strategic issue'.[116] As Burke himself put it the
question was whether the powers of the state 'should all be exercised
upon publick principles and national grounds, and not on the likings or
prejudices, the intrigues or policies, of a court'.[117]

The myth of Lord Bute's secret influence had further political consequences for the Rockingham Whigs in the remedies they proposed for
dealing with it, most notably economical reform. To reduce the influence, the offices, sinecures and pensions at the disposal of the secret
cabal seemed perfectly good sense. Their campaign began quietly and
unspectacularly in 1768 and culminated in the three measures of 1782,
Burke's, Crewe's and Clerke's Acts.[118] Along the way, a series of
other issues was treated in the context of Rockinghamite preoccupa-
tions with secret influence. The Rockinghams reacted predictably to

proposals to increase the Civil List in 1769. As Dowdeswell protested in 1770:

> It was the duty of Parliament whenever the public money was apparently squandered to bad purposes, to make enquiry how it had been so squandered; that when so large a requisition as that made last year to pay the Civil List debts, was made on the House, and for which the House could get no accounts but such as were neither satisfactory nor intelligible, it became absolutely necessary to ask for further accounts.[119]

The rhetoric deployed against secret influence could condition the Rockinghamite stance on other vital issues. On the Middlesex election issue in 1769 Rockingham himself had laid it down 'that the great and continual increase of the power and influence of the Crown in the course of this century (if the Crown should unfortunately be led by weak, wicked and arbitrary ministers and surrounded by evil counsellors) would operate most dangerously to the Constitution.'[120] In 1771 the Rockinghams opposed North's Lotteries bill. 'Though we cannot entirely annihilate the practice of corruption, let us check its ravages, where it bursts out with the greatest violence'.[121] Richmond summed up their convictions at this time:

> Yet we have not been able to succeed in destroying that System of Government which has prevail'd almost constantly during this Reign, the grand Principle of which, is to make the King govern by His Own Power and the weight of His Influence, instead of the old system of governing by that Party or Set of Men who had most personal Influence in the Country.[122]

Not surprisingly, then, the Rockinghams reacted with horror when North brought forward the Regulating Act in 1773 with the objective of subjecting the affairs of the East India Company to supervision by the executive. 'The Lucrative Offices, and appointments relating to the E.I. Company's Affairs, will virtually fall into the Patronage of the Crown ... [adding] to the ways and means of corruption, which is at least equal to all the Appointments of the Crown, in Army, Navy, and revenue, Church etc'.[123]

The myth of secret influence determined the Rockinghamite interpretation of the colonial rebellion in America. The court system, of course, had goaded the colonists into resistance, then rebellion. If, now, that rebellion were put down then there would be no possibility of controlling the system of secret influence. Rockingham was exceedingly worried.

> If an arbitrary Military Force is to govern one part of this large Empire, I think & fear if it succeeds, it will not be long before the whole of this Empire will be brought under a similar Thraldom ... I confess I begin to

believe that the Quintessence of Toryism (wich may synonimously [*sic*] be called the Kings Friends system) is both ready and willing if any opportunity offers to reak [*sic*] their vengeance upon us with the assistance of a King of the Brunswick Line, just as they would have been if any of their attempts to reinstate *a Stuart* had succeeded.[124]

Was the King implicated? At first, they may have felt some sympathy for the young and inexperienced monarch. 'I am very sorry that the king, who I am sure has good sense and good nature, can be so governed and blinded', wrote the benevolent Devonshire in December 1762.[125] There seemed, however, to be very little mutual love lost between them. The King seems particularly to have disliked Rockingham. In 1767 Rockingham told the monarch roundly that the revolts against the repeal of the Stamp Act in 1766 had proceeded 'not intirely with his Majesty's inclination', a most significant qualification.[126] In the *Thoughts* in 1770 Burke seems resigned to the involvement of the monarch in the plots and cabals of secret advisers and he studiously avoids exculpating the King from the charges and denunciations which he accumulates.[127] Rockingham himself told the House of Lords on 22 January 1770 that he deplored the maxim of the reign of George III: 'That the royal prerogative alone was sufficient to support government to whatever hands the administration should be committed'. He proceeded to trace the operation of this principle through every act of government in the preceeding ten years.[128] By the late 1770s they had come to accept George III's involvement in the politics of the Court system.[129] In 1782–3 Fox had learned to detest the King and was openly referring to him as a Satan.[130] The myth (and reality) of secret influence which had originally done so much to alienate the Newcastle and Rockingham Whigs from the monarchy of George III had now vindicated and confirmed their political status in opposition. In opposition, first reformist and then, in the 1790s, radical remedies were to be tried for the ills of the body politic. The fundamental divide in politics in the late eighteenth century was not between Whig and Tory but between those who accepted the monarchy and political system of George III and those who saw them as a threat to both liberty and stability. That divide owed much to the myth of Lord Bute's secret influence. Paradoxically, that myth was to do much to generate the reforming impulses of Charles James Fox's Whig party and, ultimately, to establish the conviction among late eighteenth- and early nineteenth-century radicals that executive government depended upon the manipulation of secret influence. In the end, both these tendencies were to reshape the pattern of politics and institutions with which Lord Bute himself had once been so familiar and in which he had played so spectacularly controversial a part.

NOTES

1. See especially Edmund Burke, *Thoughts on the Causes of the Present Discontents* (1770).
2. For the role of Horace Walpole in the evolution of a Whig historiography, see I.R. Christie, 'Horace Walpole: the gossip as historian', *History Today*, IV (1954), 291–300, esp. 297–9; J. Brooke, 'Horace Walpole and King George III', in *Statesmen, Scholars and Merchants: Essays in 18th century History presented to Dame Lucy Sutherland*, ed. Anne Whiteman, J.S. Bromley and P.G.M. Dickson (1973), 263–75. See also Brooke's introduction to his superb edition of Walpole's *Memoirs of King George II* (3 vols, New Haven, CT, 1985), xxvii–xxxii.
3. H. Butterfield, *George III and the Historians* (1957), especially 42–8, 52–7, 98–104, 113–15.
4. Strictly speaking, the essay was Professor Christie's inaugural lecture, delivered in University College, London, on 11 May 1967. It was printed in Christie, *Myth and Reality in Late 18th Century British Politics* (1970), 27–54.
5. Among the works on the 1760s which have appeared since Christie, *op. cit.*, the following books may be mentioned: J. Brooke, *King George III* (1972); P. Langford, *The First Rockingham Administration, 1765–66* (1973); P.D.G. Thomas, *British Politics and the Stamp Act Crisis* (1975); F. O'Gorman, *The Rise of Party in England: the Rockingham Whigs, 1760–82* (1975); J. Brewer, *Party Ideology and Popular Politics at the Accession of George III* (1976); M. Peters, *Pitt and Popularity* (1980); Peter D. Brown and Karl W. Schweizer (eds), *The Devonshire Diary: William Cavendish, Fourth Duke of Devonshire: Memoranda on the State of Affairs, 1759–62* (1982); P. Lawson, *George Grenville: a Political Life* (1984)
6. Christie, *op. cit.*, 28.
7. Sir Lewis Namier, *England in the Age of the American Revolution* (1961), 97.
8. R.R. Sedgwick (ed.), *Letters from George III to Lord Bute* (1939), 44–6.
9. Lord Hardwicke to the Duke of Newcastle, 29 Oct. 1760, BL Add. MSS 32913 fos. 426–9, partly quoted in Namier, *op. cit.*, 123.
10. Brown and Schweizer, *op. cit.*, 9 Apr. 1761, 93.
11. One of the earliest judgments on Bute in the new reign came from Devonshire. 'For it was plain by every step that he meant to be the minister over them all and yet he had no plan of administration, or even thought of the practicability of effecting it. It appeared plainly to be his intention to confine all the ministers to their separate departments, thinking by that means to direct them all; how far that ought or could be submitted to was a matter of future consideration' (*ibid.*, 43).
12. *Ibid.*, 53.
13. *Ibid.*, 66.
14. Newcastle to Mansfield, 18 Mar. 1761, BL Add. MSS 32920, fos. 295–6. In February, however, Devonshire had been undecided. 'I had often thought business would perhaps go on better if Lord Bute was in a responsible office, yet it was a nice question and I was not clear whether it would do well or not', Brown and Schweizer, *op. cit.*, 12 Feb. 1761, 82.
15. It was characteristic of Newcastle's uncertainty that he did so after assuring Bute privately of his support against Pitt while insisting that the promotion be rendered as inoffensive to Pitt as possible; see 'Substance of what pass'd in my Conversation with Lord Bute This Day', 10 March 1761, BL Add. MSS 32920, fos. 64–71. The account in Namier, *op. cit.*, 163–6, of the incident fails to do justice to the position of the Old Whigs.
16. Newcastle to Devonshire, 23 July 1762, BL Add. MSS 32941, fos. 36–9.
17. Horace Walpole, *Memoirs of the Reign of George III*, ed. G. Barker (4 vols, 1894), I, 43–4. For Walpole's

astonishment at the paucity of the changes in the early months of the reign of George III and his praise of Bute's restraint and moderation, see Butterfield, *op. cit.*, 115.

18. Newcastle to Devonshire, 14 Oct. 1761, BL Add. MSS 32929, fos. 253–4.
19. Peters, *op. cit.*, 179.
20. J. Brewer, 'The misfortunes of Lord Bute: a case study in 18th century political argument and public opinion', *Hist J* XVI, no. 1 (1973), 11–12.
21. Newcastle to Devonshire, 9 Oct. 1761, in G. Harris, *Life of Hardwicke* (3 vols, 1847), III, 29.
22. George III to Lord Bute, 18 Nov. 1761, in Sedgwick, *op. cit.*, 69–70.
23. The treatment of the resignation of Newcastle in Namier, *op. cit.*, 313–26, is hostile, cruel and derisory. In fact, Namier was guilty of a serious error in attributing Newcastle's resignation to the activities of Treasury subordinates. It was the repudiation of Newcastle's foreign policy which caused the breach. See also O'Gorman, *op. cit.*, 38–40; Brewer, *Party Ideology and Popular Politics*, 125–6, 297–8.
24. Newcastle to Sir Joseph Yorke, 14 May 1762, in Harris, *Life of Hardwicke*, III, 355–8.
25. Newcastle to Rockingham, 14 May 1762, BL Add. MSS 32938. fos. 262–4; Newcastle to Hardwicke, 25 May 1762, BL Add. MSS 35421, fos. 263–4.
26. George III to Lord Bute, 19 May 1762, in Sedgwick, *op. cit.*, 107–8.
27. BL Add. MSS 32943 fos. 90–1, partly quoted in Namier, *op. cit.*, 343.
28. Devonshire had retained his office of Lord Chamberlain but had ceased attending the Cabinet since Newcastle's resignation. Refusing an official summons to attend the Cabinet in early October he was unceremoniously and insultingly stripped of his office, with the maximum demonstration of the King's annoyance; see Namier,

op. cit., 370–3; O'Gorman, *op. cit.*, 42–4.
29. Lord John Cavendish to Devonshire, 28 Oct. 1762, Chatsworth MSS.
30. Rockingham to Devonshire, dated Nov. 1762, Chatsworth MSS.
31. Newcastle to Hardwicke, 19 Dec. 1762, BL Add. MSS 32945 fos. 315–16.
32. For the debates on the peace preliminaries see O'Gorman, *op. cit.*, 50–5.
33. Newcastle to Hardwicke, 22 Dec. 1762, BL Add. MSS 32945, fos. 313–14.
34. Hardwicke to Newcastle, 21 Dec. 1762, BL Add. MSS 32946, f. 4.
35. Devonshire to Newcastle, 23 Dec. 1762, Chatsworth MSS; Rockingham to Devonshire, 23 December 1762, Chatsworth MSS. The beneficiaries of the Massacre in Rockingham's rein would be Lord Bute's '*Tory* friends'.
36. G. Armytage to Rockingham, 2 Jan. 1763, Wentworth Woodhouse MSS, Sheffield Public Library.
37. *The Briton*, 25 Nov. 1762.
38. *The Annual Register* (1763), 41.
39. J. Almon, *A Review of Lord Bute's Administration* (1763), 77–8. This is a very common theme in the opposition pamphlets of the time. See the almost identical wording of John Butler, *Letter to the Cocoa Tree from a Whig* (1762): 'An unpopular minister has not the principal thing necessary towards his stability in a free country, *the confidence of the people*'.
40. A serious charge in the early 1760s. For an analysis of the potential danger to the constitution inherent in the idea of the independence of the King, see Brewer, 'The misfortunes of Lord Bute', 27–8.
41. Almon, *op. cit.*, 78.
42. For the grotesque unpopularity of Lord Bute, the object of the most vituperative ridicule and fanatical hatred witnessed since the days of Walpole, see Brewer, 'The misfortunes of Lord Bute', 12–22; Peters, *op. cit.*, 251–2.
43. So exhausted had Bute become by his

period of office that at the time of his resignation he certainly wished to 'retire in quiet, and pass the autumnal part of life, unruffled by the little infamous scenes, the black ingratitude etc. etc. etc. that decorates every hour of my present situation'. Bute to Dr Campbell, 30 Jan. 1763, Bute MSS, printed in Sedgwick, *op. cit.*, lxi–lxii.

44. BL Add. MSS 32938, fos. 227–30.
45. W. Smith (ed.), *The Grenville Papers*, (4 vols, 1852–3), III, 220.
46. Christie, *op. cit.*, 36.
47. Lawson, *George Grenville*, 163.
48. *Ibid.*
49. Newcastle to Devonshire, 30 Apr. 1763, BL Add. MSS 32948, f. 204.
50. Brooke, *George III*, 103. I do not wish to carry a brief for the Newcastle Whigs, and I certainly have no wish to bite the hand that feeds me, in this case Professor Christie's pioneering work on the myth of the double Cabinet, but I find it astonishing that scarcely a cursory reference is made to Bute's role in politics in these months. What Christie, *op. cit.*, 34n.2, does say, in a little-noticed footnote, is that 'The ministers had ground for irritation at times about this but ... the net effects were of little importance'.
51. See Thomas, *The Stamp Act Crisis*, 11. According to Sedgwick, *op. cit.*, lxi–lxii: 'There can be no doubt, however, of the sincerity of Bute's desire to rid himself of political entanglements in March and April 1763. He had sorely underestimated the amount of resentment that his promotion to the Treasury would create and the outcry against the Cider Excise early in 1763 was only the final straw which broke Bute's nerve. Quite simply, office was too much for him. He bore all the symptoms of a man facing physical exhaustion and nervous breakdown: "my health is every day impairing; a great relaxation of my bowels of many years standing is increasing on me continually; the eternal, unpleasant labour of the mind and

the impossibility of finding hours for exercise, and proper medicine, the little time I get for sleep, the little I ever enjoy, even when abed, become invincible obstructions to the cure of an old inveterate illness; my health therefore dictates retirement from the greatest weight, that ever lay on any man in this country."'

52. Sedgwick, *op. cit.*, lxiv–lxv, 225–6, 234. Although Egremont boasted in May that he would resign if Bute interfered, he had not done so in April (Egremont to Hardwicke, 13 May 1763, in Harris, *Life of Hardwicke*, III, 352). Professor Lawson, *op. cit.*, 150–3, mounts an eloquent plea on Grenville's behalf that he did have some say in the appointments to his own administration but the fact remains that at this stage Grenville refused to stand up to Bute.
53. Thomas, *op. cit.*, 11–12. See also Newcastle to Hardwicke, 9 June 1763, Harris, *Life of Hardwicke*, 111, 503.
54. Thomas, *op. cit.*, 12, and sources there given. Grenville, writing to Egremont, 4 Aug. 1763, complained of the King's 'want of confidence and communication, the evident marks of that superior influence to which it is owing', Smith, *op. cit.*, II, 85–8, 202–4.
55. George III to Lord Bute, 14 Apr. 1763, in Sedgwick, *op. cit.*, 220–1.
56. Lord Fitzmaurice, *Life of Shelburne* (2 vols, 1912), I, 199–208. Recent accounts of the negotiations may be consulted in O'Gorman, *op. cit.*, 75–7; Thomas, *op. cit.*, 13; Lawson, *op. cit.*, 159–63.
57. On balance possibly not quite. By 28 August George III had decided to end the negotiations with Pitt and although he needed the reassurance of Bute's endorsement of his own decision it does not appear that Bute effected the King's change of mind. (See, however, the story in the Grenville Diary [II, 197] that Bute's friends persuaded Bute against a Pitt

administration on the morning of 28 August whereupon Bute worked upon the King.) There is other evidence, however, to indicate Bute's continuing satisfaction with the terms the King had negotiated with Pitt (Fitzmaurice, *op. cit.*, I, 207–8).

58. Newcastle to Devonshire, 25 Aug. 1763, Chatsworth MSS.

59. Smith, *op. cit.*, II, 101, 197–201, 208–10. There had been considerable discussion about Grenville's successor, whether Bedford or Pitt, insisting on Bute's exclusion from business and withdrawal from London. See Fitzmaurice, *op. cit.*, I, 202–3; N.S. Jucker (ed.), *The Jenkinson Papers*, 371–2. Jenkinson believed that Bute had made a specific undertaking: 'that Lord B. would retire into the country and not come near the Court for a certain time and would not in the least interfere with government' (*ibid*, 393).

60. Fitzmaurice, *op. cit.*, I, 209. As early as 4 September Bute had written to Shelburne that he had 'absolutely abandoned all thoughts of interfering more in business having seen every honest wish and endeavour, every action of my life, turned in the most fake and cruel light' (*ibid.*, 207).

61. Smith, *op. cit.*, II, 202 , 214–16; Lawson, *op. cit.*, 166–7.

62. Smith, *op. cit.*, II, 232; Jucker, *op. cit.*, 395–6.

63. Smith, *op. cit.*, II, 498–9; Jucker, *op. cit.*, 396–7.

64. They met regularly at Kew with the Princess Dowager, where they both had houses. See Smith, *op. cit.*, III, 214–220; Jucker, *op. cit.*, 397.

65. Lord George Sackville to Charles Townshend, *post* April 1764, HMC, *Stopford-Sackville*, 61–2. Jucker, *op. cit.*, 397–8. For the disputes see Lawson, *op. cit.*, 213–14; Thomas, *op. cit.*, 115–19.

66. George Grenville to Lord Strange, 23 May 1765, in J. Tomlinson (ed.), *Additional Grenville Papers, 1763–65* (1962), 270–72.

67. The Regency Bill effected by the King would reserve to the King the name of the Regent. Throughout the spring, the King kept the ministry at arms length while he carefully kept his own counsel. See D. Jarrett, 'The Regency crisis of 1765', *EHR*, LXXX (1970).

68. Jucker, *op. cit.*, 399. 2.

69. *Ibid.*, 400. George III to Lord Bute end of May 1765, Sedgwick, *op. cit.*, 240–1. This letter reads very much like a periodic report upon the King's own health and upon his view of his ministers.

70. Mackenzie was to go and, once again, Bute was to be banished from politics. See Smith, *op. cit.*, III, 41; Sir John Fortescue, *The Correspondence of George III, 1760–83* (6 vols, 1927–8) I, 113–15; Sir Lewis Namier, *Additions and Corrections to Sir John Fortescue's Edition*, (1937) 30.

71. Newcastle to Cumberland, 24 May 1765, BL Add. MSS 32966, f. 464. For the King's unhappiness at having to break his promise to Bute, see the Memorandum printed in Fortescue, *op. cit.*, I, 169–73.

72. 'For His Royal Highness's Consideration', 21 May 1765, BL Add. MSS 32966, fos. 436–7.

73. Lord Albemarle, *Memoirs of the Marquis of Rockingham* (2 vols, 1852), I, 219. Newcastle would have liked the King to express his favour towards those who have always been 'true friends to the Revolution and the Protestant succession', 'Measures', 27 June 1765, BL Add. MSS 32967, f. 124.

74. Cumberland to Newcastle, July 1765, BL Add. MSS 32968, f. 381. For more of the same, see M. Bateson (ed.) 'A narrative of changes in the ministry, 1765–67', *Camden Society*, n.s. LIX (1898), 28–31.

75. BL Add. MSS 32967, f. 193; Thomas, *op. cit.*, 121.

76. Thomas, *op. cit.*, 121–2.

77. Bateson, *op. cit.*, 31.

78. Bute to J. Wemyss, 17 June 1766, Sir W. Fraser, *Memorials of the Family of Wemyss of Wemyss* (Edinburgh, 1888), III, 223, quoted in Langford, *op. cit.*,

52. He wrote to Hardwicke on 26 July
1766: 'I know as little, save from
newspapers, of the present busy
scene, as I do of transactions in
Persia, and yet am destined for ever
to a double uneasiness, that of
incapacity to serve those I love, and
yet to be continually censured for
every public transaction, though
totally retired from courts and public
business' (Albemarle, *op. cit.*, I, 360).
Bute was, in fact, quite happy to
remove himself from the political
limelight; see Langford, *op. cit.*, 53.
79. George III to Lord Bute, 10 Jan.
1766, Sedgwick, *op. cit.*, 245–6.
80. Langford, *op. cit.*, 133.
81. *Ibid.*, 158.
82. Rockingham to Charles Yorke, 25
Jan. 1766, BL Add. MSS 35430, fos.
37–8, quoted in Albemarle, *op. cit.*, I,
288; Christie, *op. cit.*, 35.
83. Bute spoke against repeal in the
House of Lords on 6 Feb. 1766,
whereupon Rockingham retaliated,
making use of the King's name to
rally support for repeal. On 10
February, a friend of George III,
Lord Strange, the Independent MP
for Lancashire, put it about on the
King's authority, that the King
favoured modification. It took a most
uncomfortable interview between
Rockingham and the King before the
Marquis extracted a signed statement
from the monarch that he was in
favour of repeal, although he insisted
on adding 'The Conversation having
only been concerning That or
Enforcing'. A few days later, a Lord
of the Bedchamber, Lord Denbigh,
spread the news that the King 'never
was for the Repeal'. Once again,
Rockingham had to persuade the
King to sign a paper declaring his
support for the Repeal. See Fortescue,
op. cit., I, 266–9; Namier, *Additions and
Corrections*, 50–2; Bateson, *op. cit.*, 51;
Albemarle, *op. cit.*, I, pp. 301–2;
Wentworth Woodhouse MSS R–161;
Newcastle to the Archbishop, BL
Add. MSS 32974, fos. 5–7.
84. Professor I. Christie, *The Crisis of

Empire (1966), 64, has tried to defend
the King, making allowances for 'the
King's well-known nervous
volubility' and his 'unintentional
indiscretion'. What the King actually
said to Strange, however, seems to me
to be quite deliberate and
premeditated. 'I therefore authoriz'd
him to declare to whoever declar'd
that to be my idea, the very words I
now acquainted him with' (see
O'Gorman, *op. cit.*, 165–6). There
seems nothing in the least accidental
about such a remark.
85. The King to Lord Bute, 10 Jan.
1766, in Sedgwick, *op. cit.*, 242.
86. George III to Lord Egmont, 7
February 1766, BL Add. MSS 47012
f. 114, Egmont MSS.
87. Lord Egmont to George III, 11
February 1766, *ibid.* f. 116.
88. Lord Egmont to George III, ? 1766, f.
124.
89. George III to Lord Bute, 3 May 1766,
12 July 1766, in Sedgwick, *op. cit.*,
246–54.
90. Langford, *op. cit.*, 225–6.
91. Hardwicke to Rockingham, 10 July
1766, Rockingham MSS; Christie,
Myth and Reality, 37. Rockingham
wished to give 'the credit of being the
secret spring of the late Events' to
'Lord Bute and *the Lady*'
(Rockingham to Portland, 28 Aug.
1766, Portland MSS.)
92. Newcastle to Portland, 14 Dec. 1766,
Portland MSS.
93. Rockingham to Portland, 4 Dec.
1766, Portland MSS.
94. Rockingham to Scarborough, 20 Nov.
1766, Rockingham MSS. For further
references of the same type see Lord
Macclesfield to Charles Jenkinson, 7
Dec. 1766, in Jucker, *op. cit.*, 438–9:
'Who would have thought of this last
turn Lord Chatham endeavouring a
connexion with the Earl of B[ute] as
the only means of supporting
himself'.
95. Sedgwick, *op. cit.*, 253.
96. August 1766, in Sedgwick, *op. cit.*,
255–8.
97. Burke to Charles O'Hara, 15 Jan.

1767, in T.W. Copeland (ed.), *Correspondence of Edmund Burke* (1958), 290–2.

98. See O'Gorman, *op. cit.*, 554–5, 38.

99. Professor Brewer stresses the Rockingham Whigs' detestation of George Grenville as a further element which defined their party views but that, surely, was a secondary consideration; see Brewer, *Party Ideology and Popular Politics*, 86–92.

100. Rockingham to Hardwicke, 2 July 1767, Rockingham MSS, partly printed in Albemarle, *op. cit.*, II, 50–4.

101. Rockingham to Dowdeswell, 20 Oct. 1767, Dowdeswell MSS.

102. Rockingham to Dowdeswell, 9 Sept. 1767, Rockingham MSS. See also the very similar letter from Rockingham to Portland, 15 Sept. 1767, Portland MSS, misdated 17 Sept. in Albemarle, *op. cit.*, II, 57–9.

103. Newcastle went to his death in 1768 firmly convinced that Bute was active. In a letter to Rockingham of 10 June he observed that 'the Present Scheme of Administration is a Thorough Union between the Graftons, the Bedfords, supported by My Lord Bute' (Rockingham MSS).

104. Professor Brewer has assembled a few examples in 'The misfortunes of Lord Bute', 9–10.

105. Not just his writings. In 1769 Burke lectured Parliament oñthe Court system, its policy of ruling the great factions by dividing them and by breaking family and friendship ties. See W. Cobbett, *The Parliamentary History (1806–20)*, xvi, 391–2.

106. *Observations on a Late Pamphlet Intituled a State of the Nation* (1769). *The Writings and Speeches of Edmund Burke*, ed. P. Langford, II, 111.

107. Burke, *Thoughts on the Causes*.

108. *Ibid.*, 275–6.

109. For continued attacks on Bute in the 1770s see Brewer, 'The misfortunes of Lord Bute', 4, n.4. See Christie, *Myth and Reality*, 45, n.2, for evidence of discrimination against Bute's family. The political nation enjoyed having a

scapegoat, however, and Bute was replaced in that role by Charles Jenkinson: 'As Lord Bute gradually retired into the shade of private life, and became insensibly forgotten, Mr. Jenkinson proportionably came forward in his own person, and on his own proper Merits ... His intercourse with the King, and even his Influence over the Royal Mind were assumed to be constant, progressive, commensurate with, and sometimes paramount to, or subversive of, the Measures proposed by the First Minister' (Sir Nathaniel Wraxall, *Historical Memories of My Own Time* (1904), 329). See also Jucker, *op. cit.*, xxv–xxviii.

110. Professor Christie, *Myth and Reality*, 42–5, lists a number of these instances, great and small, in the 1770s.

111. Burke to Rockingham, 29 Dec. 1790, *Burke Correspondence* (1966), eds A. Cobban and E.A. Smith, VI, 174–6.

112. Professor Christie, *Stress and Stability in Late 18th Century Britain: Reflections on the British Avoidance of Revolution* (1984), 38–44, has collected a number of such references for the period 1784 to 1806. See also Brewer, 'The misfortunes of Lord Bute', 4, n.5. Rockingham's widow believed that with the Portland–Pitt coalition of 1794, Lord Bute and the Tories had triumphed yet again over the Whigs. She condemned this attempt 'to blend *Whig* and Tory, to *break all Connections* and to dispense with *Parties*' (Lady Rockingham to Fitzwilliam, 9 Sept. 1794, Rockingham MSS.)

113. J. Brooke, *The Chatham Administration* (1956), 47.

114. See, for example, the explanations offered by the Rockingham Whigs for their replacement by Shelburne in July 1782, *The Parliamentary History*, XXIII, 152–201.

115. Brewer, 'The misfortunes of Lord Bute', 36–8.

116. Butterfield, *op. cit.*, 273.

117. Burke, *Thoughts on the Causes*.

118. Dowdeswell's scheme of 17 Feb. 1768 is the first detailed Rockinghamite economical reform commitment known to me. This would have checked Crown and Treasury influence by disfranchising revenue officers. This was the origin of Clarke's Bill, ultimately passed in 1782; see West to Newcastle, 17 Feb. 1768, BL Add. MSS 32988, f. 355.
119. The North government defeated Dowdeswell's motion by 162 to 104: see *The Parliamentary History*, XVI, 926.
120. Rockingham to Burke, 29 June 1769, *Burke Correspondence*, ed. Copeland, II, 35–40.
121. Cornwall in the Commons, 11 Apr. 1771, *The Parliamentary History*, XVII, 183.
122. Richmond to Rockingham, 10 Sept. 1773, Rockingham MSS, printed in A.E. Olsen, *The Radical Duke* (1961) 154–6.
123. Rockingham to Charles Turner, 7 Apr. 1772, Rockingham MSS. Burke commented that 'Next to the grand object of the destruction of Wilkes, the leading object in the Politicks of the Court, is to seize upon the East India Patronage of Offices' (Burke to Dowdeswell, 27 October 1772, *Burke Correspondence*, ed. Copeland, II, 351).
124. Rockingham to the Duke of Manchester, 28 June 1775, copy in Lady Rockingham's hand, Rockingham MSS. It is not at all clear why the Rockinghams must suffer part of the blame for causing the American War of Independence. To blame them for not taking office in 1767 and thus injecting a more cautious and amicable tone into imperial policy seems a massive exercise of historical hindsight (Christie, *Myth and Reality*, 53).
125. Devonshire to Newcastle, 29 Dec. 1762, Chatsworth MSS.
126. Rockingham to Hardwicke, 26 July 1767, Rockingham MSS. This letter is quoted without comment in Brooke, *The Chatham Administration*, 210–11, and, equivocally, in Christie, *Myth and Reality*, 46–7.
127. See, for example, the fairly brusque (and unapologetic) passage: 'The power of the Crown, almost dead and rotten as Prerogative, has grown up anew with much more strength, and far less odium, under the name of Influence' (Burke, *Thoughts on the Cause*, 258). See also *ibid.*, 258–63, 266–7. 'A great Prince may be obliged ... to sacrifice his private inclination to his public interest' (*ibid.*, 267). 'It must be remembered, that since the Revolution until the period we are speaking of, the influence of the Crown had been always employed in supporting the Ministers of State, and in carrying on the public business according to their opinions' (*ibid.*, 269). See also *ibid.*, 321–2. Parliament 'will be willing and able to teach the Court that it is the true interest of the Prince to have but one Administration'.
128. *The Parliamentary History*, XVI, 742.
129. Christie, *Myth and Reality*, 49.
130. I.R. Christie, *Stress and Stability*, 43.

4

Lord Bute and the Press:
the origins of the Press War of 1762
reconsidered

Karl W. Schweizer

On 5 October 1761, William Pitt, Secretary of State for the Southern Department, formally resigned office in consequence of a Cabinet disagreement concerning Spain and the Family Compact.[1] Initially, news of this event – the first major political upset of the new reign – was expected to incite popular indignation against the remaining ministers. Before such criticism gained momentum, however, it was arrested by the rumour that the 'Great Commoner' had accepted a royal sinecure: a yearly pension of £3000 for three lives plus a peerage for his wife. At first, Pitt's city supporters led by William Beckford strenuously denied these suggestions and the evening papers denounced them 'as a design to tarnish the luster of a certain great character',[2] but when on 10 October the official announcement appeared in the *Gazette*[3] (with appeasing news from Spain printed in close proximity), speculation had become fact and scepticism turned to disillusionment and anger. 'The city and the people are outrageous about "Lady Cheat-em" as they call her and her husband's pension', wrote one observer, '. . . they say that his Majesty has broke his word with them by this bounty to Pitt, for that he promised he would not govern by corruption'.[4] Public disapprobation of Pitt, immediate and widespread, was expressed in a variety of ways – satirical prints, burned effigies,[5] cancelled city addresses[6] – though ultimately it was the press that proved most active if not critical of all with political commentary engendering fervent controversy and debate. Such was the clamour that by mid-October, Pitt, on the advice of Lord Temple[7] decided to clarify matters and defend himself by means of a letter to Alderman William Beckford explaining the reasons for his resignation and emphasizing that the pension was 'unmerited' and 'unsolicited';[8] an obvious attempt to negate suggestions, then current, that he had been bribed to resign by the Court.[9] The letter – reprinted in the *Public Ledger*, the *Gazetteer* and other papers[10] – readily restored Pitt's popularity in the City,[11] yet also revitalized political contention by intensifying the resignation debate, raising questions of constitutional significance[12] and exposing Pitt to further hostile scrutiny in the Press. Historians traditionally have maintained that these Press attacks, before Pitt's justifying letter but especially after, were initiated and vindictively promoted by the government – specifically Lord Bute – as part of a concerted scheme to publicize the pension, compromise Pitt's 'patriot' reputation[13] – a major reason for his popular credibility and appeal – and thereby destroy his political credit should he decide to enter into opposition. 'The fierceness of the debate', writes one scholar,

> was the result of a deliberate attack, with a degree of Government support unequalled since the days of Walpole. The attack, a combination of personal abuse with substantial argument about policies, was designed to overwhelm Pitt's supporters, block off every channel of reply and to destroy once and for all Pitt's popular reputation.[14]

This contention reflects the still prevailing influence of the old 'Whig conspiracy' theory as advanced originally by John Almon, Horace Walpole and others[15] – a theory which is totally inconsistent, as this paper aims to demonstrate, with Bute's actual political objectives at this time. These can be properly understood only by re-examining the pension itself, conventionally viewed in the same conspiratorial context as Bute's other allegedly hostile activities during these months: as a clever ruse to make Pitt appear the object of Court favour, ruin his patriot image – acceptance of a pension being incompatible with the tenets of true patriotism – and so render him more vulnerable to vilification in the Press.[16] Seen in this light, the pension and the Press attacks are mutually reinforcing and dependent: the desired impact of one was necessarily contingent upon the implementation of the other.

While there is circumstantial evidence that at least some within the government intended the pension to discredit Pitt – certainly Newcastle made insinuations to that effect[17] – Pitt's reward, as I have shown elsewhere,[18] was in fact the key feature of a political strategy aimed at neutralizing the feared impact of the great minister's resignation in two ways: first, by showing that the present administration could direct national affairs and pursue the war effort as vigorously as Pitt; second, by pacifying parliamentary and popular opinion in providing a legitimate and expected recognition for Pitt's contributions to the war.[19] Pitt's own financial situation was far from secure and pensions *were* the normal way of providing for retiring statesmen – particularly for one of such stature as Pitt. Hence his rewards were both natural and politically expedient: made official in the *Gazette*, the peerage and pension were not only public evidence of royal obligation to distinguished service; they also demonstrated that Pitt bore no grudge against his former colleagues and the King; that he had resigned voluntarily under no pressure from above. The implication was clear: had he fallen victim to intrigue or been expelled from office, he would hardly have accepted anything from those responsible.[20] Bute's concern to clarify the reasons for Pitt's departure also explains the Spanish clause in the *Gazette*. In order to avoid all ambiguities about the resignation and to justify the decision of the Cabinet with regard to Spain, he decided to publicize the issue in question. The obvious divergence between the report from Madrid, reaffirming Spain's peaceful intentions, and Pitt's recommendation for immediate hostilities explained not only why the latter had resigned but also why the majority of the Cabinet had voted against aggressive measures at this time.

Political stability then – the minimization of domestic tension and unrest, not disparagement of Pitt – was Bute's foremost concern in the autumn of 1761. One must question, therefore, why Bute would deliberately initiate a Press war, bring himself and his ministry to public attention and virtually guarantee repercussions – that is, Pitt's formidable oratory – in the Commons, the very thing he hoped to avoid.[21] Pitt had, after all, made it clear that, although having no intention of going into opposition, he would defend himself publicly if 'fallen upon' in the Press or if 'his resignation should be misrepresented';[22] and since Bute was only too aware of Pitt's popular following, especially in the City,[23] it was in his interest to maintain a low profile and avoid fanning the ever volatile compound of urban radicalism and mob violence.[24]

But motive aside, it is also difficult to understand how Bute could have been anxious to implement a propaganda campaign, given, first, his ambivalent attitude towards the Press – conscious of its importance yet fearful of its unpredictability and radical trends – and secondly, his initially limited resources, in facilities and personnel, essential for manipulating national opinion on the government's behalf. Despite the repeated urgings of Dodington and Henry Fox,[25] both experienced in handling the Press, Bute had so far made only sporadic and ineffectual attempts to establish a ministerial paper (the scheme was not to reach fruition until the summer of 1762), had formed no connection with existing political journals, nor (other than for Dr John Campbell, a journalist and old personal friend) had he recruited any political writers to supplement the handful of propagandists – W. Guthrie, James Ralph, David Mallet and several others – already enlisted and pensioned by Newcastle.[26] Indeed, so far from being keen to use the Press, Bute had to be repeatedly reminded of the need for greater activity in that sphere. As James Ralph observed to him on 7 October 1761: 'My Lord, I am afraid a little writing will be necessary to bring the people to their senses and such documents as shall be thought proper to elucidate the late resignation will be sufficient for the present'.[27] The Yorke faction too were critical of Bute's hesitant dealings with the Press and persistently urged the need for better replies to the *Monitor* and other papers expounding opposition views. Lord Hardwicke clearly testified to the ministry's languid press policy when he wrote to his son:

> I agree with every word you say as to the neglect and obstinacy in not publishing proper answers to the ribaldry with which the papers abound against the administration, nor proper defences of their own conduct ... In truth, ministers should retain persons who can write well to do that business for them, but if they neglect that, it is not to be expected that their friends, however zealous, should expose themselves to the personal resentments and animosities of their enemies by doing what they decline to do for themselves.[28]

As in political journalism, so in the realm of graphic and pictorial satire. Though ultimately assaulted by a barrage of seditious prints and cartoons (totalling over 400 by 1762), Bute made practically no attempt at pictorial defence or counter-attack.[29] His most important artist, Hogarth, was not engaged until 1762 and then primarily to defend the peace negotiations with France rather than specifically to vilify Pitt.[30] Such few anti-Pitt prints as have survived, dating mainly from 1761, are anonymous and generally ignore the pension episode, tending to concentrate more on personal satire, humorously distorting or exaggerating Pitt's physical oddities and traits.[31]

If, however, Bute had neither sufficient motive nor personnel for an all-out literary offensive, who then was responsible for originating the controversy which so greatly sharpened political tensions following Pitt's resignation and finally led to the notorious 'Press war' of 1762? Certainly some of the initial comment – especially the criticism of Pitt in the newspaper press – was spontaneous and unsolicited; a matter not of ministerial connivance but general disillusionment, hardly surprising given Pitt's well-known stand on sinecures and rewards.[32] In short, Pitt came under fire for compromising the patriot ideal – the image of independence, virtue and honour cultivated throughout his career – and the bitterness with which even Horace Walpole, so familiar with the political world, and the poet Gray reflected on his conduct[33] demonstrates that negative reactions to the pension were not confined to any one element and evidently required little official incitement.

Also, as Marie Peters has shown,[34] what really started the whole

controversy, ignited the Press debate that was to ensue, were not
government efforts but the initiatives taken by *Pittite* supporters in
inundating the Press with provocative rumours, speculations and mis-
leading reports designed to heighten anxiety over the resignation and
reflect adversely on current ministerial policies. Some of these allegations
may have emanated from the City and Common Council who 'were
very violent upon the subject of Mr. Pitt' and warned 'that there would
be a bad peace';[35] others may have been planted by Lord Temple
whose oppositionist sentiments found ample expression in Beckford's
Monitor – the leading anti-government paper, or John Almon who, as
we know, wrote factional letters to the *Gazetteer*.[36] As the *Annual Register*
properly pointed out:

> The friends of Mr. Pitt raised the most violent clamours for displacing a
> *minister* whose measures had raised the nation from the most abject state
> to the highest pinnacle of glory. They said that 'he was in fact displaced
> when he was compelled to resign by not being suffered to carry into
> execution these measures which he knew to be necessary to the honour
> and safety of his country. That the check which this minister had received
> would most unreasonably revive the drooping hopes of France ... and
> would show Spain with what impunity she might insult the honour of the
> British Crown' ... However, the editor emphasized ... a strenuous defense
> was made on the part of the remaining ministry.[37]

Indeed, it was precisely in reaction to these allegations, 'misrepresentations' as Hardwicke called them,[38] that the Yorkes launched
their first government defence and criticism of Pitt in the *London Chronicle*,
and ultimately it was the controversy generated by these polemics and
the replies they provoked which in turn disconcerted Pitt and prompted
his famous letter of justification. Only after these developments,
towards late October, when the resignation debate was already well
under way – in fact just intensified by Pitt's communication to Beckford
– did Bute finally acknowledge the need for greater efforts to mobilize
and broaden public support. It is from this point onwards (and not
before, as John Brewer maintains) that Bute made any sustained
attempts to create a favourable press: instructing James Ralph to
produce drafts of projected weekly papers, recruiting runners and
coffee-house spies to monitor opinion and cultivate connections in the
city,[39] encouraging Bedford to collaborate with pacifist pamphleteers,[40]
and above all, prompting his pensioned writers to refute the opposition
Press and generally vindicate government policy on major issues of
public concern. Yet even then his press activities were anything but
adequate, hampered as he continued to be by his aversion to public
controversy, his profound dislike of literary hacks and grub street

tactics and finally by his abiding hesitation to do anything that might
unduly annoy or provoke Pitt. Thus, when James Ralph abused Pitt in
a scurrilous work, unnamed (possibly *The Right Honourable Annuitant
Vindicated*, an unprecedentedly scathing attack),[41] Bute intervened and
advised a more moderate line. As Ralph ruefully apologized:

> I am extremely mortified to find that I have misjudged the services
> expected from me. My opinion of the person and the cause was that
> neither the one nor the other could be treated too severely. And that there
> was no such thing as opening the eyes of the people without a thorough
> dissection of both. But ... it does not become me to opinionate anything
> with your Lordship – my next effort shall be accomodated to the best of
> my capacity to the ideas now communicated to me by your Lordship.[42]

Similarly, Lord Royston, who had been continuing his contributions
to the *Chronicle* and other papers in response to the Pittite *Monitor*,
suddenly found his endeavours censured by Newcastle and Bute because
'they would irritate Mr Pitt and give him a handle to be troublesome in
parliament'.[43] Royston consequently complained to his father that the
administration was not making its public case nearly firmly enough:

> The articles in Tuesday's *London Chronicle* were purely defensive and
> opposed to a torrent of calumny and falsehoods which proceeded from the
> other quarter. So little encouragement has been given to writers on our
> side and so little truth has been circulated in return to *ribaldry* and lies that
> the field has been left quite open to the enemy and great mischief has
> resulted from it to our cause. It is weakness to think Mr Pitt will want a
> handle to oppose. The Seals were scarce out of his hands but the press
> swarmed with libels against those who had opposed his extravagant views
> and still continued to do so. If under these circumstances those are dis-
> couraged or disowned or disapproved who have the courage to face the
> storm when so many in office and under obligation are timid and waver-
> ing, what will ensue but defeat?[44]

Hardwicke agreed, replying:

> I must confess that I have, not only now, but formerly observed too much
> timidity and weakness upon such points and have often animadverted
> upon it. Nothing can be more mistaken to think things of this nature will
> alter Mr Pitt's conduct ... The material point is to set the public right as
> to measures and not to let misrepresentations take root.[45]

Admittedly, Bute was by now utilizing such journalistic support as
he could muster; still it should be noted that much of this propaganda
did not primarily aim at maligning Pitt (though obviously criticism of
the former minister remained a factor) but as with Dr Campbell's
writings, was intended 'to set the nature of the resignation in its true
light', to counteract 'as much as possible the factious dialect in the

city',[46] to vindicate the government's cautious policy towards Spain,[47] and later to advance arguments in favour of a moderate peace.[48] Even the first pamphlets issued from the government's side, such as William Guthrie's *A Letter to the Right Honourable Earl of Bute* and *Second Letter to ... Bute*, were not personal attacks on Pitt but basically objective, well-reasoned commentaries on the political situation, minimizing the effects of Pitt's resignation, demonstrating the necessity of imminent peace and urging an end to Britain's military commitments abroad.[49] Various later pamphlets did become increasingly vehement in tone and widened in scope: criticizing Pitt's rewards, mocking his patriot professions and inconsistencies, his claims to 'guide' or pretentions to 'absolute power',[50] and (like *The Patriot Unmasked*) projecting these indictments over his public career as a whole. Remarkably few of these, however, can be clearly identified as officially endorsed. Altogether there are only five or possibly six pamphlet publications definitely attributable to writers with government connections: Guthrie's three *Letters to Bute* which appeared between October 1761 and January 1762; *The Right Honourable Annuitant*, perhaps composed by James Ralph – the evidence remains ambiguous – *Mr. Pitt's Letter versified* and *A letter from the Anonymous Author*,[51] two exceptionally caustic contributions, both verifiably the works of Philip Francis who, however, acted under the influence of Henry Fox and not Bute at this time.[52] Perhaps the most devastating attacks of all, the latter two pamphlets – a reaction to Pitt's defence and the City's response – pushed the Press war to new heights, gave a personally hostile tone to debate and touched on major questions of constitutional significance – issues such as the relationship between King and minister and among ministers – which, more fully developed elsewhere, continued to be the focus of public discussion for the remainder of the decade. As for the other pamphlets appearing between November and January, these were either attempted defenses of Pitt – for the most part ineffective[53] – or, more commonly, rebuttals of the pro-Pittite *Monitor*[54] or attacks reiterating the established objections to the peerage and pension, Pitt's letter to Beckford, Beckford's alleged reply, and the violent proceedings of the Common Council which Pitt was considered to have encouraged. But again, we cannot be certain how many of these critiques had official sanction; probably Israel Mauduit's *Occasional Thoughts on the Present German War*, published in December, since Mauduit enjoyed Bute's favour and subsequently received a government post;[55] others most likely were unsolicited: spontaneous contributions to a public controversy rather than polemics manipulated by interested groups.

At any rate, the picture of Bute's Press activities that has emerged from our discussion indicates the need to modify historical opinion regarding Bute's responsibility for the literary strife or 'Press war' of 1761–2. Instead of being the 'original belligerent', as John Brewer maintains, Bute seems to have been caught up in the same polemical vortex as Pitt, his growing involvement with the Press forced upon him by the widening parameters and intensification of political debate during the months following Pitt's retreat from office. Not until the commotion attending Pitt's published letter of defence – towards the end of October – did Bute make any noticeable efforts to cultivate the Press – a generally hesitant, cautious improvisation, neither sufficient to gain the initiative nor ultimately to counteract the adverse publicity which would haunt him for the remainder of his career and (as Brewer has shown) even beyond.[56]

Defence is usually more difficult than attack but Bute's propaganda system (such as it was) proved especially inadequate, partly because of poor organization and lack of consistent direction from above but also due to Bute's peculiar vulnerability: detested personally and politically, the focal point for disparate national grievances and phobias, Bute was *persona non grata* with virtually every sector of contemporary society, a fact no amount of Press activity could change. Although, by mid-1762, Bute had at last established his own weekly newspapers – the *Briton* and the *Auditor*, he still found it all but impossible to win support for his policies, construct an adequate defence or develop public rapport. Smollet, Bute's editor, even when supported by Arthur Murphy, proved no match for the journalistic skills, wit and daring of John Wilkes, whose *The North Briton* played upon popular prejudices, associating Bute with those controversial or emotive issues best calculated to place him in an unfavourable light and evoke the most hostile reactions from the nation at large.[57]

At the same time, it must be stressed that the Press was less one-sidedly in favour of Pitt during these months than has often been claimed. The circumstances of his resignation, the compromises of office, the inconsistencies of his career, the changing configuration of politics under George III, all combined to weaken the popular basis of his political strength – a decline clearly reflected in the fluctuations of public opinion throughout 1761–2. Thus, during the pension controversy, initial reactions in the newspapers tended to be predominantly negative, becoming more favourable and sympathetic once Pitt's letter of explanation appeared and as the debate developed; the pamphlets and reviews, on the other hand, initially supportive, grew steadily more hostile, the balance in favour of Pitt turning eventually against him.[58] During the debate over peace, the London papers – the

Monitor and *London Evening Post* especially – were bitterly opposed to
Bute's peace policy, as were the cartoons and political prints; yet the
magazines and literary periodicals – publications such as the *Gentleman's, London, Royal* and *Imperial Magazines* – took a more balanced
stand, expressing neither strong approval of ministerial measures,
nor endorsing the expansionist ambitions of London's mercantile
interests.[59] Most of the other newspapers (other than those coming
from the Pittite Press), reviews and pamphlets supported peace – even
Bute's controversial terms – particularly once these had passed the
Commons. As the *Critical Review* put it: 'if we may judge from the stile
of the pamphlets, the popular tide seems to have taken a turn favourable to the pacific measures of the present administration'.[60] These
limited gains in the press no doubt owed more to fortuitous factors than
improved government journalism: notably, Pitt's failure to rally his
political and extra-parliamentary support, Bute's growing *rapprochement*
with leading Tory elements in the city (who, it seems, used their
influence to defend the peace),[61] general reaction against the financial
strains of war and, above all, the terms of the peace itself, described by
one observer 'as substantial and equal to the expectations of moderate
men'.[62]

However, nurtured by the controversies surrounding the position
and policies of Lord Bute, the Press war of 1762 was in a wider sense
the climax of developments going back to the literary strife of the
previous autumn, that in turn proceeded directly from the resignation
and pension debate itself, a connection the nature and significance of
which has never been clearly recognized or explained. Any assessment,
however, of Bute's Press policy must take place in this broader context.
Indeed, for this essay, the main interest of the pension is the way in
which popular reaction to it rebounded against Pitt and Bute alike, the
resultant political upheaval forcing Pitt on the defensive, weakening his
political position while also compelling Bute to utilize the Press in order
to counter the arguments and claims advanced by the opposition on
behalf of Pitt. From this perspective, the propaganda conflict of 1761
was not the deliberate creation of a vengeful government but more an
accelerating debate sparked initially by Pitt's resignation, stimulated
by the furore over the pension and given momentum with the input
from both ministerial and opposition sources, as the discussion unfolded and as new, contentious issues arose. Moreover, the constitutional questions explored in the process – those of ministerial responsibility and power – gradually broadened the dimensions of debate
and foreshadowed the controversy over Bute's position that was to
follow. Finally, Pitt's resignation and its repercussions illustrate all too

clearly the predicament of Bute's political career as a whole: namely, any action, however legitimate and well intentioned, was bound to be turned against him. Ignoring Pitt's achievements would have aroused public resentment, yet in providing a pension and giving it publicity in the *Gazette*, Bute helped precipitate the very outburst of dissension and partisan clamour that he wanted to avoid. So anxious was he to clarify the reasons for Pitt's resignation, to avert political divisions and to justify his own policies that he presented his case to a nation which neither liked nor trusted him. The consequences are known only too well.

APPENDIX: DOCUMENTS ILLUSTRATING BUTE'S AVERSION TO PRESS CONFLICT IN THE AUTUMN OF 1761

Document 1[63]

Chiswick
October 7th 1761

My Lord

I never was so angry with the Gout as at present. .... I am sensible I ought to be now at your Lordship's gates in expectation of your commands; and yet cannot stir out of my chair.

Having my hands at liberty, however, I am in hopes I shall be honoured with them either from your Lordship immediately or by the intervention of Lord Melcombe.[64]

My Lord; I am afraid a little writing will be necessary to bring the people to their senses: and such documents as shall be thought proper to elucidate the late resignation will be sufficient for the present: of which your Lordship may rely upon it, I will make the best use in my power.

Sure as I am, that His Majesty has reason as well as power and authority on his side, I take it for granted as much firmness and spirit will be manifested now and as may secure him from the like audacious treatment forever hereafter.

I write in haste my Lord, that this note may reach your hands the sooner and most humbly beg pardon for all defects.

Having the honour to be, with the utmost zeal, sincerity and esteem

My Lord
Your Lordships most obliged and
most devoted, humble servant
James Ralph

Document 2⁶⁵

Oct. 28 – 1761

My Lord

I am extremely mortified to find that I have misjudged the service expected from me . . . My opinion of the person and the cause was that, neither the one or the other could be treated too severely . . . and that there was no such thing as opening the eyes of the people without a thorough dissection of both . . . But my Lord it does not become me to opinionate any thing with your Lordship . . . and my next effort shall be accommodated to the best of my capacity to the ideas now communicated to me by your Lordship.

I have the honour to be, with all possible esteem and respect
My Lord
Your Lordship's most obliged and
most devoted humble servant
James Ralph

Document 3⁶⁶

Richmond October 16th 1761

My Lord

I find by a short conference I had with Mr. Jones,[67] just before I set out for this place, that the paragraphs which have been inserted in the papers, tending to set Mr. Pitt's extraordinary conduct in its true colours, are disapproved of at Newcastle House. What he said was 'that he hoped no person of consideration had been so imprudent as to send them, or be concerned in them'. I presume he spoke the sentiments of others rather than his own. He seemed to think they would irritate Mr. P. and give him a handle to be troublesome in Parliament.

For my part, I know of no paragraphs which have been inserted in the papers – in defense of those with whom Mr. P. has thought proper to break – but the article in Tuesday's *London Chronicle* and those I sent to the *St. James*, I am sure, the latter were purely defensive, and opposed to a torrent of calumny and falsehood which proceeded from the other quarter. So little encouragement has been given to writers on our side – and so little *truth* has been circulated in return to *ribaldry* and *lies*, that the field has been left quite open to the enemy and great mischief has resulted from it to our Cause. It is weakness to think Mr. P. will want a handle to oppose. It is his element. He has *flourished* in it and has even carried on his Administration by arts of opposition. The Seals were scarce out of his hands, but the press swarmed with libels against those who had opposed his extravagant views, and still continues to do so. If under these circumstances those are discouraged, or disowned, or disapproved, who have the courage to face the storm, when so many in *Office*, and under *obligations*, are timid and wavering – what will ensue but a second defeat and the triumphal entry of Mr. P. into Administration? Mr. P. was never on such bad ground before and if no use is made of it, we shall smart for it when repentance can do no good. People must be employed according to their talents and the press and the tongues have both their distinct utility in a free country.

I had drawn up a paper in answer to the foolish observation on my report but shall actively suppress it for though I think it should have done some good if those I principally meant to serve at a crisis (that if not improved, will be irrecoverable) think otherwise, I shall defer to their superior judgment, submitting, but not convinced.

I hope your Lordship will excuse the freedom with which I have explained my sentiments on this subject. They are drawn from me out of the zeal of my heart, and my vexation to see that when the tide is turning with regard to the popularity of a certain person,[68] our own hands are employed in checking it.

> I am
> My Lord
> With the greatest respect
> Your most dutiful and
> Obliged Servant
> Royston

Document 4[69]

> Grosvenor Sq.
> Saturday Oct. 17th, 1761

Dear Royston

I return enclosed Sir Joseph's[70] letter and thankyou for communicating it. I find Joe is lower than usual, and don't like the state of things. I own I have not liked it for some time, either on the side of Westphalia or of Silesia; but this last blow and upon the King of Prussia[71] is surprising; and one cannot help thinking that there must have been some treachery, or gross mistakes or negligence in it. Neither do I like the situation of the Russian Army, for, instead of marching back into Poland, as we were assured, they seem to aim at Brandenburg and Berlin again.

I agree with every word you say as to the neglect and obstinacy in not publishing proper answers to the ribaldry, with which the papers abound against the Administration, nor proper defenses of their own conduct. As to what you were told was said at Newcastle House, I am sure it was not meant with regard to the paragraphs in the *St. James's Chronicle*, but to such, as have been published reflecting upon, and provoking to, Mr. Pitt; whereas those in that *Chronicle* were extremely decent and civil to him, and only stated facts in their true light. But I must confess that I have, not only now, but formerly, observed too much timidity and weakness upon such points, and have often animadverted upon it. Nothing can be more mistaken than to think things of this nature will alter Mr. Pitt's conduct. His provocations, as well as his conduct, will be taken from higher sources. The material point is to set the public right as to measures and facts, and not to let misrepresentations take root. That was the view of the paragraphs in the *St. James's Chronicle*; and extremely well executed it was; and I think you have been much in the right to condemn the trifling foolish *remarks* made upon those paragraphs. The weakness and emptiness of them appear upon reading, and they did not deserve an answer. In truth, Ministers should retain persons, who can write well to do that business for them; but, if they will neglect that, it is not to be expected that their friends, how ever zealous, should expose themselves to the personal resentment and animosity of their enemies, by doing what they decline to do for themselves.

But I suppose now that everybody, however great, will think fit to appeal to the Mob in this way. I never was more surprized in my life than with the letter published in the public *Ledger* of this day.[72] I had not seen it but by being told of it and was told at the same time (i.e.) between one and two o'Clock that those papers sold for five guineas apiece. I would not honour it with such a price, but procured a M.S. copy of it, which I enclose to you. It is the copy of a letter from Mr. P. to Ald. Beckford. I am told the King, as he justly may, is extremely offended with it;[73] But I should hope it will rather do good than harm. You will observe four things strongly marked in it. 1. He avows the sole cause of his resignation to be the point of Spain. 2. He publishes the proceedings and opinion of the Cabinet, which ought to be secret, and to which the Councillors are sworn. 3. The King clearly and strongly approved, and followed that opinion, though he drops that. 4. He betrays the strongest sensibility of having lost the good opinion of many of his friends, and a passionate resentment for it. You will make other remarks for yourself.

Mr. Prowse[74] hs declined the Speaker's Chair mostly on account of his health, – Diabetes and shortness of breath; and it is said the causes alledged are true. Where will they go? . . . [75]

> I am always,
> Yours most affectionately,
> H.

NOTES

I wish to thank the present Marquis of Bute for permission to consult and reprint items from the papers of the 3rd Earl; His Grace the Duke of Devonshire for allowing me to utilize the manuscripts at Chatsworth; and the Trustees of the British Library for permission to consult their collections and reproduce material from the Hardwicke Papers. I would also like to thank the Social Sciences and Humanities Research Council of Canada and the Bishop's University Research Fund for generous research support. An earlier version of this essay was read at Ian Christie's seminar on the eighteenth century at the Institute of Historical Research, London on 11 May 1983 and I am grateful to Dr John Dinwiddy and Dr E. Cruickshank for their helpful comments. Above all, I wish to acknowledge the encouragement and unstinting advice of Dr Marie Peters during the various stages of this paper without, of course, committing her to the views expressed in it.

1. For the events leading to Pitt's resignation see Peter D. Brown and Karl W. Schweizer (eds), *The Devonshire Diary: William Cavendish, 4th Duke of Devonshire; Memoranda on the State of Affairs, 1757–1762* (1982), pp. 17–140; P.C. Yorke, *The Life and Correspondence of Phillip Yorke, Earl of Hardwicke* (1913), III, 271–80, 318–29; W. Hunt, 'Pitt's retirement from office, Oct. 5, 1761', *EHR*, XXI (1906), 119–32.

2. Robert Rea, *The English Press in Politics 1760–1774* (Lincoln, 1963), 20. Duke of Albemarle (ed.), *Memoirs of the Marquis of Rockingham and his contemporaries* (2 vols, 1852), I, 51–2. Birch to Royston, 12 Oct. 1761, BL Add. MSS 35399, f. 258.

3. *London Gazette*, 10 Oct. 1761, no. 10146, 699.

4. J. Russell (ed.), *The Correspondence of John 4th Duke of Bedford* (1846), III, 51–52. Cf. Birch to Royston, 17 Oct. 1761. BL Add. MSS 35399, f. 260.

5. Russell, *op. cit.*, III, 51–5. Basil Williams, *The Life of William Pitt, Earl*

of Chatham (1915), II, 118–19. F.G. Stephens, *Catalogue of Prints and Drawings in the British Museum: Political and Personal Satires 1761–1770* (1883), IV, nos 3814–15.

6. Marie Peters, *Pitt and Popularity: the Patriot Minister and London Opinion during the Seven Years' War* (1980), 211–13.

7. Russell, *op. cit.*, III, 53.

8. W.S. Taylor and J.H. Pringle (eds), *The Correspondence of William Pitt, Earl of Chatham* (1838), II, 158–9.

9. *Gentleman's Magazine*, XXXII (1761), 460, 466. *Monthly Review*, II (1761), 316–17. *London Chronicle*, 10–13 Oct. 1761.

10. Williams, *op. cit.*, 120. Peters, *op. cit.*, 208–9. Pitt to Beckford, 15 Oct. 1761, in Taylor and Pringle, *op. cit.*, II, 158–9.

11. Holdernesse to Jenkinson, 20 Oct. 1761, BL Add. MSS 38198, f. 17. Birch to Royston, 17 Oct. 1761, BL Add. MSS 35399, f. 259. Newcastle to Hardwicke, 20 Oct. 1761, BL Add. MSS 32929, fos. 406–7. *Devonshire Diary*, 144.

12. See the paper by Marie Peters (Chapter 5) in this volume.

13. On the function and importance of the patriot concept in Pitt's career, see Peters, *Pitt and Popularity*, 63–5, 265ff; John Brewer, *Party Ideology and Popular Politics at the Accession of George III* (1976), 96–111.

14. Peters, *Pitt and Popularity*, 208.

15. John Almon, *Anecdotes of the Life of William Pitt* (1810), I, 371–2. *Memoirs of John Almon: Bookseller of Piccadilly* (1790), 14–15. Horace Walpole, *Memoirs of the Reign of George III* (1894), I, 63–5. *A Review of Mr. Pitt's Administration* (1763), 144–145.

16. Williams, *op. cit.*, II, 116. Brewer, *op. cit.*, ch. 6.

17. Newcastle to Devonshire, 9 Oct. 1761, BL Add. MSS 32929, fos. 139–42. Hardwicke to Royston, 12 Oct. 1761, BL Add. MSS 35399, fos. 257–8.

18. Karl W. Schweizer, 'Lord Bute and William Pitt's resignation in 1761', *Canadian J. of History*, VII (September 1973), 111–25.

19. *Ibid.*, 115. After all, in March of the same year Holdernesse had received an annuity of £4000 and the Wardenship of the Cinque Ports merely for vacating the Northern Secretaryship for Bute. As Lord Temple, no friend of the Court, observed to Wilkes on 16 October, 'when I returned to town, I found the King, upon Mr. Pitt's resignation, had not only acknowledged his great and eminent services in the highest terms and most gracious manner, but insisted likewise on rewarding them which was finally done in the way the *Gazette* sets forth, thus confirming by the testimony of the sovereign all those honours which the public had heaped upon him with such unanimous approbation.' (quoted in G. Nobbe, *The North Briton: A Study in Political Propaganda* (New York, 1939), 17).

20. G.F. Elliot, *The Border Elliots* (1897), 370.

21. Brown and Schweizer, *op. cit.*, 142.

22. Hardwicke to Newcastle, 13 Oct. 1761, BL Add. MSS 32929, fos. 227–8. Dr Campbell to Bute, 31 Oct. 1761, Bute MSS 1/165.

23. John Carswell and L.A. Dralle (eds), *The Political Journal of Bubb Dodington, Lord Melcombe* (1965), 426. Bute to Newcastle, 6 Oct. 1761, BL Add. MSS 32929, fos. 74–5. Brown and Schweizer, *op. cit.*, 140–1.

24. On the whole subject of London's political significance, its municipal government and proclivity for radicalism and opposition, see Nicholas Rogers, 'London politics from Walpole to Pitt: patriotism and independency in an era of commercial capitalism, 1738–63' (Ph.D. thesis, University of Toronto, 1975). Brewer, *Party Ideology and Popular Politics*, chs 9–12. Lucy Sutherland, 'The City of London in 18th century politics', in *Essays Presented to Sir Lewis Namier*, eds. R. Pares and A.J.P. Taylor (1956), 49–74. John Stevenson (ed.), *London in the Age of Reform* (1977).

25. Carswell and Dralle, *op. cit.*, 406. Cf.

H. Fox-Bourne, *English Newspapers*
(1887) I, 153.
26. Rea, *op. cit.*, 15; L.W. Hanson,
Government and the Press 1695–1763
(1967), 199. N.S. Jucker (ed.), *The
Jenkinson Papers, 1760–1766* (1949), XII,
69–70.
27. James Ralph to Bute, 7 Oct. 1761.
Bute MSS, 5/126. Reproduced at the
end of the paper as document I.
28. Hardwicke to Royston, 17 Oct. 1761.
BL Add. MSS 35352, fos. 202–3.
Reproduced as document IV.
29. D. George, *English Political Caricature:
A Study in opinion and propaganda* (1959),
I, 118–25.
30. Thus the famous *Times* plate was not
primarily an attack on Pitt but on the
commercial interests in the City who
opposed much needed peace in order
to foster their own ends. D. Jarrett, *The
Ingenious Mr. Hogarth* (1976), 189–90.
Stephens, *op. cit.*, 188–90.
31. Herbert Atherton, *Political Prints in the
Age of Hogarth* (1974), 257–8.
32. Precisely what Pitt himself had
predicted. As he told Lord Granville,
'his acceptance of a reward which bore
the name of a pension would create
much clamour among his friends and
much triumph among his enemies',
Grantham MSS, L31/108.
33. W.S. Lewis (ed.), *Horace Walpole's
Correspondence with Sir Horace Mann*
(1960), 541. W.H. Lecky, *A History of
England in the 18th Century* (1892), III,
200 n.i.
34. Peters, *Pitt and Popularity* 206–7.
35. Memorandum, 8 Oct. 1761, BL Add.
MSS 32929, f. 113. Cf. 'To the writers
of the *Daily Gazetteer* or *London Chronicle*
signed *Veritas*', BL Add. MSS 38198,
fos. 7–9. *London Chronicle*, 13 Oct. 1761,
359. *Public Ledger*, 9 Oct. 1761. no. 546.
See also Newcastle to Devonshire, 11
Oct. 1761, bemoaning attacks against
him in the *Monitor*, BL Add. MSS
32929, f. 428.
36. John Almon, *The Correspondence of the
late John Wilkes* (1805), I, xi. *Memoirs of
Almon*, 14–16. Robert Haig, *The
Gazetteer 1735–1797* (Carbondale,
1960), 50–1. On the importance of the

Monitor see: Marie Peters, 'The *Monitor*
on the Constitution, 1755–1765: new
light on the ideological origins of
English radicalism', *English Historical
Review*, LXXXVI (1971), 714–29; and
idem, *Pitt and Popularity*, chs. II, III.
37. *The Annual Register* (1761), 45–6.
38. Hardwicke to Royston, 17 Oct. 1761,
BL Add. MSS 35352, f. 202v.
39. James Ralph to Bute, 13 Dec. 1761,
Bute MSS 695. Rea, *op. cit.*, 21–3.
Brewer, *Party Ideology and Popular
Politics*, 222–3.
40. E. Johnson, 'The Bedford connection:
the 4th Duke of Bedford's political
influence between 1732 and 1771'
(Ph.D. thesis, University of
Cambridge, 1980), 277.
41. I owe this suggestion to Dr John
Shipley, University of Chicago, who on
the basis of circumstantial evidence
(i.e. the pamphleteer's obvious
acquaintance with Chandler's
parliamentary debates, which Ralph
helped edit) concludes that Ralph may
have been the author. For further
details see J. Shipley, 'James Ralph:
pretender to genius' (Ph.D. thesis,
Columbia University, 1963).
42. James Ralph to Bute, 28 Oct. 1761,
Bute Papers.
43. Lord Royston to Hardwicke, 16 Oct.
1761, BL Add. MSS 35352, fos. 199–
200. As late as March 1762, Dodington
deplored the unhampered activity of
the opposition Press 'with no proper
steps taken to defeat it'. Carswell and
Dralle, *op. cit.*, 436. Cf. Devonshire to
Newcastle, 24 Oct. 1761, BL Add.
MSS 32930, fos. 3–6: 'not a moments
time should be lost in answering that
curious epistle of Mr. Pitt, in stating
facts to open the eyes of mankind
against those who are endeavoring to
throw the country into a state of
confusion in a time of war ... every
engine of the press should be set to
work to paint these gentlemen and
their conduct in their true light'.
44. See document III.
45. See document IV.
46. Campbell to Bute, 28 Oct. 2 Dec. 1761.
Bute MSS.

47. James Ralph to Bute, 13 Dec. 1761, Bute MSS: 'I shall continue to send paragraphs in different papers in order to counteract the infamous falsehoods that are every day published in respect to the conduct of Spain.'
48. Campbell to Bute, 14 Jan. 1763, Bute MSS.
49. Peters, *Pitt and Popularity*, 214, 222, 227.
50. See, for instance, *The Patriot Unmasked, or a word to his Defenders; The Case of the Late Resignation set in a True Light; Impartial Reflections on the Present State of Affairs, in a Letter to a Friend; A Letter to the Right Hon. W – P – by a citizen; An Impartial Inquiry into the Conduct of a Late Minister; Remarks upon a popular letter; A Letter to the Right Honourable Author.*
51. *A Letter from a Right Honourable Person and the Answer to it, Translated into Verse* popularly known as *Mr. Pitt's Letter versified.* Advt. *Public Advertiser*, 14 Nov. 1761; *A Letter from the Anonymous Author of the Letters Versified to the Anonymous Writer of the Monitor.* Advt. *Public Advertiser*, 30 Dec. 1761.
52. Fox to Francis, Dec. 1761; 5 Jan. 1762, BL Add. MSS 51405, fos. 2–3. Fox to Shelburne, 7 Jan. 1762, Bute MSS.
53. See for example: *An Answer to a Letter to ... Bute; Reflections occasioned by the Resignation of a certain Great Man; A Full Vindication of the Right Honourable Wm. Pitt and Wm. Beckford Esqrs.*
54. I.e. *The Case of the Late Resignation set in a True Light.*
55. Karl W. Schweizer, 'A Note on Israel Mauduit's *Considerations on the Present German War*', *Notes and Queries*, XXVII. 1 (Feb. 1980), 45–6.
56. John Brewer, 'The misfortunes of Lord Bute: a case study in eighteenth century political argument and public opinion', *Hist J*, XVI, 1 (1973), 3–43.
57. Rea, *op. cit.*, 28–41. Nobbe, *op. cit.*, 34–50. Cf. Karl W. Schweizer, 'Lord Bute and anti-Scottish feeling in 18th-century English political propaganda', in *Scottish Colloquium Proceedings*, ed. A. Brodie (Guelph, Ont., 1974), 23–33.
58. Peters, *Pitt and Popularity*, 216–39.
59. Robert Spector, *English Literary Periodicals and the Climate of Opinion During the Seven Years War* (The Hague, 1966), chs III, IV. Karl W. Schweizer, 'The Court Magazine 1761–1765' and *idem*, 'The Imperial Magazine' in *British Literary Magazines: The Age of Johnson*, ed. A. Sullivan (Westport, Conn., 1983), 52–7, 167–8; and Peters, *Pitt and Popularity*, 244–7.
60. *Critical Review*, XIV (1762), 316.
61. Thus, through his secretary, Charles Jenkinson, and his City contact, Edward Richardson, Bute managed to forge links with several city Tories – among them, the immediate past Lord Mayor, Sir Mathew Blakiston and Sir James Hodges, an influential force in City politics; see Brewer, *Party Ideology*, 223–4. Richardson to Jenkinson, 20 Oct. 1762, BL Add. MSS 38200, fos. 53–4.
62. R.J. Phillimore (ed.), *The Memoirs and Correspondence of George, Lord Lyttelton* (1845), II, 636.
63. James Ralph to Bute, 7 Oct. 1761, Bute MSS 5/126.
64. George Bubb Dodington, 1st Baron Melcombe and political supporter of Bute.
65. James Ralph to Bute, 28 Oct. 1761, Bute MSS 5/127.
66. Royston to Hardwicke, 16 Oct. 1761. BL Add. MSS 35352, fos. 199–200v.
67. Hugh Valence Jones, secretary to the Duke of Newcastle.
68. I.e. Pitt.
69. Hardwicke to Royston, 17 Oct. 1761, BL Add. MSS 35352, fos. 202–3.
70. Sir Joseph Yorke, Lord Hardwicke's third son, then British Minister at the Hague.
71. A reference to the Austrian capture of Schweidnitz, a major Prussian fortress in Silesia (cf. Mitchell to Bute, 6 Oct., 12 Oct. 1761, PRO SPF 90/78).
72. Pitt's letter of explanation to William Beckford.
73. See Hardwicke to Newcastle, 17 Oct. 1761, BL Add. MSS 32929, fos. 332–33. Brown and Schweizer, *op. cit.*, 147.
74. Thomas Prouse, MP.
75. For Bute's efforts to find a new Speaker following the retirement of Arthur Anslow, MP see Karl W. Schweizer, 'A Lost Letter of John Stuart, 3rd Earl of Bute to George Grenville, 13 Oct. 1761', *Hist J*, XVII. 2 (1974), 435–42.

5

Pitt as a foil to Bute: the public debate over ministerial responsibility and the powers of the Crown

Marie Peters

More than ten years ago, John Brewer drew attention to the constitutional issues raised by 'The misfortunes of Lord Bute' in the 1760s.[1] The crucial significance of these issues – those of ministerial responsibility and the power of the Crown – in the longer-term development of the English constitution had been analysed even earlier by Clayton Roberts.[2] Brewer's work showed how important the public discussion of the 1760s was in exploring them further. It did not fully recognize, however, that the propaganda attack which, in May 1762, initiated the misfortunes of Bute, was not the first occasion on which these major questions were raised in George III's reign. They had already appeared a few months earlier in the public controversy stirred by the resignation of William Pitt from the coalition ministry with the Duke of Newcastle which had so successfully waged the Seven Years War. It seems worthwhile, therefore, to examine the constitutional arguments provoked by Pitt's resignation. Such an examination can throw light upon the assumptions on which discussion started, on the way the debate unfolded, and on the deep differences which emerged over the application in practice of constitutional principles which had appeared to be generally accepted.

Public discussion of Pitt's resignation began immediately after it was unofficially reported in the newspapers of 6 October 1761. Controversy was fuelled when the official *Gazette* announcement of 9 October was coupled with the report that the king had granted a pension to Pitt and a barony to his wife. Debate was intensified further when Pitt felt compelled to answer criticisms by writing in a letter to his City of London supporter, Alderman William Beckford, and the letter found its way into the papers on 17 October. Through October the discussion was conducted chiefly in the newspapers, where opinion remained

divided more or less equally for and against Pitt. When, in November
and December, pamphlets largely took over the debate, the balance
of argument turned much more clearly against Pitt, who was left
with the weekly essay paper, the *Monitor*, as his chief defence. By
mid January 1762 the debate was largely over and interest moved
to the recently declared war against Spain. However, when the
vitriolic attack on Bute as a royal favourite was begun in May 1762,
it was initiated by protagonists of Pitt – probably out of deep frustration
over the eclipse of their favourite's reputation.[3]

The resignation debate was concerned with attack on and defence of Pitt, not with attack on Bute.[4] Its major thrusts were the
validity or otherwise of Pitt's popular reputation and his claim to
be a 'patriot', and the merits or otherwise of his war policies. Constitutional issues were seldom predominant. Nevertheless they were
drawn out explicitly often enough to be important. The argument over
them was in fact an exploration of the constitutional significance of the
unique position in the wartime coalition which public opinion had
accorded to Pitt.

Brewer has said that the success of the Press campaign against Bute
can be attributed to 'the nerve it touched in the nation at large'
particularly concerning its relevance to basic constitutional presup-
positions.[5] The same could equally well be said of the success of the
wartime Press campaign for Pitt. Whatever the constitutional, political
and administrative realities of his position as Secretary of State for
the Southern Department may have been,[6] a quite extraordinary
dominance in the coalition was attributed to him by much of the
wartime propaganda. He was seen as the 'patriot minister', above the
dirty work of politics, pursuing the best interests of his country regardless of personal gain; he was widely regarded as the chief architect of
Britain's victories while 'mistakes' and defeats were attributed to others.
This view of Pitt was shaped by the strongly populist character of much
of the opposition 'country' rhetoric which prevailed in the Press.[7]
Undertones of criticism of the prevalent opinion of Pitt were always
present.[8] Nevertheless, because 'patriotism' and 'popularity' were seen
to be the bases of Pitt's predominance, he did not attract anything like
the volume of criticism for being an unconstitutional 'prime minister'
which had been heaped on Walpole, for example.[9]

It was on this assumption – that Pitt had enjoyed an extraordinary
dominance in the administration – that discussion of his resignation
began. He was 'Will the Coachman', the 'body coachman of us all',
presumed to have been directing affairs, one to whom, it was said,
Parliament had cheerfully granted all and of whom the public approved.[10]

To 'his' administration the successes of the war were widely credited.[11] His speedy reinstatement was hoped for.[12] As speculation grew over the circumstances or reasons for his resignation, it was soon claimed that, when his policies were opposed, he could not have been expected to remain 'to be a cypher', so he was fully justified in resigning.[13] Furthermore, he could not be said to have deserted his post when his country needed him because he was still in a position to offer advice and serve his country in Parliament.[14] No doubt much of this comment emanated from the same Pitt supporters who were able, with apparent ease, to plant in the newspapers provocative rumours and reports designed to heighten anxiety over the resignation.[15] The constitutional implications of the comment are significant none the less.

Criticism of these claims in defence of Pitt was not long silent, however. Pitt, it was soon suggested, was not the only man of ability in the nation; those who seemed set to be 'perpetual ministers' were a worse source of grievance than septennial parliaments.[16] Those who attributed all successes to Pitt were said to be running into the error of supposing him to be 'a *first*, a *sole*, nay an *independent* minister', such as was inconsistent with the principles of British government.[17] It was also held by several critics that to claim that Pitt still had power to serve his country, although he was out of office, through promoting his views in the House of Commons was to set him up as the 'DICTATOR of the People'. This uncomplimentary title for Pitt was first suggested in a highly ironic set of questions and answers which appeared initially to many to be a defence of Pitt. In fact they distilled the ambivalent constitutional implications of claims to 'popularity' and gave a new constitutional turn to wartime criticisms of the supposedly ill-founded and misused nature of Pitt's popular reputation.[18]

So by the time that Pitt felt it necessary to defend his resignation in his letter to Beckford of 15 October 1761, the main constitutional issues – Pitt's status in the coalition and the appropriate conduct when his policy suggestions were not accepted – had been clearly adumbrated. His letter, with its firm statement that 'a difference of opinion with regard to measures to be taken against Spain' lay behind his resignation, and that he resigned 'in order not to remain responsible for measures which I was no longer allowed to guide', brought these constitutional issues to the forefront of debate, while also explicitly raising the question of 'responsibility'.[19]

Arguments on both sides were now further elaborated, first in the newspapers in the latter part of October, then in the pamphlets of November. Pitt's defenders developed a full statement of the principles of ministerial responsibility as they saw them, including justification of the need for a 'prime minister'. In response, those who criticized Pitt evolved a case that, when fully developed, put much greater emphasis on the role of the King in government.

The case for Pitt took up the argument that he could not have remained 'to be a cypher'. In the *Public Ledger* of 21 October 1761,[20] 'Brito' maintained that if a minister found that what he considered to be right measures were opposed then he should resign; to submit to the judgment of other ministers was the behaviour of one overfond of office, not that of a patriot. Although the requirement in the Act of Settlement that all Privy Councillors should sign resolutions which they assented to had been rightly abandoned as too restrictive of freedom of debate, yet still, 'Brito' maintained, 'the constitution of Great Britain considers every man who fills a post, as being answerable for the consequences, even tho' his measures may have the approbation of parliament'.

> This ministerial amenability ... is coeval with the English government, and is a principle more deeply rooted perhaps, than any other in our constitution. That the King can do no wrong, is a constitutional maxim. But Britons would be the greatest slaves under the sun, should ministers not be accountable for their master's measures.

On similar grounds, another writer answered criticisms of the supposedly haughty tone of Pitt's letter.[21] The ministers of the Crown in former reigns, he maintained, had been too subservient in public to 'the diadem', thus using 'its lustre' to screen their own oppressive acts and 'private personal insolence to Majesty'; in contrast, Pitt's behaviour had properly upheld the dignity of the Crown.

Several writers applied this doctrine of responsibility particularly to the Secretaries of State. The other servants of the Crown, the heads of 'the great departments of public business', were not ministers so much as officers of state, serving the King 'in his civil and legal capacity; that is as being connected with his people and parliament'. Their proper behaviour was laid down by law and specific statements of their duties. In contrast, the Secretary of State dealt with prerogative matters, by definition not bounded by law, and served the King in his personal capacity. A particular burden of responsibility for the King's actions therefore rested on him. Thus Pitt, as Secretary of State, had a special status among the King's ministers.[22]

This statement of ministerial responsibility, especially when coupled by 'Brito' with reference to Sir Robert Walpole's alleged acceptance of responsibility 'even with his head, for all the measures of government', might seem to elevate the Secretary of State into a prime minister, having a special responsibility for the policies of the administration –

conveniently forgetting, as hostile critics were soon to point out, that there were two Secretaries of State.[23] However, some who took this line drew back into a much more strictly departmental view of the Secretary's responsibility. What he would be called to account for was not what he advised about the 'great operations and concerns of government' which were 'equally objects of deliberation, with every Privy Councellor [*sic*]', but for what was executed through is 'department of public business'.[24] As another writer put it, when a minister's 'plan' became a 'measure' through being given the approval of the 'Cabinet Council', then the Secretary of State 'becomes answerable for the execution of the measure, so far as depends upon issuing proper orders on the authority of the King's Signet of which the Secretary had custody'. Arguments about the particular responsibility of the Secretary should not be understood 'as meaning that a Secretary of State by his post is a first, far less, a sole, minister'.[25]

Most defenders of Pitt were, however, prepared to argue that there was more to his special position than simply his status as Secretary of State. Their point was put simply by a writer in the *St James's Chronicle* at the end of October: 'Was not Mr Pitt looked upon by the Nation in general as sole minister?' If he had acquiesced in any measure, then, he would have been held responsible for any miscarriage. Even 'Brito', while putting forward his departmental view of responsibility, had said:

> The public voice has pointed him out as the chief Director of all measures during the present war, and even that opinion would have rendered him accountable for the consequences, even though he had not the seals, but he was doubly so while he possest [*sic*] them'.[26]

The argument was developed much further in early November by the first substantial pamphlet defence of Pitt, *The conduct of a Rt. hon. gentleman ... justified*. Pitt, said its author, had been pointed out as a suitable head of the administration to the late King by 'the peoples voice'; he had been promoted both by his sovereign's will and the public voice to the office of first minister and was certainly 'considered by the nation' in that 'dangerous character' and supposed to be directing foreign affairs. For these reasons, certainly, the 'public would have considered *him* alone as responsible'. The office of a minister of state or prime minister might indeed be unknown to the constitution or laws of Great Britain; 'but it is necessary', the writer claimed – and in every reign since the conquest there had in fact been such a minister who had suffered as a scapegoat for the sins of government. Pitt's situation, it was asserted, was therefore highly unusual. He held not only this office of 'first minister' pointed out by the people (an office which if the constitution recognized at all it did so in the person of the Lord Chancellor and on less dangerous terms). He was also Secretary of State, a post 'more dangerous, and ticklish, than that of any other minister in this country' because 'of the directive power, which by the nature of his office he is obliged to exercise', without the guidance of the law or precedent, as counsellor of the King in matters of government. There could therefore be no question of Pitt's sacrificing his opinion to that of others in order to maintain a desirable unanimity. If he was in the highly unusual situation, for a first minister, of being unable to influence those others to agree with him, then he had no alternative but to resign. In doing so he was exercising the right of 'free agency' which was the test of liberty. This freedom to resign had been allowed, indeed guaranteed, to a minister by the (Glorious) Revolution, which at the same time had given his country the power of 'overhauling his conduct' while denying him any plea in excuse.[27]

This wider argument – that Pitt was in some sense a prime minister because he was seen by 'the people' to be so, and that therefore he bore a special responsibility over and above what was his as one among other ministers or as Secretary of State accountable for the execution of the business of his office – became the standard Pitt case.[28] It was briefly reflected if hardly elaborated in later pamphlets, and put forcefully in one late newspaper article.[29] In answer to the arguments of Pitt's critics, which were by then well developed, this newspaper writer maintained that Pitt was 'to sight at least and in the general estimation, a Prime Minister'. True, he said, such a position was not acknowledged by the constitution. But neither was the Cabinet Council, 'yet there was not a child, who hath not frequently heard, and without surprise, of both among us'. Both prime minister and Cabinet Council were increasingly necessary, the writer held, to the proper transaction of public business – and what better sanction could there be for them than 'general estimation'? As 'Prime Minister' he went on, Pitt was presumed to have such influence over his 'brother-courtiers, that the joint act of them all in concert, is universally understood to be *his* only'. He therefore had a special responsibility: he could not plead, as Laud and Strafford had done, that his was only one voice among many, or act like Clarendon, supporting in public for the sake of unanimity what he had opposed in council. Otherwise, the newspaper writer concluded, there would be no protection against wicked or weak ministers.

The argument that 'general estimation' could legitimately create an office of prime minister otherwise unknown to the constitution merely drew out the constitutional logic of the eminence accorded to Pitt by wartime propaganda. It was occasionally accompanied by hints about the part which 'general estimation' should play in the selection of ministers, hints which were usually linked with rumours that Pitt was to be reinstated. A 'historical extract' suggested that to

> replace a bad Minister, a Prince need only consult himself; to replace a good one, he must consult the Publick, and fix upon him who is unanimously pointed out by the voice of the People. A State is happy when the King has no other Favourite than his People: more happy when the Minister of the Prince is their advocate.[30]

For the present, these hints were not developed as they were to be within months, when the King's choice of Bute as in some sense a successor to Pitt became the focus of discussion. Even so, they confirm the far-reaching implications for relations between King and ministers of the interpretation of the constitution which underlay the defence of Pitt's resignation. This interpretation, with its fully-developed case for the 'responsibility' of a prime minister pointed out by 'general estimation', can rightly be termed a 'populist' interpretation.[31] It is indeed remarkable for how little reference it makes to anything more than a formal role for the King in government and how clear a distinction is stated, or obviously implied, between the King's public or 'civil and legal'[32] capacity and his private and personal one. The basic assumption, clearly there from the beginning of the debate, was that ministers governed – and this seems an instinctive assumption, not merely propaganda drummed up to suit the needs of the moment.

This assumption was, however, soon challenged. In the case against Pitt developed to answer his defenders, a view of the role of ministers was evolved which placed a far greater emphasis on the King's personal part in government. Ironically, this new emphasis was foreshadowed – in traditional 'country' vein – by the *Monitor*.[33] In its first puzzled response to the news of Pitt's resignation, the *Monitor* reverted to its standard explanation of unwelcome developments – the claim that the schemes of the 'patriot' had been undermined by the covert activities of a malignant 'faction' in the administration – and by implication urged the King to assert 'his natural right of judging, and his legal right of determining in all debates, where he sits as judge for his country'.

This emphasis on the personal role of the King was not prominent in the case against Pitt as it was initially developed in the newspapers. There the case ran along two main lines. It was maintained, first, that, as no one member of the Council could be held singly responsible for its acts, Pitt could quite properly have given in to the opinions of others. The King was justified in choosing to be guided by the majority.[34] Secondly, Pitt's claim to 'guide' was held to be not only an arrogant

and peevish claim to infallibility which other ministers should not
allow; it was also an unconstitutional claim to a position of dictatorship.
This, rather than his allegedly corrupt acceptance of rewards, it was
said, was the real charge against Pitt; an arbitrary minister was quite
as bad as an arbitrary king. In an alternative form of the 'cypher'
argument it could be said that

> If our Affairs were to be conducted entirely by the minister; if it were in
> his Power to make War or Peace, without consulting King, Council, or
> Parliament; why then King, Council, and Parliament, being three Cyphers,
> might as well be abolished, and the arbitrary Minister set upon the throne
> with the Title of Lord Protector.[35]

There was only a hint of any special deference to the King in urgings to
'show more respect to our gracious sovereign, than to let him see that
we place our whole dependence upon any subject whatever'.[36]

However, once the pamphleteers took up the case against Pitt from
newspaper writers, their constitutional arguments, like their general
attacks, were elaborated much more fully and frequently, and over a
much longer period, than his defence was stated. Particularly in two
important and relatively early pamphlets, the way Pitt should have
behaved was further described. Certainly, it was admitted, he had the
constitutional right to resign. But he would have better protected his
reputation as a patriot and deserved the confidence placed in him by
the public if he had made concessions to unanimity, especially in a
time of crisis, when his was a single voice, differing on a single issue
only.[37] (In contrast, a pamphlet defending Pitt had blamed the
opposition to him for the breach of unanimity among the ministers and
had argued that, in the circumstances, the only way to prevent the evil
effects of such division was for Pitt to resign.)[38] Pitt's critics further
maintained that he could still have served effectively and his advice
would still have been valued, even though it was not accepted in every
detail; he should have stayed to fight for his views, while trusting
the judgment of the King.[39] His critics consistently denied that his
behaviour could be justified on the grounds of any special status which
might be attributed to him as Secretary of State. Indeed, it was even
maintained that Pitt's advice would carry as much weight now that he
was simply a Member of Parliament and a private citizen as it had
done when he was in office.[40] Nor, it was argued, could he properly
claim any special status on grounds of 'popularity'. It was acknowledged that the 'popular voice' may indeed have attributed some
unusual standing to him and given him credit for Britain's success in
war. But for Pitt to claim special status on those grounds would be a
gross misuse of 'popularity', a 'flagrant instance of pride and ostentation'

which would seem 'to concentrate in himself alone all the democratical powers of the constitution'.[41]

So the pamphlets reiterated again and again the charge that Pitt's refusal to be responsible for measures which he was not allowed to guide was not merely arrogant but was also a claim to unconstitutional dictatorial powers. This was the charge most frequently made in the constitutional argument: however great his abilities, one writer stated, an 'independent minister, even an all-directing minister, is a greater solecism and more inadmissible in the British Government, than an arbitrary king', whose private virtues might well compensate for his despotism.[42] The charge was put in its most extreme form, perhaps, late in November, in a pamphlet attributed to John Shebbeare, which said that Pitt appeared to expect a God-like plenitude of power and to demand the sort of passive obedience for upholding which he was wont to attack the Jacobites.[43] Such expectations, his critics said, were quite inconsistent with attacks Pitt had made earlier in his career against former 'sole' ministers, notably Walpole.[44] Pitt apparently wanted to be 'lord paramount of all public affairs' when as Secretary of State he should have been 'the servant of the king and the kingdom'.[45]

Thus Pitt's pamphleteering critics would allow him no special responsibility which might have justified his resignation. Certainly they would acknowledge no grounds for a public defence of his action: 'he had done his best to acquit himself already' to the King; 'if he was accountable to Parliament, it was in Parliament his Defence was to be made'; and 'it is a very new doctrine, that a Minister is to put himself upon his Country, for having resigned his office'.[46]

One of the more moderate of Pitt's critics, William Guthrie, in his *Second letter to ... B[ute]*, was prepared to allow some need for 'ministerial power', even for a 'directing minister', on the grounds that the 'nature of government itself implies, that trust and power ought to be some-where or other reposed' and that 'the laws and constitution' could not be 'laid out by a plummet and rule'. But such a 'directing minister', Guthrie said, could be held responsible only for those measures which had been implicitly accepted without explanation by other ministers because they recognized the need for secrecy and had confidence in him. In the present case, however, he could see no such implicit acceptance of necessarily secret advice; quite the contrary.[47]

Much more often, however, Pitt's critics drew out the implications of their strictures on his conduct in such a way as to play down the whole notion of ministerial responsibility. Not only did they deny any special responsibility to Pitt. They also maintained a very restricted view of the individual responsibility of any minister. It was implicitly conceded,

although certainly not emphasized, that ministers had a limited responsibility for the business of their own departments.[48] However, in
the public controversy, the real argument was indeed, as one critic said,
not over Pitt's right to 'guide' the affairs of his own department, but
over determining the measures to be guided[49] – that is, the general
policies to be implemented through the various departments. In this
respect Pitt's critics continued to insist that all voices in the Council
were of equal weight. Thus no one person could be held accountable,
not even for measures he had proposed, once they had been agreed to
by the Council. At most, it was maintained that since the Revolution
ministers could be held responsible only for advice they had signed –
and it was pointed out that they were no longer formally required by
law to sign the advice they gave. Certainly no one could be made
accountable for measures he had specifically disavowed in writing, as
Pitt had done.[50] Talk of individual responsibility in any of these circumstances was 'ministerial, that is, self-important, language'.[51] One
late pamphlet seemed to insinuate that charges of responsibility more
often arose out of partisan feeling or self-interest than from constitutional
principle. The argument for individual responsibility was mocked by a
rhetorical question in another later pamphlet: would Pitt have been
prepared, the writer asked, to accept responsibility had his advice been
agreed to and the consequent actions had been unsuccessful? And how
silly, he commented, the complaisance of the rest of the Council would
then have looked.[52]

However, although this argument required individual ministers to
submit to the majority, the right to determine measures was not held to
belong to the ministers collectively, nor even to them in concert with
the King. In most of the pamphlets critical of Pitt, the right to decide
was given clearly to the King. To claim otherwise, it was said, was to
seek to 'control his Majesty's Prerogative; to take from Him his private
Right of judging'. The King was the 'merchant who plans the voyage'
as distinct from the captain of the ship; he was the master who directs
the coachman.[53] Pitt was accused not mainly of making the Council
'pauns' [sic], or of reducing them to 'so many Noughts', but above all of
making the King a 'chess board king', putting him 'in leading strings',
leaving him nothing but his 'Royal Name', forcing him to submit 'his
sceptre, dignity and Crown' and seeking to become 'Master in his
stead'.[54] Certainly, it was maintained, the constitution did properly
limit the absolute power of the King. But it did so not by requiring
him to submit to the advice of one minister but rather by urging him
to govern with the advice of 'his Council, his parliament, and his
officers of state'.[55] However, no means were suggested whereby this

requirement could be enforced. No concept or machinery of collective responsibility was developed in place of those of individual responsibility. Instead the authority of the King was emphasized even to the point of claiming that he was 'so far from being obliged to observe the opinion of a majority of his council, that he may constitutionally pursue measures directly opposite, if he pleased'.[56] The people were urged to put their trust not in ministers, who could be removed, but in the King.

Not all the major pamphleteering antagonists of Pitt went as far as this. William Guthrie, for example, even in his *Third letter ... to B[ute]*, published in January, never took up the emphasis on the constitutional role of the King.[57] The thrust of his argument was much more a political one: if Pitt had in fact been 'guiding' affairs for some years, could he not be justly criticized for not taking up British grievances against Spain much earlier?[58] Nevertheless, as the implications of the constitutional criticisms of Pitt's behaviour were drawn out, they could be said to amount to a strong, remarkable and amply reiterated case for personal monarchy. This royalist or Court case was clearly juxtaposed by its protagonists to the 'populist' view of the constitution which underlay the defence of Pitt. 'Make use of a minister, if you can', said one of them, only 'when you have no hope of a King' and employ popularity [only] as an engine to control the excesses of Royalty.[59]

Public discussion of Pitt's resignation had begun, however, with the 'populist' view uppermost. The initial strength of a view which legitimized the position accorded to Pitt by wartime propaganda by justifying the 'responsibility' of a prime minister based on 'popular estimation' is the first conclusion of interest to be drawn from a close examination of the constitutional issues in this primary stage of the 'Press war' of 1761–2.[60] Arguments about the proper role of 'the people' in the constitution were not new. But the justification of a prime minister in these terms, although in some ways a natural development, was new – and it is perhaps the most clearly novel element in the debate.

True, this interpretation was soon overwhelmed, at least temporarily, by the second major feature of the debate: an assertive and in some ways equally novel 'royalist' case. Ideas of Divine Right personal monarchy were, of course (as J.C.D. Clark has recently so cogently demonstrated), by no means new in Hanoverian political argument and were, in various forms, widely accepted.[61] But the working out in detail of their practical implications for the relations of King and ministers was new – at least at this level of Press and pamphlet debate. In such debate, since 1714 anyway, Tory or 'country' propaganda had been preoccupied with attacks on the Whig oligarchy or on an all-powerful minister – in which respect for the royal prerogative was more assumed than closely argued – rather than with issues of responsibility and the respective roles of King and ministers.[62] The emergence now of the 'royalist' case – as strong in criticisms of Pitt as in the later defence of the appointment of Bute to high office where it was more obviously both natural and necessary – owes something, perhaps, to the release of long pent-up feelings of indignation at the *hauteur* of Pitt. It owes much more, probably, to enthusiasm for the new young British King 'who desires and designs to make a *popular* use of his Royalty' – and so bears out J.C.D. Clark's suggestion that the existing widely diffused Divine Right personal monarchy ideas could be readily attached to the person and regime of George III.[63] And it can be strongly suggested that much of the fever of the hostility to Bute soon evinced in the Press attack on him was a reaction to this powerful 'royalist' case, novel in focus if deep-rooted in origins, mounted in answer to defences of Pitt's resignation.

However, in weighing the significance of the opposing cases, the point at which the debate began must not be forgotten. The 'royalist' case was evolved in this form in answer to the development of an equally cogent 'populist' view of the constitution on the question of responsibility. Both the initial strength of the 'populist' view and the later fevered attacks on Bute are reminders that, at least in this 'low-level' political debate, other modes of argument were as readily available for use. At the same time, the marked shift in the specific focus of the argument of both ideological inclinations, 'royalist' and 'populist', draws attention once again to fundamental alterations in political circumstances around 1760. The accession of George III may have been the most profound, but the partly associated resignations of Pitt and, later, of other Whigs were not without repercussions also.[64]

Interpretations advanced in public debates by propagandists should not lightly be taken as generally accepted by contemporaries. The chief protagonists in the events giving rise to debate may well have viewed their actions differently. Indeed, Pitt's refusal 'to be responsible for nothing but what he directed' was stated by him in his last Cabinet meeting, and even in his letter to Beckford, in a way that could readily be construed as no more than a claim to be allowed to 'guide' the correspondence of his own department. In fact Pitt himself so interpreted it when he again repeated the claim in the House of Commons, in answer to Beckford's assertions of the need for *'one* minister'. Nor did Pitt appeal in an unqualified way to 'the voice of the People' in justification of his position. On the other hand, when, at that last ministerial meeting, Granville challenged Pitt's view of his responsibility for the measures of his department, he did so on the grounds of 'the opinion of the majority of the council', not the King's overriding right to decide.[65] There was obviously some gap between the terms of public debate and the way in which politicians perceived their actions – although there was a closer accord, it would seem, between the 'royalist' case and the intentions of George III and Bute.[66]

Nevertheless, an examination of the public debate confirms that significant constitutional issues were raised by those actions. As Brewer has shown, in acknowledging this one does not need to revert to the discredited Whig view of the early years of George III's reign. The debate demonstrates that, however clearly solutions may have been adumbrated in the seventeenth century, there was as yet no received eighteenth-century understanding of some central issues of 'responsibility', namely 'the collective responsibility of the Cabinet, the particular responsibility of the departmental head, and the special responsibility of the Prime Minister' – just as the Bute debate was soon to show that the notion that the King should choose his ministers from those who had the confidence of Parliament was by no means always fully accepted. Extremists on the Court side could even implicitly question, more perhaps than Brewer allows, the general concept of ministerial responsibility for the King's actions.[67] The consequent practical issues concerning relations between King and ministers, and among ministers, were highlighted by the debate over Pitt's resignation – just as those concerning the choice of ministers were to be the focus of attention when the debate turned to Bute's position. These were major issues in the transition from personal to constitutional monarchy, issues that were to be resolved only gradually over the next hundred years or so, as political circumstances changed. For the time being, whatever the practical needs of government, personal monarchy apparently still had a strong case.

Meanwhile, the public debates of the 1760s had their political as well as constitutional effects. There is little doubt that, just as Bute's unpopularity helped 'immeasurably' to ruin him politically, so Pitt's popularity helped to give him a status he did not entirely deserve.[68] This was just one of a number of ways in which, in the unsettled 1760s, the 'Favourite of the Prince' and the 'Favourite of the Mob' were foils one to another.[69]

NOTES

The present locations of the pamphlets cited are given in the bibliography of Marie Peters, *Pitt and Popularity: the Patriot Minister and London Opinion during the Seven Years' War* (1980), 288–9.

1. John Brewer, 'The misfortunes of Lord Bute: a case study in eighteenth-century political argument and public opinion', *Hist J*, XVI (1973), 3–43; cf. John Brewer, *Party Ideology and Popular*

Politics at the Accession of George III (1976), ch. 7.

2. Clayton Roberts, *The Growth of Responsible Government in Stuart England* (1966).

3. Marie Peters, *Pitt and Popularity: the Patriot Minister and London Opinion during the Seven Years' War* (1980), 240–1. The course of public discussion of Pitt's resignation is fully described in ch. 7. See also the paper by Karl W. Schweizer on Lord Bute and the Press in this volume (ch. 4).

4 The pamphlet cited by Brewer, 'The misfortunes of Lord Bute', 12 n.48, is not in fact an attack on Bute but a defence of Pitt.

5. *Ibid.*, 18, cf. 23–8, 31, 32.

6. These are discussed by Richard Middleton, *Bells of Victory. The Pitt–Newcastle Coalition and the Conduct of the Seven Years' War, 1757–1762* (1985), especially 20–1, 49–50, 69–70, 211–13, 219–32. Cf. *idem*, 'Pitt, Anson and the Admiralty, 1756–61', *History*, LV (1970), 189–98; *idem* 'The Administration of Newcastle and Pitt: the Departments of State and the conduct of the war, 1754–1760, with particular reference to the campaigns in North America' (Ph.D. thesis, University of Exeter, 1968), especially introduction, chs. 1, 2, and conclusion; E.J.S. Fraser, 'The Pitt–Newcastle coalition and the conduct of the Seven Years' War 1757–60' (D.Phil. thesis, University of Oxford, 1976), 42–65; Karl W. Schweizer, 'William Pitt, Lord Bute and the peace negotiations with France, May–September 1761', *Albion*, XIII (1981), 262–75 (reprinted with some revisions in ch. 2 of this volume).

7. Pitt's wartime reputation is thoroughly explored in Peters, *op. cit.*, and, with reference to the provincial Press, in Austin Gee, 'English provincial newspapers and the politics of the Seven Years' War, 1756–1763' (M.A. thesis, University of Canterbury, 1985), especially ch. 5. Fraser, *op. cit.*, 52–3, points out that it was not only propagandists who attributed this

dominance to Pitt. On the 'populist' character of 'country' thought, see Marie Peters, 'The *Monitor* on the constitution, 1755–1765: new light on the ideological origins of English radicalism', *EHR*, LXXVI (1971), 714–17, 724.

8. Peters, *Pitt and Popularity*, e.g. 120–1, 128–9, 134–8, 154–6.

9. Fraser, *op. cit.*, 53, suggests that Pitt escaped criticism as a 'prime minister' because he could and did rightly claim that he had neither the confidence of the King nor a majority in Parliament; Newcastle enjoyed these supports. This explanation carries some weight but underrates the importance of Pitt's 'popularity' as a justification of his dominance, at least in the public debate.

10. *London Chronicle*, 8–10, 15–17 Oct. 1761; cf. *London Evening Post*, 8–10 Oct. 1761 (item attributed to the *Public Ledger*), *Lloyd's Evening Post*, 7–9 Oct. 1761.

11. For example, *London Evening Post*, 6–8, 8–10 Oct. 1761; *Public Advertiser*, 9 Oct. 1761; *Lloyd's Evening Post*, 7–9 Oct. 1761.

12. *London Evening Post*, 6–8, 8–10 Oct. 1761; *Lloyd's Evening Post*, 5–7 Oct. 1761; *Owen's Weekly Chronicle*, 3–10 Oct. 1761.

13. *St. James's Chronicle*, 10–13, 17–20 Oct. 1761; *London Chronicle*, 17–20 Oct. 1761; *Public Ledger*, 20 Oct. 1761; *Monitor*, 24 Oct. 1761; *An earnest address to the people of Great-Britain and Ireland: occasioned by the dismission of William Pitt, Esq. from the office of Secretary of State*, [Oct.] 1761, 48–9.

14. *An earnest address*, 50; *A certain great man vindicated. By a lover of his country*, [Oct.] 1761, 2, 3.

15. Peters, *Pitt and Popularity*, 206–7 and n.7.

16. *London Chronicle*, 10–13 Oct. 1761 ('Publicola' and 'A Z'); *A letter to the right honourable the earl of B[ute], on a late important resignation and its probable consequences*, [Oct. 1761], especially 8–16.

17. *A letter to B[ute]*, 14.

18. *The patriot unmasked, or, a word to his defenders. By John Trott, cheese-monger and statesman,* [Oct.] 1761, 17–18, where the questions and answers are attributed to the *Gazetteer,* 16 Oct. 1761; but see also *St. James's Chronicle,* 13–15 Oct. 1761; *Public Ledger,* 16 Oct. 1761; *Lloyd's Evening Post,* 14–16 Oct. 1761.
19. William Stanhope and J.H. Pringle (eds), *Correspondence of William Pitt, Earl of Chatham* (4 vols, 1838–40), II, 158–9. These issues had also been raised in exchanges at Pitt's last ministerial meeting on 2 Oct. 1761. See pp.110–111 below.
20. Cf. *London Chronicle* and *London Evening Post,* 20–22 Oct. 1761.
21. *Public Ledger,* 28 Oct. 1761.
22. 'Brito' in *Public Ledger,* 21 Oct. 1761; 'The Dignity of A Secretary of State's Place. By Sir Robert Cecil', *Lloyd's Evening Post,* 21–23 Oct. 1761.
23. For example, *A letter to the right honourable author of a letter to a citizen,* [Nov.] 1761, 12; *A letter from the anonymous author of the letters versified to the anonymous writer of the Monitor,* [Dec.] 1761, 22.
24. 'Brito' in *Public Ledger,* 21 Oct. 1761.
25. *Ibid.,* 28 Oct. 1761.
26. *St. James's Chronicle,* 29–31 Oct. 1761; 'Brito' in *Public Ledger,* 21 Oct. 1761. Cf. *Monitor,* 31 Oct. 1761.
27. *The conduct of a Rt. hon. gentleman in resigning the seals of his office, justified, by facts, and upon the principles of the British Constitution. By a Member of Parliament,* [Nov.] 1761, 4, 33, 39, 46–8, 49–50, 51–5 (quotations, in the order cited, from 4, 33, 51, 55, 54). On 'free agency', cf. 'Brito' in *Public Ledger,* 21 Oct. 1761.
28. Cf. *Monitor,* 14, 21, 28 Nov. 1761; *Reflections occasioned by the resignation of a certain great man. Particularly addressed to the citizens of London,* [Nov.] 1761, 13–14; *A full vindication of the right honourable Wm. Pitt and Wm. Beckford, Esqurs ... ,* [Dec.] 1761, 16–17; *A consolatory epistle to the members of the Old faction; occasioned by the Spanish War,* [Jan.] 1762, 14, 84.
29. *London Chronicle,* 24–26 Nov. 1761.
30. *London Evening Post,* 29–31 Oct. 1761; cf. *Lloyd's Evening Post,* 28–30 Oct. 1761, where it follows reports of rumours that Pitt was to be reinstated; and *Monitor,* 14 Nov. 1761.
31. See above, n.7. Cf. Brewer, *Party Ideology,* 130.
32. 'Brito' in *Public Ledger,* 21 Oct. 1761.
33. *Monitor,* 10 Oct. 1761; cf. 17 Oct. 1761. 'Country' thinking, especially as illustrated in Tory newspapers like the *Monitor,* typically upheld a high view of monarchy and blamed constitutional and political ills on abuse of their power by ministers.
34. *London Chronicle,* 20–22, 22–24 Oct. 1761.
35. *Ibid.,* 20–22 Oct., 3–5 Nov. 1761; *Lloyd's Evening Post,* 21–23 Oct. 1761; *St. James's Chronicle,* 22–24 Oct. 1761.
36. *London Chronicle,* 22–24 Oct. 1761.
37. *A second letter to the right honourable the earl of B[ute]. By the author of the first,* [Nov.] 1761, 16–18; *The case of the late resignation set in a true light,* [Nov.] 1761, 6–8, 11.
38. *The conduct of a Rt. hon. gentleman ... justified,* 45–51.
39. *The case of the late resignation set in a true light,* 11; *A letter to the right honourable author of a letter to a citizen,* 4.
40. *A second letter to B[ute],* 57; *A letter to the right honourable author of a letter to a citizen,* 11–12.
41 *A second letter to B[ute],* 9–10; *The case of the late resignation set in a true light,* 3–4; *Remarks upon a popular letter. By a citizen of London,* [Nov.] 1761, 16–17 (quotation).
42. *A second letter to B[ute],* 3. Cf. *Remarks upon a popular letter,* 15–16; *Impartial reflections upon the present state of affairs. With incidental remarks upon certain recent transactions. In a letter to a friend,* 38; *The coalition: or, an historical memorial of the negotiations for peace, between his high mightiness of C[lare]m[oun]t, and his sublime excellency of H[a]y[e]s. With the vouchers. Published by authority of one of the contracting powers,* [Dec.] 1761, 11–12; *An impartial enquiry into the conduct of a late minister,* [Dec.] 1761, 29–30.
43. *A letter to the right honourable author of a letter to a citizen,* 14–15; cf. *A letter*

from a right honourable person and the answer to it, translated into verse, [Nov.] 1761, 7n.8.

44. *A letter to the right honourable author of a letter to a citizen,* 78; *An impartial enquiry into the conduct of a late minister,* 30.

45. *A letter to the right honourable author of a letter to a citizen,* 12; cf. *The case of the late resignation set in a true light,* 11.

46. *The case of the late resignation set in a true light,* 7.

47. *A second letter to B[ute],* 20–1; cf. *London Chronicle,* 24–26 Nov. 1761; see pp.103–4 above.

48. For Example, *A letter to the right honourable author of a letter to a citizen,* 8–9.

49. *Ibid.,* 8; cf. *A letter from a right honourable person ... translated into verse,* 7n.8.

50. *A second letter to B[ute],* 18, 20; *The case of the late resignation set in a true light,* 11; *A letter to the right honourable author of a letter to a citizen,* 12–13; *An impartial enquiry into the conduct of a late minister,* 28. Cf. 'Brito' in *Public Ledger,* 21 Oct. 1761; see pp. 101–2. Both critics and defenders of Pitt agreed that the provision of the Act of Settlement requiring advice to be signed had been properly dropped because it was too restrictive; they disagreed over whether constitutional convention still imposed an individual responsibility.

51. *A second letter to B[ute],* 20, cf. 18.

52. *A fair and compleat answer to the author of the occasional thoughts on the present German war, with a reply to the considerations on the same subject,* [Dec.] 1761, 6–7; *A third letter to the right hon. the earl of B[ute]. In which the causes and consequences of the war between Great Britain and Spain are fully considered; and the conduct of a certain right honourable gentleman further examined,* [Jan.] 1762, 64–5.

53. *A letter from a right honourable person ... translated into verse,* 7 n.8; *A letter to the right honourable author of a letter to a citizen,* 9.

54. *A second letter to B[ute],* 12–13, cf. 4; *An impartial enquiry into the conduct of a late minister,* 29, 30; *The case of the late resignation set in a true light,* 3, 12; *A letter to the right honourable author of a letter to a*

citizen, [4].

55. *An impartial enquiry into the conduct of a late minister,* 30; *A second letter to B[ute],* 72 (quotation).

56. *A letter to the right honourable author of a letter to a citizen,* 10; *The case of the late resignation set in a true light,* 13.

57. For the argument of his *Second letter ... ,* see above, p.108 (notes 50 and 51), p.108 (note 55); cf. *A third letter to B[ute],* 64–5.

58. *A second letter to B[ute],* 22–40; *A third letter to B[ute],* 9–14 and *passim.*

59. *The case of the late resignation set in a true light,* 13.

60. Contrast Brewer, *Party Ideology,* 119, where he maintains that the 'populist' view came to be fully expressed because of the political conspicuousness of Bute. True, Bute's conspicuousness turned attention to the question of the choice of ministers, but there was already a strong populist case on their responsibility.

61. J.C.D. Clark, *English Society 1688–1832. Ideology, social structure and political practice during the ancien regime* (1985), especially ch. 3.

62. Issues of responsibility had arisen from time to time, most notably in the Pelhams' struggle with Carteret between 1744 and 1746 – see, for example, John B. Owen, *The Rise of the Pelhams* (1957), chs. 6, 7 – but as far as I know (cf. Brewer, *Party Ideology,* 133) they did not give rise to any extensive Press discussion.

63. Peters, *Pitt and Popularity,* 202; *The Case of the late resignation set in a true light,* 13; Clark, *op. cit.,* 173–89 (especially 184), 201–16. It is significant, perhaps, that in defending Pitt the formerly Tory *Monitor* never entirely abandoned its high view of monarchy. See, for example, *Monitor,* 14 and 21 Nov. 1761, and note 33 above.

64. See Clark, *op. cit.,* especially 202, 210 and 81, for the term 'low-level' discussion. Cf. Brewer, *Party Ideology,* Part II, especially 130–5; Peters, *Pitt and Popularity,* 240.

65. For Newcastle's account of Pitt's last

ministerial meeting, see Philip C.
Yorke, *The Life and Correspondence of
Philip Yorke, Earl of Hardwicke, Lord
High Chancellor of Great Britain* (3 vols,
1913), III, 279–80; and *EHR*, XXI
(1906), 130–2 (for a full account of
Granville's reply to Pitt); for the
exchange in the House of Commons
see Horace Walpole, *Memoirs of the
Reign of King George the Third; first
published by Sir Denis Le Marchant bart.*,
ed. G.F. Russell Baker (4 vols, 1894),
I, 75, 88–9, 92; cf. Middleton, *Bells of
Victory*, 203; Middleton, 197, puts a
limited interpretation on Pitt's claims,
but see Sir Lewis Namier and John
Brooke, *The History of Parliament. The
House of Commons 1754–1790* (3 vols,
1964), 295, for a statement of Pitt's
which cannot readily be construed as a
claim to authority only in his own
department. Cf. also Richard Pares,
George III and the Politicians (1953),
177. It is interesting that Hardwicke
could, when it suited, claim for the
King the right to decide. See
Middleton, *op. cit.*, 167, and cf.
Hardwicke to Newcastle, 17 Oct. 1761,
BL Add. MSS 32929, f. 333,

commenting on Pitt's letter.
66. See, for example, Peter D. Brown and
Karl W. Schweizer (eds), *The
Devonshire Diary. William Cavendish
Fourth Duke of Devonshire Memoranda on
State Affairs 1759–62* (1982), 43 (27 Oct.
1760), 51 (1 Nov. 1760), 53–4 (3 Nov.
1760). Cf. Hardwicke's views cited in
n.65 above. They suggest, perhaps, a
general initial sympathy at Court
with the King's and Bute's stance, at
least until events revealed its
implications. For Hardwicke's more
usual views see, for example, Sir
Herbert Butterfield, 'Some reflections
on the early years of George III's
reign', *Journal of British Studies*, IV
(1965), 80–3.
67. Roberts, *op. cit.*, 429 (quotation),
438–40; Brewer, *Party Ideology*, 135–6,
116–7, 114. Cf. Middleton, *Bells of
Victory*, 21.
68. Brewer, 'The misfortunes of Lord
Bute', 40–1; cf. Peters, *Pitt and
Popularity*, especially ch. 9.
69. *Auditor*, 17 June 1762 (cf. *London
Evening Post*, 17–19 June 1762,
Gazetteer, 18 June 1762); Peters, *Pitt and
Popularity*, 243–4.

6

Lord Bute, James Stuart Mackenzie, and the government of Scotland

Alexander Murdoch

Scotland should be considered as 'any other part of the United Kingdom', Lord Bute told the Duke of Newcastle in April 1761. At the same time, he astounded Newcastle by speaking of himself 'as having little to do in Scotland; or at least, as being in no degree, particularly concerned about it.'[1] Thus the man who had taught the young George III to 'glory in the name of Briton' announced his intention of staying aloof from Scottish affairs. Bute may have seen himself as the sort of 'Briton' he wanted the King to be, but if the King had to overcome the fact that his family was German, so Bute could not escape the fact that he was born a Scot. Bute did not just hold a Scottish peerage, he was a member of the family which had, more than any other since the union of the Crowns of Scotland and England in 1603, dominated public life in Scotland. One cannot understand Bute unless one understands the importance of him family connections in Scotland.

It was Bute's family and his birth which forced him to acknowledge his Scottish background, and it was his background which, more than anything else, his enemies would use in arousing the hostility in England which would help to drive him from office, and more important, from Court. Bute's background, in fact, presented him with two very different problems which in the end he could not resolve. The first was that the Scots, because of his family as well as his birth, insisted on claiming him as a Scotsman and looked to him for leadership in all aspects of their national life and their desire to 'compleat the union'. The second problem was that most of the English viewed Scots as crypto-Jacobite traitors, strangers to the principles of English law and liberty, who were exploiting the Union for their own gain at the expense of the honest English subjects whose nation was the cornerstone of the King's dominions. William III had his Dutchmen, George I his Germans, and George II had favoured Hanover over England. Now George III was going to favour the Scots. As had happened since opposition to the Crown first expressed itself in Parliament, this was the issue which would provoke a genuine response in England at large.

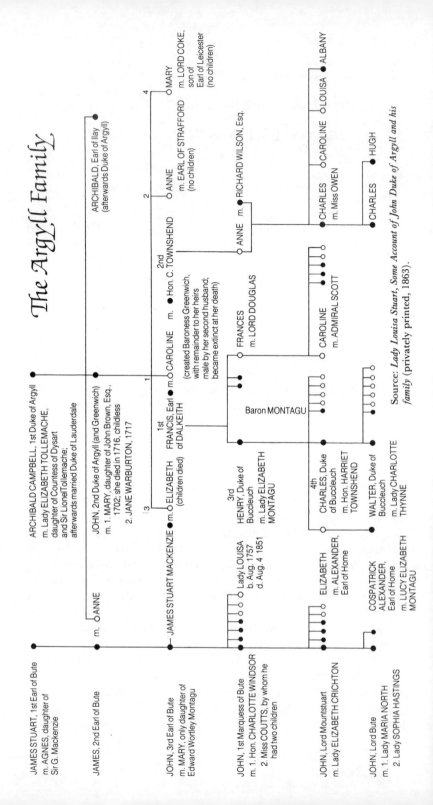

The Argyll Family

ARCHIBALD CAMPBELL, 1st Duke of Argyll
m. Lady ELIZABETH TOLLEMACHE, daughter of Countess of Dysart and Sir Lionel Tollemache; afterwards married Duke of Lauderdale

JOHN, 2nd Duke of Argyll (and Greenwich)
m. 1. MARY, daughter of John Brown, Esq., 1702; she died in 1716, childless
2. JANE WARBURTON, 1717

ARCHIBALD, Earl of Illay
(afterwards Duke of Argyll)

ANNE

1. ELIZABETH (children died) m.

2. CAROLINE m. o
FRANCIS, Earl of DALKEITH
(created Baroness Greenwich, with remainder to her heirs male by her second husband; became extinct at her death)

2nd m. ● Hon. C. TOWNSHEND

ANNE
m. EARL OF STRAFFORD (no children)

MARY
m. LORD COKE, son of Earl of Leicester (no children)

ANNE m. RICHARD WILSON, Esq.

CHARLES
m. Miss OWEN

CAROLINE

LOUISA

ALBANY

CHARLES

HUGH

FRANCES
m. LORD DOUGLAS

Baron MONTAGU

CAROLINE
m. ADMIRAL SCOTT

3rd HENRY, Duke of Buccleuch
m. Lady ELIZABETH MONTAGU

4th CHARLES, Duke of Buccleuch
m. Hon. HARRIET TOWNSHEND

WALTER, Duke of Buccleuch
m. Lady CHARLOTTE THYNNE

JAMES STUART, 1st Earl of Bute
m. AGNES, daughter of Sir G. Mackenzie

JAMES, 2nd Earl of Bute

ANNE m.

JAMES STUART MACKENZIE ●

JOHN, 3rd Earl of Bute
m. MARY, only daughter of Edward Wortley Montagu

JOHN, 1st Marquess of Bute
m. 1. Hon. CHARLOTTE WINDSOR
2. Miss COUTTS, by whom he had two children

Lady LOUISA
b. Aug. 1757
d. Aug. 4 1851

JOHN, Lord Mountstuart
m. Lady ELIZABETH CRICHTON

ELIZABETH
m. ALEXANDER, Earl of Home

JOHN, Lord Bute
m. 1. Lady MARIA NORTH
2. Lady SOPHIA HASTINGS

COSPATRICK ALEXANDER, Earl of Home
m. LUCY ELIZABETH MONTAGU

Source: *Lady Louisa Stuart, Some Account of John Duke of Argyll and his family* (privately printed, 1863).

The genealogical chart reproduced on p.118 (taken from a memoir of the family by Bute's youngest daughter) shows us just how deeply Bute was enmeshed in an extended aristocratic kin network which he regarded as an encumbrance to his ambitions at Court, but which many others, both English and Scots, saw as an inheritance he could not deny. Bute's maternal uncles were the two most influential Scottish peers of the eighteenth century. His elder uncle, John, 2nd Duke of Argyll, had carried the Treaty of Union with England through the Scottish Parliament of 1707 and had commanded the army that frustrated Jacobite hopes in the 1715 rebellion. Bute's younger uncle, Archibald, Earl of Ilay, became 3rd Duke of Argyll after the 2nd Duke's death in 1743. 'Duke John' had been trained as a soldier, 'Ilay' was trained as a lawyer. Together they extended the influence their family had held in seventeenth-century Scotland by allying themselves with the rising star of Sir Robert Walpole. Walpole could count (eventually) on their support in Parliament and at Court, and in return he (eventually) gave them his support in Scotland. By 1725, after helping Walpole to still the unrest aroused in Scotland by the extension of the English malt tax there, Argyll and Ilay were secure in their domination of Scottish politics. Almost anyone in Scotland who wished preferment had to seek it from them. Walpole allowed them to dole out commissions in the Army and Navy, customs and excise appointments, and legal preferment on the understanding that they would both keep the Jacobites quiet and ensure that the 16 Scottish representative peers in the House of Lords and the 45 MPs from Scotland in the House of Commons supported Walpole. This the Campbells, to give them their surname, did with varying degrees of success until the elder brother broke with Walpole in 1737.[2]

'Ilay' continued to support Walpole, and suffered a brief eclipse after Walpole's fall from power. His succession to the Argyll peerage in 1743 (the Scottish title was tied to descent through the male line of the family), and the incompetent handling of the 1745 Jacobite rebellion by those responsible for Scottish affairs, ensured that 'Duke Archibald' (as he has often been called to distinguish him from his brother) continued to play a prominent role in Scottish affairs and Scottish patronage for the rest of his life. Henry Pelham decided that Argyll could be useful to the ministry, so despite the hostility of the King and the Duke of Cumberland, Argyll in his old age (he was 63 when he succeeded to the title as Duke) renewed and maintained the dominance that he had enjoyed in Scotland under Walpole, but with some of the stature of an elder statesman. Newcastle's efforts to drop him after Henry Pelham's death did not succeed. Argyll had been so important in

Scottish government for so long that it was impossible to run Scottish government without him.[3]

Bute's family connections with Scotland were more extensive than his immediate relationship with his uncles, who were responsible for his upbringing after the death of his father in 1723 (when Bute was ten). Bute's younger brother James married one of his first cousins, 'Duke John's' third daughter, Elizabeth (known as 'Lady Betty'). James inherited estates in Angus and Ross-shire which their grandmother had brought to the Bute family as daughter of Sir George Mackenzie of Rosehaugh, Lord Advocate of Scotland from 1682 to 1686 (and founder of the Advocate's Library in Edinburgh). For this reason James took the additional surname of Mackenzie.[4] Caroline, eldest daughter of 'Duke John' and Bute and Mackenzie's cousin, inherited her father's English estates and his Edinburgh residence (which he had named 'Caroline Park'), but kept a strong connection with Scotland by marrying the Earl of Dalkeith, son of the second Duke of Buccleuch. Dalkeith died young, however, and by 1754 Caroline's young son was 3rd Duke of Buccleuch, with a vast estate in the border country of Scotland.[5]

Bute's heritage was Scottish, but his upbringing, by and large, was not. His uncles had both been taught the importance of influence at Court, and the Court was in England. Both had been sent to Eton, and both married English women. Bute was groomed for the same sort of life. He was sent to Eton at the age of seven, and did not return to Scotland 'till almost a man'.[6] Ilay later forced him, however, to study civil and public law at Groningen and Leiden for three years,[7] on the grounds that a Scottish peer should have training in the civil law. His marriage to Mary Wortley Montagu in 1736 changed his prospects entirely (for his wife was heiress to a large estate in England), but in early adulthood Bute had to live on the modest (if one wished to live at Court) proceeds of his estate on the Isle of Bute, and on what his uncles could get for him.[8] They arranged his election as a Scottish representative peer in 1737, and a sinecure place on the Commission of Police for Scotland.

Bute's uncles ceased to order his life when they quarrelled over continued support for Walpole. Both Bute and his younger brother took the part of their elder uncle. The tenor of the argument is well illustrated in a letter from the 2nd Duke of Argyll to James Stuart Mackenzie which is among the few Stuart Mackenzie papers at Mount Stuart:

> My brother Ilay, wants to make all his friends Tools to Walpole because he finds his ends in so doing, your brother Bute and I would have all our friends Independent of Walpole & all other Ministers Whatsoever, My

Brother Ilay prefers his Places to all other Considerations; friendship, Honour, Relation, gratitude & Service to his Country Seem at present to have no weight with him. Your Brother Bute & I think it Our Honour that these considerations should weigh with us,. . . . [9]

Bute lost his places, and retired with his wife and his family (when he was still only 28) to the Isle of Bute, where he interested himself in his estates and his family, and began the botanical hobby which he pursued in later life. The sojourn in Scotland was broken by the rebellion of 1745, which took Bute back to London and the fringe of Court, never to return to Scotland.[10] Bute's mother-in-law, Lady Mary Wortley Montagu, observed of this:

As regards Lord Bute and my daughter's coming to town, it may be owing to the advice of the Duke of Argyll [the former Ilay]. It was a maxim of Sir R. Walpole's that whoever expected advancement should appear much in public. He used to say, whoever neglected the world, would be neglected by it, tho' I believe more families have been ruined by that method than raised by it.[11]

The story of Bute's subsequent rise to influence in the circle surrounding Frederick Prince of Wales is relatively well known.[12] Since Bute had broken with the Court over Walpole, it was not surprising that he held the Pelhams, as the heirs to Walpole's system, objectionable. His relationship with his surviving uncle was an uneasy one, never coming to an open break, but never very close, as Argyll's instincts were all for seeking favour from the Court. Thus when the Princess Dowager of Wales began to contemplate encouraging an opposition after the 1754 general election, Bute was able to use his influence with several of the younger Scottish MPs, such as his brother James Stuart Mackenzie, Gilbert Elliot, and William Mure, to build up a personal following inclined to Bute and the opposition and Bute's admiration for Pitt.

There is evidence that Bute hoped that Argyll, at that time in dispute with Newcastle over Scottish affairs, would join him in opposition. Argyll played a canny game, encouraging Bute and the enthusiastic Elliot (who owed his election to Parliament in 1754 to Argyll's influence), and at the same time leaving the ministry the chance to make him enough concessions to continue his support for it. When Henry Fox agreed to lead the Commons for the ministry (Pitt had pitched his demands too high), Argyll decided to stay with the ministry if they would give in to a series of demands concerning Scottish patronage. Newcastle did, and Argyll stayed his hand, though Elliot had hoped that Argyll would 'employ his great capacity & experience, at this critical juncture, rather than upon the little turns of provincial faction.'[13]

Why did Newcastle collapse so suddenly in the face of Argyll's

demands in the autumn of 1755? Certainly he had reason to fear Argyll
in opposition, but there was something just as important, related to
Argyll's respect for Fox. 'The King wants me to employ him [Argyll] to
get *a certain Lord of his country* [Bute]', wrote Newcastle.[14] In due course
Argyll was employed, through the offices of William Murray (soon to
be Lord Mansfield), and negotiations to get Bute to turn his back on
Leicester House, in exchange for a suitable reward, carried on through
the summer of 1756. They ended with the King accepting that Bute
would have to be allowed office in the Prince's household as Groom of
the Stole. Argyll's letter of congratulations to Bute, however, added
a heavy hint that Fox's help had been significant in dealing with
Newcastle and the King.[15]

In the following years Fox chose the lucrative offstage role of Paymaster General, leaving the way clear for Pitt to stride centre stage.
Argyll and Bute played their roles in the intricate political manoeuvres
of the period, the older man continuing to favour Fox, the younger
adhering, for a while, to Pitt. There were times when Argyll thought
that Bute might supplant him as Scottish minister (in 1757), but he was
too useful in managing the day-to-day business of Scottish affairs, and
too ready to accommodate, for any ministry to make a point of excluding him from influence. As the war progressed, Argyll's help in
raising highland regiments gave him real influence with Pitt and even
the King, so that he became stronger as the war wore on.[16]

These years saw the real break between Bute and Scotland. His
influence at Leicester House gave him a role which was not connected
with Scotland in any way, and freed him from any link to Argyll. He
had overcome the long years in obscurity without capitulating to his
uncle's advice to trim his sails to catch current influence. He was
educating the future King, who would, he hoped, have little to do with
the ways of the Pelhams and his uncle, and free the ministry of corruption and the use of influence. We can glimpse this sort of mentality
through the comments his brother James Stuart Mackenzie later made
when Lord Temple left the government and returned to opposition in
October 1761:

> He will not find it so easy to talk Himself in again, in the Reign of George
> the 3d as He may have done in that of George the 2d. A prince on this
> Throne, who on every occasion that offers, shows His strong Predilection
> to this Kingdom, and views the happiness of His people as his great
> object; ... such a Prince it will be difficult to give the Law to, as may have
> been the case in former times.[17]

Bute knew (or thought he knew) that he would always have a place in
the affections of the future King, and he knew that his wife would soon

inherit vast estates in Yorkshire, Cornwall and Wales that would free him from any need of preferment or monetary reward. Scotland, in contrast, held nothing for him but association with political defeat and obscurity.

Bute's place about the Prince of Wales, however, brought with it unforeseen attention from those who sought influence in the new reign. It was not surprising that many of those who approached Bute were Scots. George II was only a few years younger than Argyll. Both were expected to die in the near future. The Septennial Act ensured an election by 1761 at the latest, earlier if George II should die. Some Scots seeking parliamentary influence, looking to ministerial favour, began to wonder if they should not look to their connection with Bute and the Prince as well as Argyll and the King. Bute, disenchanted with Pitt by 1758, saw no reason to discourage them.

This led to some confusion. No one was more confused than the Duke of Newcastle, torn between a desire to serve the King and the urge to curry favour with the heir to the throne. Newcastle's confusion over plans for the general election in Scotland, expressed in a long, neurotic, self-justificatory memorandum in his private papers, has misled some historians, though Sir Lewis Namier got it right when he wrote that 'Argyll tried to join up the conflict in his own family with that between George II and his grandson, as a sure means to gain the King's support.'[18] Argyll, indeed, went so far as to tell Newcastle and the King 'that Lord Bute had set up the Prince of Wales's standard in Scotland against the King'.[19]

What Bute had done, in fact, was countenance the ambitions of the 10th Earl of Eglinton in Ayrshire and, more to the point, in the Ayr district of burghs. This affair has been examined elsewhere, but briefly, in a district of five Scottish burghs the votes of a majority in the town council of three of them were enough to choose the Member of Parliament. The little burgh of Rothesay on the Isle of Bute always voted as Lord Bute directed, and the burghs of Inveraray and Campeltown in Argyll were in the pocket of the Duke of Argyll. In the past, Bute and Argyll would agree on a suitable candidate and so choose the Member of Parliament between them. Now Bute allied himself with the Earl of Eglinton, who had forced his way to influence in the burgh of Irvine, and who assumed that the remaining burgh in the group, Ayr, would back the candidate supported by the favourite of the Prince of Wales.

Political life in a Scottish burgh was more complicated than this, however, particularly as Ayr was known as a '*free* Town, under no Influence but that of *internal Faction*', whose town council would not be overawed by the great in making their choice.[20] A colourful and time-consuming campaign ensued. Eglinton, however, was an indifferent practitioner of the art of jolly drinking with town councillors, and Bute's friend William Mure, MP for the neighbouring county of Renfrew, was left with much of the work of electioneering with the Eglinton–Bute candidate. Soon Argyll fought back by setting up a rival candidate from a prestigious Ayrshire family. For good measure, he encouraged opposition to Mure in Renfrew, and when Eglinton sought a sinecure appointment in the winter of 1760, Argyll went to the King himself with the story that Bute was fomenting opposition in Scotland. Newcastle found the King 'most violent for supporting the Duke of Argyll against my Lord Bute.'[21]

The death of George II transformed the situation. Though Argyll could not now oppose Bute's will, Bute now had more important things to think about than sinecures for the Earl of Eglinton. Instead, Bute sent his friend Gilbert Elliot to call on Argyll when he returned to London from Scotland, to ask Argyll to help his nephew with Scottish affairs. Elliot reported that Argyll 'seems mighty well disposed to be the instrument to execute your Lordship's commands in Scotland.'[22] And so, relatively simply, reconciliation was effected. Bute would not have done this unless he wanted Scottish affairs kept out of his way. He did not approve of his uncle's career, but he was willing to use him if Argyll would act in 'subordination'.[23]

Newcastle, having spent the previous year trying to keep peace between the two, found the change in attitude all a bit breathless, as he reported to the Earl of Hardwicke after seeing Argyll: 'He [Argyll] told me in general, that he had had a conversation with the King; and I scarce know by his own report, which of them commended my Lord Bute the most.'[24] So Argyll agreed to tidy up affairs for the general election in Scotland on behalf of the government, and to guide the various routine renewals of commissions and offices made necessary by the accession of a new king through the government departments in London.

Then, on 15 April 1761, Argyll died. 'Indeed, he [Bute] told me himself the very night of the Duke of Argyll's death that he had by that event lost more than any man in Britain', one MP wrote later.[25] 'See, My Brother the perverseness of human fate' Bute wrote to his brother just after Argyll's death.

> I have been these 5 months carefully avoiding all Scotch affairs; & now they are thrust upon me in a manner not to be resisted; the Patronage alone I could despise; & give the power to another without the least regrett; but to deliver My Uncle's friends, My friends into the hands of their enemys, when they implore my protection, is not honourable; Judge

then what a load of business comes upon me; sinking under the former load;. . . . [26]

Bute went on to plead with his brother to return from his duties as a British diplomat in Italy to help Bute with Scottish affairs.

Why replace Argyll at all? Why not consider Scotland as 'any other part of the United Kingdom'? Bute told his brother that he despised, or could do without, Scottish patronage, and they both continued to hold to this line in the years that followed. Why then, should Bute choose a replacement for Argyll, and why did his brother, against his inclinations, give up his diplomatic post and his hopes of promotion in the diplomatic service abroad to return to London to take charge of Scottish patronage?

The answer lies in Bute's reference to delivering 'My Uncle's friends, My friends into the hands of their enemys, when they implore my protection'. This, however, only leads one on to further questions. Why should Bute care about Argyll's friends, and who were the enemies who might harm them? Reference to the Duke of Newcastle's correspondence with the Earl of Hardwicke gives one an idea of the sort of enemies Bute had in mind. Newcastle and Hardwicke regarded the Argyll interest in Scotland as crypto-Jacobite in effect, if not intention, and Hardwicke actually used the words 'the Highland Influence' in reference to that group.[27] If Bute took no interest in Scottish affairs, the Duke of Newcastle would, and he intended to bring in a very different, and much more Anglicized regime in Scottish affairs if he could.

Bute very probably did not care what Newcastle did with Scotland, but the fact that his 'friends' (like William Mure) and those who had been attached to his uncle (like the judge, Lord Milton) 'implored his protection' must have appealed to his conscience and to his sense of family. We have discussed how closely he was related to the Argyll family, and discussed how closely that family had been linked with the Court interest in Scotland. Though their real influence at Court fluctuated, as did their influence in Scotland, the house of Argyll had often been perceived as the Court party in Scottish politics throughout the first half of the eighteenth century. Neither of the great dukes of Argyll had a son; the new Duke of Argyll was their cousin General John Campbell of Mamore, a safe, unassuming, elderly soldier. His sons had still to make their way. It was natural, then, for all eyes in Scotland to turn to Bute, both as his uncles' nephew, brought up under their tutelage, and as the Scot most highly placed in British government and at Court. If Bute had comparatively little in common with 'Duke Archibald', there were many who would think of 'Duke John', and find similarities between the attitudes of uncle and nephew to politics.

Having considered why Bute should assume that there must be a
minister for Scotland, perhaps we should alter the question and ask
why there seemed to be an assumption in Scotland that a minister was
necessary. There always had been those Scots who felt that there
should not be a Scottish minister. The best-known expression of this
view was a comment by Duncan Forbes (Lord Advocate and later Lord
President of the Court of Session) written in 1725:

> if any one Scotsman has absolute power, we are in the same slavery as
> ever, whether that person be a fair man or a black man, a peer or a
> commoner, 6 foot or 5 foot high, and the dependence of the country will be
> on that man, and not on those that made him.[28]

Another exponent of this view was James Boswell, who expressed it
quite forcefully in the early 1780s, just before the political power of
Henry Dundas became entrenched in Scotland. He recorded a conversation with Bute's son, Lord Mountstuart, in 1783, in which Boswell
asked 'Why always an agent, a salesman for us like cattle? Archibald
Duke of Argyll drove us up like bullocks for an age. Then came
[Henry] Dundas, the same. Why not let us speak ourselves, every duke,
every peer, every baron?' Perhaps the answer Boswell received from
Mountstuart reflects something of Bute's own experience. Boswell was
told that 'it was better for Scotland to have a Minister, one man
to act provided he was a man of great consequence and a good man.'[29]
   There were many in Scotland who did not share Forbes's or Boswell's
impatience. One should note that Boswell confined his list of
those who should 'speak ourselves' to dukes, peers, and barons. Many
others in Scotland looked for a patron, a great man who could wrest
what Scotland needed from the government, and keep the English from
poking into Scottish affairs. There had been 'great men' dealing with
Scottish affairs from the time that James VI had gone south to his
wealthier kingdom in 1603. The Earl of Haddington and the Duke of
Lauderdale were the most obvious seventeenth-century examples.[30]
The dukes of Argyll partly had fallen heir to this tradition (the first
duke had married Lauderdale's stepdaughter), though the removal of
the Scottish Parliament in 1707 and the Scottish Privy Council in 1708
had abolished two key institutions for the focus of political life. The
power of the house of Argyll was less formal because it was never tied to
a specific office or manifest in a particular institution in Scotland, but
its continuance as an informal Court party reflects the strength of the
seventeenth-century precedent. Of course the Campbells were not
disinterested servants of either the Crown or their Scottish consti-
uency, but to those in Scotland it must have seemed that any hope of

obtaining something from the government, whether it be an Act of Parliament, a linen bounty, or just a job, had to be obtained through the dukes of Argyll.

This status must account for the continued influence of the 3rd Duke of Argyll, particularly after the 1745 rebellion when English ministers turned their attention to Scotland. Most often glimpsed through superficial pen portraits by those like Horace Walpole or Lord Hervey, who had no reason to like him, it is easy to dismiss Argyll's importance.[31] If one reads the comments of those whose horizons were limited to Scotland, however, a different, if overly flattering, impression emerges. This may explain the extraordinary demonstration at Argyll's funeral in Edinburgh in May 1761, when Argyll lay in state at Holyrood Palace, and the references to him at the time as Scotland's 'father' and 'protector'. It may come as no surprise that his closest political associates described him as the 'protector' of Scotland, but there were others, such as Sir Alexander Dick of Prestonfield, who spoke for a larger group: 'We may really say the Country had lost a father whose place it will not be easy to supply'. Adam Fairholme, then a prominent merchant, also lamented the loss of 'my country on being deprived of a Father & Protector'.[32] Nor did this perception of Argyll soon die away, as comments in memoirs written at the turn of the century indicate, like those written by Carlyle of Inveresk, Thomas Somerville, and Ramsay of Ochtertyre.[33] There were many who came to look back nostalgically to Argyll's period of power, like the writer in the *Caledonian Mercury* in 1784, who asked rhetorically 'Whether is not the patriotic genius of Archibald Duke of Argyll, or Provost Drummond, awanting, to turn the minds of our people of rank and fortune to promote something that may give bread to the industrious poor?'[34] One may quibble that Argyll was not the disinterested elder statesman that many thought him, but this cannot negate that fact that, to many Scots, he filled that role in the 15 years immediately following the 1745 rebellion.

There was thus a strong precedent for Bute to appoint a Scottish minister on both family and political grounds. Some expected Bute to fill the place himself,[35] but there were too many pressing matters taking Bute's attention away from Scotland. There was the King, of course, who wanted Bute to take the lead in the ministry and in making peace with France. There was his wealth, for not only had George II and the Duke of Argyll died, but so also had Bute's father-in-law, Edward Wortley Montagu, leaving Bute and his wife in possession of a vast fortune which reduced their Scottish estates, in effect, to insignificance.[36] Bute, from a material standpoint, could turn his back on Scotland. Nor was the King alone in urging Bute to take a prominent role in public life. There were those, like Gilbert Elliot, who also urged Bute to consider himself as having a role to play as a Briton rather than as a Scot.[37] Elliot, who looked after Scottish business at Westminster for a short period following Argyll's death, considered Scottish matters provincial. 'I protest I do my part in it from a mere sense of duty,' he wrote to Lord Milton, 'for this detail is to me no amusement, and hardly comes within the pale of what is called ambition'.[38] It was Elliot who would tell David Hume, aghast at the hostility towards Scots aroused by Bute's favour with the King, that 'Notwithstanding all you say, we are both Englishmen; that is, true British subjects, entitled to every emolument and advantage that our happy constitution can bestow. Do not you speak, and write, and publish what you please?'[39]

If Bute had, like Elliot, become too much a Briton to remain a Scot, what of his brother, upon whom he proposed to bestow responsibility for Scotland in succession to their uncle? James Stuart Mackenzie had just succeeded in getting himself returned as Member of Parliament for Ross-shire, where his maternal great-grandfather's estates lay. He had additional property in Angus and Perthshire, and was married to one of the 2nd Duke of Argyll's daughters. More than Bute, who had married English and Welsh property, his interests should have been Scottish. His ambitions, however, were for a diplomatic career, and it was with reluctance, and only from a sense of brotherly duty, that he obeyed his brother's pleas to return to London to superintend Scottish affairs. Indeed, Mackenzie would spend much of his time from September 1761 until early 1763 encouraging Bute in his efforts to achieve a peace treaty that would end the Seven Years War. There were rumours, by 1763, that Mackenzie would succeed the Duke of Bedford as envoy to France once the peace settlement was approved.[40] In the meantime, Scottish affairs were run as a private department with Mackenzie and Bute's secretary Charles Jenkinson dealing with matters as they arose, almost as a nuisance rather than as a concern.[41]

This approach caused trouble in Scotland. There Bute had retained the services of Lord Milton, who had served Argyll as his 'subminister' for so many years. Many had hoped that Argyll's death would break Milton's influence, but Bute's clear support left Milton with almost as much power as before, and ensured a smooth transition. Bute had also arranged with the Duke of Newcastle that his friend William Mure, who had been MP for Renfrew, was appointed as a judge (or 'Baron') of the Scottish Court of Exchequer, probably with the idea that Mure would eventually succeed the elderly Milton. These two became Mackenzie's principal correspondents, with Mackenzie speaking to Bute about any matter which might require his influence.[42] If Bute served the King, Mackenzie served Bute. The relationship was that personal, and that remote from any other influence.

If Mackenzie did not experience the sort of virulent abuse that Bute attracted in England, the brothers soon alienated many Scots who felt that they were worthy of their attention. An excellent example was the town of Edinburgh, where Dr Richard Sher has shown us the sort of trouble that Bute and Mackenzie provoked by leaving their local agents too free a hand.[43] Even before the 'Drysdale affair' they had chosen an MP for Edinburgh (to stand at a by-election) in such a way as to provoke local opposition.[44] Lord Milton had been concerned, on first entering into correspondence with Mackenzie, that he had heard that Lord Bute 'did not think that procuring an interest in the city of Edinburgh was worth notice'. To which Mackenzie replied that, while Bute was not disinterested,

> he and I are both of opinion that gold may be bought too dear, in that case, 'tis not a purchase to be envied; tho' if the showing of an attention to them, and of being of service to them when proper opportunities offer, can produce the desired effect, my brother is extremely well inclined towards them.[45]

This sort of patronizing attitude led to the resentment which expressed itself in the Drysdale affair. By 1764 the following comparison, which was not unique, was being made between the way Argyll had treated the city, and the pose adopted by Edinburgh's new patron.

> A correspondence betwixt the town and the late Duke of Argyll existed for about forty years, the whole power of the country was in his hands, and no attempt made, under the Jesuit-like pretext of our good, to force down our throats patronage, which imperiously deprives us of our once-enjoyed privileges. But this new minister, made in a heat, is no sooner helped into the saddle, than like the genius of conceit, he is resolved to try the highest feats of horsemanship.[46]

Another example of the sort of approach to patronage which may have been forthright, but which was not good politics, was Bute and Mackenzie's treatment of Daniel Campbell of Shawfield, MP for Lanarkshire, whose family owned the island of Islay off the Kintyre peninsula in the county of Argyll. The feu duties due to the Crown from the island were granted by the Crown, through Bute's influence, to Bute's cousin Lord Frederick Campbell (younger son of the 4th Duke of Argyll). Campbell of Shawfield never forgave Bute, and went into opposition.[47] Yet in 1763 Lord Milton wrote to Mackenzie that Lord Frederick Campbell, though aware of the 'high obligations' he owed to Bute and Mackenzie, felt that he was never consulted or kept informed by them, 'and this is a common complaint from all your best friends'.[48]

So matters stood when, in April 1763, Bute resigned. He had negotiated the Peace of Paris, thereby consolidating Britain's possession of
Canada and India, but, irony of all ironies, to get the approval of
Parliament for his treaty he had to employ his uncle's old crony Fox,
who had stood for all that Bute detested in politics. Fox, enjoying the
full backing of King and ministry for the first time, marshalled Parliament as if it had been on parade, but Bute had tired of politics. John
Brooke has called him 'the most finished example in British history of
the don in politics', which agrees with Samuel Johnson's observation to
Boswell: 'That Lord Bute, though a very honourable man, a man who
meant well, a man whose blood was full of prerogative, was a bookman,
and thought this country could be governed by the influence of the
Crown alone.'[49] John Brewer has shown us just how intensely he was
vilified by the opposition outside Parliament, as well as distrusted by
those within it.[50] Alexander Forrester, whom Argyll once had intended
as MP for Edinburgh, noted at the time that 'one who was a sort of
parent', meaning Argyll, 'who knew men and things much better than
he', had advised Bute of the wisdom of 'keeping behind the curtain
where he might make and unmake ministers'.[51] This may have been
possible in the past, though Lord Carteret (favourite of George II in
later years) had not been especially successful. Both Argyll and his
elder brother had been Court politicians, and their nephews followed in
this tradition, but Bute had too much pride and too little stomach to
face those now ranged against him. He had secured the peace, and that
would be enough. 'Our friend has been long tired of the anxiety, envy,
and disgust of a situation, ill suited to his temper, health, or habitudes
of life', Gilbert Elliot wrote to William Mure in Scotland at the time of
Bute's resignation of his offices.[52]

Part of Bute's arrangements, on leaving the Treasury, was to get his
brother office, exchanging a pension for the post of Lord Privy Seal of
Scotland, and making the new ministry headed by George Grenville
promise the King that all Scottish appointments would be channelled
through Mackenzie. Argyll's old lieutenant Lord Milton expressed
reservations, but Mackenzie loftily responded

> that when I am no longer supported, I will no longer have anything to do
> with the Scotch business; I know well what my uncle went through, at
> times, in that department, and sure I am, that ten times the power he ever
> had, would not tempt me to submit to the same ... [53]

It would not be long before Mackenzie wanted no more to do with 'the
Scotch business'. Throughout his brief public career Bute had overestimated the power of the Crown. Mackenzie's appointment was one

of the most obvious examples of this misconception. Bute and the King were planning a separate minister for Scotland answerable only to the King.[54] Though Argyll had maintained this appearance in Scotland, and people like Newcastle called him, at the time of his death, 'absolute governor of one of his majesty's kingdoms',[55] his power rested on a fragile basis, and it was only in the last years of his life that he ever enjoyed direct access to the King. Argyll really served Walpole, Pelham and Newcastle, not the King, though he himself did not like to think so. Bute's son Mountstuart pointed this out to Boswell in 1783:

> Lord Mountstuart said Archibald Duke of Argyll was not so great as he made us believe; Duke of Newcastle kept him hanging on. And his way was, when he found Duke of Newcastle for a different man than one whom he recommended, he gave us his own and recommended that one. So he prevailed.[56]

The brevity of Mackenzie's tenure as Scottish minister indicates just how unsound were his and Bute's ideas on Scottish government. Their ideas were not alien to the bulk of the Scottish political nation, who never really opposed them and if anything closed ranks behind Bute in response to the vilification he suffered at the hands of the English.[57] Mackenzie took an interest in the Commission for Annexed Estates, the Forth–Clyde canal, Smeaton's bridge over the Tay at Perth, the extension of a daily post to Scotland from London, and even a bill to abolish fictitious votes in Scottish county elections. Thus if Mackenzie was bad at distributing patronage, he was undoubtedly diligent at seeking to further Scottish interests, in a limited way, with the government in London.[58]

Mackenzie, however, was not able to develop a working relationship with Grenville after Bute's resignation because he saw himself as serving Scotland, his brother, and the King, while Grenville wanted his loyalty to be to the ministry. The 3rd Duke of Argyll had come to terms with this conflict of interest, which perhaps gave him his reputation as a trimmer with the English. Mackenzie, like John, 2nd Duke of Argyll, did not. Since Mackenzie often distributed patronage without regard to influencing Members of Parliament, whose loyalty was a priority with the ministry, Grenville was bound to clash with him. Soon Scottish politicians in London were attempting to deal directly with Grenville, and, after the Duke of Bedford joined the ministry in December 1763, pressure increased as Bedford's Scottish followers clamoured for patronage that Mackenzie had allocated elsewhere, often to those without parliamentary influence.[59]

Mackenzie expressed his feelings on his work in a letter written in April 1765:

People who are so happy as to live remote from the busy scene where Power & Authority reside, for ever conclude, that those who are invested with it, can at all times provide for any one they please; tho a week's Experience of the Fact, convinces them of the numberless Difficulties which render that Idea impossible to be carried into Execution by any body in any Country; but still more in Scotland, where the demands so infinitely exceed the small number of offices to be given away. This is no ministerial Language, but mere matter of Fact, as many can well inform you, tho perhaps you may not credit me; for I observe that you eye in me so much the *Minister*, that you lose sight of the Man.[60]

The Duke of Atholl's brother recorded his thoughts on his dealings with Mackenzie over a period of several years, in a letter written in 1767:

I should be glad to know if Mr. Stewart McKenzie (now that he & his are in power) is as desirous to be of service to me as he seem'd to profess to me, so often, by what I can judge of him hitherto he's more a man of words than deeds, it is with him, as with the world in general, out of sight out of mind, ...[61]

We glimpse here the proud and forthright attitude of Mackenzie, a man incapable of dissembling, but also little capable of compromise. Haughty yet generous and warm, diffident but well intentioned; he inspired loyalty in those close to him, but had not social facility enough to avoid offending many who with more attention might have been friends. A good example of this process was the one contested parliamentary by-election which occurred while Mackenzie was minister under Grenville. This was in Perthshire, where the sitting MP, John Murray of Strowan, inherited the estates (and later the title) of his uncle and father-in-law, the 2nd Duke of Atholl, in December 1763. Pressing his claim for the title, it was clear that Murray would resign his seat. Bute and Mackenzie, without consulting Murray, decided that this was an opportunity to reward the loyalty of David Graeme of Gorthy, an old associate of Bute's who had been employed in arranging the marriage of George III to Charlotte of Mecklenburg, afterwards becoming her secretary. It can be imagined how the appointment of a Scot as secretary to the Queen had been received by the English opposition. Murray, however, had committed himself to a local gentleman who had supported his return in 1761. 'I could have taken my measures accordingly,' he complained, 'but now my honour is too far engaged to allow me to recede.'[62] 'Ministry shall always find me their friend whilst I think the measures they pursue are good,' he declared, 'but never their SLAVE.'[63]

As a result, like the Edinburgh 'Drysdale Affair', Bute and Mackenzie again blundered into provoking an opposition where the issue became the power of the Crown. Mackenzie was incredulous that anyone would dare oppose the candidacy of the Queen's secretary. Like Bute turning to Fox in order to secure parliamentary approval for the Peace of Paris, so Mackenzie turned to old Lord Milton, whose two younger sons secured promotion in the Army as a result of his services.[64] Despite the opposition of Murray, by now confirmed as 3rd Duke of Atholl, and most of the resident freeholders, Milton and Mackenzie were able to secure Graeme's election. 'I really think it will do,' Milton allowed, 'if proper attention is paid to the lesser interests of that country, which are so numerous and a good many of them unconnected'.[65] Atholl, as his lawyer recalled years later, could not prevent 'a Dutch officer to be Stuck into your County & seat in place of a Land holder of more Respectable Metal'.[66] The Duke did not go into opposition, but, as the preceding remark indicates, the episode did not fill Atholl with zeal for the cause of the house of Bute. 'It was indeed a very muddy Affair,' wrote Milton to Mackenzie, 'Such a Number of Voters, such Various Interests to combine, such Variety of Means to be Used, That I have seldom seen any Thing of the kind require more Attention.'[67]

Soon, however, Milton entered his last illness, Mackenzie was to be dismissed from office, and Grenville and his colleagues were refusing to continue their ministry unless it was demonstrated that Bute had no influence with the King or the government. Though there was no real opposition to them in Scotland similar to the Wilkite opposition in England, Bute and Mackenzie had alienated too many of their peers by their aloof attitude and lack of knowledge of local affairs. Those, like Atholl or the town council of Edinburgh, or even Gilbert Elliot, who would naturally look to them for leadership, would not exert themselves in their support. Others, like Lord Garlies or Lord Fife, would gloat over their eclipse.[68]

The surprise, however, was that Mackenzie was not replaced. Grenville had not intended this. He wanted to turn Scottish affairs over to the sons of the 4th Duke of Argyll, the Marquis of Lorne and Lord Frederick Campbell. They were at that time in political alliance with the Duke of Bedford, who occupied a key role in Grenville's government.[69] It was hardly a new approach to call on the House of Argyll to run Scotland for a ministry. One set of cousins would be replaced by another who were less attached to the King and more attached to the ministry. Grenville, however, did not have the chance to implement his plans. The King was Mackenzie's strongest supporter. He had promised Mackenzie that he would be Lord Privy Seal of Scotland for life and Grenville had forced him to break his promise. The Marquis of

Rockingham was persuaded to form a government, though such was the infamy attached to Bute, that Rockingham refused to restore Mackenzie to office.[70] Nor did Rockingham make any provision for a Scottish minister, despite the urgings of the elderly Duke of Newcastle. He listened to those who advanced the arguments put forward earlier in the century by Duncan Forbes and later by Boswell, writing to the Earl of Breadalbane 'that it was the opinion of the King's servants and of many Scotch noblemen and commoners that there ought to be no ministry for Scotland, but that all the business of the United Kingdom should go thro' the same channel.'[71]

Rockingham, of course, lost office in October 1766. Part of the price for the return of the elder Pitt to office was his promise to restore Mackenzie to his place as Lord Privy Seal. This did not, however, mean that Mackenzie resumed his role as minister for Scotland.[72] Bute's influence with the King was waning rapidly, and the opprobrium that he continued to suffer from all ranks of the population made it impossible for any English politician to be identified with him, though Bute and Mackenzie were rumoured to have power in the ministry.[73] Rockingham had also commented to Breadalbane in 1765 'that the opinion of the great officers of Scotland would naturally be asked on many occasions, but that a particular minister for that department was not intended.'[74] This seemed to continue to be the pattern under the ministries of Chatham, Grafton and North. 'The Government here seems again Running into Anarchy & Confusion, and the Northern Department [responsible for Scotland] still Worse', the Duke of Atholl wrote in January 1767.[75] 'Of late years,' Andrew Stuart wrote to the Duchess of Argyll in 1773, 'those who are at the Head of the different departments of the State have been allowed the power belonging to their Stations, more absolutely and independently of the first Minister than was the case in former times.'[76] Bute's son Lord Mountstuart complained to Boswell in 1775

> that each Secretary of State insisted on giving away the offices in his own department without consulting Lord North. I [Boswell] said that we were at present governed by an aristocracy of ministers. That the King should either govern himself, or by a minister as his deputy, who should solely be supreme.[77]

Each English minister, then, attended as best he could to the Scottish affairs which came within the purview of his department.

This left the Scots with no clear channel of government to London, whether it be for the classic eighteenth-century purpose of patronage, or an attempt to secure action from the government on Scottish issues like the construction of the Forth–Clyde canal, the completion of a building to house the national records of Scotland, relief for the clergy from the window tax, or the construction of Edinburgh's New Town.[78] There were those Scots who questioned the wisdom of this arrangement, like the Duke of Atholl's lawyer, John Mackenzie of Delvine:

> However this had happen'd, The Cry here is as high as Elsewhere to clear the houses – Caballs & Mobs may perhaps be Least Dangerous where greatest property is at Stake But this Quarter may soon grow Mutinous, If there Continues, No viceroy in our Israel, and there has been none Since Archd D. of Argyle dyed – This merits Some Attention for Riots here are Generally more serious than Elsewhere & John Wilkes principles have hitherto mett with no countenance But we are ripening for Mutiny Unless some Countryman is pointed out to whom Supplicants May Look up – Lord Privy [James Stuart Mackenzie] will never Stifle Grievances if once they are raised.[79]

'I am now so happy (and a great satisfaction it is to my Mind) as to have no sort of Concern in the Disposal of Offices in Scotland', James Stuart Mackenzie wrote in 1767, 'nor in the Elections of Members of either House of Parliament, and that from my former situation, I am more shy to interfere in matters of that kind, than any private Individual need be, who never filled the department I did.'[80]

Mackenzie increasingly gave way to Bute's son, Lord Mountstuart, in speaking for the Bute interest in Scotland, after the latter came into Parliament (for an English constituency). Mackenzie concentrated on his estate in Perthshire and Angus and his interests in astronomy and other matters, including the management of his brother's estate on Bute.[81] Mountstuart achieved brief notoriety in 1776 upon introducing a bill in the House of Commons to extend the militia laws to Scotland, but the bill failed, and its failure demonstrated the limitations of the Bute interest.[82] Bute retreated, with some bitterness though with more relief, to the life of a book collector and botanist, spending his fabulous fortune on his extensive properties in England.[83]

Both brothers, indeed, withdrew to the world of the wealthy Anglo-Scot, of which they in fact were early examples: Scottish by birth and property (though this changed for Bute in middle life), yet English in speech, education and taste. In this they shared in a general move away from politics by the wealthier Scottish peers and many of the landed gentry. Indeed, Bute's experience of metropolitan politics and the depth of national prejudice by the English against the Scots in the 1760s must have had much to do with this emerging attitude. The 3rd Duke of Atholl expressed this reaction vividly in 1766, when contemplating entering Parliament as a Scottish representative peer:

By all I can Judge publick affairs never Was in Such Confusion Since Britain was a Country, nor do I see how those who are, or may be at the Helm will be able to mend them; besides the difficulties in America the mob at Home seem to me to have every day a greater aversion to all sort of Order or Government, and there are daily papers Published in the English News which I take in, that 5 Years since a man would have run a Risk of Hanging for Publishing – They are afraid of both Houses of Parliament so now Level all the Scurrility Higher; We are greatly too much upon a Levelling principle at present; and if the Republican Principle increases an Oliver Cromwell may be found; for My own Part did I think I could in the least Contribute to the Welfare of my Country by mixing in the present busy scenes I would think it my Duty to Sacrifice my Private Satisfaction; but the more I see of the ways of the World at present, the more I am Convinced that the Post of Virtue & Happiness as well as of Honour is a Private Station – With Pleasure and Satisfaction amongst our peaceable Rocks and mountains I view the distant Voice of Faction & Licentiousness; and the more so at Having Myself so Lately Escaped Storms where those now at Sea were Cool Spectators.[84]

Shortly before this letter was written the old Duke of Newcastle found it impossible to interest any of his Scottish connections in assuming responsibility for Scottish affairs for the Rockingham administration, largely on the same grounds that Atholl had for wishing to remain in the countryside; that residence on one's estates was the true place for a landowner, rather than attendance to politics in the southern metropolis.[85]

By the time the general election of 1768 was held, without ministerial intervention, electoral corruption had developed into a free-for-all, leaving those like Atholl, or Bute, with little inclination to intervene. It was one of the most corrupt general elections of the eighteenth century, if not *the* most corrupt, as burghs sought patrons and family interests clashed in the counties.[86] The amount of electoral litigation which followed was enormous. 'Had D. Archibald been alive we shoud not have seen this nor many things we have seen and probably will see', Lord Auchinleck [Boswell's father] wrote to the Earl of Loudoun at the time.[87]

Bute's sympathies were with those who stayed close to their estates. James Boswell recorded the following conversation with Bute in 1781:

His Lordship regretted the old land proprietors of Scotland estranging themselves from their estates. 'Now,' said he, 'Mountstuart has been in Bute, and loves it, as indeed it is the prettiest place I ever saw. But his son has never seen it, and perhaps never will.' 'Pray, my Lord,' said I, 'give me leave to ask, when was your Lordship last there?' HE. 'Not these thirty years.' I. 'Allow us to lament. Though the Stuart of Bute is very well as we see him in South Audley Street.'[88]

Here we witness an expression of the nostalgia of the wealthy Scottish landowners of the late eighteenth century for the days when their estates were an inherent part of their identity. Bute, like his brother and the Duke of Atholl, would have retired to Scotland and seldom come to London, but his English fortune diverted him elsewhere.

Perhaps this was because Bute had aroused such emotional feelings in the English towards the Scots during his short political career, leading him to distance himself as much as possible from the land of his birth. He was resented as a royal favourite, but paradoxically this hostility was often transmuted into hatred of Bute as an alien Scot, blighted by Jacobitism (his sharing his surname with the Jacobite royal house was not ignored) and incapable by birth of appreciating the glories of the English constitution. John Brewer has made the point that the most important aspect of Bute's political career was what he came to symbolize in English and British politics, just as John Wilkes, whom Brewer has termed Bute's 'political antonym' came to play an equally symbolic role whose importance lay not so much in the actual career and thought of the man, but the assumptions, ideas and attitudes of those who took the trouble to hate him.[89]

An essay on Lord Bute and Scotland cannot, therefore, ignore this aspect of Bute's importance. Professor Brewer has dealt with the use made of Bute's nationality by those opposing him. All sorts of aspects of what had come to be associated with Scots in the popular mind were used in the flood of pamphlets and caricatures aimed at Bute. Most interesting, in this strain of abuse, was the implication that Bute and the Scots in general were alien to the English political system and therefore could not hold a place in it. Even before Bute, there were Scots, like James Campbell of Cawdor, James St Clair or Alexander Hume-Campbell, who were denied British office on account of their nationality. Campbell was ruled out as a potential Chancellor of Exchequer in 1755 because he was a Scot. St Clair had been suggested as Commander-in-Chief in 1760 by Pitt, but was passed over because he was a Scot. Hume-Campbell's attempt to secure the Chancellorship of the Duchy of Lancaster was blocked by Lord Chancellor Hardwicke on the grounds that it, as Hume-Campbell wrote to his brother, 'was an English Law place and I was a Scotchman, that that objection cut me so deep I could not depart from it.'[90] For some reason William Murray, Lord Mansfield, was considered fit for the English bench, but then he, as Doctor Johnson had said, had been 'caught young'.

Even before the death of George II, there were insinuations that there was a limit to the ambitions that Bute, as a Scotsman, could set himself. John Dalrymple of Cranstoun, an ambitious Scottish lawyer, wrote to Charles Townshend in October 1759 that 'I have often heard it said by English people that the English would never bear to be ruled by a Scotch Minister.' Why? asked Dalrymple:

> They [the English] have born three foreign princes without grumbling, they bore two very low men Lord Oxford and Lord Orford long to reign over them, who had nothing but their own abilitys & their princes favour to support them, men of low birth & of no connexions: & is it to be supposed they will rebel against L:B:, a man of high birth, of more imposing manners, who will have near a whole country at his back, ... the favorite of his sovereign, & of a young & therefore probably obstinate sovereign.[91]

It never occurred to Dalrymple that Oxford and Orford had the benefit of an extensive following in the House of Commons. Henry Fox, writing after the storm had burst, took a cynical view which revealed something of the temper of the times:

> the Press is with more vehemence that I ever knew set to work against Ld. Bute. And it would be very surprizing to see how quick & fiercely the fire spreads, but for the consideration that it is fed with great industry, & blown by a national prejudice which is inveterate and universal. Every man has at some time or other found a Scotchman in his way, and everybody has therefore damned the Scotch: and this hatred their excessive nationality has continually inflamed. A peace is thought necessary to Lord Bute; therefore a peace on any supposed terms is exclaimed against.[92]

The most persistent theme in the attack on Bute and the Scots, and the most coherent, was that he and they would not respect the constitution. Various prints published in the 1760s show Bute and other Scots putting the Magna Carta to a variety of contemptuous or filthy uses.[93] This sort of attack was still current as late as 1778. 'The imputation of Jacobitism would have served their turn as well', wrote a Scots pamphleteer,

> but it would have been too gross to have called us all so, seeing so many of us have fought and died in the cause of the House of Hanover; but as they were determined that not a man of us should escape the publick hatred, they stigmatised those to whom they could not impute Jacobitism, with the odious name of Tories, a character than which nothing can be more heterogenous and repugnant to our genius, education and prejudices.[94]

'Boot' had become a subject of English abuse. 'Macboote, Macboote, Macboote, of W-les, beware; Avoiding him, nought else is worth thy care' went one squib published at the time.[95] The *Caledonian Mercury* published a story on 20 August 1763 relating how an English representative of some London merchants had refused to drink to Lord Bute's

health after concluding his business with local merchants in an unnamed town in the west of Scotland.

> The Gentleman who give it insisted; but the rider instead of complying,
> went out of the room, and returning with a boot and a whip, 'This,' says
> he, striking the boot several times with his whip, 'this is the way we drink
> Lord Bute in England;' then advancing to the table, he filled a bumper,
> and drank health to Wilkes, and d————n to Lord Bute.

The subsequent humiliation of the rider was then narrated, and the
Scots were reported to have ordered the man thrown out of the inn
where they were meeting, as 'that pitiful rascal Wilkes ought to be
treated by every honest man.'

Indeed, Wilkes entered Scottish popular mythology to become as
much of a bogey in Scotland as Bute was in England. 'Squint-eyed,
hollow-nosed, buck-teethed, snarl-looking wretch', 'a most shocking
dog to look at';[96] Wilkes was burned in effigy after a mock trial at
Stirling in 1763, and burned in effigy by mobs of apprentices at
Edinburgh and Leith in 1768.[97] For years afterwards, every year on
the King's birthday, effigies of Wilkes were burned by the boys of
Edinburgh and Leith at Parliament Square off the High Street, and at
the Gallow Lee on Leith Walk, as well as other places in the town.
According to the two most authoritative histories of Edinburgh published at the end of the nineteenth century, this practice continued until
well into the reign of Victoria, and occurred in other parts of Scotland
as well.[98]

Wilkes even attracted the attention of the Gaelic song writer and
poet Duncan Ban Macintyre, at that time one of the Town Guard of
Edinburgh, where his wife kept a dram shop. His *Song to John Wilkes*
(*Oran Iain Faochag*) is a model of loyalty to the Crown. Macintyre is not
alone in punning on Wilkes's name by calling him 'the Whelk', and
though the English translation naturally cannot convey the fluency of
the Gaelic original, it is worth quoting as an illustration of the sentiments involved.

> Thou hast spoken much nonsense
> behind the back of the noble Earl of Bute,
> an honoured champion verily,
> stoutly defending the kingdom;
> he is highly respected and beloved
> at the court of the King and Queen,
> despite the Whelk and such rascals
> as would deign to be his allies.

> Thou hast talked unsparingly of Scotland,
> and thou hadst better have kept silent;
> wert thou to come near the Roughbounds,
> woe to one in thy position:
> thou wouldst be in prison all thy days,
> in spite of those who might support thee;
> and, in requital for the mischief thou has wrought,
> the gallows for death-blow would be assigned to thee.[99]

The Scots and the English had divided on national lines again because of Bute and Wilkes. The English, wrote a correspondent of the *London Chronicle* on 30 June 1768, opposed Bute because he did not respect English liberty and the Magna Carta. The Scots, retorted a correspondent to the *Caledonian Mercury* on 25 July of the same year, had seen Wilkes revive 'the antient enmity between the two nations' by stirring the 'unthinking' mob. The Scottish aristocracy and gentry retreated into a period of genteel insularity, taking up literature and agricultural improvement. The English experienced a revival of radical, libertarian politics that would encourage a similar kind of opposition across the Atlantic. As early as 1766, the Duke of Atholl remarked, ironically, that 'Mr. Grenville had better have Contented himself with Opressing our little Kingdom, and not have Pushed the Joke so far as America; two millions of People ten Thousand Miles Distant will think for themselves'[100] The majority of the Scots would expand on the new identity they had embraced during the Seven Years War as enthusiasts for Empire and imperial glory when the American war renewed their opportunity to prove their loyalty and enthusiasm for the concept of Britain.[101] It was the national aspect of Lord Bute's brief career at Court which confirmed them in this course. Bute had provided a chance for talented Scots like Gilbert Elliot or James Oswald in politics, or Allan Ramsay (the younger) in art, or Robert Adam in architecture, or William Robertson, Hugh Blair and many others in literature, to glimpse what might be possible for themselves through access to a wealthier state and a larger market. Wilkes symbolized the resentment of the English, drawing on a long tradition, at finding themselves part of a larger entity without being able to monopolize all the advantages it made possible. Bute and Wilkes, then, like Pitt, symbolized forces at work in a new imperial politics now centred at Westminster, where narrow English concerns were just as parochial as those which were exclusively Scottish, Irish, West Indian or American. It would take the loss of America, the expansion of British power in India, and the Napoleonic wars, before some sort of new British entity would evolve. That process is not yet fully understood.

NOTES

This essay is dedicated to the memory of Catherine Armet, late archivist to the Marquess of Bute, whose devotion to the Stuarts of Bute was only exceeded by that to the Society of Friends and the cause of peace.

I am grateful to the Trustees of the National Library of Scotland and the British Library for permission to use manuscripts from their collections in this essay. The copyright owners of several other collections of manuscripts are acknowledged in the footnotes. Special thanks are due to the Duke of Atholl and the Marquess of Bute for permission to use material in their possession.

I am also grateful to the following scholars, who were kind enough to give me their comments on an earlier draft of this paper: H.T. Dickinson, William Ferguson, Rosalind Mitchison, John Robertson, Karl Schweizer, Richard B. Sher and John M. Simpson. Naturally, however, I am responsible for the views expressed in this essay.

1. Newcastle to Hardwicke (copy), 17 Apr. 1761, BL Add. MSS 32922, fos. 15–20. See Also 'Memo of a Conversation with Lord Bute', 21 Apr. 1761, BL Add. MSS 32922, fos. 108–10.

2. See John M. Simpson's excellent essay, which repays close attention, 'Who steered the gravy train, 1707–1766' in *Scotland in the Age of Improvement*, eds N.T. Phillipson and Rosalind Mitchison (1970), pp. 48–72. This can be supplemented by P.W.J. Riley, *The English Ministers and Scotland, 1707–1727* (1964) and Richard Scott, 'The politics and administration of Scotland, 1725–1748' (Ph.D. thesis, University of Edinburgh, 1982); both works of acute scholarship. Other works of interest are listed in the bibliography of Richard B. Sher, *Church and University in the Scottish Enlightenment* (1985), 347. See also Bruce Lenman, 'A client society: Scotland between

the '15 and the '45', in *Britain in the Age of Walpole*, ed. J. Black (1984), 69–93. I have used the contemporary (anglicized) spelling 'Ilay' employed by the Earl of Ilay in his correspondence, rather than the modern spelling of the name of the island from which he took his title.

3. This paragraph is based on Alexander Murdoch, *'The People Above': Politics and Administration in Mid-Eighteenth-Century Scotland* (1980), ch.2. The description 'elder statesman' is from Rosalind Mitchison, *A History of Scotland* (2nd edn, 1982), 343.

4. Bute's brother was usually referred to as 'Mr. Mackenzie' or 'Lord Privy Seal' but if he did use both his surnames, he tended to use the 'Stewart' spelling. However, I have followed the modern practice of the family, which has settled on the 'Stuart' spelling.

5. See the relevant entries in *DNB*, and Lady Louisa Stuart, *Some Account of John Duke of Argyll and His Family* (1863), reprinted (without the 'Pedigree of the Argyll Family' reproduced here) in *Lady Louisa Stuart: Selections from her Manuscripts*, ed. J.A. Home (1899).

6. See Stuart, *Some Account of John Duke of Argyll.*

7. See J.W. Reed and F.A. Pottle, *Boswell: Laird of Auchinleck, 1778–1782* (1977), 344.

8. See the entry for Bute in *DNB*. John Davies, *Cardiff and the Marquesses of Bute* (1981), 6, indicates just how much of an influence on Bute's life was 'the use of the Wortley fortune', as Davies puts it.

9. John, 2nd Duke of Argyll to James Stuart Mackenzie, 9 Jan. 1741/2, Bute MSS. I am grateful to the Marquess of Bute for permission to quote from the Bute papers.

10. *DNB.*

11. Lady Mary Wortley Montagu to Edward Wortley Montagu, Avignon,

1745, printed in Mrs. E. Stuart Wortley, *A Prime Minister and His Son* (1935), 13.

12. See J.L. McKelvey, *George III and Lord Bute: The Leicester House Years* (Durham, NC, 1973), ch.1; John Brewer, 'The Earl of Bute' in *The Prime Ministers*, ed. H. van Thal (1974), I, 103–13; Betty Kemp, 'Frederick, Prince of Wales' in *Silver Renaissance: Essays in Eighteenth-Century History*, ed. A. Natan (1961), 38–56.

13. Gilbert Elliot to Bute, 31 Aug. 1755, Bute MSS, Box 1, 48/1755. Some light is shed on Argyll's actions in Historical Manuscripts Commission (HMC), *Report on the Manuscripts of the Right Honourable Lord Polwarth*, ed. H. Paton (1961), V, 297–300. Many, including the 3rd Earl of Marchmont, considered Argyll's behaviour 'dark and ambiguous'; see Marchmont to Andrew Fletcher, Lord Milton, 23 Apr. 1755, NLS MS 16690, f. 238. Bute to Gilbert Elliot, 27 Apr. 1755, NLS MS 11014, fos. 6–7, described Argyll's behaviour as 'mysterious as ever'.

14. Newcastle to Hardwicke, 18 Oct. 1755, BL Add. MSS 35415, fos. 110–11.

15. Argyll to Bute, 2 Nov. 1756, Bute MSS 95/1756: 'I had private notice some time ago that Your Lordship was to be Groom of the Stole from one who has all along taken that side of the Question'. The day after he wrote to Bute, Argyll wrote to Fox that 'I hope Ld. Bute will act wisely and temperately, He, The Young Royal family, and above all the Publick owe much to the part you have acted'. Argyll to Fox, 3 Nov. 1756, BL Add. MSS 51430, f. 23.

16. See Murdoch, *op. cit.*, 39–51, for a detailed account. For the English context, see W.A. Speck, *Stability and Strife: England 1714–1760*, 258–74. The works of J.C.D. Clark touch on this subject at times.

17. Mackenzie to Milton, 17 Oct. 1761, Saltoun Papers, NLS MS 16721, fos. 186–9.

18. Sir Lewis Namier, *England in the Age of the American Revolution* (2nd ed, 1961), 117–18, in contrast to McKelvey, *op. cit.* 137.

19. Namier, *op. cit.*, 117–18, quoting Newcastle to Hardwicke (copy), 28 Feb. 1760, BL Add. MSS 32902, fos. 453–6.

20. W. Mure to Bute, 4 June 1759, Bute MSS 88a/1759.

21. Newcastle to Hardwicke (copy), 6 Sept. 1759, BL Add. MSS 32911, fos. 101–2. This affair can best be followed in W.L. Burn, 'The general election of 1761 at Ayr', *EHR*, LII (1937), 103–9; the relevant essays in Sir Lewis Namier and J. Brooke, *The History of Parliament: The House of Commons, 1754–90* (1964); and Murdoch, *op. cit.*, 86–92.

22. G. Elliot to Bute, 16 Dec. 1760, Bute MSS 194/1760, quoted in Murdoch, *op. cit.*, 95.

23. Bute to Mackenzie, 17 Apr. 1761, Bute MSS uncatalogued 'with him dy'd all my resentment, indeed I had forgot it long before; and was determin'd, to have done all in my power to make his old age easy, happy; while he on his side had taken his part, & was acting in perfect subordination'.

24. Newcastle to Hardwicke (copy), 3 Jan. 1761, BL Add. MSS. 32917, f. 90, quoted in Murdoch, *op. cit.*, 95.

25. Alexander Forrester (1705–87), at that time MP for Okehampton, quoted in Namier, *England*, 162, N .2; also quoted in Simpson, *op. cit.*, 63. For a sketch of Forrester's career see Namier and Brooke, *op. cit.*

26. Bute to James Stuart Mackenzie, 17 April 1761, Bute MSS. The full letter is quoted as an appendix to Murdoch, 'The People Above' (Ph.D. thesis, University of Edinburgh, 1978), but was not included in the published version of 1980.

27. Hardwicke to Newcastle, 16 Apr. 1761, BL Add. MSS 32922, fos. 3–4.

28. D. Forbes to John Scrope, 31 Aug. 1725, quoted in Simpson, *op. cit.*, from D. Warrand (ed.), *More Culloden Papers* (1923–30), II, 322.

29. I.S. Lustig and F.A. Pottle (eds), *Boswell: The Applause of the Jury* (1982), 144–5. I would like to thank David Brown, now of the SRO, for drawing this passage to my attention. Quotation by permission of Yale University and the McGraw-Hill Book Company.
30. The work of Professor Maurice Lee, Jr., explores this theme in *Government by Pen: Scotland Under James VI and I* (Urbana, IL, 1980) and *The Road to Revolution: Scotland Under Charles I 1625–37* (Urbana, IL, 1986). There has also been some recent work on Lauderdale: Roy Wallace Lennox, 'Lauderdale and Scotland: a study in Restoration politics and administration, 1660–1682' (Ph.D. thesis, Columbia University, New York, 1977).
31. Horace Walpole, *Memoirs of the Reign of King George II*, ed. Lord Holland (2nd edn, 1846), I, 278; *A Selection from the Papers of the Earls of Marchmont*, ed. Sir G.H. Rose (1831); HMC, *op. cit.*; John, Lord Hervey, *Some Materials Towards Memoirs of the Reign of King George II*, ed. R. Sedgwick (1931 edn, repr. New York, 1970), II, 708; Horace Walpole, *Memoirs of King George II*, ed. J. Brooke (1985), I, 187–8.
32. *Edinburgh Evening Courant*, 16 May 1761; *Scots Magazine*, XX (May 1761), 278; Saltoun Papers, J. Maule to Lord Milton, 16 April 1761, Saltoun Papers, NLS MS 16722, f. 11; Sir Alexander Dick to Milton, 20 April 1761, Saltoun Papers, NLS MS 16721, f. 193; A. Fairholme to Lord Milton, 30 April 1761, Saltoun Papers, NLS MS 16720, fos. 122–3.
33. J. Ramsay of Ochtertyre, *Scotland and Scotsmen* (Edinburgh, 1888) I, 87; [David Erskine, Earl of Buchan], *Printed Recollections Respecting the Family of the Fletchers of Saltoun* (1803); Alexander Carlyle, *Anecdotes and Characters of the Times*, ed. J. Kinsley (1973), 193; Thomas Somerville, *My Own Life and Times, 1741–1814* (1861), 379–81.
34. *Caledonian Mercury*, 11 Feb. 1784; 'Queries addressed to the Citizens of Edinburgh', no. 38, signed 'Diogenes', reprinted on the wrappers of the *Scots Magazine*, Feb. 1784.
35. P. Craufurd to 'a friend', 17 Nov. 1760, Bute MSS, quoted in Namier, *op. cit.*, 162.
36. See Davies, *op. cit.*, 6.
37. Namier, *op. cit.*, 162–3.
38. Gilbert Elliot to Milton, 11 June 1761, Saltoun Papers, NLS MS 16720, f. 55.
39. G. Elliot to David Hume, n.d., in G.F.S. Elliot, *The Border Elliots and the Family of Minto* (privately printed, 1897), 387.
40. *Edinburgh Evening Courant*, 2 April 1763; *Caledonian Mercury* 5 May 1764. Mackenzie also, among other things, negotiated the purchase of the magnificent art collection of Joseph 'Consul' Smith at Venice on behalf of George III in 1762; see J.H. Plumb and H. Wheldon, *Royal Heritage* (1977), 172.
41. See James Stuart Mackenzie Letterbook, *passim*, Bute MSS; Mackenzie to C. Jenkinson, 15 Oct. 1762, Bute MSS 532/1762; Mackenzie to Milton, 22 May 1762, Saltoun Papers, NLS MS 16725, f. 141.
42. Stuart Mackenzie Letterbook, Bute MSS; Caldwell Papers, NLS MSS 4941–4; correspondence with Mackenzie, Saltoun Papers, NLS MSS 16718, 16725, 16728, 16731, and 16733.
43. R.B. Sher, 'Moderates, managers and popular politics in mid-eighteenth-century Edinburgh: the Drysdale bustle of the 1760s', in *New Perspectives on the Politics and Culture of Early Modern Scotland*, ed. J. Dwyer *et. al.* (1982).
44. *Edinburgh Evening Courant*, 1 Feb. 1762; *A Letter from a Citizen in Town to his Friend* (1762) (in the NLS); Milton to Mackenzie, 21 Jan. and 4 Feb. 1762, Saltoun Papers, NLS MS 16725, fos. 110, 121 (drafts).
45. Lord Milton to Mackenzie, 19 Oct.

1761, Saltoun Papers, NLS MS 16721, f. 194 (draft); Mackenzie to Milton, 27 Oct. 1761, *ibid.*, fos. 197–8.

46. *The Citizen Number I* (1764) (in the Edinburgh Room of the Edinburgh Central Public Library); also see *A Letter from a Citizen.*

47. Lord Digby to Lord Holland, 31 May 1765, *Letters to Henry Fox, Lord Holland*, ed. G. Strangeways, Earl of Ilchester (Roxburghe Club, 1915), 219–21; Horace Walpole, *Memoirs of the Reign of George III*, ed. Sir D. Le Marchant (1845), I, 178.

48. Milton to Mackenzie (copy), 22 Oct. 1763, Saltoun Papers, NLS MS 16731, f. 182.

49. J. Brooke, *King George III* (1972), 47; Johnson to Boswell, 14 Apr. 1775, *Boswell; the Ominous Years, 1774–76*, ed. C. Ryskamp and F.A. Pottle (1963), 143. Quotation by permission of Yale University and the McGraw-Hill Book Company.

50. J. Brewer, *Party Ideology and Popular Politics at the Accession of George III* (1976); and more particularly, *idem*, 'The misfortunes of Lord Bute: a case study in eighteenth-century political argument and public opinion', *Hist J*, XVI, no.1 (1973).

51. Alexander Forrester to Sir Andrew Mitchell, BL Add. MSS 30999, fos. 16–17, quoted in Namier, *op. cit.*, 162. John Simpson made this point, and used this quotation, in *op. cit.*, 63.

52. Elliot to Mure, 7 Apr. 1763, in W. Mure (ed.), *Selections from the Family Papers Preserved at Caldwell* (Maitland Club, 1854), Part II(1), 175–6.

53. Mackenzie to Milton, 21 Apr. 1763, Saltoun Papers, NLS MS 16731, fos. 121–2.

54. Bute to W. Mure, 9 April 1763 in Mure, *op. cit.*, Part II(1), 176; R. Sedgwick (ed.), *Letters from George III to Lord Bute*, no. 294, 4 April 1763; G. Grenville to Mackenzie, 29 April 1763, Bute MSS, uncatalogued.

55. Newcastle to Hardwicke (copy), 16 Apr. 1761, BL Add. MSS 32922 f. 5 .

56. *Boswell: The Applause of the Jury*, 144–5. Quotation by permission of Yale

University and the McGraw-Hill Book Company. For a general discussion of this point see Richard Scott, 'The politics and administration of Scotland, 1725–1748'; Murdoch, *People Above*, and Simpson, *op. cit.*

57. The Scottish Press of the time, particularly the *Scots Magazine*, *Edinburgh Evening Courant*, and the *Caledonian Mercury* illustrate this point, corroborated by sources such as those cited in notes 93–96, 98–101 below.

58. Stuart Mackenzie Letterbook, 34, 83, 100, 103, Bute MSS; correspondence between Mackenzie and Milton, 1762, Saltoun Papers, NLS MS 16725, fos. 135–7, 139–40, 149–50; Mackenzie to Milton, 26 Aug. 1763, Saltoun Papers, NLS MS 16728, fos. 153–5; Mackenzie to Milton, 1764, Saltoun Papers, NLS MS 16731, fos. 66–7, 138; Mackenzie to Milton, 18 March 1765, Saltoun Papers, NLS MS 16733, f. 90; N. Jucker (ed.), *The Jenkinson Papers* (1949), 314–15, 317, 330–2, 337–8; Mure, *op. cit.*, Part II(1), 232–4, 236–7, 260–3, 280–3; II(2), 8–11, 12–15, 19022.

59. Murdoch, *People Above*, 110–23.

60. Mackenzie to 'Mrs. Agnew', 19 April 1765, Bute MSS, Stuart Mackenzie Letterbook, 107.

61. Capt. James Murray to Atholl, 11 March 1767, Atholl MSS, Box 49, section 6, no. 31. I am grateful to the Duke of Atholl for permission to quote from the Atholl MSS.

62. J. Murray of Strowan to Mackenzie (copy), 25 Jan. 1764, Atholl MSS, Box 49, section 3, no. 48.

63 J. Murray of Strowan (later 3rd Duke of Atholl) to A. Drummond of Meginch (copy), 27 Jan. 1764, in J. Stewart Murray, 7th Duke of Atholl (ed.), *Chronicle of the Atholl and Tullibardine Families* (privately printed, 1908), IV, 8–9, corrected from Atholl MSS, Box 49, section 3, no. 56.

64. Saltoun Papers, NLS MS 16724, f. 188; NLS MS 16726, fos. 132–3; NLS MS 16729, f. 80; NLS MS 16731, fos.

98–9, f. 162; NLS MS 16732, f. 93; J. Abercrombie to the Earl of Loudoun, 15 May 1773: 'Some people are surprised Stuart Mackenzie takes no part in the contest [to choose a successor to Graeme as MP for Perthshire], because on a similar occasion it got Fletcher a Regt' (Loudoun MSS, 1772, bundle B).

65. Milton to Mackenzie (draft), 26 Jan. 1764, Saltoun Papers, NLS MS 16731, fos. 70–1.

66. Mackenzie of Delvine to Atholl, 24 Dec. 1770, Atholl MSS, Box 54, Section 1, no. 244.

67. Milton to Mackenzie (draft), 2 Apr. 1764, Saltoun Papers, NLS MS 16731, f. 124.

68. For Edinburgh, see Sher, 'Moderates, managers and popular politics'; for Atholl, see Atholl, *op. cit.*, IV, 8–9, and the relevant correspondence in the Atholl MSS, calendared in NRAS survey 234; for Elliot, see Elliot to W. Scott, 22 Mar. 1765, Scott of Harden MSS, GD 157/2250, no. 12, cited by permission of Lord Polwarth; for Fife, see Fife to Grenville, 2 Aug. 1764, in J.R.G. Tomlinson (ed.) *Additional Grenville Papers* (1962), 169–70, also 161–4, 166–7. For Garlies, see Garlies to Grenville, 19 and 23 Dec. 1763, Bedford MSS, HMC 8, XLVIII, f. 214; Garlies to Bedford, 16 Jan. 1764, *ibid.*, f. 22, cited by permission of the Marquess of Tavistock and the Trustees of the Bedford Estates.

69. See the entry for Lord Frederick Campbell in *DNB*; Namier and Brooke, *op. cit.*, and W.J. Smith (ed.), *The Grenville Papers* (1852–3), III, 187–8. Dr N.T. Phillipson pointed out to me many years ago how natural it was for Grenville to turn to Lorne and Lord Frederick Campbell as an alternative to Bute and Stuart Mackenzie.

70. P. Langford, *The First Rockingham Administration 1765–66* (1973).

71. Breadalbane to the second Earl of Hardwicke, 18 Oct. 1765, BL Add. MSS 35451, f. 161.

72. See J. Brooke, *The Chatham*

Administration 1766–68 (1956); Bute to James Wemyss (copy), June (?) 1766, Bute MSS, quoted in Namier and Brooke, *op. cit.*, III, 622; Mackenzie to the Earl of Findlater, 2 Nov. 1767, Seafield MSS, GD 248/572/4. I am grateful to Lord Seafield for permission to quote from the Seafield MSS on deposit at the SRO.

73. *Ibid.*, Bute MSS and Seafield MSS. Also the letter by James Murray cited in note 61.

74. Letter by Breadalbane cited in note 69.

75. 3rd Duke of Atholl to J. Mackenzie of Delvine, 27 Jan. 1767, Mackenzie of Delvine Papers, NLS MS 1405, fos. 161–2.

76. Andrew Stuart to the Duchess of Argyll, 30 July 1773, in J. Campbell, 9th Duke of Argyll (ed.), *Intimate Society Letters of the Eighteenth Century* (1910), II, 155–60.

77. *Boswell: The Ominous Years*, 119, 3 Apr. 1775. Quotation by permission of Yale University and the McGraw-Hill Book Company.

78. Queensberry to the Earl of Findlater, 28 May 1767, Seafield MSS GD 248/572/4.

79. Mackenzie of Delvine to Atholl, 15 Dec. 1770, Atholl MSS, Box 54, section 1, no. 238.

80. Mackenzie to the Earl of Findlater, 2 Nov. 1767, Seafield MSS, GD 248/572/4.

81. See the entry on Mackenzie by Lady Haden Guest in Namier and Brooke, *op. cit.*, and D. Gavine, 'James Stewart Mackenzie (1719–1800) and the Bute MSS', *J. for the History of Astronomy*, v (1974), 208–14.

82. See the entry on Mountstuart in Namier and Brooke, *op. cit.*; and the account in John Robertson, *The Scottish Enlightenment and the Militia Issue* (1985), 130–2.

83. Davies, *Cardiff and the Marquesses of Bute*, 6; Stuart Wortley, *A Prime Minister and His Son*. See also the paper by P.D. Brown in ch. 10 of this volume.

84. Atholl to Mackenzie of Delvine, 25

Feb. 1766, written from Dunkeld, Mackenzie of Delvine Papers NLS MS 1405, f. 49.

85. BL Add. MSS 32968, f. 367; BL Add. MSS 32969, fos. 82, 86–7, 279–82; BL Add. MSS 32970, fos. 371–2, 375–6; G.W.T. Omond, *The Arniston Memoirs* (1887), 178–9.

86. See William Ferguson, 'The electoral system in the Scottish counties before 1832', in *The Stair Society: Miscellany Two*, ed. David Sellar (1984), 261–94.

87. Auchinleck to Loudoun, 25 March 1768; Loudoun MSS, 1768, bundle 6; also see Atholl MSS, Box 49, section 7, no. 16, Mackenzie of Delvine to the third Duke of Atholl, 18 Feb. 1768.

88. J.W. Reed and F.A. Pottle (eds), *Boswell: Laird of Auchinleck, 1778–1782* (1977). One can see Bute and Mountstuart's interest in Bute as improving landlords through their correspondence with their factor: Ian H. Adams (ed.), *Papers of Peter May Land Surveyor 1749–1793* (1979), 200–62.

89. Brewer, 'The misfortunes of Lord Bute'.

90. Namier and Brooke, *op. cit.*, I, 167–8.

91. John Dalrymple of Cranstoun to Charles Townshend, 5 Oct. 1759, Charles Townshend MSS. Quoted with the permission of the William L. Clements Library.

92. 'Political Sketch 1760–1763', in *The Life and Letters of Lady Sarah Lennox*, ed. the Countess of Ilchester and Lord Stavordale (1902), 68. Also see Karl Schweizer, 'Lord Bute and anti-Scottish feeling in eighteenth century English political propaganda', in *Procs of the Eighth and Ninth Colloquia on Scottish Studies*, ed. A. Brodie (Guelph, Ont., 1974), 23–33.

93. See Herbert Atherton, *Political Prints in the Age of Hogarth* (1974), 208–77; Michael Duffy, *The Englishman and the Foreigner*, vol. 3 of *The English Satirical Print 1600–1832*, ed. Michael Duffy (1986); and *Catalogue of Prints and Drawings in the British Museum Division I, Political and Personal Satires*, IV and V.

94. *Scotch Modesty Displayed* (2nd edn, 1778), 40.

95. *The Three Conjurors; a political interlude stolen from Shakespeare* (1762).

96. [Andrew Henderson (my attribution)], *A Letter to the Author of the North Briton. ... (1763); A Letter from Scots Sawney the Barber to Mr Wilkes an English Parliamenter* (1763).

97. *Edinburgh Evening Courant*, 6 Apr. 1768; also see the *Caledonian Mercury*, 6 Apr. 1768. See the *Edinburgh Evening Courant*, 30 May 1763, regarding Wilkes being burned in effigy at Stirling.

98. James Grant, *Old and New Edinburgh* (1881–3), III, 157 (Grant gives the first occurrence of burning Wilkes in effigy as 1770, but see n.97); Sir Daniel Wilson, *Memorials of Edinburgh in the Olden Times* (2nd auth. edn, 1891) I, 281, which corroborates Grant's account.

99. *The Songs of Duncan Ban Macintyre*, edited with a translation by Angus Macleod (1952), 396–405. The song first appeared in 1768. See the *Caledonian Mercury*, 18 April 1768, for another reference to Wilkes and whelks, there spelled 'wilks').

100. Atholl to Mackenzie of Delvine, 4 March 1766, Mackenzie of Delvine Papers, NLS MS 1405, f. 516.

101. See, for example, Sher, *Church and University*. See also D.B. Swinfen, 'The American Revolution in the Scottish Press' in *Scotland, Europe and the American revolution*, ed. O. Dudley Edwards and G. Shepperson (1976), 66–74; and D. Fagerstrom, 'Scottish opinion and the American Revolution', *William and Mary Q.*, 3rd ser., XI (1954), 252–75.

7

Lord Bute and the
Scottish universities 1760–1792

Roger L. Emerson

One vital facet of Lord Bute's extra-political career – his patronage of the Scottish universities, a major contribution to Scottish cultural life – has never been fully examined. It is the purpose of this essay to trace the outlines of these often obscure activities and to argue that it was his men and his outlook which marked three of the five Scottish universities during the period from *c*.1760–1780. Before entering upon this task, it is necessary to say something about the nature of the Scottish colleges and their relation to political figures.[1]

In 1760, when Bute first became active in university affairs in Scotland, the Kingdom possessed five universities and six colleges. Each had unique features of government but they all possessed formal characteristics which it is important to describe. These structured the bodies within which patronage was dispensed and control exercised by those with legal rights of appointment and others who believed they had proper concerns with the corporations. These structures both limited and at the same time made possible Bute's interference in the university recruitment of new faculty members.

All the universities had or claimed the right to elect chancellors. These heads of the universities or their *vices* controlled or could try to control university administration through the university's court, over which they were entitled to preside and in whose proceedings they could interfere. Chancellors also had executive responsibilities and formally admitted men to office except at King's College and University and at Edinburgh. At King's this right was exercised by the Commissary of Aberdeen who was thought still to possess the rights of the Vice-Chancellor even though the bishops for whom he had once deputized had been replaced by presbyterian functionaries after 1689. At Edinburgh the Chancellors' post was sometimes claimed by the city's Lord Provost while their functions were exercised by the town council, its university committee or by the 'college baillie' who normally dealt with matters relating to administration.

All the universities but Edinburgh had Rectors in whose courts sat Assessors. The Rectoral Court was the disciplinary body for the university and the place where corporate privileges were defended, defined and sometimes in these ways substantially changed. At Edinburgh these functions also belonged to the town council. Elsewhere they were exercised by men usually chosen from outside the corporation who were alumni of its colleges. Deans of Faculty also existed at Glasgow, St Andrews, and Marischal College. These were usually notable local ministers, physicians or even professors whose political connections were also of interest to the masters who elected them. Glasgow University also possessed Visitors who were active throughout the eighteenth century. This committee was composed of the Rector, Dean and Minister of Glasgow who were empowered to audit accounts, to inquire into and settle grievances and to make rules in conformity with the foundation's charters which they could construe and enforce. Other university bodies which were directly or indirectly involved in filling professorial chairs included the Procurators of the Four Nations at King's and the *ad hoc* bodies at Glasgow and St Andrews which chose the Rectors whose votes in college meetings were sometimes crucial to the election of a professor.

The corporate structures of the colleges were generally simpler. Their heads, the principals, had wide powers of administration and the colleges' meetings attended by the masters or professors named in the charters or foundation documents, possessed even greater authority. Principals and/or masters[2] admitted men to college livings, assigned them rooms and teaching times, authorized their payment and the sums needed to equip laboratories, disciplined them for collegiate offences and exercised a general oversight of every aspect of the corporation. Again, Edinburgh was an exception to this rule because its college meetings lacked these legal powers. Only after the early 1760s did Principal William Robertson manage to assert a moral leadership of the corporation which was generally respected both by the town council and politicians of a grander sort until *c*.1780.

The colleges had other figures who were concerned with appointments even though they were not members of the corporations. At the beginning of the eighteenth century the most important of these were private patrons enjoying the right to nominate men to chairs founded by their forebears or their corporations. Before 1715 their influence was greatest at Marischal College, where the Earl Marischal appointed five of the seven professors. His rights were forfeited to the Crown in 1715 because the Earl had helped to lead the Jacobite rebellion of that year. At Marischal College the town council of Aberdeen chose the Professor of Divinity, held a virtual veto over the choice of Principal and supervised the competitive examinations held to choose the Professor of Mathematics. In 1732 Ramsay of Balmain founded a Chair of Oriental Languages to which his representatives retained rights of nomination. Neighbouring King's College was less open to outside influence since eight of its ten livings were filled either by the masters or by them and the Procurators of the Four Nations, an *ad hoc* body which they could control if they were united. The Crown had here only one regius chair and, while the Synod of Aberdeen elected the Professor of Divinity, King's was virtually a closed corporation. At St Andrews University the Kennedys of Cassillis and the Scots of Scotstarvit appointed two men while the Crown named the four masters at St Mary's College along with the other principal(s) and the Professor of Mathematics. Edinburgh had no individual private patrons but the city's lawyers had corporate rights to nominate men to fill the chairs of Humanity, Civil History, Civil Law and Scots Law. Medical men (professors, Fellows of the Royal College of Physicians and members of the Chirurgeon's Company[3]) had similar privileges but they enjoyed them not by right but by custom. Because it was economically important to the burgh to appoint only first-class men to its medical chairs the advice of doctors and surgeons had to be heeded.[4]. Glasgow had no private or institutional patrons but it frequently sought advice about appointments from lawyers, medical men and clerics. By the time of Bute's accession to power the most important outside patron in the universities and colleges was the Crown. In 1760 the Crown appointed to 21 of the 71 chairs. Its ministers could easily influence the selection of some other professors since they controlled the principal Edinburgh botanical garden and gave small salaries to some medical professors honoured by the designation of King's Physician. And, they could and did influence most other appointments in some way although they could not make them. The formal power of the Crown to appoint had often been increased by new administrations. During Bute's period of power one more regius chair was added to the system by him, the Edinburgh Professorship of Rhetoric and Belles Lettres. When he left office in 1763 the real power of the Crown to intervene in university affairs during normal times had never been greater.

The structures of the universities and colleges and the complex vesting of rights to appoint insured that every politically important group in Scotland played a role in the appointment process and that several of them could veto nominations or at least bargain effectively before appointments were made. Local magnates and gentlemen served as chancellors, rectors, assessors, procurators and so on. Their protégés would be considered for jobs and their polite and generally enlightened interests were well supported by the universities throughout the Scottish Enlightenment. Through them, through MPs and other local men of influence, all the universities but King's were usually well connected to politicians. The latter, if long in power, also generally had parties of loyal clients in the colleges who often cast their votes for men whom the politicians wished to see installed – often, but not always.

Professors, if they opposed an appointment, could make an unwelcome colleague miserable and the value of his place little more than its generally small salary which might be paid only after legal wrangling.[5] The Kirk in 1760 still enjoyed its traditional and legal right to supervise educational institutions in Scotland. Its courts had a right to inquire into the beliefs and morals of all professors who were required to subscribe to the Westminster Confession of Faith before some official or a judicatory of the Kirk. Actively engaged in the politics of clerical appointments and preferment, Scottish ministers had formal and legally guaranteed rights which, if they chose to use them, amounted to veto powers over appointments. Finally, merchants, town councillors and professional men could all expect to be consulted when some chairs were filled. In those negotiations they also affected other chairs. Such a patronage system did not work smoothly when political power in Scotland was held uncertainly by men not enjoying the full confidence of the King and his ministers in London. Throughout the period from 1746 to 1760 that confidence had generally been possessed by Bute's uncle, Archibald Campbell, 3rd Duke of Argyll, the greatest Scottish politician of the century. Bute's own achievements as a university patron[6] built upon and continued the work of the man whose political machine he inherited. Without that legacy he could certainly have made the five appointments to regius chairs which he did make before 1764 but his long-term impact upon the colleges would not have been so great, for reasons set out below. It is important then to consider briefly Argyll's contribution to Bute's success.

Bute inherited a university system full of men who shared and reflected his uncle's broad cultural interests. Argyll had been an improver and something of a virtuoso who knew more than a little about mathematics, science, medicine, history, law and the philosophy to which it was usually related. He seems to have wanted to appoint polite, accomplished and meritorious gentlemen to university chairs; generally he did so. He also managed the business of appointments to create in every school but King's a party devoted to his interests and capable of defending them. By 1760 he had shaped the colleges somewhat in his own image. As a politician, Argyll had created a political machine which was efficiently run in Edinburgh by a Court of Session judge, Andrew Fletcher of Saltoun, Lord Milton. After about 1755 both Milton and Argyll had come to rely for advice about church and university affairs upon the men who were in these years creating the new moderate party in the Kirk – John Home, Adam Ferguson, John Jardine and others connected with them.[7] By 1760 the ties of this group also ran directly to Bute through his secretary, John Home, and through Gilbert Elliot of Minto and other polite Scots gentlemen involved with affairs in London.

When Argyll died on 15 April 1761 Bute inherited his political machine. That made the transition to his regime easy. No time was lost in organizing or in battling for control. Bute did change the way the machine worked. In Edinburgh Lord Milton was retained as an adviser but he was displaced as the principal adviser by four younger men. William Mure of Caldwell, who became a Baron of the Scottish Exchequer in February 1761, was by the summer of 1761 giving advice about university affairs which carried more weight than Milton's although the older man's political skills and knowledge were still much needed.[8] At the London end, Gilbert Elliot of Minto (until August 1761) and then Bute's brother, James Stuart Mackenzie, handled patronage matters with some help from Home.[9] Where there had been formerly a leader and principal assistant there were now four men close to Bute who could assess merit but who lacked Milton's skill and long experience in the use of patronage for political ends. Each of the four had ties to Scottish intellectuals. Those of Bute and his brother ran to scientists and botanists such as Dr John Hope, Sir James Naysmith and the Reverend John Walker. Mure was a close friend of David Hume and of others in his circle. Elliot belonged to that group, too, but probably more to that of the Moderates; those men were a bit different in their interests and in their social situation since fewer were independent, landed and laymen. Bute's team was even more insistent than Argyll had been that merit and known achievements be the criteria for university appointments. Their attitude could work in the short run because they had come to power with few Scottish debts and because Argyll had operated on quite similar bases in the universities although he was not given to making self-righteous statements about his rules for negotiating university jobs. The new men did not radically change the system they inherited but they quite consciously and more openly used it for the advantage of the Moderates and the enlightened. This can be seen in the correspondence concerning the 12 appointments made between 1761 and 1764 which should be assigned to Bute and his friends.

Bute's first university appointment was effected before Argyll died in 1761 and seems to have been secured without the Duke's intervention. The chair was the Edinburgh Professorship of Botany and Materia Medica; the man appointed was Dr John Hope, an Edinburgh physician whom Bute probably had met in London during the late 1750s.[10] The chair was nominally in the gift of the town council which gave the professor a small salary and control over the Town Garden at Trinity Hospital.[11] But the chair was not really theirs to give. The Surgeons' Company had some purchase on the appointment process because the endorsement of the Surgeons meant that surgical apprentices would attend the classes and that no competing garden would be created under their auspices. The Surgeons' Company unanimously recommended John Hope on 21 January 1761.[12] The Crown also had a part to play in this appointment because it had in the past appointed Regius Professors of Botany in the city and Regius Keepers of the Royal Garden at Holyrood Palace. Should it do so again and not choose Dr Hope, the University post would perhaps not be very valuable.[13] It is not known when Lord Bute began to act on his behalf to secure the offices in the gift of the Crown but it is certain that he did so, for Hope later wrote 'It was to his Lordship I owed my office(s)'.[14] Hope's appointments in April 1761 secured his monopoly over the gardens and teaching rights and gave him £77 as Regius Professor and £50 as Regius Keeper. By 1768 the chair was worth not only £127 but more; £272 came from the Materia Medica lectures alone. It also brought fees from botany students and doubtless increased the doctor's medical practice as well.[15] Not all posts were as lucrative as this but university patronage could be as great a reward to friends as many offices in the military or civil administration. Bute, however, probably saw this appointment not in financial or political terms but in relation to his own botanical interests.

By 1760 Dr Hope was already contemplating projects in which Bute was to be deeply interested. The doctor wished to produce a *Flora Scotica* and had begun work on this project.[16] He was also keenly interested in taxonomic problems and hoped to find a more natural system of classification than Linnaeus had produced. That desire did not, however, prevent him from laying out the Edinburgh garden according to Linnaeus's system or keep him from adopting a Linnaean binomial nomenclature. By 1760 the Professor had also probably begun the anatomical and physiological investigations for which he was later known.[17] Bute had picked an unknown man but one who showed great promise and whose activities deserved the support which he continued to receive. By 1762 Hope was asking for Treasury grants to move and

consolidate the city's gardens at a site on Leith Walk. The Earl secured for him £1330 1s. 2½d., a £69 annual payment and very likely the
£25 per annum grant from the town council.[18] It is not surprising
that Hope should have remained in correspondence with his patron.
Throughout the 1760s and 1770s Sir John Hill's volumes of the 'vegitable
System' were regularly sent to Hope for transmission to the Royal College
of Physicians to which Bute had earlier given books.[19] Little remains of
this correspondence but it is obvious that Bute would have been informed of the activities of the Edinburgh botanists some of whom he
would occasionally have met.[20] That he was kept abreast of Hope's
surveying activities is clear from surviving letters of David Skene. In
1768 the same correspondence shows that Hope and the Earl were
discussing corralines, other zoophytes and problems of classification.[21]
Occasional unflattering references to Hill in Skene's papers may also
point to more lost correspondence. That some of it involved university
patronage after 1763 is also clear. In 1768 Hope tried to sell his Chair of
Materia Medica to Dr Skene. It was during those negotiations that he
seems to have taken pains to make Bute aware of this learned and
ingenious Aberdeen botanist.[22] The same letter mentions Dr Robert
Ramsay, an Edinburgh physician then in London, where he moved in
botanical circles. In 1770 the Earl probably acted along with Lords
Loudoun, Buchan and Breadalbane to secure the creation of a new
Regius Chair of Natural History at Edinburgh for this man.[23] Ramsay
had a good reputation as a naturalist and botanist but he made of his
chair a sinecure position and did nothing to improve the Museum of
the University which mouldered away under his keeping.

The Earl's first appointment was very much his own although it
would have pleased the men in his entourage and certainly Lord
Hopetoun who was also Dr Hope's patron. His second was equally
distinguished and marked out a new course of historical and legal
analysis in Scotland as distinctive as the botanical inquiries which
Hope inculcated upon a generation of Scottish medical students. It did
so because it placed in the Glasgow Regius Chair of Civil and Scots
Law John Millar, a protégé of Henry Home, Lord Kames, an exponent
of historical and sociological jurisprudence. Millar was the first man to
lecture on public law in a British university.[24] Bute appointed him but
he did not find him. That honour belonged to Kames, Adam Smith and
other members of the Glasgow faculty. Because the previous incumbent
of the chair had long been ill, recommendations about his successor
had doubtless been received by Bute before 2 June 1761 when the
Professor died. On the following day the faculty wrote Bute requesting
that Millar be appointed.[25] The college wanted a bright lawyer who

would make his career in the lecture hall and not as an advocate who
would seek fame and fortune at the bar or on the bench. In Millar they
found such a man, one whom Bute was happy to support. Indeed, he
wrote to them on 10 June 1761:

> the present opportunity of supporting the application of so many respect-
> able personages I embrace with real pleasure; & I hope in a few days to
> transmit the Royal Nomination, which from the Character I have seen
> drawn of Mr Millar, cannot fail to do Honor to our Young Sovereign from
> whose Parental Eye the University of Glasgow is not concealed.[26]

The King's confidence in Bute had made quick work of this business
but Bute's judgment had been determined by the Glasgow professors
and probably such lawyers as Kames, Baron Mure and others in their
Edinburgh set.

About a month after Bute secured Millar's chair he got to make
another appointment at Glasgow. The aged Principal, Neil Campbell,
died on 22 June 1761 after a long illness during which many of his
duties had been carried out by the Professor of Divinity, William
Leechman, who was then also Vice-Rector. This post was important
for the management of the Kirk. It was also a well-paid place reserved
for a worthy cleric in a church whose livings were not rich and where
pluralism was not much practised. Numerous candidates had for some
time been angling to succeed Campbell. Among them were Patrick
Cuming, Alexander Carlyle, William Ruat and William Leechman.
The strongest claim was Cuming's. He had served Argyll for many
years as an adviser and manager of clerical business. He claimed the
post had been promised to him. Two days after Campbell's death Lord
Milton wrote to Gilbert Elliot reminding the Earl of this obligation:

> It was the intention of the Late Duke of Argyle to give upon Principal
> Campbell's Death his Principality & Chaplaincy to Mr Cuming one of the
> Ministers of Ed[r] who upon obtaining that place should give up his church
> & his office of Professor of Church History [in Edinburgh University] the
> salary of which is a Hundred pounds a year in the gift of the Crown and
> for life. If the Crown does not dispose of the Principality in thirty days
> after the death it falls into the hands of the College. I know Mr Cuming
> was always a favourite of the Duke of Argyle was trusted by him and will
> always be faithful to the Earl of Bute.[27]

To have given Cuming his reward would seem to have been normal,
decent and good politics since it would have allowed three other men to
be promoted – one to Cuming's chair, another to his Edinburgh parish
and a third to Campbell's chaplaincy. It would also have provided a
decent place of retirement for one whose advice was no longer wanted

or needed. This was not done for reasons easily found. As a Professor of Ecclesiastical History, Patrick Cuming had been old-fashioned and a near sinecurist. At age 65 he was hardly likely to become a vigorous Principal. Moreover, he had throughout the latter 1750s been opposed to the ecclesiastical policies of Bute's Moderate friends. Promoting him would have sent wrong signals to the Kirk while giving the chair to a Moderate would have made clear Bute's own attitudes about church politics.[28] The post would go to one of the other three contenders.

Carlyle's pretensions were slight. He was a clubbable man who was to play a considerable role in church affairs but he was no scholar, no deep divine or great preacher. He had small and mostly anonymous accomplishments.[29] Among them were pamphlets defending John Home's *Douglas* which had caused a scandal among many clerics who believed ministers should neither write nor act in nor go to plays. Carlyle's role in the *Douglas* furore would have made his appointment objectionable even though he had the support of the Buccleuch interest then managed by Charles Townshend, stepfather to the 3rd Duke of Buccleuch.[30] Bute probably dismissed Carlyle's application for these reasons.

William Ruat's case was little better. He was a Moderate and a kinsman, friend and nominee of Baron Mure who no doubt wished to be seen to have some importance in the giving of places. Ruat was also an absentee Professor of Ecclesiastical History, away from Glasgow without leave as tutor to Lord Hopetoun's son. He was to be deprived of his chair on 26 November 1761;[31] his appointment would have ended his difficulties with his colleagues but it would not have been a brilliant one. On 2 July 1761 Bute sent Mure his opinion of Ruat's nomination which the Baron had submitted:

> One of [the recommendations] seems made *par manière d'acquit* because he was your relation. You might save yourself trouble in such cases, by assuring the person at once, that tho Ld Bute has the greatest friendship for you, he in things of public concern will neither regard your relation, nor his own one minute, but turn his thoughts to a worthy subject.[32]

The 'worthy subject' was William Leechman. Moderate in his views, he had proven to be an able teacher. He had published a number of sermons, a short essay on 'The Character of a Minister' (1740, 1741) and a life of Francis Hutcheson prefixed to an edition of Hutcheson's *System of Moral Philosophy* (1755) which he had seen through the press. Leechman was known to be a forceful administrator and had the added virtue of being personally connected to and also recommended by Baron Mure whose tutor he had been. On the day Bute wrote to the

Baron, who had lukewarmly supported Leechman's pretensions, Elliot wrote to Lord Milton:

> But as Mr. Leechman has acted for many years in the University of Glasgow as Professor of Divinity with the greatest Character for Learning, Virtue & Piety & as this Gentleman has now applied to be Principal, his health in some sort disabling him to perform the functions of his former profession, His Lordship thinks it incumbent upon him to recommend Mr Leechman to his Majesty on this occasion.[33]

On 6 July 1761 Leechman was appointed, giving Bute's friends a powerful voice both at Glasgow and in the Kirk.

Throughout the period in which these chairs were being filled another Regius Professorship was being created at Edinburgh for Hugh Blair, the unsalaried Professor of Rhetoric and Belles Lettres. The idea of founding such a chair went back at least to 1756 when John Home, now Bute's secretary, had tried to promote the creation of a chair 'of Eloquence' to be filled by Adam Ferguson.[34] Ferguson had been taken care of but Blair, who began to give rhetoric lectures in 1759, had not been. Home, Blair, Ferguson and Gilbert Elliot were all members of the Select Society which in 1754 had been founded to provide a place in which members could practise public speaking on important and current topics. Its origins were thus intertwined with the feelings which had led Lord Kames and others since 1748 to sponsor extra-mural lectures on rhetoric and *belles lettres*, lectures given by Adam Smith, Robert Watson, Thomas Blacklock and now by Blair.[35] While these lectures were somewhat theoretical, they had the practical aim of polishing the English diction and style used by Scots who habitually spoke their own Lowland dialect rather than standard English. To promote the latter was to promote polite letters and to sharpen the skills of men committed to the Union of Scotland and England. These commitments in 1762 and 1763 were made even clearer when Thomas Sheridan was invited to Edinburgh by a subsidiary of the Select Society to give public lectures on elocution.[36] The promotion of Blair's chair thus related to a programme of cultural improvement with political overtones. Bute could be expected to approve and sympathize with the old aims of his secretary who was also Blair's friend. The town council of Edinburgh created a Chair of Rhetoric for Blair on 27 June 1760[37] but his friends wanted more.

By April 1761 Elliot, Blair, Home, John Jardine and Robertson were again discussing a matter they had mulled over before.[38] On 2 August 1761 John Home proposed to Lord Milton that a salaried place be made for Blair.[39] By the end of August it had been decided that this should be a regius professorship. Bute had undertaken to secure the necessary grants.[40] Ironing out the details took some time but Blair was eventually given his warrant as Regius Professor on 7 April 1762 and on his own terms. Bute's interest had been increased in a perfectly traditional way since most of the Regius Chairs created during the eighteenth century seem to have been founded to reward supporters and to increase a political interest in one or other of the corporations. Blair's appointment provided for a useful friend who was an able seconder of the policies of William Robertson whose appointment as Principal of Edinburgh was the next move made by Bute and his friends on the university scene.

Nominally the right to appoint a principal of Edinburgh University was vested in the town council but this body always knew on which side its bread was buttered. On 18 February 1762 Baron Mure informed the Earl that the Council's right 'will make no difference with regard to the disposal of the place . . . It will be equally as your Lordship shall direct'. Comforting though that message was it is also revealing that Bute's men did not initially know who had the rights to appoint.[41] They clearly had been proceeding without Lord Milton's advice but they were to find it helpful before they finished because this appointment could not be made in London but required the manipulation of the town council. First, they had to pick a candidate.

During the illness of Principal John Gowdie a number of men had been drumming up support. When he died on 19 February 1762 there were seven in the field. Hugh Blair's candidacy was not serious since there were plans afoot to provide for him.[42] John Jardine, the son-in-law of Lord Provost George Drummond, refused in the end to stand, throwing his considerable influence behind William Robertson.[43] George Wishart offered to exchange his Clerkship of the General Assembly for the Principality which had been earlier held by his father and brother. Nothing came of that offer.[44] Daniel MacQueen, the high-flying candidate backed by Baillie Stewart, the Reverend John Erskine and Professor George Stewart, recognized that his cause was hopeless and did not make a run even though he was a distant kinsman of the Earl. His support also went to Robertson who was Erskine's colleague at Greyfriars' Church.[45] That left two other serious contenders: Adam Ferguson and Patrick Cuming. Ferguson was initially supported by Lord Milton, whom he had served as a secretary and whose sons he had tutored, and by John Home.[46] Neither man prevailed. Bute explained to Milton on 27 February 1762 that he had

'several months ago laid before the King, for a favorite undertaking, in which Dr. Robertson was to be employ'd, a project which does not leave me at liberty at present to offer my assistance to procure that office for any person but Him ... Dr Robertson is the Person I wish may succeed to the vacancy'.

Milton was to make the necessary arrangements.[47] That left only Patrick Cuming who had, like Ferguson, applied for the job the day Gowdie died.[48] It was now time to do something more for him since he could not have the Principal's Chair which came to Robertson on 10 March 1762.

Cuming's claims to patronage had probably been recognized in 1761 when his son Patrick was made Professor of Oriental Languages at Glasgow. Again, this chair was not in the gift of the Crown but was filled by the masters. They had not appointed the younger Cuming when he sought the professorship in the spring of 1761.[49] At that time Robert Trail, a friend of Lord Deskford, was elected over the objections of Principal Leechman and other professors.[50] In September 1761 Trail was promoted to the Chair of Divinity, again with the backing of Lord Deskford, who sought Baron Mure's influence in the matter.[51] Since Trail was a distant relative of the Baron, he may have had help from Bute's friends as he certainly did in 1762 when he became Moderator.[52] That vacated the Chair of Oriental Languages to which Patrick Cuming now succeeded. For over 30 years he offered courses in French and Italian but was not remarkable for the teaching of Hebrew.[53] Probably many believed the elder Cuming had been adequately paid off and that Bute could safely ignore his uncle's promises of a principality to this man. In the end he chose to pay the debt, but not as Cuming wished. Throughout the spring of 1762 the elder Cuming seems to have haggled with Lord Milton. In March he promised to resign his Chair if his eldest son Robert were allowed to succeed to it. This arrangement was probably accepted with reluctance in London but by 22 May 1762 Robert Cuming's commission as Regius Professor of Ecclesiastical History had been prepared.[54] In Edinburgh the new Principal Robertson was still opposing this appointment as late as 12 August 1762. What was worse, he was casting up to Elliot words which sounded much like the Earl's. Robertson promised to give, and said he gave, honest evaluations and recommended only the fit.[55] Bute in this case was prepared to accept a man Robertson thought a dull incompetent. Perhaps he was also just a bit suspicious because the man Principal Robertson recommended, the Reverend John Drysdale, was Robertson's own relative.

The Bute interest at Glasgow was strengthened again in 1762 when the absent William Ruat was replaced. On 27 October 1761 the Earl had wanted Ruat's place declared vacant. A month later (26 November) the Faculty deposed him.[56] Three candidates immediately appeared to seek a post again in the gift of the Crown. Bute's opinion was made known to the professors through Lord Erroll, who in 1761 had been chosen as Rector. The Earls would be for 'the man who is recommended as the fittest for filling the Place properly'.[57] The masters recommended James Oswald, a common-sense philosopher but not a Moderate.[58] Robert Spens was a Moderate but his backing did not come from the heart of this Edinburgh-based clique.[59] The post went in June 1762 to Alexander Carlyle's cousin, William Wight.[60] This has sometimes been seen as just a bit of jobbery but it probably involved a real difference of opinion about what the historian ought to teach. Oswald is likely to have taught Church history; Wight's principal course was a secular Western civilization course which stressed such topics as the growth of commerce and the economic interests of Great Britain. It touched upon the relation of these to manners and was exactly the sort of course the *literati* could be expected to approve.[61] Bute's endorsement of their man added a new subject to the Glasgow curriculum and in later years a conservative voice which deliberately tried to counter the Foxite Whiggism of John Millar.

One other complex appointment deal was sanctioned by Bute and his friends before the Earl left office in 1763. This was an Edinburgh shuffle designed to remove from the Chair of Moral Philosophy James Balfour, a near sinecurist more interested in income than in teaching. Balfour, already Sheriff Substitute of Edinburgh, was to get a better judicial post. His place would then be filled by Adam Ferguson, who held the Professorship of Natural Philosophy. That job was to go to James Russel, an eminent Edinburgh surgeon known for his mechanical abilities and his skill as an experimenter. Plans for such a shuffle went back at least to 1756. By 1761 Balfour was willing to move but he demanded that Bute secure for him the Edinburgh Sheriff Depute's post then held by Lord Torphichen. Negotiations dragged on through 1761, 1762 and 1763, with Balfour's greed the real obstacle to a settlement. Finally in 1764 a deal was struck with the details worked out by Stuart Mackenzie. Balfour got the sinecure Chair of Public Law worth about £300 a year but did not receive an honourable and lucrative law post until 1779.[62]

Bute's success in gaining these appointments depended upon his ability to secure regius chairs and to manipulate elections to others. Doing this he had been able to strengthen the interests he had inherited at both Glasgow and Edinburgh universities. By 1764, seven of the 19 men teaching at the latter had come by their jobs with his support or that of his brother. When other friends of the *literati* and the Moderates are added to this list it is clear that the *Senatus*[63] would be controlled by these men for a long time. The same was true at Glasgow where five of 13 men owed their jobs to Bute. Recommendations to the town council of Edinburgh, to the Crown, and appointments made by the Glasgow faculty would long reflect the Earl's regard for merit. And they would continue to find it in the studies, ideas and values of those whom he had preferred. The Earl's retirement from office in 1763 also did not mean the end of the influence of those whom he had employed. Baron Mure, Gilbert Elliot, James Stuart Mackenzie, Erroll and other gentlemen of his connection continued to exercise influence in London. During the long period of ministerial instability following 1760, these men could be and were disproportionately influential because there were no strong and capable managers of Scottish patronage until Henry Dundas secured this function in *c.*1780. Until then, Bute's appointees at these two universities exercised a great deal of influence in the Church and colleges because they possessed in the Moderate Party the only real political machine left in Scotland by 1765. Their success can be seen not only at the two largest universities but also at St Andrews where Bute himself had not been able to fill any positions.

At St Andrews there already existed a nucleus of Moderate professors by 1760. Over the next 20 years most of the vacancies in the two colleges there were to be filled upon the recommendation of men whom Bute had placed or those of their friends among the *literati*. Between 1765 and 1787 the latter were to be greatly aided by Robertson's friend Thomas Hay, 9th Earl of Kinnoull who became the University's Chancellor in 1765. Seventeen men were installed during those years. Thirteen received support from him or at least one other known Moderate leader. Kinnoull's patronage policies much resembled Bute's in their attention to and definition of merit.[64] He also seems to have resisted the nepotism which overtook St Andrews during the regime of its next Chancellor, Henry Dundas (1788–1811).

Lord Bute had, it seems, no impact upon King's College and University. No deaths there gave him opportunities to interfere and the loyalties of the ten professors were neither to him nor his friends.[65] Marischal College, however, presents a very different case. In 1760 the professors were totally loyal to Argyll, whose influence had secured the places of most of them. Argyll also served the College as *de facto* Chancellor although he lacked a legal claim to this title which is sometimes bestowed upon him.[66] This is not without interest because in 1761 Lord Bute was elected to 'succeed' his uncle as Chancellor of the University. Thomas Gordon, a Regent at King's College, described this curious business in a polemical essay written *c.*1786:

This high university office remained unfilled until some time after the death of the Earl of Ilay [Argyll died on 15 April 1761], who, notwithstanding his declining the acceptance & acting [of the Chancellorship of King's College in 1761], yet always had this among his titles – Chancellor of the University of Aberdeen. Nothing can equal the effrontery of Members of the Marischal College, who pretend that the E. of Ilay was Chancellor of their supposed University &, as is informed, to induce Lord Bute to accept the office of Chancellor of the Marischal College, they set forth, that his Uncle Archibald Earl of Ilay had accepted the nomination to the said office of Chancellor.[67]

There is evidence to support Gordon's belief about Ilay's title but less to show that in 1761 the Masters knew that Argyll had never been Chancellor and could not be elected by them without permission from the Crown to whom the right of election had apparently reverted.[68] Given Bute's relationship to George III it would have made little difference. The professors chose a protector and they chose well. Bute as Chancellor of Marischal College left his mark in three areas. He changed the way in which appointments were managed; he promoted science within the corporation; and he nursed schemes of union with King's College which he lacked the power to bring about.

Between 1761 and Lord Bute's death on 11 March 1792, 13 men were chosen to fill professorships in the University or College. Four were made by the town council and two more by the professors.[69] The other seven were Regius appointments with the recommendations to the Secretary of State and later to the Home Secretary normally going through the Chancellor, who could oppose them or refuse to give them in if he chose to do so. Bute's policy regarding his recommendations was quite different from that of his uncle. Argyll had allowed the town council of Aberdeen a great deal of say about appointments. The consequence of this had been the placement of burgesses' sons and nephews whose relatives helped Argyll manage burgh politics to the advantage of his party. These university appointments were of a generally high standard but they were unmistakably linked to parliamentary politics. By the time Lord Bute got to make his first professorial recommendation in 1771, he had long ceased to be greatly concerned with elections in the North-East. Instead of allowing the town council to nominate a man he gave this privilege to the professors whom he no doubt regarded as better judges of academic talent.[70] This he continued to do. In 1788 he won a final tussle with the council when Henry Dundas and Lord Sydney informed the magistrates 'that the respect due to the Earl of Bute both as Chancellor of the University, and as a munificent Patron of learning, was such, that the Person recommended by him would undoubtedly have the preference'.[71] From other sources it seems clear that the condition under which the professorial recommendation would be accepted by the Earl was unanimity.[72] This protected him from unwanted challenges to his authority and maximized the influence of the professors.

Bute clearly preferred the opinion of polite and learned men over that of practical businessmen. One also suspects that the professors were shrewd enough to recommend to him candidates in whom he would be interested. Five of the seven men whom he presumably nominated to the Crown were scientists of somewhat more than local note. George Skene (1775) seems to have been a good naturalist and he certainly expected Bute to take an interest in his career.[73] Patrick Copland (1775) was an astronomer who also acted as an industrial consultant, ran classes for artisans and promoted technological development in the Aberdeen area.[74] By 1800 he was equally well known in London. Robert Hamilton (1779), an amateur botanist, applied his mathematical skills not only to local insurance schemes but also to taxation.[75] William Morgan (1788) brought to Aberdeen from the West Indies a valuable natural history museum whose purchase price seems to have exceeded £300.[76] When he died he was replaced by James Beattie II (1788), a naturalist who discovered several new species of Scottish plants.[77] Marischal College had long paid particular attention to the sciences;[78] Bute, as its Chancellor, clearly encouraged this development. While he allowed two of Professor James Beattie's relatives to be appointed, they were also men who had already taught satisfactorily. James Hay Beattie, the poet's son, was also keenly interested in history and might have produced something of interest had he not died in 1790. The other man appointed during Bute's tenure, John Stuart (1781), was a notable antiquary.

To appreciate Bute's record, it should be contrasted with that of Henry Dundas at St Andrews or with the one compiled by the 4th Duke of Gordon at King's College after 1793. Those were characterized by the appointment not of men of distinction but of some political usefulness. When Bute died the Chancellors who followed him again allowed Marischal College patronage to be used by Dundas for the management of the burgh politics.[79]

References to the Earl as a patron of science were certainly justified by other aspects of his record in Aberdeen. The professors and town fathers had long been interested in having medicine taught in the city. In 1780 abortive efforts at Marischal College to create a botanical garden were undoubtedly related to this dream.[80] A year later, and again in 1783, Bute seems to have promised to contribute a medical library to the College. In 1786 1,300 volumes (about 250 titles) were sent north from Luton.[81] It was a magnificent present which included incunabula, as well as many sixteenth-, seventeenth- and eighteenth-century works. When medical teaching began in Aberdeen a few years later it was to be based largely on Marischal College.[82] The College was not unappreciative and asked Sir William Fordyce to wait upon Bute in London to convey its thanks.[83]

The Earl's generosity touched instruction in the arts classes, too. By 1764 the College had founded a museum to aid in the teaching of civil and natural history.[84] Bute seems to have made donations to this and promised additions to it in 1784.[85] He was more clearly generous to Patrick Copland, the Professor of Natural Philosophy, who in 1780 began a fund drive to improve the College Observatory and to furnish it more completely. Bute gave two telescopes, one an 'Equatorial', and some other instruments of the best quality.[86] Given the size and splendour of the Earl's own collection of instruments, these gifts were perhaps not wonderful, but they certainly were appreciated by a college which lacked such telescopes. In financial terms they also represented a contribution of well over £500.

The other great favour which Lord Bute did for the College was to give support to schemes which would have amalgamated the King's and Marischal Colleges. Proposals for such a union had been discussed in 1770–2 and 1784–8.[87] They were primarily pushed by Marischal College professors who in each case stood to gain most from the contemplated union.[88] It is clear that Bute backed the plans and almost certain that he would have retained his Chancellorship in the reorganized university.[89] Although he had been willing to bring 'into Parliament a Bill for uniting the Colleges' in 1770–2, he was probably not greatly concerned in this scheme since he did not know in 1784 why it had failed.[90] Perhaps his professors had felt embarrassed to tell him that the men at King's College believed that their Marischal College counterparts and perhaps Bute himself were bamboozling them into a scheme not in the end to their advantage and not in the end requiring their full and explicit consent.[91] The 1784–8 proposals were to founder on the same objections. It is slightly ironic that union schemes were revived in 1784 by Bute's query about the failure of the plans made in the 1770s.

During the summer of 1784 Patrick Copland went to London where he paid a visit to the Chancellor. In conversation Bute was told Copland's version of why the plan to join the two small universities only a mile apart had failed.[92] This seems to have elicited from Bute comments which showed that he would still support such a union and, more interestingly, a suggestion about how it could be accomplished. The Earl had speculated that the union might be accomplished by a Royal or Parliamentary Visitation Commission empowered, as they usually had been, to regulate and order the affairs of the bodies visited. This may have been a casual remark not deeply considered but Copland was obviously struck with it. When he had returned to Aberdeen he reported his conversation to his colleagues who quietly mulled over the ideas until Copland again visited London and Lord Bute in the summer of 1785.[93] On this occasion it seems that he discussed the unification of the colleges by a Visitation Commission not only with Bute but with others whom he chose not to mention – probably James Stuart Mackenzie and Sir William Fordyce.[94] On his return to Aberdeen he again mulled over these matters with his colleagues and he also informed Professor William Ogilvie and Principal John Chalmers of King's College of Bute's renewed interest in the union of the colleges.[95] He did not tell either of them of the proposal for a visitation. Not long after his return the Marischal College faculty held a meeting at which

> they unanimously resolved that such of the gentlemen of King's College, as had not been already informed of the scheme [of union] should be as soon as possible, and of the encouragement we had to hope that it would meet with support from persons of rank, when application should be made to Parliament, and for this purpose most of those present undertook to open the matter to some or other of the Members of that College, who were all named, that none might be forgotten ... The only thing which we agreed not to mention was that a Visitation had been suggested, in case of obstacles, otherwise unsurmountable.[96]

The meeting probably also decided not to impugn the motives of the opponents to the plan, a decision to which they could not in the long run adhere either privately or publicly. In fact, it broke down shortly thereafter at the annual convivial dinner held by the King's and Marischal College professors each autumn before the beginning of term. It did so because the King's faculty members had already got wind of what was going on.

Some days before the dinner Dr George Skene seems to have told one or more of the King's men of Bute's interest.[97] By the time the professors all met, third-hand rumours had given the King's professors worse news: Bute 'was to procure a Visitation: that he had already settled the matter with the Ministry, and that his brother Mr. Stuart McKenzie was to be the Visitor'.[98] Exaggerated as the rumour was, it could and did revive fears about a disadvantageous and forced union which the events of 1770–2 tended to confirm. Knowing that Marischal College had met to discuss all this some time before, but not knowing what had been decided, only added to the worries and anger which some King's professors brought to the dinner meant to be convivial. This it was not.

King's College men were again told in general terms that union had been discussed in London and that it would have support. They were not told of the visitation plans and they were denied further information on the grounds that private conversations should remain private and collegiate business remain closed to outsiders.[99] King's Professors Gordon, Gerard and Leslie seem to have taken and given offence which, their opponents later noted, 'shewed us, that measures had been concerted for opposing us'.[100] In the end matters were smoothed over by the King's Sub-Principal, Roderick McLeod, who said everyone was really for a union which he toasted.[101] Some days later Professors Thomas Gordon and Alexander Gerard waited upon Principal George Campbell of Marischal College, demanding to see all correspondence which had or might in the future pass between Bute and his College. Principal Campbell promised only to put their demands before the College meeting; he could have done no more. Gerard said this was unacceptable. He and Gordon left 'at freedom to take their own measures'. What they did was to write directly to Lord Bute.[102]

Principal Chalmers's letter to Bute asked if he was indeed backing the union plans which it gave him reasons to abandon. Signed by only seven of the King's faculty, it also indicated that unanimity did not exist on this issue at that College.[103] Bute probably already knew this. Principal Campbell had either already written or shortly thereafter was to inform him of what had transpired.[104] He asked for continued support for the visitation and offered to find more locally by getting up

> a Petition for that purpose to be laid before his Majesty (if this should be a proper means), signed not only by all the Members of our University, & by two or three others,[105] but further strengthened, as we flatter ourselves, by the names of several Noblemen & Gentlemen, who from their connection with this Country, are interested in the success of the scheme, and have already honoured it with their approbation.

He went on to name the Duke of Gordon and his uncle, Lord Adam Gordon, who, he wrote, 'from a thorough conviction of its utility have offered their good offices, if there should be occasion in advancing any measure your Lp may judge necessary for carrying the plan into execution'. Campbell was not only pointing to parliamentary support but he probably believed he was naming at least one visitor. The letter also impugned the motives of his adversaries before closing in a way meant to involve Bute more deeply in the College's business:

We therefore only wait for your Lordship's advice and that you may be possessed of any necessary information on the subject I have the honour to inclose for your Lordship's revisal & correction the general outlines of the Plans of Union attempted in 1755, and in 1770, together with such alterations & improvements as have at this time been suggested to us by the Members of either University.[106]

Bute received these letters sometime in the autumn of 1785. He made no reply to Chalmers but continued to support Marischal College proposals and doubtless gave advice about the petition which Campbell wished to circulate.[107]

During the winter and spring of 1785–6 the two camps gathered support. By 5 June 1786 Bute, James Stuart Mackenzie and Sir William Fordyce had met to draw up a petition to the King.[108] Twenty-four days later this had been approved by Baron Cosmo Gordon, the Marischal College Rector, whose cousin, the 4th Duke of Gordon, was now known to support the union.[109] With their approval a plan of Union was 'now respectfully submitted' by Patrick Copland to Henry Dundas who was told that it was supported unanimously by the men of Marischal College and by 'some Professors of Kings College'. The latter included James Dunbar and William Ogilvie who is said to have drafted the petition. Dundas was also informed that a petition for a Royal Visitation was being prepared and his support for this was solicited.[110] By then Dundas had probably been approached by the Duke of Gordon, Dr James Dunbar, Dr George Skene and Sir William Fordyce who was to give the petition to Lord Sydney, the Home Secretary. It had been decided that he, not Bute, should present the petition; Bute was a party to the cause and would benefit from its success because he would remain Chancellor. Fordyce, in explaining all that to George Skene on 6 June 1786, had also noted that the petition had the Chancellor's 'most heartily approbation'.[111] Everyone involved should have paid more attention to the cautious reply made by Dundas on 12 July 1786: 'Give me leave only to observe that unless there is a general Concurrence of opinion among yourselves, the objection ag^t Innovation will naturally have the advantage in any discussion which the subject may undergo before His Majesty's Servants'.[112]

From mid-July 1786[113] until well into the following year Marischal College professors circulated in Scotland and England their printed plan of union along with letters asking for support for their petition. Each seems to have contained a reference to Bute's adherence to the scheme, like that sent to the Earl of Kintore on 17 July 1786:

The measure has been recommended to us by our Chancellor, the Earl of Bute, who is pleased to interest himself very warmly in the matter and who has little doubt of the success of such an application, especially when supported by the voice of the Principal Noblemen and Gentlemen of the North of Scotland, who have always favoured such a Scheme, and we have every reason to believe will still honour it with their approbation.[114]

By September support for the plan and petition had been indicated by many gentlemen in the northern counties, by the town councils of Aberdeen, Banff, Elgin, Forres, Nairn and Wick, by a few presbyteries and by some pamphleteers.[115] As this support crested, Sydney was approached late in August by Sir William Fordyce who submitted the petition for a Royal Visitation and carried a verbal message from Bute indicating his approval of the projected union and of the propriety of such a Visitation to bring it about.[116] Dundas was not convinced and Sydney would not accept the petition as it stood.[117] The opposition had been busy as well.

Principal Chalmers had undoubtedly looked about for allies and found a few. One was Lord Fife who controlled a sizeable electoral interest in the North-East and who had bought from King's College superiorities which had extended his influence. Visitors might well inquire into this and other dubious transactions which had enriched the sitting professors at King's by alienating the property of the corporation.[118] When Fife received his letter from Marischal College he refused to sign its petition.[119] Two days later, on 25 July 1786, Principal Chalmers 'cast himself' on the 'goodness' of Lord Sydney to whom he complained about the unfairness of the way in which Marischal College was proceeding and of the illegality of tampering with property rights and chartered liberties. Visitors could reform but they ought not to abolish or void regulations they were meant to enforce. Behind his letter were the ideas expressed by Gordon and Gerard in 1785 and subsequently by pamphleteers. Chalmers modestly asked only for a hearing 'before the desire of the petition be granted'.[120] The opposition had also engaged an Edinburgh Writer to the Signet who was to set out the legal case against a Visitation. They very sensibly chose William Tytler, an antiquary whose son was friendly with Dundas.[121] He seems to have done his work skilfully. The Marischal College agent, Walter Ross, reported late in August that, although Dundas was sympathetic and would please the Duchess of Gordon, the idea of a Visitation bothered him as a lawyer while the King's claims about property and patronage rights also presented obstacles.[122] He would also have found Fife's action interesting. It was that which had brought into play the Duchess of Gordon who responded to a request from Patrick Copland to write to Dundas. She seems to have lobbied him and Lord Sydney and to have reported the progress of the petition drive to Bute and his brother. That Dundas was still unmoved showed that King's had made a legal and political case even though it was losing the paper war carried on in the Press.[123]

Throughout the autumn of 1786 the opposing lawyers prepared their cases aided by professors who searched for precedents. Both sides probably expected to appeal to the House of Lords. Bute was still eager to have a petition for a Royal Visitation presented and he helped to rework a draft sent to him by Walter Ross before 12 September 1786.[124] This the Earl was to give in to Dundas but again its presentation was delayed by Dundas's doubts and demands for more information. Bute's reaction to all that is clearly recorded in a letter to Sir William Fordyce written on 15 September. 'I still remain of the same opinion relative to this business'. He had supported and did support a visitation, for which he found precedents, as a means of ascertaining facts. He was 'sorry to find in one of these letters [sent to him] that Mr Dundas is of another opinion' even though 'His arguments appear to me refuted by three Visitations'. Bute still hoped that more or plainer 'facts may probably induce that Gentleman to change His Opinions, & this should certainly be attempted, for I see little hopes of success in any application for a Visitation when any of those whose opinion His Majesty confides in, hesitate about his power to grant it'.[125] Dundas's doubts would not have been lessened by the letter sent to him on 27 September by Principal Chalmers. The Principal again raised the issues concerning property rights, corporate and chartered rights, and he again asked for a formal hearing before any action was taken. Accompanying his letter was a longer printed pamphlet by Thomas Gordon and Alexander Gerard. This set out more reasons not to unite the colleges.[126] While the lawyers and antiquaries ground away, time was running against Bute and his friends. Sometime in late September or early October the Duke of Gordon suggested to Professor Thomas Gordon 'the measure of Arbitration'. He was rebuffed politely but firmly, being told 'arbitration in this case is incompetent, & *ultra vires*'.[127] In October Henry Dundas finally was presented with the Marischal College case and petition.[128] Rather than acting on it and presenting it to the Ministry, he delayed until late in January or February 1787 and then referred it to the Lord Advocate and Lord Justice Clerk for their opinions.[129] By then both sides expected some decision since they had retained counsel for a parliamentary hearing. But in the spring of 1787 the Marischal College professors gave up. They refused to get the opinion of the Lord Advocate and Lord Justice Clerk. They would not sign the final petition prepared for them by Walter Ross. They had boggled earlier at Ross's bill and they were not willing to pay more than the £14 the affair had cost each of them – the equivalent of an Aberdeen labourer's yearly income.[130] Bute's reaction to the outcome is not known but he too must have recognized that this was an uncertain business which Dundas did not favour.[131]

The union affair and the appointments made in 1788 ended Bute's important involvement with Marischal College. His activity, however, probably had a further impact upon King's. The union debates of 1770–2 and 1784–7 came at times when King's lacked a Chancellor. It is doubtful that the King's professors could have found a satisfactory Chancellor who would not have sold them out as at least one of their Rectors, Sir William Forbes, was prepared to do.[132] After the Earl's death, when their choice would not embarrass him, they chose as their Chancellor the one prominent nobleman who had been for arbitrating their disagreements – the 4th Duke of Gordon. By promoting the union issue Bute had perhaps inadvertently saddled King's with a meddlesome man who was to put political loyalties above the values of politeness, learning, innovation and faculty independence which Lord Bute had encouraged at Marischal. The union affair had also made it clear that Bute lacked the influence to bring about a needed reform. If this and other favours were to be obtained in the future, they would have to be sought from Henry Dundas and would be pursued by younger and more energetic men whom the affair had introduced into the Marischal College business. After 1793 this fact was recognized by the election of Chancellors and rectors at both King's and Marischal who were clearly in the Dundas political machine.

In some respects Bute's influence upon the Scottish colleges was salutary but short-lived. His rigid insistence that the best man get the job came quickly to seem outmoded and as quixotic as some of his friends must have found it. But then other politicians who came after him did not inherit a well-functioning political machine active in both state and Church. They could be neither as high-minded nor, as was the case with Henry Dundas after 1785, were they willing to be. To promote twice a union between two colleges a mile apart now seems very sensible but neither Bute nor a later Parliamentary Visitation in 1826 were able to bring it about. It was to come in 1859. In these matters Bute made no lasting impact on the Scottish universities. For his legacy we must look elsewhere.

The Earl's gifts of books and instruments at Aberdeen were important to its development as a centre of practical astronomy and scientific and medical education. Similarly, his contribution to the teaching museum of John Walker, after 1778 the Edinburgh Professor of Natural History, were also of use to the first man who taught geology in a British university.[133] That collection has long since vanished, as have Bute's gifts to John Hope. What has not disappeared but grown and prospered is the great Royal Botanic Garden in Edinburgh which Bute did so much to establish. His friend, John Hope, published little but taught well. His students spread through the old and new British Empires which gave them new fields for the anatomical, physiological and taxonomic inquiries which he had taught them to pursue. Hope never published a *Flora Scotica* but he, Walker and David Skene aided John Lightfoot who did so in 1778. Bute may have been mistaken in his patronage of John Hill but his Scottish protégés amply made up for that shortcoming.

Lord Bute's greatest impact upon the Scottish universities cannot be measured easily. It built upon and continued the enlightened patronage long exercised by his uncle, the 3rd Duke of Argyll. Together they endowed the Kingdom with an enlightened professoriate which turned out to be able to perpetuate its influence for nearly a generation after Bute left office in 1763. It was their appointees and protégés who established Edinburgh and Glasgow as great centres of medical education, as seats of polite learning and as the places to which botanists, chemists and those with scientific interests should resort. To a lesser extent, Bute's recommendations for chairs at Marischal College had a similar consequence. The enlightened professors who made all that possible also helped to change the outlook of the Kirk. After *c*.1760 it not only did not oppose the enlightened but sometimes even furthered their activities as was the case in its support of the natural history surveying work carried on by Bute's friend, John Walker. The divinity halls after *c*.1760 were also staffed by Moderate professors who no longer encountered the sort of clerical and collegiate opposition which their forerunners had suffered during the 1730s and 1740s. The sort of minor cultural politics played by Argyll, Bute and other gentlemen who dispensed patronage and defended their protégés may in the long run have been more significant for Scotland than anything else these men did in the British Parliament. The 20 or so men whom Bute helped to Scottish university chairs played a disproportionate role in the process of defining what Scottish culture was to become. This was probably Bute's most important political legacy and it is one directly related to his role as a dispenser of university patronage.

NOTES

I should like to thank a number of people whose comments, references to manuscripts or other aid is unnoticed in this paper. Among them are Dr Paul Bator, Professor Arthur Donovan, Dr Alexander Murdoch, Professor Richard Sher and Dr P.B. Wood who all read or heard a version of this essay. I am also grateful to Mr Colin McLaren and Dr Dorothy Johnston of the Aberdeen University Archives and especially to Jean Dalgleish, my wife, who saw the paper being written during part of our planned vacation.

1. The following two sections of this paper draw upon my unpublished study of patronage in the Scottish universities 1690–1800.

2. Masters were those professors established by the original charters who had the right to manage college affairs.

3. This became the Royal College of Surgeons of Edinburgh in 1779.

4. By the 1780s perhaps half of the students of university age studying in Edinburgh were medical students enrolled at either the University or the extra-mural school kept at Surgeons' Square. They numbered around 600, while arts students numbered about 400; law and divinity added 250 more. For the years after 1790 precise figures are given in the *Annals of Medicine*, III (1800), 537.

5. Fees and perquisites were more important sources of remuneration for most professors than were salaries; see J.B. Morrell, 'The University of Edinburgh in the late eighteenth century: its scientific eminence and academic structure', *Isis*, LXII (1971), 165. Many professors also increased their incomes by boarding aristocratic boys.

6. In 1760 it is likely that over half of the professors owed their appointments to Argyll or to his loyal supporters who could secure chairs for their friends.

7. These men have recently been the objects of study by Richard Sher, *Church and University in the Scottish Enlightenment: the Moderate Literati of Edinburgh* (Princeton, NJ, 1985).

8. Edith, Lady Haden-Guest, 'William Mure' in *The History of Parliament: The House of Commons 1754–1790*, ed. Sir Lewis Namier and John Brooke (3 vols, 1964), III 181–2. Bute to Baron Mure, 2 July 1761, in W. Mure (ed.), *Selections from the Family Papers Preserved at Caldwell* (1883), Part II(1), 127.

9. Gilbert Elliot to Andrew Fletcher, Lord Milton, 21 Apr. 1761, NLS MS 16720, f.4. Lady Haden-Guest, 'Gilbert Elliot', in Namier and Brooke, *op. cit.*, II, 390–4. That Elliot remained concerned with university patronage is borne out by numerous papers in the NLS Minto MSS. On Bute's relationship with Home see R. Sher, ch.8 of this volume.

10. For details of Hope's career see A.G. Morton, 'John Hope 1725–1786, Scottish botanist' (Edinburgh Botanic Garden Trust, 1986).

11. The history of the Chair of Botany is best given in Horn, 'Chair of Botany', EUL MS Gen. 1824/I; H.R. Fletcher and W.H. Brown, *The Royal Botanic Garden, Edinburgh 1670–1970* (1970), 38–41, 57–8.

12. Minute Books of the Royal College of Surgeons of Edinburgh, 21 January 1761, RCSL.

13. Fletcher and Brown, *op. cit.*, 58; Robert Kerr, *Memoirs of the Life, Writings and Correspondence of William Smellie* (2 vols, 1811), I, 103.

14. Hope to Lord Loudoun, 14 Jan. 1768, Loudoun MSS, Bundle 7. Hope went on, 'it is to his Lordship – the University owes the establishment of the Botanic Garden'.

15. Morton, *op. cit.*, 16; Hope to Dr David Skene, 28 Dec. 1767, David Skene MSS, MS 38.

16. Morton, *op. cit.*, 17–18. There are numerous letters in the Skene MSS

from John Ellis, Hope and the Revd
Mr John Walker (later Professor of
Natural History at Edinburgh) which
relate to the surveying, listing and
cataloguing of Scottish plants. It is of
some interest that Hope and his
friends saw themselves as following in
the footsteps of Sir Robert Sibbald
(1641–1723) whose list of Scottish
plants printed in *Scotia Illustrata*
(1684) provided their starting point.
Ellis in 1765 was 'surprised Lord
Bute does not encourage' a *Flora
Scotica* while Skene in 1768 expressed
his happiness 'in ye thoughts of a
British Herbal under ye direction of
Ld B[ute]'. John Lightfoot's *Flora
Scotica* (1778) contained information
willingly supplied to him by this
group of Scottish botanists. Ellis to
Skene, 22 Oct. 1765; Skene to Hope,
11 Apr. 1768; Hope to Skene, n.d.
[1768?], Skene MS 38. The last letter
says that Bute intended John Hill to
write 'a British Herbal or history of
English Plants with figures'.

17. Morton, *op,cit.*, 21–27, 43.
18. *Ibid.*, 11–13; see n.14.
19. Bute's gifts to the Royal College of
Physicians are noted in the Minute
Books, e.g. 27 June 1767, 2 May 1769,
7 Nov. 1769, 2 Feb. 1773, 6 Aug.
1776. Bute was made an Honorary
Fellow of the College on 3 November
1761. Another link to the Edinburgh
Scientific community came through
the Philosophical Society to which
Bute and James Stuart Mackenzie
were elected on 17 June 1762: R.L.
Emerson, 'The Philosophical Society
of Edinburgh 1748–1768', *British J. for
the History of Science*, XIV (1981), 139.
20. Among other Scottish scientists
clearly in touch with Bute were Sir
James Naysmith, Dr Robert Ramsay,
Sir Alexander Dick and almost
certainly the officers of the
Philosophical Society. See John
Walker, 'Adversaria' [*c*.1766], GUL,
Murray MS 327; Morton, *op. cit.* 13,
39; R.L. Emerson, 'The Edinburgh
Society for the Importation of Foreign
Seeds and Plants, 1764–1773',

Eighteenth Century Life, VIII (1982), 91
n.14; Ellis to Skene, 3 Dec. 1766,
Skene MS 38; Lord Morton to Bute, 8
Sept. 1764; Sir Alexander Dick to
Bute, 23 Feb. 1763; Sir John Pringle
to Bute, 25 June 1762, Bute MSS.
21. Ellis to Skene, 28 July 1768, Skene
MS 38.
22. Skene to Hope, 11 April 1768, *ibid.*
23. 'Chair of Natural History', Horn, *op.
cit.*; Kerr, *op. cit.*, II, 106–7; Hope to
Lord Loudoun, n.d. [1766 or 1767],
Loudoun MSS; 'Extracts from Lord
Buchans Diaries', Murray MS 502/
66; William Robertson to Gilbert
Elliot, 8 Feb. 1763, NLS, Minto MSS.
24. The most recent work on Millar is
David Walker's *The Scottish Jurists*
(1985), 248–266; see also M.
Ignatieff, 'John Millar and
individualism', in *Wealth and Virtue*,
ed. I. Hont and M. Ignatieff (1983),
317–43; I.S. Ross, *Lord Kames and the
Scotland of His Day* (1972), 95–97.
25. William Leechman to Bute, 3 June
1761, Bute MSS; J. Coutts, *History of
the University of Glasgow* (1909), 234–5.
26. Bute to Leechman, 10 June 1761
(copy), Leechman to Bute, 16 June
1761, Bute MSS. Leechman's reply
notes that Bute answered by the first
post which implies that he, like the
professors, had made a decision some
time earlier. There were almost
certainly other candidates. William
Ruat to Robert Simson, 10 July 1761,
GUL MS 660.
27. Andrew Fletcher, Lord Milton to
Gilbert Elliot (copy), 24 June 1761,
Saltoun Papers, NLS MS 16720, fos.
66–9. Milton had been asked by
Cuming on the same day to write this
letter. Cuming offered to give up his
chair but not the prospective
chaplaincy. Cuming to Milton, *ibid.*;
Cuming to Milton, n.d., Saltoun
Papers, NLS MS 16719, f. 167.
28. Sir Alexander Grant, *The Story of the
University of Edinburgh* (2 vols, 1884),
II, 308–9; Sher, *op. cit.*, 96–9.
29. Sher, *op. cit.*, 331–3, 156–65;
more information about Carlyle's
activities can be found in D. Raynor,

Sister Peg: a pamphlet . . . (1983),
4–8.

30. Carlyle's request was for either the
Principalship or the Chair of Oriental
Languages. Carlyle claimed that the
3rd Duke of Argyll 'had marked my
name down in his private notebook for
Principal of the College of Glasgow . . .
and had said to Andrew Fletcher
junior, to whom he showed the note,
that it would be very hard if he and I
between us could not manage that
troublesome society': *The Autobiography
of Dr Alexander Carlyle*, ed. John Hill
Burton (1910), p. 401. If Carlyle
is correct here, it shows that the
Moderates would have come to
places of power even though Bute
had not been a minister. Lord
Milton to Gilbert Elliot, 24 June
1761, Saltoun Papers, NLS MS 16720,
f. 69.

31. College Minutes, 26 Nov. 1761,
GUA.

32. Mure, *op. cit.*, 127–8. Ruat later, on 30
September 1761, thanked Mure for
trying to get the Principality for him,
ibid., 133. In the same letter the still
absent professor expressed his
disbelief in Bute's willingness to see
him removed from his post: 'I
scarcely think either his Lordship, or
the warmest friends I have in the
College seriously incline to litigate the
point, viz. that there is really no
vacancy'. The threatened legal action
was ignored.

33. Milton to Gilbert Elliot, 2 July 1761,
Saltoun Papers, NLS MS 16720, f. 72.
There was little if anything wrong
with Leechman's health. For the next
24 years he battled robustly with
various colleagues who found him
autocratic and litigious.

34. John Home to Milton, February (?)
1756, Saltoun Papers, NLS MS
16696, f. 74.

35. These developments are the subject of
a forthcoming paper by Paul Bator;
see also Wilbur Samuel Howell,
*Eighteenth-Century British Logic and
Rhetoric* (Princeton, NJ, 1971), 543–
44; Sher, *op. cit.*, 108–09, 115.

36. R.L. Emerson, 'The social
composition of enlightened Scotland:
The Select Society of Edinburgh,
1754–1764', *Studies on Voltaire and the
Eighteenth-Century*, CXIV (1973), 298–
9; Howell, *op. cit.*, 233–43. The
Edinburgh Society for Elocution still
formally existed in 1765 when a list of
its directors appeared in the *Universal
Scots Almanack*. Both it and the
Edinburgh Society, which appears
there too, seem to have lasted longer
than has generally been realized.
Hugh Blair had helped to promote
the Elocution Society which he served
as a director.

37. Alexander Morgan and Robert Kerr
Hannay (eds), *University of Edinburgh
Charters, Statutes and Acts of the Town
Council and the Senatus 1583–1858*
(1937), 177.

38. Blair to David Hume, (?) April 1761,
Hume MSS; John Jardine thanked
Gilbert Elliot, on 11 July 1761, for
securing the post for Blair, NLS,
Minto MSS. [The Minto MSS have
been catalogued and foliated since I
used them; since, however, they are
catalogued by the names of
correspondents the references can be
easily checked.] The decision on a
chair and its occupant had been made
by early July.

39. NLS MS 16720, f. 88. I am indebted
to Professor Paul Bator for this
reference.

40. Blair to Elliot, 3 Sep. 1761, NLS,
Minto MSS.

41. Mure's letter to Bute makes it clear
that the former did not know who had
the legal right to appoint the
Principal. Mure to Bute, 18 Feb.
1762, transcription in Horn, *op. cit.*
See also the accounts of this
appointment by Sher, *op. cit.*, 112–16;
Jeremy J. Cater, 'The making of
Principal Robertson in 1762', *Scottish
Historical Review*, XLIV (1970), 60–84.

42. Blair to David Hume?, before June
1762, NLS MS 3211; Sher, *op. cit.*,
116.

43. John Jardine had been a candidate
for the principalship in 1753; Lord

Provost George Drummond to Milton, 15 May 1753; John Jardine to Milton, 12 May 1753, Saltoun Papers, NLS MS 16682, f. 176; NLS MS 16683, fos. 136–7; Robertson to Elliot, 26 Feb. 1762, NLS, Minto MSS.

44. Mure, *op. cit.*, Part II (1), 248.

45. George Stewart to Milton, 20 Feb., 13 March 1762, cited in Cater, *op. cit.*, 83.

46. Milton's obvious interest in Ferguson's candidacy is testified by the numerous drafts of letters to Bute nominating him. They begin in February at the onset of Gowdie's illness and continue until after Gowdie's death; see Saltoun Papers, NLS MS 16725, fos. 127–33. John Home supported Ferguson's candidacy as early as 12 May 1761. Ferguson applied to Milton for this post on 18 Feb. 1762 and again on 19 Feb.; see Cater, *ibid.*, 81–2; Saltoun Papers, NLS MS 16724, f. 37.

47. Bute to Milton, 27 Feb. 1762, Milton to Bute (copy), 5 and 6 March 1762, Saltoun Papers, NLS MS 16726, fos. 129–30, 206–7. Bute had earlier (in 1761) considered the founding of a new history Chair for Robertson. Sher, *op. cit.*, 112.

48. Cuming to Milton, 19 Feb. 1762, Saltoun Papers, NLS MS 16723, f. 204; Cater, *ibid.*, 81. Cuming earlier had sought this Chair in 1753 when he asked for the principalship and the reversion of his Chair for his son Robert; Cuming to Milton, 12 May 1753; Saltoun Papers, NLS MS 16682, f. 114 among his competitors then had been John Jardine and William Robertson; Saltoun Papers, NLS MS 16681, f. 63; NLS MS 16682, f. 176.

49. Robert Cullen to Adam Smith, 24 June 1761, GUL Gen. 1035/135–77. Others were also recommended but the place went to Robert Trail, a protégé of Lord Deskford, who beat Alexander Carlyle who also had sought the post; William Mure, *op. cit.*, 129–30; Bute's friend the Earl of

Erroll nominated James Crombie who seems to have not been much considered; see E.C. Mossner and I.S. Ross (eds), *Correspondence of Adam Smith* (1979), 87.

50. It appears from the Glasgow Faculty Minutes that Trail's election was opposed by Leechman and thus perhaps by the men who had made Leechman Principal. Glasgow University Minutes, GUA, 5 June, 15 July, 26 Aug., 1 Sept. 1761.

51. Cuming by then had the backing of some of the Edinburgh *literati*; J.Y.T. Grieg, *The Letters of David Hume* (2 vols, 1932), I, 346.

52. If Trail was the candidate of Bute and his friends one should note David Hume's obituary for him: 'Dr Trail, he declared, is dead and now knows whether there be any truth in all those doctrines which he taught, and of which he did not believe a word while alive' (Grieg, *op. cit.*, II, 303.

53. Coutts, *op. cit.*, 231, 324.

54. George Drummond to Milton, (?) March 1762, Saltoun Papers, NLS MS 16723, f. 204; Patrick Cuming to Milton, 22 April 1762, *ibid.*, f. 206; Milton (scroll) to James Stuart Mackenzie (?), 5 March 1762, Saltoun Papers, NLS MS 16726, f. 207; Mackenzie to Milton, 22 May 1762, Saltoun Papers, NLS MS 16726; Mackenzie recorded in the patronage register among his papers at Mount Stuart that Robert Cuming had come 'in Room of His father who resigns for His Son's Benefit'. It is probably worth noting that Lord Milton found this chap not dull but 'a good man and good scholar & well qualified as he had studied Church History several years, & will have an opportunity of being perfected at the feet of Gamaliel'. Milton to Bute (scroll), Saltoun Papers, NLS MS 16726, f. 207.

55. Robertson to Elliot, 12 Aug. 1762, NLS, Minto MSS.

56. Lord Erroll to Adam Smith, 27 Oct. 1761, in Mossner and Ross, *op. cit.*,

78; College Minutes, GUA, 26 Nov. 1761.

57. College Minutes, GUA, 22 Jan. 1762; Erroll's letter to the College was dated 11 Nov. 1762; his recommendation of James Crombie came too late to be acted upon.

58. College Minutes, GUA; Coutts, *op. cit.*, 324.

59. College Minutes, 22 Jan. 1762; Henry Spens to Mure, 22 Jan. 1762 in William Mure, *op. cit.*, 140.

60. Carlyle, *op. cit.*, 445.

61. A syllabus of Wight's course was printed: 'Heads of a Course of Lectures on the Study of History given Annually by William Wight' (1767).

62. The known details of the various schemes are too extensive to list but see Sher, *op. cit.*, 117–18. Balfour was already the holder of a legal office which kept him busy but which paid poorly and lacked dignity; see Alexander Murdoch, *The People Above* (1980), 23.

63. Technically the Edinburgh faculty members had no power but after 1761 they began to act as if they had and the town council proved willing to heed them; Morgan and Hannay, *op. cit.*, 212–13, 241–58.

64. Typical of Kinnoull's statements about merit is the following which concluded his letter of 11 June 1767 to Baron Mure recommending Robert Watson for the Glasgow Chair of Greek: 'it will be always my wish that every Chair of every Professor in every University should be filled up with the ablest, the fittest and the best men', Mure, *op. cit.*, Part II(2), 110.

65. James Ogilvie, 7th Earl of Findlatter, became Chancellor of King's College and University in 1761. He was not unfriendly to Bute but neither was he honourably employed by him.

66. Ilay had apparently rejected the King's Chancellorship when it was offered to him in 1716 because his political power was waning. He may, however, have kept a sealed diploma naming him as Chancellor. If he did, and if

the Duke of Roxburghe knew he had, it is understandable that the latter should also have declined the office. Thomas Gordon, Collections Regarding King's College, 'Chancellors', AUL, Gordon MS, K 34, 5–6. Another account says Roxburghe got a diploma which had visible erasures showing Ilay's name and arms: AUL MS KC/4/4/2, f. 25. [The spelling of Ilay is that which he followed in his own correspondence.]

67. Gordon, 'Chancellors'; *Fasti Academiae Mariscallanae Aberdonensis*, II, *Officers graduates and alumni of the Marischal College and University of Aberdeen 1593–1860*, ed. P.J. Anderson (1893), 6. Thomas Gordon believed Bute's election illegal because he thought the University was not properly constituted and, because, if it were, the right of election vested in the Crown without whose consent no valid election could be held. Legal opinion in the eighteenth and nineteenth centuries did not support his view. See AUL MS K144; P.J. Anderson, 'The Catanach case', *Scottish Notes and Queries*, 1st ser. I (1888), 129–31.

68. In 1727, the Marischal College 'Rector, Principal, Professors and Masters' petitioned the King to name the five-year-old Duke of Cumberland as the University's Chancellor. Nothing came of this petition but it shows that some then believed that the nomination lay with the Crown and that the office was vacant (AUL MS M.387/9/7/2; Knight MSS, M107). Bute is unlikely to have known that his uncle had never been Chancellor.

69. I have found no evidence of Bute's involvement in these appointments, the first three of which were to the Mathematic Chair, the fourth to the Chair of Divinity and the latter two to the *pro forma* Chair of Law which merely facilitated the granting of law degrees in a body which did not teach the subject or have a law faculty.

70. There are no references in the town council Minutes or Letter Books to these appointments, a lack explained by James Beattie in a letter to Sir William Forbes, 20 Oct. 1788: 'There was a violent opposition on the part of the Magistrates and Town-Council of Aberdeen, who wanted to wrest from the College that influence in the choice of our own members, which we have been in possession of ever since Lord Bute became our Chancellor in the year 1761' (NLS MS 4796, Box 94). This had been stated earlier by Beattie in a letter to his son James Hay Beattie, 3 Aug. 1788, AUL MS 30/1.

71. James Beattie to Sir William Forbes, 20 Oct. 1788, NLS MS 4796.

72. Numerous letters from faculty members dealing with appointments make that clear.

73. The Botanical Garden was planned while he held the Chair of Natural and Civil History (1775–88); Marischal College Minute Book, 6 May 1780.

74. John S. Reid, 'Patrick Copland 1748–1822: aspects of his life and times at Marischal College', *Aberdeen University Review*, CLXXII (1984), 359–79; *idem*, 'Patrick Copland 1748–1822: connections outside the College courtyard', Aberdeen University Review, CLXXIV (1985), 226–50.

75. This is borne out by Hamilton's papers, AUL MSS 36, 451–8.

76. Morgan was probably related to Daniel William Morgan, a Royal Chaplain in 1762 who was awarded a D.D. by Marischal College. The Chaplain, it was then noted, 'is patronized by the Earl of Bute', see *Fasti Academiae Mariscallanae, op. cit.*, I: 84. Beattie to Forbes, 20 Oct., 31 Oct. 1788, NLS MS4796, f. 92; Beattie to James Hay Beattie, 19 Oct. 1787, 3 Aug. 1788, AUL MS 30/ 2; Knight MSS, M 109/433.

77. Baron Cosmo Gordon to Beattie, 24 Sep. 1788; this letter makes it clear that Beattie did not initially apply to Henry Dundas but only to Bute when he sought this place for his namesake.

78. This is treated in a forthcoming essay by P.B. Wood, 'Science and the Aberdeen Enlightenment'.

79. This happened almost immediately with the appointment of Dr William Livingstone to the Chair of Medicine in 1793. The professors had recommended their old colleague Dr George Skene; Knight MSS, M 109/ 92, p. 385. But the town council secured the post for Dr Livingston; see Alexander Allardyce to the Magistrates of Aberdeen Town Council Letter Book 13, Town House Aberdeen: George Skene to Lord Buchan, 3 Sep. 1797, NLS MS 3873, fos. 253–4.

80. Knight MSS, 109/35 and M 111/995.

81. Knight MSS, M 111/1107; 'Catalogue of medical books presented to the Library of Marischal College by John Earl of Bute 1783', AUL MS M362. The library had 43 titles in folio, 63 in quarto and 144 in octavo.

82. There is no adequate account of the Aberdeen Medical School, but see G.A.G. Mitchell, 'The story of anatomy in Aberdeen', *Aberdeen University Review*, XXVI (1938–9), 22–32; *idem*, 'The founder of the Aberdeen Medical School', *Aberdeen University Review*, XXVII (1939–40), 17–30, Bute may have played a greater role than is now thought.

83. Sir William Fordyce to My Lord [Sydney], 20 and 24 Aug. 1786 (copies), AUL MS U 558.

84. *Marischal College Minute Book 1729–1790*, 13 Dec. 1764; Knight MSS, M 111/1267. It may not be accidental that the museum was established soon after Bute came to be Chancellor.

85. Knight suggested that Bute may never have given the natural curiosities promised in 1784; see AUL M 107. If he did they would have been in the Natural History Collection purchased by James Beattie II in 1788. That consisted of 100 books, 'a good chemical apparatus' and other materials

copious enough to fill a large room. Many had been brought from the West Indies by William Morgan. James Beattie I to Sir William Forbes, 31 Oct. 1788, NLS MS 4796, Box 92.

86. Knight MSS, M 111/1248 and M 109/35; John S. Reid, 'The Castlehill Observatory, Aberdeen', *J. for the History of Astronomy*, XIII (1982), 87–89. Bute's gift made Aberdeen a potentially important observatory but the potential was never realized.

87. The most complete account of these efforts during Bute's period is contained in *A Complete Collection of Papers Relating to the Union of the King's and Marischal Colleges of Aberdeen* (1787). The copy in the Aberdeen University Archives identifies the authors of the pamphlets. A union proposal from 1765 seems to be referred to there on page 22.

88. Most of the King's College professors were elderly and would have been expected to retire on lower incomes than they might otherwise have had. They would also have lost the ability to patronize younger relatives: see Patrick Copland to the Duchess of Gordon (copy), n.d., AUL MS U 557/3, Principal George Campbell to Bute (copy), n.d. [Aug.–Oct. 1785], AUL MS M 387/16/4/7; Knight MSS, M 113/1909.

89. 'Outlines of a plan for uniting the King's and Marischal Universities of Aberdeen', 18 July 1786; it was not proposed to abolish a chancellorship because there was then only one serving Chancellor, Lord Bute. His office would seem to be protected by items V and VI of the plan; *Complete Collection*, 24, 128–32.

90. *Ibid.*, 154, 128.

91. This had certainly been the case in 1754 when the town council had promoted a union and had engaged the 6th Earl of Findlatter as a mediator of disputes between the Colleges. They already knew he was biased in favour of Marischal College; Aberdeen Council Register 60, 14, 20,

21 Nov. 1754; 25 Mar. 1755; *Complete Collection*, 154.

92. *Complete Collection*, 28, 128, 153.

93. Robert Hamilton to his colleagues, 12 Aug. 1784, AUL MS M 387/16/4/13. This has written on its cover 'but should have been 1786'. The original date is probably correct since Marischal College had already decided by 6 June 1786 to petition for a Royal Visitation. Debate in the Aberdeen Press had begun by at least 20 July 1786. Sir William Fordyce to George Skene, 6 June 1786; AUL MS M 387/16/4/17/1; *Complete Collection*, 13, 130.

94. *Complete Collection*, 28–30; 156.

95. Ogilvie and Dr James Dunbar at King's supported the union schemes, perhaps, as their colleagues bitterly alleged, 'as much for their private party purposes, as for promoting an Union' (*ibid.*, 28, 170); William R. Humphries, 'William Ogilvie and the projected union of the colleges, 1786–1787', *Aberdeen University Studies*, CXVII (1940). Ogilvie in particular was to be very active in the pamphlet war and very acerbic and scathing about seven of his nine colleagues.

96. *Complete Collection*, 130.

97. *Ibid.*, 142, 148, 156.

98. *Ibid.*, 156.

99. *Ibid.*, 28–9, 132–4.

100. *Ibid.*, 135.

101. *Ibid.*, 136.

102. *Ibid.*, 140–2, 157.

103. *Ibid.*, 142.

104. Campbell's draft letter told Bute of the likely legal arguments against union by a Visitation before going on to say that the men at King's 'dispose of [places] and also of the Revenues of the University entirely at their Pleasure and not always to the Public satisfaction – This, my Lord, we believe to be the true cause of their opposition, and from this likewise arises their dread of a Visitation ... We would therefore humbly submit to your Lops the expediency of such a measure'. These lines are partially crossed out but there is little doubt

that Bute learned what they contained. Campbell to Bute, n.d., AUL MS M 387/16/4/7.

105. James Dunbar, William Ogilvie and John Ross; Ross was a neutral in the beginning but came gradually to support the majority of his King's College colleagues.

106. Campbell to Bute, n.d., AUL MS M 387/16/4/7.

107. *Complete Collection*, 32, 142.

108. Knight MS, M 113/1913. Knight is wrong in saying that Bute had 'speedily drawn back' from the idea of a Visitation. Bute seems not to have publicly supported the petition because he did not wish to insult 'the [seven] old Town Professors' who had appealed to him to oppose it. On 9 June he thought 'a Memorial requesting a Visitation [should] be immediately made out, & after being signed by Noblemen Gentlemen & c sd. be presented to Lord Sidney'. Plans had also been made to approach Skene of that Ilk, the Duke of Gordon, General – Grant and Henry Dundas; see David Gordon to Dr George Skene, 9 June 1786, AUL MS M 387/16/4/17/2, AUL. The petition as it then stood is probably that dated 12 July 1786 and found in the papers of James Beattie, AUL MS 30/2/512. Another short version was sent to him on 16 July 1786 by Patrick Copland, AUL MS 30/2/514.

109. Baron Cosmo Gordon to Patrick Copland, 29 June 1786, AUL MS M 387/16/4/17/3.

110. Copland to Dundas, 26 June 1786, AUL MS U 557. With this letter went a 'Memorial' approved by Bute and signed by Ogilvie, Dunbar and all the Marischal College professors.

111. Sir William Fordyce to George Skene, 6 June 1786, AUL MS M 387/16/4/17/1.

112. Dundas to ?, 10 July 1786, AUL MS M 387/16/4/17/4. Here he also asked for more information.

113. Just when the printed plan for union was circulated with a covering letter asking for subscriptions to the petition

for a Royal Visitation is not clear. Some of the peers of the North-East had received it and replied by 17 July; see, for example, Kintore, AUL MS M 387/16/4/17/6. The printed *Outlines of a Plan for Uniting the King's and Marischal Universities of Aberdeen, with a View to render the System of Education more complete*, is dated 18 July 1786.

114. Principal George Campbell to Kintore, 17 July 1786, AUL MS 2954.

115. *Ibid.*; AUL MS M 387/16/4/17/5, 9–11; Patrick Copland to the Duchess of Gordon, 9 Aug. 1786, AUL MS U 557/3. Aberdeen's medical men also supported a measure designed to give the city a medical school, see AUL MS M 387/16/4/15/1.

116. Copland to the Duke of Gordon, 9 Aug. 1786; Fordyce to Sydney, 20 and 24 Aug. 1786, AUL MS U 557; 558. Fordyce had waited 'last week' on Bute, who indicated that the proposal for a Visitation 'had his approbation'. Bute still declined publicly to 'take any partial part about it'.

117. Knight MSS, M 113/1915.

118. The political interests of 11 other men might also have been affected; see Humphries, *op. cit.*, 10.

119. Fife to George Skene, 23 July 1786, AUL MS M 387/16/4/17/13; Fife protested that the consequences of the Visitation and union would affect the 'rights of others' and that 'the Petition and the whole matter had been kept [*sic*] a secret from almost every Member of [King's College]'.

120. Chalmers to Sydney, 25 July 1786, AUL MS U 557.

121. Walter Ross to Patrick Copland, 12 Sep. 1786, AUL MS M 387/16/4/17/13.

122. In 1782–3 and 1785 Dundas had fended off requests for Visitations to Edinburgh and Glasgow made by two Whigs, the Earl of Buchan and John Anderson, Professor of Natural Philosophy at the latter University. He would not have wanted to set a precedent in Aberdeen. A man as

deeply conservative as Dundas may genuinely have worried about the legal niceties of this case but he was probably merely procrastinating, perhaps with the hope that the dispute could be arbitrated. See Ross to John Stuart, 31 Aug. 1786, AUL MS M 387/16/4/19/16; Knight MSS, M 113/1915–17.

123. Copland to the Duchess of Gordon, n.d. [probably late July or August 1786], AUL MS U 557/3.

124. Ross to Copland, 12 Sep. 1786, AUL MS M 387/16/4/19/13: 'The forwarding the Petition to the Earl of Bute was a proper step & nothing less than he was entitled to'. It presumably went with copies of George Campbell's 7 September letter to Henry Dundas answering queries about patronage, past visitations and the proposed medical establishment which had provoked 'jealousy to some of the Members of the University of Edinburgh'. AUL MS M 387/16/4/8 and U 557.

125. Bute to Sir William Fordyce (copy), 15 Sep. 1786, AUL MS M 387/16/4/18/1.

126. Chalmers to Dundas, 27 Sep. 1786, AUL MS U 557; *Complete Collection*, 24–41.

127. The Duke of Gordon had clearly mentioned such a proposal earlier to Patrick Copland since it is referred to as having being rejected by the King's College men by 8 Aug. (cf. n. 115); Thomas Gordon to the Duke of Gordon, 7 Oct., AUL MS M 387/16/4/12/2.

128. Ross to (?), 9 Oct. 1786, AUL MS M 387/16/4/19/11.

129. Knight MS M 113/1919; AUL MS M 387/16/4/19/8.

130. *Ibid.*;Principal Campbell to James Beattie, 17 April 1787, AUL MS 30/1/542. Because the unification affair was not an official College matter those who pursued it shared the legal costs to which Bute does not appear to have contributed. Knight MSS M 113/1908.

131. As late as 27 Nov. 1787 Ross had not come to that conclusion. He was in favour of proceeding even though the Presbytery of Skye and the Synod of Aberdeen had recently announced their opposition to a union; see Knight MSS, M 113/1919–20.

132. Forbes's support for the union proposals had been announced in the *Aberdeen Journal* on 16 Oct. 1786. It had probably been gained by James Beattie; Patrick Copland to James Beattie, n.d., 1786, AUL MS 30/2/513. Forbes was not elected Rector for the customary second term, a decision protested by William Ogilvie; AUL, King's College and University Rectoral Minute Book, 14 May 1786, 5 Jan. 1788.

133. Walker seems to have exchanged both plant materials and geological specimens with Bute whom he regarded along with William Cullen as one of 'the best Judges of fossils I have ever known'; GUL MS Gen. 1061.

8

'The favourite of the favourite': John Home, Bute and the politics of patriotic poetry

Richard B. Sher

In 1775 James Boswell conversed with Samuel Johnson about the propriety of 'John Home's going into Lord Bute's room before the first people in England' during Bute's administration. Bute's eldest son had defended the practice, arguing that it was better for a minister to see people in the order in which they had come than according to their 'rank'. 'Yes', Johnson retorted, 'But Home should not have come to the levee to be in the way of people of consequence. He saw Lord Bute at all times, and could have said what he had to say at any time as well as at the levee.'[1]

The very fact that Boswell and Johnson had such a conversation a decade after Bute's political demise shows how much contemporary interest there was in the fascinating and long-neglected relationship that forms the subject of this essay. Johnson took it for granted that Home, in his capacity as Bute's personal secretary, 'saw Lord Bute at all times'. What particularly disturbed him was the public side of their relationship. There was simply no precedent for a man of Home's religious, national, political, and social background to be seeing the chief minister of state while dukes and earls waited their turns.

Henry Mackenzie's biography of John Home confirms that contemporary concern over this matter was not limited to Boswell and Johnson. Writing of Home's relationship to Bute, Mackenzie observed that 'persons of high rank, and great political influence ... saw, with indignation, those private interviews which were refused to them, granted to this obscure man of letters.'[2] Isn't this the mirror image of Bute's own relationship with George III? If one major source of political opposition to Bute was the impropriety of a politically in-experienced Scottish peer gaining political power solely on the basis of a personal relationship with the King, another source of opposition was the impropriety of that peer giving private and public preference to a politically inexperienced Scottish playwright and Presbyterian minister for equally personal reasons. Just as in the contemporary idiom Bute was 'the favourite', so was John Home, in Sir Walter Scott's phrase, 'the favourite of the favourite', owing all his influence to his friendship with his lord.[3]

The aim of this essay is to examine the Bute–Home relationship in as much detail as the sources permit. In particular, I shall seek to explain why a wealthy, powerful, high-born politician like Bute would have chosen an 'obscure man of letters' like Home for his chief assistant and closest adviser. I believe this puzzle admits of no simple solution. It will be necessary to consider a wide range of factors, including personality, politics and ideology, in order to understand the Bute–Home relationship in all its complexity. Such an investigation will be well worth the trouble, however, not only for what it will reveal about Bute but also for what it will reveal about Home, the Scottish Enlightenment, the London stage, and mid-eighteenth-century politics.

Since John Home's name may not be familiar to all readers of this volume, it will be useful to begin with a brief biographical sketch.[4] Home (pronounced Hume) was born in 1722 in Edinburgh's port city of Leith, where his father was town clerk. He attended Leith Grammar School and took the arts and later divinity courses at Edinburgh University, earning an M.A. in 1742 with a thesis entitled 'De republica vel imperio civili'. During his university years he joined a student circle that included William Robertson, Adam Ferguson, Hugh Blair, and Alexander Carlyle – all of whom would eventually become the recipients of Bute's patronage. With them, Home would devote much of his life to upholding the principles of the intellectually and culturally liberal, but socially and politically conservative, Moderate party in the Church of Scotland. And with them, too, he would occupy a central position in the Scottish Enlightenment during the second half of the eighteenth century.

The years 1745 and 1746 were particularly momentous ones for Home. Early in 1745 he finished his divinity studies and had his 'trials' or examinations before the Presbytery of Edinburgh. He was then licensed to preach the gospel as a 'probationer' in the Church. While he was awaiting an appointment or 'presentation' to a parish, the Jacobite rebellion of 1745 broke out. As staunch Presbyterians and Whigs, Home and his friends naturally opposed the rebellion, but in their case opposition was translated into military zeal. Home, who was one of the most militant members of his circle, not only joined his friends as a member of the College Company of Edinburgh Volunteers and a night watchman for General Cope's army but subsequently became an officer in another regiment of volunteers. At the Battle of Falkirk in January

1746 Lieutenant Home and a small group of his men were captured by Charles Stuart's forces and imprisoned high in Doune Castle. According to his own account of this incident in the history of the '45 that he published late in life, Home led an escape by tying bedsheets together to make a rope that was lowered out of a window. Later in 1746 – after the uprising had been quashed at Culloden – Home was selected by the patron of the little rural parish of Athelstaneford in East Lothian to be minister there.

These events of 1745–6 reveal a fundamental paradox in Home's life. On the one hand, he was trained for a career as a Presbyterian clergyman, preaching and pastoring to his flock in some peaceful Scottish parish. When he was duly ordained and inducted as the minister of Athelstaneford in 1747, he settled down to a quiet life of this kind. Home seems to have been a good preacher and was very well liked by his parishioners. If things had worked out differently he would probably have lived out his days in that way, writing poetry in his spare time like his immediate predecessor Revd Robert Blair (author of 'The Grave') and making frequent visits to Edinburgh to be with his literary friends.

On the other hand, Home was intellectually and emotionally drawn to a strange blend of classical republican and romantic or sentimental values. As a student he earned a reputation as a respectable classicist and studied Roman history and culture with Charles Mackie. His M.A. thesis probably grew out of the sort of topics that Mackie discussed.[5] It was particularly the heroic, martial aspect of the classical civic ideal that appealed to him. Like his good friend Adam Ferguson, Home was a lifelong admirer of classical ideals of military virtue. His experiences during the '45 provided an opportunity to act on those ideals, and later in life he campaigned aggressively for a Scots militia and served as an officer in a regiment of Scottish 'fencibles' (so called because their sole concern was national defence). Home differed from Ferguson as a poet differs from a philosopher; he expressed his ideals not through the Stoic and civic humanist rhetoric that Ferguson championed but through appeals to the emotions. For Home, emphasis was always placed upon the glory, the heroism, the poetry, the romance of military life. It is not coincidental that Home was the discoverer and chief promoter of James Macpherson's Ossian, for Macpherson's Ossianic poetry embodied both the sentimentalism and the ideal of martial virtue that Home found so attractive.[6]

Home, then, was part Presbyterian minister, part romantic sentimentalist, and part civic humanist with a strong military bent. The element that held these diverse and sometimes conflicting tendencies together was 'virtue'. On Sundays he would preach Christian virtue from the pulpit, and on other occasions he would discuss the concept at Edinburgh debating clubs and tavern gatherings. But it was only through poetry, particularly dramatic poetry, that Home discovered a satisfactory medium for expressing his civic and sentimental concerns. Between 1757 and 1778 six of his tragedies were produced on the London stage. Almost all of them were morality plays that sought both to draw tears from the ladies and to rouse their husbands to a high pitch of patriotic enthusiasm. Perhaps more than any other eighteenth-century dramatist, Home was the playwright of 'pathetic' patriotism and sentimental civic humanism.[7]

For the purposes of this study, the most important of Home's plays were the first three – *Agis* (the first to be written, though the second to be staged), *Douglas*, and *The Siege of Aquileia* – which I shall call the Leicester House tragedies. All three were written or revised with the help of Bute, to whom Home was supposedly introduced by the Duke of Argyll by 1755 at the latest.[8] And all three were staged during the first four years of the Seven Years War, when Bute was consolidating his hold over the Prince of Wales and his Leicester House entourage. William Pitt, who was allied with Bute during most of this period, was Home's earliest theatrical patron, and it was he who arranged the London production of *Douglas* at Covent Garden in 1757 after Bute's influence with David Garrick proved insufficient to arrange a production at Drury Lane.[9] But as Bute and Pitt drifted apart, Home, along with his friend Gilbert Elliot, gravitated to the former.[10] *Agis* and *The Siege of Aquileia* were both produced by Garrick at Drury Lane with the help of Bute's influence, and shortly before the death of George II in October 1760 Home republished all three plays at London as *The Dramatic Works of John Home*, with a long dedication 'To His Royal Highness, George, Prince of Wales'.

Had Home remained, as for several years it appeared he would, a closet dramatist, he would probably have remained the minister of Athelstaneford. The stage productions of *Douglas* produced such a furore of clerical opposition in Presbyterian Scotland, however, that Home thought it prudent to resign his church in June 1757, accepting employment soon after as Bute's personal secretary and adviser.[11] He seems to have continued in that position at least until Bute's resignation in 1763, during which time he lived part of the year in Bute's household in London and the other part in Scotland. For nearly four years after leaving the manse at Athelstaneford his only fixed income was a £100 per annum pension from the Princess of Wales. The Leicester House tragedies each earned him hundreds of pounds, and a few months after the accession of George III his pension was raised to £300. Bute was undoubtedly instrumental in arranging these pensions, but Home's public flattery of the Prince of Wales helped, too. Even with £300 a year, however, Home was not well off in expensive London until Bute got him a £300 per annum sinecure as conservator of Scots privileges in Campvere (Holland) in 1763.

After that appointment Home was financially comfortable, in spite of his notorious inability to manage his money efficiently. 'J. Home is not only Conservator, but retains his pension, so that you may hope for a Botle [sic] of good claret when you come to Killduff', wrote one of his friends to another in 1763.[12] Killduff was Home's farm in East Lothian, to which his former parishoners now welcomed him not as a minister but as a laird. The reference to claret had nationalist connotations, as readers of this epigram that Home published the year before would have appreciated.

> Haughty and fierce the Caledonian stood;
> Old was his mutton, and his claret good.
> Let him drink port, an English statesman cried;
> He drank the poison, and his spirit died.[13]

Relations between England and 'Caledonia' were tense indeed during the 1760s, and resentment surfaced over cultural matters concerning claret and Ossianic poetry as much as over political questions involving the Scots militia and Lord Bute. As a leading supporter of all four of these Scottish causes, Home was something of a marked man in England. His fourth tragedy, an Ossianic adaptation called *Rivine*, was performed at Drury Lane in 1769 with the Anglicized title *The Fatal Discovery* because of the 'jealousy and dislike which prevailed at that time against Lord Bute and the Scotch.'[14] Even so, it was said that the play failed the moment Home revealed himself as the playwright. The next year Home married the plain and sickly daughter of his cousin Revd William Home, joking to his friend David Hume that if he hadn't married her no one else would have. Upon hearing the news in Venice, Bute wrote his 'worthy bard' a warm letter on the joys of love and marriage.[15]

In 1773 Garrick produced Home's *Alonzo*, which had some success despite being a thinly veiled reworking of *Douglas*. 'Now he is Master of the Stage', crowed his friend Alexander Carlyle upon learning that *Alonzo* had triumphed at Drury Lane. According to Carlyle, this demonstrated 'how little Gall there is in John Bulls fat Body; and that Patriotism, I mean the mock Patriotism that consisted chiefly, in hatred to Ld Bute & the Scottish, is now dead & Buried.'[16] Actually, Home's dramatic talent and theatrical stature were greatly overestimated by Carlyle and other members of Home's circle of Scottish literati. With the complete failure of his last tragedy, *Alfred*, in 1778, Home's career as a dramatist came to an abrupt and humiliating end. In that year Home accepted a commission in the Duke of Buccleuch's South Fencibles. His appearance as an elder in the Church of Scotland's General Assembly of 1778, dressed in the bright scarlet uniform of his regiment, provoked an ecclesiastical opponent's quip that 'it was the *farce* after the *play*'.[17] Not long after this Home sustained a serious injury when he fell from his horse. He subsequently moved from Killduff to Edinburgh, where he spent the rest of his life except for occasional excursions to London and other places. From the account of one such excursion made in 1801, it appears that the elderly and somewhat feeble author of *Douglas* was still regarded by many in the capital as a kind of cultural hero.[18] Seven years after that London jaunt, and a few days before his 86th birthday, John Home died.

How powerful and influential was John Home during the Bute era? Because Home operated behind the scenes, it is very difficult to answer this question. Years later Alexander Carlyle referred to Home as 'the man of his [Bute's] right hand' and made the astonishing claim that Home 'might really have been said to have been the second man in the kingdom while Bute remained in power'.[19] Though probably an exaggeration, and for the most part unverifiable, Carlyle's statement deserves more consideration than political historians have traditionally given it. Merely by virtue of having 'the undisputed ear of the Prime Minister', Home was in a position to influence Bute's appointments and policies on practically everything. Surviving correspondence demonstrates that he was in the habit of advising Bute on matters of great delicacy, such as whom he should use as manager of Scottish affairs, how he should behave towards his uncle the Duke of Argyll, and what action he should take to secure a substantial office for life.[20] Of course, like all favourites, Home was rendered instantly and utterly powerless the moment his patron fell from grace, and even while Bute retained power Home sometimes fared poorly when he tried to exert his influence personally and directly.[21] As long as he employed his influence indirectly, however, he was a force to be reckoned with in British politics.

How is this force to be explained? On one level, Bute's attraction to Home was political in a narrow sense. Increasingly isolated and under incessant attack in the popular Press, Bute needed loyal publicists to defend him and his policies. Although Home has not usually been mentioned among those who served Bute in this way, there is reason to believe that he did so. At least one contemporary source put his name in the company of Arthur Murphy, Tobias Smollet, and others who warmly defended Bute in the Press.[22] This would explain the following remarks in Bute's letter to Home of 27 July 1768, written as the beleaguered earl was about to depart for the Continent: 'I know your warm heart so well, that I am certain you will not suffer me to be calumniated and abused in my absence, without taking proper methods of answering these infamous wretches, where it is necessary or expedient.'[23] The strongest evidence of Home's involvement in the paper wars of the 1760s comes from a little-known biography of Home published in the *New Monthly Magazine* in 1839–40. The anonymous author of this work, identified only as a 'near relative' of his subject, drew upon a large body of private papers that cannot now be located. Among these were 'a great mass of writings' endorsed by Home as 'Letters Political published in the Newspapers'. 'These papers are as various in their style as in their subjects', the 'near relative' states, 'but they are chiefly distinguished by the author's bold and strenuous vindication of the character of the young king, with the occasional interposition of a shield to defend Lord Bute.' They were supposedly sent to political periodicals and newspapers such as *The Briton*, the *London Chronicle*, the *Monitor*, and the *Public Advertiser*, using signatures such as 'A Friend to the Constitution', 'A Retired Officer of the Army', and 'A Foreigner'. The undated examples printed by the 'near relative' contain expressions of contempt directed at the *Monitor*'s criticisms of the King; praise of the constitution; a tirade against 'the detestable Junius ... that spider, who, in his dark chamber, spins from his bowel webs of poison and torture'; and support for a firm and unyielding American policy.[24]

Whatever the extent of Home's contribution to the political Press, this factor alone cannot fully explain his relationship with Bute. Unlike most of Bute's other publicists, Home occupied a place of true intimacy in Bute's life. In all likelihood he was Bute's closest friend. Their intimacy began very soon after their initial meeting in the mid-1750s and continued throughout their lives. In his first known letter to Home, dated 20 September 1755, Bute was already expressing confidence that his friend would pardon his tardiness in replying because 'I know you so well, that I flatter myself you will be satisfied with assurances, that no way proceeded from any want of regard or real esteem.'[25] And in his last known reference to Home, in a letter sent from his estate at Highcliffe to his son Charles on 6 April 1791, Bute wrote: 'I told Home I meant to desire you to bring him here; I would not lose the opportunity of seeing my old friend on any account; God knows, I am not in a situation to forego that pleasure.'[26]

If hack political service cannot account for this friendship, what can?

Part of the answer lies in the personalities of the two men and the particular way in which they interacted. Despite his handsome appearance, high birth, considerable intelligence and learning, and privileged position as young King George's favourite, Bute was fundamentally insecure and had great difficulty getting along with people. In social situations he invariably appeared proud, cold and unapproachably aloof, and it was said that he was the same way among his children and family. Walpole called him haughty; Chesterfield said he never made eye contact; Waldegrave observed that he affected a theatrical air; Shelburne remarked that he was always upon stilts; Henry Mackenzie commented on his shyness and reserve.[27] When Home arranged for Alexander Carlyle and a few of his other Scottish friends to meet Bute in 1758, their reception was infuriatingly 'dry and cold'.[28] Yet most of them came to have good relations with Bute once they got to know him. Carlyle, for example, related having a very agreeable conversation with him around this time when they met by chance while riding in Hyde Park, adding: 'but he was a different man when he received audience'. Carlyle considered Bute 'a very worthy and virtuous man – a man of taste, and a good belles-lettres scholar' who simply lacked the ability and disposition to cope effectively in the political arena.[29] This assessment still rings true.

John Home was just the person to relieve Bute's deep sense of insecurity. As a fellow Scot of much lower social standing, Home posed no threat to Bute. Besides the fact that they were both exceptionally vain, the two men were remarkably similar in their zeal for virtue, patriotism, piety, and lofty sentiments of every kind. Like the Earl, Home was not very witty or humorous. What he had, however, more than compensated for those deficiencies, as Alexander Carlyle pointed out:

> He had so much sprightliness and vivacity, and such an expression of benevolence in his manner, and such an unceasing flattery of those he liked (and he never kept company with anybody else) – the kind commendations of a lover, not the adulation of a sycophant – that he was truly irresistible, and his entry to a company was like opening a window and letting the sun into a dark room.[30]

Just as Home's coming into a room was like a burst of light, 'when he left the room prematurely ... the company grew dull, and soon dissolved.'[31] It is not difficult to see why the insecure and shy Bute would have been attracted to such a person. He was also attracted by what Carlyle called Home's 'unceasing flattery'. Carlyle elaborated on this characteristic in regard to Home's relationship with Bute specifically:

Besides ambition and pride to a high degree, Lord Bute had an insatiable vanity, which nothing could allay but Home's incessant flattery, which being ardent and sincere, and blind and incessant, like that of a passionate lover, pleased the jealous and supercilious mind of the Thane. He knew John to be a man of honour and his friend, and though his discernment pointed out the excess of John's praises, yet his ardour and sincerity made it all take place on a temper and character made accessible by vanity.[32]

In both these passages, as well as in a third passage elsewhere in his memoirs,[33] Carlyle tried to excuse Home's addiction to flattery by comparing that trait to the attention bestowed by a 'lover'. He pointed out that Home flattered everyone he liked – including people with no patronage to bestow – much the way he flattered Bute. In Carlyle's opinion Home judged other people in strictly personal, black-and-white terms: he had a 'blind admiration' for those who approved of him and his plays and a 'thorough contempt' for those who did not. For this reason, 'in all the periods of his long life his opinions of men and things were merely prejudices.'[34] Bute befriended Home and patronized his theatrical career wholeheartedly; Home responded with absolute devotion. Others may have flattered Bute in order to win patronage, but Home's flattery came straight from the heart. That is why his attempts to use his intimacy with Bute for personal gain were relatively infrequent, and that is why his friendship with Bute continued unabated after the Earl had lost power and influence.

Home's letters to and about Bute are the best means of observing his devotion at work. In the summer of 1760 Home learned that Bute had been ill with a fever and promptly wrote these words to him from Edinburgh:

My Dearest Lord

I never heard of your illness, till I heard of your recovery. I was in the country, & met with a newspaper of an old date which sent me in a great hurry to this town. Mr Elliot (who has had a little fever) informed me how very bad you had been for some days. I wish I had been in London. I should surely have been permitted to watch at your bed side, & to have lessened a little the great fatigue which Lady Bute underwent. I left you My Dearest Lord after the long conversation you was pleased to have with me at my going away, with a more easy mind than I have had for some time upon your account. Your opinions, judgements & resolutions seemed to be so just so wise & firm, that nothing could be added to them, & you gave me that tranquillity, which I can never have when you are not tranquill. Many a time last winter, have I watched your looks, & endeavoured by my idle discourse to amuse you, & to make you smile when my own heart was bleeding for the uneasiness which I thought I discerned in yours. . . . [35]

Later that summer Home wrote again in much the same vein:

My Dearest Lord

> I dont know how you are & therefore dont know how to write to you. I
> have never seen any letter from you but that which Elliot shoud me – &
> am afraid of fatiguing you with a long epistle upon subjects, that may not
> suit your attention or your spirits. I dont know any thing of that sort of
> fever which you have had, as that Species of illness is never seen in this
> part of the kingdom. If you are still an Invalid, I think that I could
> contribute in the least to amuse you, to ride out or play at Chess. You
> have only to say the word, & you shall see how soon I can come to
> London. ... [36]

In these letters Home comes across as a mixture of nurse, friend,
adviser, and court jester. He is deferential and yet obviously extremely
intimate with his patron. He is clearly in the habit of being admitted
not only to Bute's bedroom but to the private regions of his psyche,
where he works to ward off the bouts of depression to which the Earl
seems to have been prone. The word 'flattery' does not do justice to this
sort of behaviour, unless it be the flattery of a loved one that Carlyle
described.

If this was how Home served Bute when the latter's spirits were low
and physical condition weak, we have now to see him in action under
the opposite circumstances. The accession of George III in October
1760 raised Bute to new heights of political power, and the resignation
of his new rival Pitt a year later raised him still higher. During this
period Bute had evidently confessed to Home his personal fears, both
physical and psychological, and following Pitt's resignation he wrote
Home an optimistic letter (now apparently lost) about his prospects.
Home's reply of 12 November 1761 exudes personal joy and satisfaction at his friend's apparent good fortune:

My Dearest Lord

> I congratulate you from the bottom of my heart, upon the constancy, &
> conduct too, of your beloved friend & master. Your situation is now what
> I long have wished it to be. The career that lies before you is a thousand
> times more glorious & in my mind less difficult to force like yours than
> that hollow path thro which you have with such prudence past. Doctor
> [Sir John] Pringle is a good physician & is very much in the right, in his
> opinion of your health. Your spirits will not fail you, nor your mind
> languish. Nunc animis opus Ænea! nunc pectore firmo.[37] In my humble
> opinion my Lord, the obstacles you will henceforth meet with are scarce
> sufficient to put your strength & resolutions to a trial. Honest men will be
> of your party for the sake of your integrity, & the rogues will be with you
> since you have the bestowing of the loaves & the fishes. I have read over

your letter fifty times, to my self, & if I was to tell you how happy it made me you would perhaps infer that I had longd for it too much before it came. I shall only say that you cannot give me any thing that I like so well as a letter from you. It does me a great deal of good.[38]

Unfortunately for Home and Bute, of course, the 'rogues' referred to in this letter did not rally to Bute's standard, and the Earl was out of office less than a year and a half after his brief moment of elation. Some of Home's most interesting statements of devotion occur in letters written during the difficult years following Bute's resignation in April 1763. In September of that year, for example, he wrote to Bute:

I hear reports of various revolutions [in politics]. I consider them only thro one Medium, that is how they affect you. As to the state, it is more prosperous than its members deserve. I am longing to hear from you. I have retired to the rivers & the streams, but they do not murmur peace, whilst I think your mind is not without trouble.[39]

In the same letter he stated that 'if there was any Christian that had served the God of his life as faithfully & cordially as I have you (to the utmost of my power,) he might expect salvation.' Two years later, when Bute's situation was even worse, Home wrote to Charles Jenkinson: 'I am convinced that a vigorous defence of LB, & a bold one, would be of great use not so much with a view to gaining the people, for in my own mind I think them of no consequence but to compose & satisfy his mind which ... unanswered abuse frets & dejects.'[40] Remarks like these reveal the true extent of Home's devotion. Even after the King began to distance himself from Bute in 1766, Home never wavered. Towards the end of that year he expressed his dismay at the way Bute was being treated and praised him as the only minister 'who loved the publique & despised every object of interest who was the friend of the deserving & the friendless'.[41]

There was also a public side to Home's flattery. In his shorter poems, dedications, and sometimes even in his plays, Home praised Bute, his family, his supporters, and of course his protégé George. Mention has already been made of the dedication to the Prince of Wales that Home placed in his *Dramatic Works* (1760). There Home declared that George would have it in his power either to lead Britain to further greatness or to preside over its decline:

The envied state of this nation cannot remain precisely as it is; the tide must flow, or ebb faster than it has ever flowed. A Prince destined in such a period to reign, begins a memorable æra of perfection or degeneracy. The serious cares and princely studies of your youth, the visible tenor of your generous and constant mind, have filled the breasts of all good men with hopes of you, equal to their wishes.[42]

On the occasion of the Prince's 21st birthday in 1759, Home had published a long poem containing more testimonies to George's fitness to rule. For example:

> Mature in years, in virtue ripe before
> Science has taught the Royal Youth her lore;
> Pointed the path to which his heart inclin'd.
> And fix'd the generous purpose of his mind;
> Avow'd his purpose, and confess'd his aim,
> On Freedom's base to build a monarch's fame;
> To stand the regal guardian of the laws,
> And make the public good the prince's cause.[43]

In these writings Home not only praised George but, by drawing attention to his 'princely studies', indirectly praised the man responsible for George's education in 'patriot' principles – Bute. Home republished his poem on George's birthday in a volume of 'original poems by Scottish gentlemen' that appeared in 1762. That volume also included Home's 'Verses on Inverary' (the estate of the dukes of Argyll) and his poem honouring one of Bute's friends, 'An Epistle to the Earl of Eglintoun', which included the following stanza:

> My humble wish does not aspire
> To steed of Andalusian fire;
> Such as brave Bute delights to ride
> When *Cortes* feels his master's pride.[44]

Observing this public flattery and the rewards it seemed to bring, Bute's enemies naturally considered Home fair game for their barbs and jests. In an attack on pensions in John Wilkes's *North Briton* (21 August 1762), for example, a discussion of the horse owned by Bute's friend Lord Talbot is concluded thus:

> I leave this knotty point to be decided by the earl of *Eglinton*, because Mr. *John Hume*, alias *Home* (for so it is printed in the new sweet nosegay of *Scottish thistles*) tells the world, vol. ii. p. 230, that he is,
>
> > A friend of princes, poets, wits,
> > A judge infallible of Tits.[45]

This is followed by a reference to a 'Scottish pension', granted to a certain Mr Hume, that would be well deserved if given to David Hume but a disgrace if granted to 'Mr. *John Home*, who has endeavoured to bring the name into contempt, by putting it to two insipid tragedies, and other trash in the *Scottish miscellanies*'. In a later issue of the *North Briton* (27 November 1762) Wilkes again ridiculed 'Jacky Home' for his

> ... new-got pension, free and clear,
> Three hundred *English* pounds a year.

Wilkes's friend Charles Churchill mocked Home and other Scottish men of letters in *The Journey: A Fragment* (1765):

> Let Them with Home, the very Prince of verse,
> Make something like a Tragedy in *Erse*.

and in *The Prophecy of Famine: A Scots Pastoral* (1763):

> *Thence* Home, disbanded from the sons of pray'r
> For loving plays, tho' no *dull* Dean was there.[46]

As late as 1778 Home was still being roasted along with another Scottish man of letters whom Bute had pensioned:

> Home and Macpherson now their weambs are full
> Grow very indolent and very dull.[47]

The power to grant pensions and offices to his supporters placed Bute in a quandary. Raising Home's pension from £100 to £300, as was done early in 1761,[48] provoked the fury of English antagonists like Wilkes and Churchill. Failure to do so, however, provoked the fury of Home's Scottish friends. Adam Ferguson sent Gilbert Elliot a long, forceful letter on this subject in November 1760:

A subsistence altogether precarious however honourable for the present or big with hopes was never to my mind. Every man of worth should have a firm bottom on which he may stand however narrow it is & I may say of myself what I believe is not true of [Home] that I never could love a man entirely whilst I remain in absolute dependance on him or at least that I never could act as if I did love him so. ... I therefore wish most earnestly that every other act of Friendship for Home was thought of no avail till he is fixed in some moderate reasonable or even little provision sure for his Life.[49]

Doing justice for Home, Ferguson continued with a nationalist thrust, 'is of more consequence than half the Public measures you will pursue this Twelve Month for more than that proportion of them will result finally in getting more Victuals for John Bull, for which I do not care one single farthing.' Home's friends (i.e. Bute) should be made aware that Home will not stop writing if given a secure income, and they should be told that Home should not be kept in a state of constant dependency. Though Home is the 'boldest [man] in the world in interposing for other [people] he is shy for himself'. 'Whilst he continues in his present situation or any like it', Ferguson concluded, 'I shall always think of him with pain, as a man who is misplaced & who meets with injustice, [even] if he should otherwise meet with all the marks of kindness that ever was bestowed on Man.'

One interesting aspect of this letter is its use of the civic humanist ideal of independence to justify acts of patronage that would normally be classified as 'corruption' in civic humanist terms. As J.G.A. Pocock has shown in a number of studies, two of the cardinal tenets of eighteenth-century civic humanist, commonwealth man, or country ideology were that political virtue presupposed independence founded upon owner-ship of land and that the growth of state patronage posed a threat to the welfare of Great Britain because it added to the national debt, upset the balance of the constitution in favour of the monarch, and tended to put political power in the hands of men who lacked independence and therefore could not act virtuously. Ferguson turned this formulation on its head by arguing that government patronage in the form of a fixed pension or sinecure was the only way to provide his friend Home with the 'firm bottom' without which he would always be a slave to his political master. Patronage was therefore no longer the enemy of independence but a device for realizing it; what some commonwealth men would have termed 'corruption' had become a means to 'virtue'.

Ferguson's letter is also of interest for insinuating that Bute took unfair advantage of Home's saintly innocence and devotion. Later accounts by Alexander Carlyle and Henry Mackenzie developed this line of thought into a full-blown hagiography. Home was sympathetically portrayed as a selfless, loyal servant whom Bute deliberately kept in a position of slavish dependence 'from the indulgence' (as Mackenzie put it) 'which he found in the society of the man'. Bute got no thanks for giving Home the £300-a-year sinecure as conservator of Scots privileges at Campvere in 1763. Instead, all credit for that appointment went to Home's friends for having prodded the ungrateful Earl into action. Here is Carlyle on this subject:

> What demonstrates the artlessness and purity of John's mind was, that he never asked anything for himself, though he had the undisputed ear of the Prime Minister. Even those who envied John for the place of favour he held, exclaimed against the chief for doing so little for the man of his right hand; and John might have starved on a scanty pension (for he was required to be in attendance in London for more than half the year), had not Ferguson and I taken advantage of a vacancy of an office in Scotland, and pressed Lord Milton to procure the Lord Conservator's place for him, which more than doubled his income. But though Home was careless of himself, he was warm and active at all times for the interest of his friends.[50]

And here is Mackenzie:

He exhibited a degree of purity of mind and disinterestedness, much less common in never turning this favour and intimacy to his own private advantage. He never asked (and I cannot mention it without feeling equal surprise and displeasure,) he was never offered, any office or appointment, so many of which Lord Bute had in his power to bestow. It was solely at the suggestion of some of his friends, without the most distant hint from himself, that Lord Bute at last bestowed on him the office of *Conservator of Scots Privileges at Campvere*.[51]

These accounts may contain grains of truth, but they are somewhat unfair to Bute. For one thing, they do not take into consideration the delicate political situation with which he had to contend. Whereas Home's Scottish friends thought it perfectly proper and just that Home should get a £300 sinecure in addition to a £300 pension, Bute's critics saw matters differently, and Bute himself had to bear the brunt of their scorn. If he secured preferment for Home, he risked being denounced by his opponents for giving preferential treatment to Scottish lackeys; if he passed over Home, he would be deemed ungrateful – or worse – by his Scottish supporters. Matters were made more difficult for him by the fact that both camps refused to relinquish the high moral ground. There was probably no way to appease both sides, though a more skilful politician than Bute might have avoided attracting abuse from friend and foe alike.

Moreover, although Home was relatively unselfish in his position as Bute's favourite, he was not quite so pure as Carlyle and Mackenzie claimed. From the time of their earliest correspondence in the mid-1750s Home tried to get Bute to use his influence with the Duke of Argyll to secure a university chair for him.[52] In December 1761 he wrote letters to Bute and Gilbert Elliot requesting the Campvere conservatorship specifically.[53] After turning him down Bute grew concerned when Home did not immediately reply. 'Is Home dead?', he queried his agent William Mure late in February 1762. 'He wrote to me last year about the Conservatorship, that I could not give him, from parliamentary reasons. I hope he is not out of humour?'[54]

One year later, however, Bute was instrumental in pushing through Home's appointment as conservator despite the reluctance of his brother James Stuart Mackenzie, who was then manager of Scottish affairs.[55] Far from being responsible for that appointment, as Carlyle believed, Lord Milton advised against it for fear that it would exacerbate the local uproar over the disputed presentation of the Moderate minister John Drysdale to an Edinburgh church.[56] Milton did help to arrange the transfer of the conservatorship to Home, but only because he was told that Bute wanted it 'for particular reasons'.[57] Although we have no way of knowing just what those 'particular reasons' were, it seems logical to suppose that before resigning from office (which he did shortly after Home's appointment) Bute wanted to be certain that his loyal friend would be well provided for. Whatever Bute's motives, and however much he relied on his friend's flattery to sustain his ego, the fact is that by April 1763 Home had secured a 'firm bottom' of £600 per annum for life chiefly through the efforts of his 'dearest lord'.

By this time some of the personal reasons for Bute's attachment to John Home should be apparent. Without further consideration of Home's plays, however, we shall be very far from fully understanding the relationship between the two men. From the very outset the Leicester House tragedies were the basis of the bond that developed between Bute and Home. It appears that Home gained his introduction to Bute because of the Duke of Argyll's belief that his nephew (whose own ties with Leicester House stemmed in part from the love of amateur theatricals that he had shared with George's father Frederick)[58] would appreciate and patronize the young Scottish playwright. This belief was, of course, correct. Bute's first known letter to Home (September 1755) was chiefly concerned with the progress of the tragedy of *Douglas* ('I long to hear how *Douglas* goes on') and prospects for using influence to arrange its production; Home's first known letter to Bute (April 1756) indicated that the revised acts of that play were being sent to him.[59]

Subsequent correspondence reveals that Bute not only regularly received Home's revisions of all three Leicester House tragedies but actively participated in the revision process. In a letter about *Agis* of 17 August 1757, for example, Home wrote that he was following 'the plan which your Lordship & I laid in the Library'.[60] When Home began working on *The Siege of Aquileia* late in 1758, he stated that he had come over to Bute's opinion regarding the staging of the 'catastrophe'.[61] A few months later he announced that he was bringing four new acts with him to London, with the fifth soon to follow, 'but this & every thing else I submit to your judgement'.[62] Towards the end of 1759 he responded to Bute's criticisms of his most recent work and enclosed a new prologue to be evaluated by the Earl.[63]

Bute's involvement in the writing and revising of Home's early plays cannot be attributed to a single motive. Vanity was surely part of it, for only in this manner could Bute hope to acquire, at least vicariously, the fame and glory of a man of letters. Home continually flattered and deferred to Bute, making him feel like a penetrating critic with superb dramatic taste. Sometimes his flattery of Bute and his family made its way into the plays themselves. Discussing revisions of *Douglas* in his earliest known letter to Bute, Home wrote: 'The fourth [act] I have sent first not only because it is almost entirely new, but because there are thirty lines which I would have you see before any body else & if you please show to the Duke [of Argyll].'[64] The lines in question concern the appearance on the battlefield of 'the valiant John of Lorn', who is evidently meant to represent the dukes of Argyll. Impressed that John of Lorn had rallied his men from the safety of the hills to fight against the coming Danish invasion, the noble Lord Randolph speaks these words of praise:

> May victory sit on the warrior's plume!
> Bravest of men! his flocks and herds are safe;
> Remote from war's alarms his pastures lie,
> By mountains inaccessible secur'd:
> Yet foremost he into the plain descends,
> Eager to Bleed in battles not his own.
> Such were the heroes of the antient world;
> Contemners they of indolence and gain;
> But still for love of glory, and of arms,
> Prone to encounter peril, and to lift
> Against each strong antagonist the spear
> I'll go and press the hero to my breast.[65]

Yet vanity and flattery were not wholly responsible for Bute's attraction to Home's plays. Their virtuous, patriotic ideology was equally important. The speech just quoted, contrasting 'indolence and gain' with the 'love of glory, and of arms' in defence of one's native land, is typical not only of *Douglas* but of all three Leicester House tragedies. Those tragedies were staged, let us remember, when Bute was instilling patriot principles into his royal charge at Leicester House during the Seven Years War. Although the values propagated by Bute's teaching and Home's plays were often vague or trite, they must not be dismissed on that account by anyone wishing to understand either the politician or the playwright.

A critical assumption shared by mid-eighteenth-century ideologies that are variously termed 'patriot', 'civic humanist', 'commonwealth man', or 'country' was the belief that public virtue must take precedence over private interest if Great Britain were to avoid falling prey to 'corruption' and decay.[66] Like Home, Adam Ferguson and other civic moralists of the Scottish Enlightenment, Bute was a firm believer in (if not always a consistent practitioner of) this ideal. He believed that private faction was destroying Britain and that a true patriot king, representing the common good rather than special interests, was needed to save the country.[67]

In one form or another this theme of the public good taking precedence over private interest runs through all the Leicester House
plays. The plot of *The Siege of Aquileia* presents it as a struggle between
paternal love and patriotism, as a Roman consul must decide whether
to save his two captured sons by surrendering to the enemy or condemn
them to certain death by continuing the battle (he chooses the latter).
In *Douglas* Lord Randolph reminds Young Norval and Glenalvon that
their personal differences should be put aside until Scotland is safe from
foreign invasion:

> Thus far I'll mediate with impartial voice:
> The antient foe of Caledonia's land
> Now waves his banners o'er her frighted fields.
> Suspend your purpose, till your country's arms
> Repel the bold invader; then decide
> The private quarrel.

It is, however, the tragedy of *Agis* that most clearly reveals both the
private interest/public virtue theme in Home's dramatic writing and
the manner in which that theme became intertwined with Bute and the
politics of Leicester House. A detailed discussion of the genesis and reception of *Agis* will therefore be helpful for understanding the role of patriotic
poetry in forging the intimate relationship between Home and Bute.

Home is said to have begun writing *Agis* during the mid-1740s, about
a decade before he met Bute. The plot involved an unambiguous
struggle between civic good and evil, centring on the efforts of the
dashing young Lysander to defend good King Agis of Sparta against
the corrupt magistrate Amphares. From the beginning this tragedy was
heavily didactic, with an abundance of long, preachy odes and lofty
exchanges about public virtue and corruption. The following lines
spoken by Agis in Act I set the tone:

> The laws have been neglected, not annull'd,
> And corrupt rulers have corrupted manners.
> Authority will soon revive the laws,
> And great example yet restore the manners,
> In spite of those who have oppress'd their country,
> Deprived the people of their antient rights,
> And while the nation sunk beneath their sway,
> Still sought for wealth in an impoverish'd land.
> Even at this hour rapacious they persist,
> And, like some wretches in a stranded vessel,
> Plunder and riot in the midst of ruin.

With its allusions to 'antient rights', just laws, and good manners that
had been (and were still being) corrupted by 'rapacious' oppressors,

speeches like this one dramatized the principles of patriot or country ideology. The setting of the play was ancient Sparta, but the real topic was the state of Great Britain in the mid-eighteenth century.

Agis's journey to Drury Lane was long and arduous. David Garrick rejected it in the late 1740s, after which Home continued to revise it under the patronage of Scottish gentlemen such as Gilbert Elliot, James Oswald, and Henry Home, Lord Kames.[68] Through Oswald the play was passed along to William Pitt, who found 'great spirit and imagery' in it and offered his patronage.[69] In an early letter to Oswald, Home observed that Lysander 'all along seems, both by his principles and connections, to be incapable of private happiness without public liberty.' Later in the same letter he elaborated on the principles that lay behind the writing of this play, stressing the tension between wealth and virtue:

> The spirit of trade and manufactures runs high in this country. I wish that our other political regulations kept pace with those that promote our wealth. We are in danger of becoming *populus mercatorum, sine armis et ingenio*. The Scotch genius tends altogether to arts and arms, and must be dragged by necessity (the necessity which luxury imposes) to commerce.[70]

Clearly, civic humanism and patriotism were the stuff from which *Agis* sprang.

In 1754 there was talk of an Edinburgh stage production of *Agis*,[71] but this did not happen. Meanwhile, attention shifted to Home's second tragedy, *Douglas*, which was successfully produced at Edinburgh (December 1756) and London (March 1757). After resigning his church in June 1757, Home spent the summer in the country with his friend Adam Ferguson revising *Agis* in accordance with the 'plan' he and Bute had devised. These revisions were fuelled by Home's growing concern over the course of the Seven Years War. On 11 August, for example, he told Gilbert Elliot that 'if I was not busied in my task [i.e. revising *Agis*] which I will finish before I stir, Id come up & volunteer'.[72] A few days later he reported to Bute on the progress of his task. 'There is a particular circumstance highly favourable to Agis', he added, referring to the 'calamity of the times' which rouses men's 'sentiments of publique spirit'.[73] While in Edinburgh to have the first three acts copied for submission to Gilbert Elliot and Lord Bute, Home remarked to Elliot that his two critics, David Hume and Adam Ferguson, particularly admired the long ode in Act II,[74] which is little more than a sustained panegyric on Spartan valour and patriotism. Although by this time a love theme had been added to the play, Home and his patrons and friends were still primarily interested in the play's original civic and patriotic purpose.

Once Elliot and Bute had approved the three revised acts of *Agis*, the next step was to get Garrick's approval for a stage production. Since *Agis* was dramatically speaking far inferior to *Douglas*, which Garrick had already rejected more than once, it was widely believed that Garrick agreed to produce *Agis* solely because of Bute's influence.[75] Yet the available evidence does not support this interpretation. For one thing, a year earlier Garrick had resisted Bute's pressure to stage *Douglas*, and the Earl's political influence had not increased much since then. For another, Garrick continued to produce Home's tragedies long after Bute's fall from office, and he seems to have genuinely liked both the playwright and his plays. As an actor, Garrick enjoyed playing the virtuous heroes like Lysander in *Agis* and Emilius in *The Siege of Aquileia*. Finally, Garrick's long letter to Home of 5 November 1757, written after he had read the revised versions of the first three acts of *Agis*, betrays no signs of political pressure. 'Some of the scenes are rather heavy', Garrick conceded, and he had other criticisms, too. Yet he appears to have meant it when he stated that 'the more I read of *Agis*, the more I like it; and if the pathos rises to a proper height in the two last acts, *l'affair est faite*.'[76] No doubt Bute's influence helped, but the most likely explanation for Garrick's volte-face is the fact that *Douglas*'s triumph at Covent Gardens the previous March had transformed Home into a theatrical celebrity and raised doubts in Garrick's own mind about his earlier judgment of Home's talents as a dramatist.

Within weeks of receiving Garrick's letter Home had the last two acts of the play copied by his friend Alexander Carlyle in preparation for final submission to Garrick,[77] who was true to his word. Thus did a remarkable union between the Scottish Enlightenment, Leicester House, and the London stage give rise to the production of Home's *Agis* at Drury Lane in February 1758. Home, guided by Bute, wrote and rewrote the play, while his fellow Scottish literati, such as Hume, Ferguson and Carlyle, served as critics and copyists. The play's heavy moral message and preachy style were characteristic not only of the Moderate manifestation of the Scottish Enlightenment from which Home sprang but also of the patriot ideology with which Leicester House was then associated. Chiefly by means of Gilbert Elliot, who brought the perspective of the Scottish Enlightenment to London politics, the revised work was read and criticized by Bute and his political friends. Sir Harry Erskine, a Bute MP, even wrote the play's patriotic prologue. The task of preparing *Agis* for the theatre fell to Garrick, who was evidently less concerned with the plays' ideological and political significance than with how it would play on the stage.

Depending upon one's ideology, political connections, prejudices,

and taste, *Agis* was either praised or damned without reservation.
There was simply no middle ground. Home's Scottish friends, such as
William Robertson, were ecstatic after the opening night performance.[78]
So was Garrick, who dashed off a note to the playwright that began
'Joy, joy, joy to you!'[79] Arthur Murphy, a Bute publicist himself during
the early 1760s, saw the matter differently in the biography of Garrick
that he published in 1801:

> A strong party was formed in the fashionable world in favour of the play,
> and during a run of ten or eleven nights, the boxes displayed great
> brilliancy, while the rest of the house, feeling no emotion in their hearts,
> looked on in sedate and dull composure.[80]

An anonymous pamphlet by one of the play's zealous supporters
states the point of view of the expensive 'boxes' to which Murphy
referred.[81] 'The play breathes heroism and virtue', the author asserts.
'The moral is excellent. That the good of our country is the first human
duty'. There is praise of C[harles] T[ownshend] and his wife Lady
D[alkeith] (a relation of Bute's) for patronizing the play, and the
pamphleteer does not fail to point out that in the next box 'a lady,
overcome by the tenderness of the scene, fainted'. The strongest praise,
however, is reserved for Bute himself:

> Nothing could more charm me, than to hear that the earl of B—, patron
> and protector of every science, extends his just regard to a man injured at
> home by the too rigid, though much to be reverenced and honoured piety
> of his brother clergy: to see him stamp the bullion with his seal of praise;
> lead by the hands an unknown friendless and oppressed young man; who
> had no one recommendation but his merit; procure for him the favour of
> his prince, and give him that Encouragement, which is all the British
> want (but which they always want) to raise them to a superiority over the
> whole world.

The Prince of Wales, whom Bute had taken to the third performance,
shared in the general euphoria of the Bute camp, as the following
passage from a letter to Bute illustrates:

> I forgot to desire my Dear Friend to take the trouble of presenting Mr
> Hume with a £50 note; pray let him know that I am much indebted to him
> for my entertainment last night; I can't praise enough the noble generous
> sentiments that run through the whole play; in short both language and
> action please me so much, that I shall go again sooner than I intended.[82]

And go again he did, prompting Horace Walpole to remark that 'the
Prince of Wales went three times to see *Agis*, a new tragedy written by
John Home, and so indifferent a one, that nobody else could bear to go
to it twice.'[83]

Most English men of letters agreed with Walpole. Thomas Gray could not believe that the author of *Douglas* had fallen so low,[84] and during the latter part of *Agis*'s run James Grainger sent these disparaging remarks to Thomas Percy:

> The tragedy of Agis is much followed, and much decried. I have not seen it performed, and from the first act of it, which I have read at Strahan's [bookshop], have no curiosity. In the meantime, it is what we in the city call good mercantable ware, for it will bring Home in six or seven hundred pounds. How easily some folks make their money![85]

In early April Grainger wrote again, using stronger language:

> In truth ... never did I read a tragedy with much less merit, than this last of Mr Home's. His very friends are half ashamed of it, all but Sir Harry Erskine and Lord Bute; the former of whom wrote the prologue, and a pamphlet in praise to it, as the latter dragged the Prince of Wales twice to its representation. The author, in the mean while, if he has not much praise, has got much pudding, and that, you know, to a North Country Bard, is no small consolation.[86]

By implying that Home was chiefly interested in making money and by asserting that most of Home's friends were 'half ashamed' of *Agis*, that George had to be 'dragged' to the theatre, and (in a passage not quoted) that Garrick personally hated the play but was forced to perform it for political reasons, Grainger was almost certainly in error. Yet his charges were mild compared to those made by the anonymous author of a pamphlet called *The Dramatic Execution of Agis*, which began:

> On Tuesday the 22d of February, the Tragedy of Agis was played for the first Time in Drury-Lane Theatre, with riotous Applause on one Side, and just Contempt on the other; it being looked upon as a rank Party-Piece. ... It is certain there was not a Clap throughout, but at Party-Strokes.

The pamphleteer went on to say that *Agis* is 'stuffed with Common-Place interjective Exclamations to Liberty, Patriotism, etc. and strongly peppered with sarcastic Innuendos of Corruption, Bribery, Degeneracy, Cowardice, Venality'.[87] It was, in other words, little more than a pompous piece of opposition propaganda emanating from Leicester House.

Agis's supporters tried their best to refute these criticisms. 'I cannot believe the author aimed in any part at personalities; for it is beneath his genius', said one. Political implications had been drawn, but not by the playwright: 'Perhaps the Pit made their own application: but something there was said of *men who aimed at enriching themselves in times of general calamity*; and it was felt severely.' Similarly, when a line was

spoken on the need to face up to dangers, someone in the boxes supposedly shouted 'Rochefort' and the applause and 'huzzas' that followed
were so loud that 'the performance for some time was interrupted'.[88] A
review of *Agis* by Home's friend Alexander Carlyle employed a different
line of argument to counter the charge that the play was a mere 'party-
piece':

> To quote all the thoughts that are virtuous, noble, and in the true spirit of
> patriotism, would be almost reprinting the whole piece. The tendency of
> this play, and the sentiments with which its [*sic*] abounds are suitable at
> all times, and can never deserve the names of faction and party.

With a nod towards Bute, Carlyle concluded that

> the patronage the author of Douglas and Agis has obtained, ought to give
> great encouragement to men of merit and genius. The sanguine may per-
> haps from thence predict a new Augustan age of learning and the fine arts.
> And surely it can forbode nothing but good to Britain, that a play full of
> the high spirit of patriotism and heroic virtue, drew the attention of her
> princes, and received the most distinguishing marks of their approbation.[89]

The *Agis* affair may be viewed as a test case of the relationship
of ideology and politics in mid-eighteenth-century Britain. A pure
Namierite interpretation might say that *Agis* and John Home's other
Leicester House tragedies were little more than dramatic representa-
tions of party propaganda – the politics of personal faction played out
on the stage. Evidence to support such an interpretation is not lacking.
Bute and his followers helped to write, revise, and produce *Agis* and
made a conspicuous display at the theatre, packing the boxes and
wildly applauding all lines that seemed to have political significance.
Home had a reputation as a flatterer who would do anything for his
lord, and he was not above putting his flattery into his tragedies as in
the John of Lorn passage in *Douglas*. Bute himself was quite capable of
using men of letters for narrowly political purposes, as is shown by this
sentence from a letter of February 1761: 'Most of our best authors are
wholly devoted to me, and I have laid the foundation for gaining
[William] Robertson, by employing him for the King in writing the
history of England; he must be pensioned.'[90] Finally, the testimonies of
some of Bute's contemporaries, such as James Grainger and the author
of *The Dramatic Execution of Agis*, support this narrowly political or
factional interpretation.

Yet a purely political interpretation of the *Agis* affair cannot stand.
While it is certainly true that the Bute faction at Leicester House
turned *Agis* to political advantage when possible, no one familiar with
Home, Bute, Elliot, and Home's closest friends among the 'Moderate

literati' in Scotland can doubt the genuineness of their faith in the ideological sentiments that *Agis* expressed. We have seen that Home began writing that play, and provided a civic humanist commentary on it in a letter to James Oswald, years before he even met Bute, and that his commitment to patriotism and martial virtue can be traced all the way back to his youth. Home and his friends continued their struggle for these ideals in regard to the Scots militia cause and other issues that had little or nothing to do with the advancement of Bute's faction in the metropolis. Perhaps it is because their expressions of patriotism and public spirit were so simple-minded and 'Common-Place' (as the author of *The Dramatic Execution of Agis* put it) that commentators have found it easy to dismiss them as mere masks for concealing self-interested ulterior motives.

From the historian's standpoint, hackneyed ideology can be as meaningful as any other kind. Home and Bute really believed that Britain was in danger of decline due to the prevalence of faction, self-interest, and corruption, and that a pious patriot king was the best hope for leading a national reformation of manners and morals. In a corrupt world, the success of the virtuous prince's heroic mission was by no means assured. But the example of Agis showed that defeat, even death, in the cause of the public good is no disgrace. Faced with the prospect of a downfall brought about by treachery, Agis vows to fall 'on the ruins of virtue'. His death teaches a moral and ideological lesson that is clearly articulated in this passage from Sir Harry Erskine's Prologue to the play:

> May this sad scene improve each Briton's heart:
> Rouse him with warmth to act a Briton's part!
> Prompt him with Sparta's noblest sons to vie;
> To live in glory; and in freedom die!

as well as in the Epilogue's appeal to the ladies to employ their 'matchless charms' in a manner consistent with their sympathetic response to Agis's unfortunate fate:

> A King in bloom of youth, for freedom die!
> Our bard, though bold, durst not have soar'd so high.
>
> Ye fair of Britain's isle, which justly claims
> The Grecian title, land of lovely dames,
> In Britain's cause, exert your matchless charms,
> And rouse your lovers to the love of arms.

For Home, dying in the service of heroic virtue was a crucial aspect of dramatic tragedy. The death of Agis was meant to have both sentimental and patriotic meaning: to draw tears, perhaps even a faint, from every tender-hearted soul and to provoke the heroic fervour of every good citizen. Home's tragic muse was inspired by these goals at least as much as by the wish to flatter, make money, or spread factional propaganda. Indeed, according to Adam Ferguson, Home's own self-image was modelled on the character of the noble Young Norval (*Douglas*),[91] who also dies in the pursuit of heroic virtue. It was a character 'endowed with chivalrous valour and romantic generosity, eager for glory beyond every other object, and ... entirely regardless of the present objects of interest and ambition.'[92] Home may have been vain, foolish, or naive, but he was not insincere or crudely opportunistic. In his own life, as well as in his plays, he consistently and enthusiastically espoused civic, patriotic values. Since those values happened to be similar to the principles Bute was tryng to instil in the Prince of Wales during the 1750s, the reasons for the Earl's preference for Home must be sought in the realm of ideology as well as in the realms of personality and party politics.

Ferguson's contention that Home modelled himself on the character of Young Norval leads to some final observations about the importance of the Leicester House tragedies for understanding Bute's relationship with Home. In the tragedy of *Douglas* Norval is a poor shepherd lad who saves Lord Randolph from an attack by ruffians and subsequently learns he is really the son of the late Lord Douglas and his (now Randolph's) wife. From the time of Young Norval's first appearance in Act II the play revolves around the problem of identity and the tension between high and low birth. Norval's very first words identify him as

> A low born man, of parentage obscure,
> Who nought can boast but his desire to be
> A soldier, and to gain a name in arms.

Although Norval's 'warlike bent' is initially viewed as a freak of nature, after his true identity is revealed it becomes proof that noble blood cannot be denied ('for nature will break out'[93]). The highlight of the play is a scene in Act IV in which Young Norval learns his true identity from Lady Randolph ('Lady, who am I then? / Noble thou art; For noble was thy Sire!'), but the identity theme persists in lines like the following, spoken by Young Norval towards the end of his last meeting with his mother in Act V:

> Too soon we part; I have not long been Douglas,
> O destiny! hardly thou deal'st with me:
> Clouded and hid, a stranger to myself,
> In low and poor obscurity I liv'd.

The autobiographical aspect of Young Norval's plight is revealed not only by Ferguson's testimony but also by this passage from Sir Walter Scott's review of Mackenzie's life of Home:

> The poet, as is natural to a man of imagination, was tenacious of being descended from a family of rank, whose representatives were formerly possessed of power scarcely inferior to that of the great Douglasses, and wellnigh as fatal both to the crown and to themselves. We have seen a copy of verses addressed by Home to Lady Linloch, of Gilmerton, in which he contrasts his actual situation with his ancient descent. They begin nearly thus, – for it must be noticed we quote from memory:
>
> > 'Sprung from the ancient nobles of the land,
> > Upon the ladder's lowest round I stand:'
>
> and the general tone and spirit are those of one who feels himself by birth and spirit placed above a situation of dependence to which for the time he was condemned.[94]

Home's 'near relative' biographer took these pretensions seriously, asserting that 'John Home was within a few lives of the earldom [of Home]'.[95] Yet, for all that, Home was in reality just a town clerk's son who had achieved, in Mackenzie's words, a degree of intimacy with the King and Prime Minister 'as seldom falls to the share of any individual of his rank and situation in life.'[96] Young Norval, then, was Home's poetic *alter ego* not only in regard to his heroic character but also in regard to his successful resolution of the tension between high and low birth.

If there was something of Home in Young Norval, there was something of Bute in Lord Randolph. Throughout the play Randolph is the voice of heroic, patriotic sentiments. It is he who sings the praises of John of Lorn (Argyll) in the patriotic passage previously quoted. When Young Norval first introduces himself as 'a low born man, of parentage obscure', Randolph nobly brushes aside this circumstance:

> Whoe'er thou art, thy spirit is ennobl'd
> By the great King of Kings! thou art ordain'd
> And stamp'd a hero by the sovereign hand
> Of Nature! blush not, flower of modesty
> As well as valour, to declare thy birth.

He immediately promotes Young Norval to the same high rank as his own kinsman Glenalvon and promises to introduce him to the King, much as Bute introduced Home to the Prince who would soon claim that title.

> My brave deliverer! thou shalt enter now
> A nobler list, and in a monarch's fight

Contend with princes for the prize of fame.
I will present thee to our Scottish king,
Whose valiant spirit every valour lov'd.

Until the last moments of the play Randolph does not know Young Norval's 'true' identity, yet he is prepared to shower praise on him and stops doing so only when the false counsel of the 'matchless villain' Glenalvon leads him to believe that Norval is Lady Randolph's lover. Norval's lowly birth is simply not a barrier to success in the eyes of a truly noble figure like Randolph.

In this way Home used the theatre to express his deepest hopes and aspirations – hopes and aspirations that went far beyond the narrow political goals of the Leicester House party. Home dreamed of being raised up to his rightful place among the great. Born a Norval, he yearned to be a Douglas, standing equal to the likes of Lord Randolph. Of course, this was just a poet's fantasy. Yet when Home brushed past the peers of the realm at the Prime Minister's levées the fantasy might have begun to seem real. It might also have seemed real in 1780 when, after a quarter of a century of sending letters addressed 'My Dearest Lord' and receiving replies addressed 'Dear Home', Home got a letter from Bute that began 'Dear John'.[97] It must have been difficult for the proud Earl to write those words to his most devoted admirer. One can imagine the impression they made. Perhaps on occasions like these Home thought of Young Norval's response to Lord Randolph's generosity:

I know not how to thank you. Rude I am
In speech and manners: never till this hour
Stood I in such a presence: yet, my Lord,
There's something in my breast which makes me bold
To say, that Norval ne'er will shame thy favour.

And shame Bute's favour Home never did.

Why, then, did John Home become the lifelong favourite of the Earl of Bute? How can one explain this extraordinary relationship between a powerful peer and a playwriting parson? In this essay I have tried to show that there is no simple answer to such questions. Political interests, literary tastes, nationalist sentiments, moral and ideological beliefs, private hopes and fears, and genuine personal affection all contributed. Personally insecure and aloof, Bute liked having his ego boosted by Home's incessant, adoring flattery. Incapable of mixing comfortably in society, he was attracted to a man whose very presence was said to light up a room. Subjected to frequent and sometimes virulent abuse in the Press for both political and nationalist reasons, he appreciated the services of a writer who was eager to defend his honour and that of his native land. Deeply committed to the virtuous rhetoric of patriot ideology as well as to the practice of patronizing deserving men of letters, he was proud to be associated with a playwright whose tragedies exalted and sentimentalized heroic, martial virtue and denounced excessive, narrow-minded concern with private interest in both politics and economics. By patronizing Home's plays Bute was promoting the lofty patriot principles in which he believed, the Leicester House faction with which he was connected, the cause of polite literature and theatre to which he was devoted, and the career of a personal protégé whose plays he admired and whose advice and support he cherished. A stage triumph for one of Home's tragedies was therefore a triumph for Bute's friend, Bute's faction, Bute's ideology, and Bute himself.

NOTES

1. G. Scott and F.A. Pottle (eds), *The Private Papers of James Boswell from Malahide Castle* (18 vols, New York, 1928–34), X, 212.
2. H. Mackenzie, 'Account of the life of Mr John Home', in *The Works of John Home* (3 vols, 1822), I, 51.
3. 'Life and work of John Home', in *The Miscellaneous Prose Works of Sir Walter Scott* (28 vols, 1834–5), XIX, 316.
4. See R.B. Sher, *Church and University in the Scottish Enlightenment: The Moderate Literati of Edinburgh* (1985), 336–7, for a discussion of the major biographical sources on Home.
5. On Mackie see L.W. Sharp, 'Charles Mackie, the first Professor of History at Edinburgh University', *Scottish Historical Review*, XLI (1962), 23–45. Home's name appears on Mackie's class roster in EUL, which also contains a copy of his MA thesis. See also the comments in Mackenzie, *op. cit.*, 32, on an early essay by Home that praised the Roman republic.
6. Sher, *op. cit.*, 242–61, and R.B. Sher, '"Those Scotch Imposters and Their Cabal": Ossian and the Scottish Enlightenment', in *Man and Nature: Procs of the Canadian Society for Eighteenth-Century Studies*, ed. R.L.

Emerson *et al.*, (London, Ont., 1982), I, 55–63. Under Home's guidance Bute became the leading patron of Macpherson's Ossianic poetry as well as of Home's attempt to devise a dramatic adaptation of an Ossianic fragment. See G.R. Thomas, 'Lord Bute, John Home and Ossian: two letters', *Modern Language Review*, LI, 73–5.
7. The manner in which Home combined the heroic with the sentimental and romantic is best illustrated by *Douglas*. Throughout the play the heroic speeches of Young Norval and Lord Randolph are balanced by the sentimental appeals of Lady Randolph, who dreads warfare and exemplifies a private, non-heroic, highly emotional brand of virtue. The prologue identifies the 'test of your congenial tears' as the ultimate criterion by which the tragedy should be judged, and at the end of the play the heroic fades into what the epilogue terms 'celestial melancholy', as pointed out in F.V. Bogel, *Literature and Insubstantiality in Later Eighteenth-Century England* (Princeton, NJ, 1984), 101–8. For Home and many of his contemporaries, the tension between

heroic and sentimental virtue represented a fundamental contrast between masculine and feminine ideals; it is therefore significant that at the end of Act III Young Norval, who embodies both kinds of virtue, is said to have 'that alluring look,/Twixt man and woman'.

8. Mackenzie, *op. cit.*, 33.
9. Home to Andrew Fletcher, Lord Milton, 1 Feb. 1757, Saltoun Papers, NLS MS 16700, f. 190: 'Mr Pitt in the midst of his greatest hurry the day before he moved the house for the subsidy, fixed the acting of Douglas at Covent Garden.'
10. Adam Ferguson to Henry Mackenzie, 3 June 1812, Mackenzie, *op. cit.*, 125–6: Home's 'openness, ardour, and warmth of heart, recommended him equally to Mr Pitt and Lord Bute; but the political difference which arose and increased betwixt these personages, lost him the one in the same degree as he acquired the other.'
11. It remains unclear exactly what functions Home performed in this role. There seems to be no evidence to support the story, found in the article on Home in *DNB* and elsewhere, that Home served as tutor to the Prince of Wales during this period.
12. Alexander Carlyle to Thomas Hepburn, 5 Sept. 1763, NLS MS 10782, fos. 69–70.
13. T. Blacklock (ed.), *A Collection of Original Poems by Scottish Gentlemen* (2 vols, 1760–2), II, 167. The poem refers to attempts made by the British government during the Seven Years War to encourage the drinking of port from Britain's ally Portugal in place of claret from its enemy France.
14. J.H. Burton (ed.), *The Autobiography of Dr. Alexander Carlyle of Inveresk, 1722–1805* (1910), 534–5.
15. Bute to Home, 5 Oct. 1770, in Mackenzie, *op. cit.*, 149–50. Home was almost 50 years old at the time of his marriage, which produced no offspring.
16. Carlyle to John Douglas, then canon of Windsor, 11 March 1773, BL Egerton MS 2185, fos. 90–1.

17. B.L.H. Horn (ed.), *Letters of John Ramsay of Ochtertyre, 1799–1812* (1966), 240.
18. 'Biographical notice of the late John Home, Esq.', *New Monthly Magazine*, LVIII (1840), 171–5. Cf. the remarks by Margaret Adam in an undated letter from London on the elderly Home being 'greatly caressed here at present' and feted by 'great people' even more than when he was 'in the height of Lord Bute's patronage' (SRO, Clerk of Penicuik GD 18/4979).
19. Burton, *op. cit.*, 378, 427–8.
20. See, for example, Sher, *Church and University*, 110–11, and Home's advice to Bute in a letter of 22 April 1761 on the need to acquire a permanent office, Bute MSS, Box 3 (1761), no. 300. My thanks to the Marquess of Bute for permission to quote from the Bute Manuscripts. I would also like to take this opportunity to acknowledge more than a decade of helpful assistance by the late Miss Catherine Armet, whose kind and dedicated service as Bute Family archivist will be sorely missed.
21. I know of several instances of Home arousing resentment in Scotland when he tried to use influence. See, for example, Lord Minto's letter to his son Gilbert Elliot on the hostility towards Home among the parishoners of Leith 'for pretending to plant their Church' (10 Jan. 1765, NLS Minto MSS 11017, f. 32). In 1765, and again in 1768, Home would have stood for a seat in Parliament if Bute, Elliot, and other friends had not talked him out of it. See Burton *op.cit.*, 310, and the exchange of letters of January 1768 in the Bute MSS.
22. [John Almon], *Anecdotes of the Life of the Right Hon. William Pitt, Earl of Chatham*, 7th edn (3 vols, 1810), I, 263–4.
23. Mackenzie, *op. cit.*, 148.
24. 'Biographical notice of the late John Home', *New Monthly Magazine*, LVII (1839), 303–4, 471–2. Although these clues may someday make it possible to identify Home's political writings, I have so far been unable to find any articles with the signatures he supposedly used. My thanks to Marie

Peters for aiding me in this futile
search.

25. Mackenzie, *op. cit.*, 143–4.
26. In *A Prime Minister and His Son*, ed. E.
Stuart Wortley (Violet Hunter
Montagu) (1925), 208. On 4 Apr. 1791
John Douglas, Bishop of Salisbury
speculated to Alexander Carlyle that
on Home's coming to England on this
occasion he 'will be in so close
attendance on Lord Bute, that I have
little Chance of his paying me a Visit'
(EUL Dc.4.41, no. 29).
27. J.A. Lovat-Fraser, *John Stuart, Earl of
Bute* (1912), 96–7; Mackenzie, *op. cit.*,
50.
28. Burton *op. cit.*, 375.
29. *Ibid.*, 376.
30. *Ibid.*, 233.
31. *Ibid.*, 310.
32. *Ibid.*, 377–8.
33. *Ibid.*, 242.
34. *Ibid.*, 241–2.
35. Home to Bute, 3 July [1760], Bute
MSS, cdf. 3/81/1. Home's 'My Dearest
Lord' closely resembles George's 'My
Dearest Friend' as an intimate mode of
addressing Bute.
36. Home to Bute, 6 Aug. 1760, Bute
MSS, cf. 3/82/1.
37. Virgil, *Aeneid*, VI, 261: 'Now is the need
for courageous spirits, Aeneas, now for
a resolute heart.'
38. Home to Bute, 12 Nov. 1761, Bute
MSS, cdf. 3/85/4 (my thanks to M.A.
Stewart for helping to decipher this
passage). Home may have liked
receiving a letter from Bute more than
anything else, but he also enjoyed
receiving the more substantial gifts
that Bute showered on him, such as the
small gold watch that he always wore.
After receiving one such gift he wrote
to Bute: 'You have given me so many
things that I am all over yours, even in
the outward man, as the divines say.
How much the inward man is yours I
will not say' (n.d., Bute MSS, cdf. 3/
80/1).
39. Home to Bute, 4 Sept. [1763], Bute
MSS, cdf. 10/69/1.
40. Home to Jenkinson, 5 Aug. 1765, BL,
Liverpool MS 38204, fos. 329–30.

41. Home to Bute, 5 Dec. 1766, Bute MSS,
Box 6 (1766), no. 77.
42. Mackenzie, *op. cit.*, 185–7.
43. 'Prologue on the Birthday of the Prince
of Wales, 1759', in Blacklock, *op. cit.*,
II, 165–7.
44. *Ibid.*, 231.
45. Home's 'Epistle to the Earl of
Eglintoun' does appear on page 230 of
Blacklock's collection, though the first
word of the lines quoted is actually
'Thou' rather than 'A'. In the eighteenth
century the word 'tits' meant both
small horses (Home's usage) and loose
women (Wilkes's joke).
46. D. Grant (ed.), *The Poetical Works of
Charles Churchill* (1956), 198, 442.
47. Lines by William Mason in the *Yale
Edition of Horace Walpole's Correspondence*
(42 vols, New Haven, 1955), XXVIII,
438. 'Weambs' is a Scots word for
'bellies'.
48. Andrew Fletcher to Lord Milton, 17
Jan. 1761, Saltoun Papers, NLS MS
16523, fos. 18–19. This source courtesy
of David Raynor.
49. Ferguson to Elliot, 6 Nov. 1760, NLS
Minto MS 11015, fos. 67–8.
50. Burton *op.cit.*, 378. Fifty pages later
Carlyle adds that Home 'never asked
anything for himself, and, strange to
tell, never was offered anything by his
patron'.
51. Mackenzie, *op. cit.*, 51–2. It is likely
that Carlyle's then unpublished
memoirs were consulted by Mackenzie
when he wrote his biography of Home.
52. Home to Bute, 27 Apr. [1756], Bute
MSS, Box 1 (1755), no. 38.
53. Home to Bute, 13 Dec. 1761, Bute
MSS, Box 3, no. 698; Home to Elliot,
14 Dec. 1761, NLS Minto MS 11015,
fos. 131–3.
54. Bute to Mure, 27 Feb. 1762, in
*Selections from the Family Papers Preserved
at Caldwell* (3 vols, 1883–5), II, pt 2, 147.
55. Home to Ferguson, [Feb. 1763], and
James Stuart Mackenzie to Milton, 19
Feb. 1763, Saltoun Papers, NLS MS
16728, fos. 22 and 96.
56. Milton to Mackenzie, March 1763
(draft), Saltoun Papers, NLS MS
16728, f. 108. On the Drysdale

presentation dispute see R.B. Sher,
'Moderates, managers and popular
politics in mid-eighteenth-century
Edinburgh: the Drysdale "bustle" of
the 1760s', in *New Perspectives on the
Politics and Culture of Early Modern
Scotland*, ed. J. Dwyer *et al.* (1982), 179–
209.
57. Milton to Ferguson, March 1763
(draft), Saltoun Papers, NLS MS
16727, f. 198.
58. J. Brooke, *King George III* (1972), 91.
59. Bute to Home, 20 Sept. 1755, in
Mackenzie, *op. cit.*, 143–4; Home to
Bute, 27 April [1756] (incorrectly
dated and catalogued 1755), Bute
MSS, Box 1 (1755), no. 38.
60. Home to Bute, 17 Aug. 1757, Bute
MSS, Box 1 (1757), no. 107. Alexander
Murdoch has informed me that 'the
Library' was the name commonly
given to the Duke of Argyll's London
residence.
61. Home to Bute, 12 Dec. 1748, Bute
MSS, Box 1 (1758), no. 192.
62. Home to Bute [Feb. or early March
1759], Bute MSS, Box 2 (1759), no.
146.
63. Home to Bute, 8 Nov. 1759, Bute
MSS, Box 2 (1759), no. 184.
64. Home to Bute, 27 April [1756], Bute
MSS, Box 1 (1755), no. 38.
65. John Home, *Douglas*, ed. G.D. Parker
(1972), Act 4, lines 125–36. Home's
'near relative' identified these lines as a
tribute to Argyll in 'Biographical
notice of the late John Home', *New
Monthly Magazine*, LVII (1839), 294.
66. J.G.A. Pocock, *The Machiavellian
Moment: Florentine Political Thought and
the Atlantic Republican Tradition*
(Princeton, NJ, 1975).
67. J.L. McKelvey, *George III and
Lord Bute: The Leicester House Years*
(Durham, NC, 1973), 82–9, contains
a good summary of Bute's patriot
principles. As Alexander Murdoch
notes in ch. 6 of this volume, Bute
sacrificed his political career during
the 1730s by following his uncle, the
2nd Duke of Argyll, into a principled
opposition to Walpole, even though
this action meant banishment to his

relatively meagre estate on the Isle of
Bute.
68. See the relevant correspondence in
*Memorials of the Public Life and Character
of the Right Hon. James Oswald of
Dunnikier* (1825).
69. Pitt to Oswald, [1750], in *Memorials of
Oswald*, 112–14.
70. Home to Oswald, 1 Aug. 1750, in
Memorials of Oswald, 107–11.
71. Gilbert Elliot to Oswald, 18 Aug. 1754,
in *Memorials of Oswald*, 94–6.
72. Home to Elliot, 11 Aug. [1757], NLS
Minto MS 11008, fos. 103–4.
73. Home to Bute, 17 Aug. 1757, Bute
MSS, Box 1 (1757), no. 107.
74. Home to Elliot, 19 Oct. 1757, NLS
Minto MS 11007, f. 79.
75. See, for example, Arthur Murphy, *The
Life of David Garrick, Esq.* (Dublin,
1801), 204, and the letter by James
Grainger cited in note 86 below. Adam
Ferguson also implied this years later
when he stated that in the summer of
1757 Garrick 'was beginning to regard
the influence of Lord Bute more than
he had formerly regarded the
applications of Home.' Ferguson to
Henry Mackenzie, 3 June 1812, in
Mackenzie, *op. cit.*, 126. Cf.
Mackenzie, *op. cit.*, 84.
76. Garrick to Home, 5 Nov. 1757, in *The
Letters of David Garrick*, ed. D.M. Little
and G.M. Kahrl (3 vols, Cambridge,
MA, 1963), I, 269–70.
77. Carlyle to Gilbert Elliot, 19 Nov. 1757,
NLS Minto MS 11007, fos. 100–1.
78. Robertson to Milton, 22 Feb. [1758],
Saltoun Papers, NLS 16707, fos. 92–5.
79. Garrick to Home, 22 Feb. 1758, in
Little and Kahrl, *op. cit.*, I, 281–2.
80. Murphy, *op. cit.*, 205. Murphy's book
contains harsh criticism of Home's
plays, including much sarcasm
directed at Home, his circle, and
Scotland. Among the papers of
Alexander Carlyle in EUL is a
handwritten defence of Home against
Murphy's charges (Dc 4.41, f. 99).
Murphy's recollection of the length of
Agis's Drury Lane run was correct: the
play was performed 11 times between
21 Feb. and 14 March 1758 and

grossed the impressive sum of £2,090. For details see G.W. Stone, Jr. (ed.), *The London Stage, 1660–1800*, (4 vols, Carbondale, IL, 1962), III, 647–51. Another of Garrick's biographer friends, Thomas Davies, attributed *Agis*'s long run to 'the prodigious efforts of the manager, and of the author's friends, to support it.'; see *Memoirs of the Life of David Garrick, Esq.*, (2 vols, 1780; reprint of 1808 edn, New York, 1969), I, 250.

81. *The Story of the Tragedy of Agis, with observations on the Play, the Performance, and the Reception* (1758). This pamphlet has sometimes been attributed to Sir Harry Erskine, presumably on the basis of James Grainger's assertion (cited below) that Erskine was the author of a pamphlet defending *Agis*.

82. George to Bute, [26 Feb. 1758], reproduced, but imprecisely dated, in *Letters from George III to Lord Bute, 1756–1766*, ed. R Sedgwick (1939), 8–9. Among other reasons for enjoying the play, I suspect George particularly identified with Home's depiction of Agis's dependence on Lysander, as in this speech by Agis in Act I:

Without, the enemy; within, the faction.
What shou'd I think? I have a thousand thoughts
That rise and fall like waves upon the shore.
I need thee now, Lysander! O my friend!
I lean on thee, and thou perhaps art fall'n.

83. Quoted in Sedgwick, *op. cit.*, 9. After attending the third performance of *Agis* on 25 Feb., George ordered command performances of the play on 28 Feb. and 4 March. Stone, *op. cit.*, 647–51.

84. Cited in Murphy, *op. cit.*, 205.

85. Grainger to Percy, [early March] 1758, in J.B. Nichols, *Illustrations of the Literary History of the Eighteenth Century*

(8 vols, 1848; reprint edn New York, 1966), VII, 249. This letter could not have been written in February, as Nichols believed, because *Agis* was not published until 2 March.

86. Grainger to Percy, 4 April 1758, in Nichols, *op. cit.*, 251.

87. *The Dramatic Execution of Agis* (1758), 3–4.

88. *Story of Agis*, 9–10. The reference to those who seek to get rich in times of national emergency may have been directed at Leicester House's chief political opponent, Henry Fox, who would profit substantially from his office as Postmaster General during the Seven Years War. On the controversy surrounding the ill-fated Rochefort expedition of 1757, including Pitt's successful efforts to deflect the blame for that fiasco on to others during the winter of 1757–8, see M. Peters, *Pitt and Popularity : The Patriot Minister and London Opinion during the Seven Years War* (1980), 92–103.

89. *Critical Review*, V (March 1758), 242.

90. Quoted in Lovat-Fraser, *op. cit.*, 30.

91. Cited in Mackenzie, *op. cit.*, 6–7, 30–1.

92. *Ibid.*, 7.

93. So says the prisoner who reveals the story of Norval's upbringing and uses it to explain why, as a shepherd boy, 'night and day he talk'd of war and arms'.

94. Scott, *op. cit.*, 286.

95. 'Biographical notice of the late John Home', *New Monthly Magazine*, LVIII (1840), 165.

96. Mackenzie, *op. cit.*, 50.

97. Bute to Home, 27 June 1780, in Mackenzie, *op. cit.*, 152.

9

'My favourite studdys':
Lord Bute as naturalist

David P. Miller

That John Stuart, 3rd Earl of Bute, maintained a strong interest in science, particularly botany, throughout his long life has been noted by historians but has rarely been taken as a significant feature of the man. This interest has been treated with the dismissive tone, if not the scorn, of Shelburne's famous comment on Bute:

> his bottom was that of any Scotch nobleman, proud, aristocratical, pompous, imposing, with a great deal of superficial knowledge such as is commonly to be met with in France and Scotland, chiefly upon matters of natural philosophy, mines, fossils, a smattering of mechanics, a little metaphysics, and a very false taste in everything.[1]

That Shelburne mischaracterized Bute's scientific interests, not even mentioning his consuming passions of botany and horticulture, only further reinforces the point. To historians, then, the man's scientific interests have been a footnote to history, at best giving an insight into the peccadilloes of Bute the controversial politician and statesman. For historians of science also Bute has merited only a minor place on the tableau of eighteenth-century natural history. Even in those cases where his botanical work has been taken more seriously, the praise is faint indeed. Thus Alice Coats concluded that Bute is best remembered as a patron, rather than a distinguished practitioner, of botany. She summed up by suggesting that 'In his botany as in his politics and house building, Bute had grandiose ideas which were beyond his capacity to execute'.[2] As we shall see, there is some truth in this. But it would be unfortunate if this perception were to divert attention from the real interest and importance of a revealing life in science.

In rescuing Bute's scientific activities from 'the enormous condescension' of political historians and historians of science in particular, the main claim of this paper must be that those activities, when appropriately treated, have considerable historical interest. Botany in particular, and natural history more generally, was part of Bute. This will be illustrated by documenting the extent and nature of Bute's commitment to science. In the context of the 'vogue of natural history' which swept across Britain in his lifetime, the Earl was neither eccentric nor quirky in his chosen recreation.[3] But I would contend that Bute's interests were not predominantly those of a 'fashionable' gardener or planter. Bute was also a part of botany and the enterprise of natural history. The rescue work involved in sustaining this claim is more complicated. Essentially my argument will be that Bute was written out of eighteenth-century botany by those botanists who, in the later years of the century, sought to define the subject in their own image as part of the process of organizing its study in a delimited botanical community. In this context what we might call Bute's botanical style was rejected and condemned along with his substantive ideas on classification. Crudely, we might say that Bute can be seen as the victim of the botanical 'Whig historians'. And it has proved difficult for modern historians of science to free themselves from the grip of this tradition.

The map of human knowledge and also the criteria according to which one would judge an individual as 'interested' in natural knowledge have undergone a number of important transformations since the eighteenth century. These transformations have included: the conceptual differentiation of the sciences (from 'natural philosophy' and 'natural history' to the subjects of chemistry, physics, botany, zoology, geology, and so on); the organization and constitution of these subjects into 'disciplines' (both a conceptual and a social accomplishment); the emergence of research for publication as a major criterion for membership of a scientific community. Recognition of these transformations is vital if we are to avoid anachronism in characterizing the interests of an eighteenth-century figure in natural knowledge. Thus, Bute would subscribe to a category of 'natural history' embracing the animal, vegetable and mineral kingdoms. Although he certainly had the terms 'zoology', 'botany', 'mineralogy' (though not 'geology'), these had few if any of the disciplinary connotations they have for us. He and his contemporaries, though they might have special interests, were free to roam the natural realm. The ways of apprehending and comprehending nature were 'seizure', description and classification. By seizure I mean the physical act of appropriating nature: collecting it and exhibiting it in mineral cabinets, herbaria and gardens, sometimes, though by no means always, as a preliminary to depicting it in written descriptions and illustrations. Depiction in its turn was sometimes, though not always, part of the process of classification – 'finding' order and affinity within the numerous specimens of animal, vegetable and mineral and publishing one's results.[4] Nor must we forget that aesthetic appreciation and spiritual communion with nature and the practical uses of its products were as often the goal of 'seizure' as was understanding in a more abstract sense.

There were thus many roles which might be taken up in the activity of doing natural history. And only gradually during our period was a hierarchy firmly established in which the collector and the depicter were mere under-labourers in the 'truly scientific' task of classification. One need only remember that one of the most important and influential naturalists of the eighteenth century, Joseph Banks, published exceedingly little, to recognize the importance of informal activity to the enterprise. The publication of systems of classification and of other 'higher level' work was only the most visible part (though obviously a crucially important one) of activity in natural history. We can now attempt to place Bute in this conceptual and social landscape.

We know very little about the origins of Bute's fondness for natural history. But undoubtedly the influence and example of his maternal uncle Archibald Campbell, Lord Ilay and later 3rd Duke of Argyll, was of great importance.[5] Lord Ilay became one of Bute's guardians on the death of his father in 1723. The young 3rd Earl was brought up in England and sent to Eton in 1724. Peter Collinson, the merchant and naturalist, recalled that Lord Ilay, his 'honoured friend and great patron of all planters', had taken in a part of Hounslow Heath to add to a little farm in 1723–4,

> and began planting by raising all sorts of trees and shrubs from seeds from our northern colonies and all other parts of the world; he had the largest collection in England, and ... gave to every one to encourage planting, and raised plants on purpose to oblige the curious at this seat of his called Whitton. He had a fine collection of rare birds and beasts ... his library was scarcely to be equalled.[6]

One can only speculate that the young Bute during his vacations from Eton imbibed his uncle's interests, and through him was introduced into the circle of naturalists associated with Collinson.[7] Even more obscure is the completion of Bute's education in Holland, where he went first to Groningen and then to Leiden. We know that he matriculated at the University of Leiden in 1728 and took his degree there in 1732.[8]

Bute was at Leiden just before Linnaeus's galvanizing period there. Leiden was already a major centre of botanical activity boasting not only Hermann Boerhaave and Adrian van Royen but also the rich doctor and naturalist J.F. Gronovius.[9] A fellow student of Bute at the university there was another Scot, Isaac Lawson, who had arrived in 1730 to study medicine and botany under Boerhaave and van Royen.

Lawson became a great friend of Linnaeus, and, with Gronovius, financed the printing of Linnaeus's *Systema Natura* in 1735. On graduation as M.D. in 1737, Lawson became a physician in the British army, only to die in the Netherlands ten years later. Whilst Bute departed before the Linnaean whirlwind hit Leiden, his friend Lawson remained there throughout that period. There are grounds for believing that Lawson was for some years one of Bute's primary contacts with the Leiden group.[10]

After his marriage to Mary Wortley Montagu in 1736 and his election as a Scottish representative peer shortly afterwards, Bute divided his time between Mount Stuart, his home on the Isle of Bute, and London. On the loss of his seat at the general election of 1741 Bute began his famous period of 'retirement' at Mount Stuart, where he engaged in tree planting and the study of botany, agriculture and architecture. Despite his isolation, he also maintained his contacts with Collinson and his circle. Coats notes the fact that the *Stewartia* was named in Bute's honour during this period:

> This lovely American shrub first bloomed in England in 1742, and a drawing of it was sent to Linnaeus the following year with a request from Dr. Isaac Lawson and Mark Catesby that the plant should be named after 'a Lord of Iland Bute Scotland, an ingenious Gentleman who knows Dr. Linnaeus' Methods extremely well'. It was first illustrated as 'Steuartia' in the supplement to Mark Catesby's *Natural History of Carolina*, which was published in 1746.[11]

The 'immortalizing' of Bute as botanist at this early stage is seen as rather mysterious by Coats. But given his contact with Collinson and (through the latter) with American naturalists, as well as his friendly relations with Lawson, the honouring of Bute in this way is understandable even if its precise cause remains somewhat obscure.[12]

The first direct evidence of contact between Collinson and Bute is a letter from the latter written from Mount Stuart in 1745. But it is clear from this that they had been correspondents for some time. Bute was collecting specimens of 'all the Shells this Island [the Isle of Bute] affords', lamenting the fact that 'the Learned have proper names for very few', seizing the opportunity of accepting a box of seeds supplied by a correspondent of Collinson's and expressing the 'Infinite obligation all Lovers of Planting' had to Collinson's good nature and the delight it gave him 'to see so General an Ardour for increasing the knowledge of Nature'.[13]

Bute's correspondence with Gronovius reveals a good deal about his botanical interests at this period. Thus in the same letter in which he acknowledges receipt of Gronovius's description of his method for a *hortus siccus*, he also thanks him for seeds and dried plants many of which were new to him, especially the Siberian kinds. Bute also inquired after the 'Philosophica Botanica of the Prince of Botanists' which Dr Lawson had given him hopes of seeing soon:

> May he live to finish itt [*sic*] and see the remaining Hereticks [*sic*] in botany converted to his doctine, for he has really in a very short time done more to embellish that lovely science than all the united Pens of his forerunners.[14]

Having revealed himself a committed 'Linnaean' (at this date at least), Bute went on to apologize for the rather meagre offerings in terms of natural history specimens which the Isle of Bute could offer Gronovius in return. Though there were no 'very uncommon' plants, there were perhaps a few shells worth looking at which Bute promised to send via Collinson.

The move to London in 1746 apparently disrupted Bute's scientific pursuits for a time, for in February 1751 he reported to Gronovius that for some years he had had little time to spend on his 'once, (& indeed future) favourite studdys'. But now he had finally acquired a house with a garden near London where he had moved his library and instruments: 'here I steal a day every week in winter, with great satisfaction. I mention all this to show you that Botany & the Sciences were only dormant, not extinguish'd in my breast'.[15] Bute feared, however, that this was not the case generally because he described botany in England as at a low ebb 'for tho' the nobility & gentry are at present mad with planting American Trees the Science is absolutely neglected, both by them & gentlemen of the Aesculapian faculty'. As if to exempt himself from the guilt of neglect, Bute ended by inquiring of Gronovius where the characters could be found of the new genera which Linnaeus had formed since the publication of his *Genera Plantarum*.

We have already seen reference by contemporaries to Bute's keen interest in and knowledge of Linnaeus's methods. Although the Linnaean system was subsequently to become a solid orthodoxy in British botany, the reception of his work as it unfolded was friendly but not entirely uncritical. And Bute was prominent among the leading admirers and critics. Linnaeus, obviously interested in the reception of his work in Britain, sought information on those active in the science there. Among those he questioned was Collinson, who replied:

> You desire to know our botanical people. The first in rank is the Right Hon. the Earl of Bute. He is a perfect master of your method; by his letter to me you will see his sentiments, and those of another learned Botanist on your *Species Plantarum*. Then there is Mr Watson, Mr Ellis, Mr Ehret, Mr Miller, Dr. Willmer, Dr. Mitchel, Dr. Martyn. These all are well skilled in

your plan; and there are others. But we have great numbers of Nobility
and Gentry that know plants very well but yet do not make botanic
science their peculiar study.[16]

In this final remark Collinson makes clear that, in his opinion at least,
Bute was out of the ordinary among the nobility in the depth of his
interest in botanical science. Returning the *Species Plantarum*, which
Collinson had lent to him, Bute was critical on a number of points. [17]
First he suggested that Linnaeus had made such extensive changes to
his names and genera that the *Species* would be of little use until he
published a new edition of his *Genera*. Secondly, Bute was distressed by
the 'number of barbarous Swedish names ... I am surprised to see all
Europe suffer these impertinences. In a few years more the Linnaean
Botany will be a good Dictionary of Swedish proper names'. Finally
Bute was concerned at the 'many bold coalitions of genuses' and that
'by degrees we shall have more *confusion with order* than we had formerly
with *disorder*'. These and other observations by Bute were transmitted
to Linnaeus by Collinson.[18]

These exchanges tell us a great deal. First they illustrate the earlier
point that botanical reputation was often gained at this time purely
upon the basis of informal contact and correspondence involving
botanical topics. It was on the grounds of his participation in this
'higher level', yet still informal, activity that Bute stood out in terms of
his own self-image, and for his contemporaries, from most other noble
planters and patrons. Thus Bute loomed much larger in botany than
the application of anachronistic criteria such as 'authorship' would
indicate. Second, we see in these exchanges Bute's serious reservations
about the Linnaean approach, especially his concern that it would
produce more confusion with order than had formerly existed with
disorder. This will be considered in more depth below.

Meanwhile we can note that Bute's botanical activities continued in
the 1750s, the period when he moved decisively into the Royal Household and became increasingly a major figure at Court and in political
negotiations. During this time he continued as an active member of
Collinson's botanical circle, commenced his patronage of the work of
John Hill, and became involved in the establishment of Kew Gardens.

The patronage extended by Bute to the botanist and miscellaneous
writer John Hill (1714–75) drew the Earl into the Augustan saga of
Hill's controversial life. At the time and subsequently Bute's support of
Hill was seen by many as an example of his pernicious patronage
practices. The tale told by Hill's widow of the supposed desertion of the
author by his patron is an attractive and evocative story not least

because of its powerful Johnsonian overtones.[19] Before his association with Bute, Hill had already systematically alienated many of the most influential figures in the English scientific and learned world by his attacks upon the Royal Society. This, together with the fact that Hill was widely regarded as a scientific, as well as literary, hack also given to opportunism, undoubtedly did little to add lustre either to Bute's wider scientific reputation or to his discrimination as a patron. Nevertheless, Bute must have seen virtues in Hill, perhaps in part because of a shared concern with the utility of botany in the economic development of the colonies. In any case, as we shall see, Bute was confident in his ability to control the darker side of Hill's personality.[20]

The two probably met for the first time in 1757. Hill's first letter to Bute suggests that they were brought together by Hugh Percy, 1st Duke of Northumberland (1715–86), who had been a patron of Hill for some time. Bute had evidently spoken favourably of some of Hill's earlier work and already at this early stage of their relationship Hill expressed himself 'happy to lay before your Lordship, the slow, but, I hope not ineffectual, advances I have made toward beginning that great Plan your Lordship has been pleased to mark out to me ...'.[21] This plan, which runs through their correspondence for a number of years, involved the compilation of a complete 'Vegetable System' and the cataloguing of Bute's botanical specimens. *The Vegetable System* eventually extended to 26 volumes between 1759, when the first volume was published, and December 1775 when the last appeared. This was as lavishly produced a publication as it was lavish in conception. On the publication of the first volume, Hill explained that 'The Readers of Science are so few in England, that our Booksellers feard to engage in the Expence'. But in the hopes of support from Bute and the Prince of Wales, Hill had not 'feard to undertake it alone'.[22] With the slow fuse which was to lead to Hill's financial demise thus set, the work continued.

In the meantime, Hill undertook various tasks: at Bute's suggestion, he advised various colonial governors on the cultivation of their islands; he was a botanical adviser to Bute and the Duke of Argyll in the arrangement of the latter's gardens at Whitton Park, in the generical arrangement of trees in the gardens of the Princess of Wales at Kew and more generally in the establishment of Kew Gardens. He read, reported on and sometimes procured the latest botanical works for Bute, rarely missing an opportunity to point out their deficiencies when compared with *The Vegetable System*. Somewhat later in their association, in the early 1770s, Hill was engaged in cataloguing the Earl's enormous fossil and mineral collection. At times the two men worked closely together. For example, Bute closely supervised the writing of the introduction to *The Vegetable System,* and was active in overseeing the construction of the microscope with which Hill conducted his investigations into the construction of timber. This resulted in one of Hill's most impressive and lasting works.[23]

Although their relationship seems to have cooled somewhat in the 1760s, particularly during Bute's most politically active years, there does not appear to have been an open rift between the two men during Hill's lifetime. In the early 1770s Bute remarked revealingly:

> I think Hill is the only naturalist I have made of a rule, never to talk with Him on any Subject but what he is employed in, I have heard so much of his vanity & imprudence that I keep him at the greatest distance by which means he is quite another person with me, than he is with others ... [24]

Almost to the last Hill continued to refer to Bute as his worthy noble patron. It was Hill's wife, left to pick up the pieces, who complained of Bute's conduct, but to no avail. Bute felt that he had done all that he could and that it was Hill's improvidence rather than any bad faith on his own part which had resulted in the Hill family's straitened circumstances.[25]

Hill was undoubtedly the chief beneficiary of Bute's patronage of natural science. But he was far from the only one. Others were the botanical artists George Ehret, Simon Taylor (whome Bute employed to record new plant arrivals at Kew) and Johann Sebastian Mueller (alias John Miller) who produced the 500 plates for Bute's *Botanical Tables.*[26] Authors who dedicated botanical works to Bute included George Edwards, William Curtis, Samuel Pullein and Albrecht von Haller.[27]

Bute's best-known role in botany was in connection with the development of Kew Gardens. Kew House was leased from the Capel family by Frederick, Prince of Wales, in 1730. Its gardens had already been long known for their rare plants and Frederick set about replanning them along with his wife, Princess Augusta of Saxe-Gotha. The Princess continued the task after Frederick's death in 1751.[28] Given Bute's former place in Frederick's household, his friendship with the Princess, his tutelage of the young George, Prince of Wales, and his recognized botanical reputation it is no surprise that he became the principal manager of Kew. Bute had placed himself conveniently for the task, giving up Caen Wood House in 1754 and taking up two others, one a townhouse in South Audley Street, the other on Kew Green. At the latter Bute built extensions for his botanical library and study, thus equipping himself in an ideal location from which to supervise the

Gardens.[29] The reorganization of these got under way in the late 1750s. The architect Sir William Chambers was commissioned to design new buildings including the orangery, the pagoda and a number of temples. William Aiton (1731–93) was appointed head gardener in 1759 with immediate responsibility for the establishment of the herbaceous plant garden and the arboretum and proceeded to lay out the garden on the Linnaean system.[30] To Bute fell the overall management of the enterprise and particularly, it seems, the task of procuring through his contacts trees and plants from around the world. Some of his contemporaries felt that he succeeded admirably in this.[31] But Coats reports that, of the 5,500 species named in Aiton's *Hortus Kewensis*, Bute is credited there with the introduction of only 28. In addition 'the greater number of the species [were] introduced after 1772 when his connection with the garden had ceased'.[32] This may cast some doubt on Bute's diligence, or at least upon the amount of time he was able to devote to the Gardens. But one must bear in mind that Bute the busy politician is being implicitly compared here with his successor as Director of the Gardens, Sir Joseph Banks, who was free to devote as much time as he wished to them.

Nevertheless the Gardens were well established in the 1760s. Bute was confident enough in 1767 to state that 'the Exotick Garden at Kew is by far the richest in Europe ... getting plants and seeds from every Corner of the habitable world'.[33] The first *Hortus Kewensis* was produced by Hill in 1768. Hill not only assisted at Kew, but was also reputedly appointed gardener to the King at Kensington Palace. Hill had himself solicited the creation of such a post and, though its precise duties remain obscure, some contemporaries saw it as a reprehensible act of patronage. It elicited Horace Walpole's famous remark:

> I am sorry to say this journeyman [Hill] is one of the first men preferred in the new reign: he is made gardener at Kensington, a place worth £2000 a year. The King and Lord Bute have certainly both of them great propensity to the arts – but Dr Hill, though undoubtedly not deficient in parts, has as little title to favour in this reign, as Gideon the stockjobber in the last; both engrossers without merit ... [34]

Worse than this, and however unlikely it may seem, Kew Gardens was even brought in by the scandalmongers in the matter of the unfounded rumours of an improper liaison between Lord Bute and the Princess Dowager which so often featured in satirical attacks upon him. In May 1767 the *Political Register* carried an item which included an engraving depicting 'A View of Lord Bute's Erections at Kew; with some Part of Kew Green, and Gardens'.[35] The prime purpose of this was to indicate the existence of a door in the garden wall between the Princess

Dowager's residence and the garden of Lord Bute's house. This must have caused Bute pain since he always thought of his botanical and other scientific work as an escape from politics and scandal.

More important criticism of the naturalists at Court, which was clearly directed at Bute and also at Hill, came from John Ellis.[36] Writing to Linnaeus about the imminent conclusion of Cook's first voyage and the return of Linnaeus's pupil Daniel Solander, Ellis rejoiced in the expectation that 'as soon as he [Solander] arrives he will be introduced to the King & Royal Family and I hope to get some handsome appointment'. He continued in a darker vein: 'I mention this because the Court have been imposed on by quacks & compilers of Natural History too long and I am persuaded our King was not informed of Solander['s] character till he was just going abroad'.[37] The implication was clear: the King ought to be served in natural history and particularly at Kew by active naturalists who had taken their lives into their hands to bring back knowledge of hitherto unknown treasures rather than by armchair naturalists who (and this is a stab at Hill) merely compiled the work of others. Although undoubtedly unjust in many ways, it is probable that such a view was widely shared by those who considered themselves active naturalists.

Against this background of mounting criticism, Banks and Solander returned in triumph. The death of the Princess Dowager at about the same time deprived Bute of his chief support at Kew, and left the fate of the Gardens in the hands of a King anxious to distance himself from his former tutor and chief minister. Bute was replaced as Director of the Gardens by Joseph Banks, who, with his assistant Solander, launched Kew into a new era as a centre of botanical research and the botanical clearing-house of the Empire.[38] Had Bute remained in charge, it is unlikely that Kew would have developed as it did. But equally, Bute had laid a solid foundation upon which Banks would build.

The late 1760s were something of a watershed in Bute's life. Increasingly impotent politically, his health was also failing.[39] Travels undertaken incognito on the Continent, partly for health reasons, restored him somewhat and revitalized his interest in earth science. On his return from the last of his travels, and on the severance of his connection with Kew, he accordingly turned to his minerals and fossils.

We know from the sale catalogues of his collections that Bute had amassed an enormous collection of minerals and fossils during his lifetime.[40] Although this was almost certainly a lifelong interest, it appears that it became a consuming one during the late 1760s and 1770s. Much light is thrown on this by a sustained correspondence between Bute and John Strange during the 1770s. John Strange (1732–99) graduated from Cambridge in 1753 and shortly after, on the death of his father, the eminent lawyer Sir John Strange, inherited a large fortune. He travelled extensively in the South of France and in Italy, his travels forming the basis for papers contributed to the Royal Society and the Society of Antiquaries. He was a fellow of both societies. From November 1773 until 1788 he was British Resident at Venice.[41]

Strange, though based throughout this time in Italy, became probably Bute's closest scientific and literary contact. He procured books for Bute on all aspects of natural history, apprised him of mineral and fossil collections for sale, and reported his own work and that of other Continental naturalists in mineralogy and on the structure of the Earth. In return, Bute offered commissions, comments, collections of specimens for Italian friends, what news he could of natural history in England, and some of the most intimate glimpses we have of his life during this period.

It seems likely that Bute's new-found enthusiasm for minerals and fossils dates from his European tours of the late 1760s and early 1770s. His travel diaries[42] recount journeys from Venice to Holland through Germany during early 1769, from Dieppe to Valdagno later that year, from Venice to Holland through France in 1771, and a journey from Rome to Naples which is undated. They reveal a steady interest in the face of the country, in its minerals and fossils as well as botanical treasures. And he was a prepared traveller who knew what he was looking for. For example, whilst in the Pyrenees on one occasion he tested Buffon's notion of correspondent angles 'with the utmost attention; but without the least success; they appeared sometimes in small Ravines, form'd by Torrents ... but His System for ever fail'd In the larger valleys ... '.[43]

Like Strange, Sir William Hamilton, and a number of continental naturalists, Bute was particularly interested in volcanoes. Such interest, stimulated by a series of earthquakes (London in 1750, Lisbon in 1755) and eruptions of Vesuvius, was an important element in an emergent view of the Earth as active, and of volcanic activity as of great importance in creating the landforms now extant. The observations of such cosmopolitan travellers were an important feature of debates on the theory of the Earth. As Porter puts it:

> controversy over the role of volcanoes in the Earth's economy became translated into the mineralogical analysis of basalt, lava, tufa, pumice and related rocks. Volcanists claimed that basalt outcrops were mineralogically continuous (as well as geomorphologically similar) to rocks which were undeniably part of lava flows or associated with volcanoes.[44]

Strange was an active participant in the debates on volcanoes, publishing a number of papers on the subject.[45] His correspondent, and in some measure patron, Bute was clearly not an active 'volcanist' in the same sense. But their correspondence reveals him as a behind-the-scenes stimulus, encouraging Strange to communicate his ideas to a wider public, agreeing for the most part with his 'theory of the earth', and commenting intelligently upon the work of other students of volcanoes such as the Abbé Alberto Fortis.[46] It would be a mistake, then, to regard Bute as merely a collector of minerals, though in terms of 'achievement' this was his major contribution. We might say of Bute, as Porter says of Bute's contemporary Emmanuel Mendes da Costa: 'his scientific ambitions were essentially those of a previous century: the accumulatory strategy of natural history, the concern with specimens ... [but] this spilled over into broader concerns with the significance of these objects for a philosophy of the earth'.[47] And just as theories of the earth became more concerned with mineralogy, and, for some at least, chemical analysis of minerals became a crucial issue, so Bute too was to recognize its importance.

Back in London in 1771, Bute began trying to bring some order to his mineral collections. His barn was cleared of boxes of books so that the collections could be spread out and examined. Even as this was done, he was acquiring further materials: 'I have got a cargo lately of fossils from Switzerland a very large one from Darbyshire; & I am in treaty about a beautiful collection of minerals ... of a German General sent over here ... tho all this time I work in the dark not knowing what I am already possess'd of'.[48] Bute oscillated between periods of rational self-denial (usually precipitated by the realization that a new cargo sent over by Strange contained few specimens he did not already have) and renewed bouts of collecting mania. But he was acutely aware of the need for a philosophical approach to the material:

> I am deeper in Minerals than I ever was, but the more I look into authors that have treated on this Reign of Nature, the more I perceive confusion & uncertainty, in short this beautiful branch of nat: History is still in the Cradle I wish I had applyd my thoughts to it 30 years ago not from any opinion of the progress I might have made in it but from the opportunity I should have had of employing abler heads & hands. I see nothing is to be done witout chemical analisis; that is the only mode of getting at true distinctions; at least it is the best we can employ.[49]

Once again we see Bute as an intermediate figure, not a mindless collector with no science, but one aware to some degree of the extant literature and, most importantly, of the need for classification on a sound philosophical basis in order to give meaning and significance to the enterprise of collecting.[50] And yet he was perhaps realistically modest about his own capabilities here and sought to employ others more knowledgeable than himself. For example he employed the chemist Peter Woulfe in mineral analysis; he also made use of the services of John Hill.[51] The latter reported to his patron on his analysis of spar which 'by Linnaeus & other Moderns' was classified as a salt or many salts 'as species of nitre'. But according to Hill's experiments it was found to be composed of 'Lime stone & sulphur'. For Bute, this illustrated nicely the 'great difficulty attending a true methodical distribution of minerals'.[52] In his awareness that the methodical arrangement of minerals by external characters (as used by Linnaeus and most other naturalists up to that time) ought to be complemented by one based on chemical analysis, Bute was very up to date. Helped by Woulfe, he made a serious attempt to master the fundamental principles of chemical analysis.[53] And yet the outcome of all this activity is uncertain, there being no published record.

There are, however, a few clues. Hill informed Linnaeus in early September 1772 of an arrangement of fossils for the ordering of Bute's collection. This work was supposedly going through the press.[54] At about the same time Bute reported to Strange that 'Hill has been at work on a new Method of Mineralogie & fossills, that I chalkd out for Him, of which you shall hear more'.[55] Then in March of the following year we find Bute sending to Venice '2 copys of [the first volume of] a Methodical System of fossills I set Hill about; to serve as a rule to range my collection'. But we learn also, rather paradoxically, that Bute had insisted that Hill *avoid* chemical analysis as a basis of distinctions wherever possible, 'this on Lady Bute's account, who is extremly fond of fossils & minerals & no chymist'.[56] It is unclear whether we see here a number of classificatory efforts – some pursuing chemical analysis in a serious fashion, as Bute apparently wanted to do earlier, and others avoiding it for his good Lady's benefit – or whether the ambitious schemes of the previous year had been effectively abandoned. Certainly Woulfe remained a close associate, being involved as late as 1782 in the importation of yet more minerals and fossils for Bute's collection.[57] But the death of Hill in 1775, and the frequent absences of Woulfe, made it increasingly difficult to sustain the 'experimental' activities of the early 1770s. Moreover, Hill's death was to lead Bute back to his first love, botany.

The demise of his long-time associate within sight of the completion of *The Vegetable System* was a blow to Bute:

I have lost poor Hill very unexpectedly, 4 months longer of life would
have given us the Supplemental Volume [of *The Vegetable System*], in which
a multitude of little Errors, occasiond by too much haste, & many omiss-
ions would have been ... corrected, as it is there is no work I know
containing half the number of figures of plants, for the most part correct.[58]

Although he thus expressed some pride in the outcome of the work
which he had suggested to Hill some 16 years before, Bute was not
entirely happy with it. He was to explain this in the introduction to his
Botanical Tables:

Had the person employed by me, formerly, to execute this scheme, lived
to give a new edition of his work, the many errors (unavoidable in so vul-
uminous [*sic*] an undertaking) carefully corrected, might have answered
every purpose – but his death left the whole design so imperfect, so
altered from the original idea, that I discovered with difficulty the out-line
of my plan. It became necessary therefore to review the whole subject.[59]

In short, in Bute's view at least, *The Vegetable System* and his own
completed works of the 1780s, the *Botanical Tables* and *A Tabular Distribution of British Plants*, were all attempted realizations of his 'great
Plan', the latter a response, at least in part, to the imperfect way in
which Hill had performed the task originally set out for him. In fact
Bute did not stop there, as the existence of further printed materials
shows:[60] he intended to extend the application of his plan from British
plants to the plant kingdom as a whole. Thus he saw himself as
presenting a fully generalized system of classification. This larger work
was probably still in progress at his death and nothing other than the
printed introductory matter has come to light.

What was this 'great Plan'? Bute sought to offer an avowedly *artificial*
system of classification which was rigorously methodical. He was react-
ing quite specifically to the problems which he perceived in Linnaeus's
system. It is well known that Linnaeus's ultimate goal was a natural
system of classification. The sexual system which he developed, though
artificial, was intended as a scaffolding upon which a natural system
would eventually be built. Linnaeus's goal was not realized, but he did
believe that the sexual system was at least partially natural and argued
that, in the absence of an entirely natural system, the merits of various
classifications were to be judged on the basis of the number of natural
orders which they contained.[61] Bute regarded this approach as an
equivocation, and a dangerous one at that. Though he professed admiration for Linnaeus as an unrivalled 'philosophick Botanist', he felt
that the Linnaean botanical system had by no means the same merit:

for waving [*sic*] all other considerations, it is sufficient at present to
observe, that there are more exceptions to his classical characters, more

plants ranged under heads they do not suit; than in any one method I am acquainted with. This proceeds in some measure from attempting to unite a natural with an artificial System – two objects so extremely different, that no mode of combining them, can ever with any probability be expected.[62]

Whilst Bute agreed that a perfect natural system, in which all the vegetable productions of nature could be organized into classes, orders and genera without 'separating affinities, or mixing improper plants', would surpass all other systems, he did not think such a system could be realized. First, there was the practical problem of ever discovering and gathering together absolutely all the members of the vegetable kingdom. But even if this were done, a perfect natural system would be elusive:

From these considerations I incline to think, a natural method impossible at present; nay, I am tempted to go further, for I suspect it can never be attained. This may appear to be a bold assertion, but when I see all Nature composed of one entire chain, whose links are so intimately connected and blended together, that the transition from animals to vegetables, from them to minerals, is scarcely perceptible; how much more difficult will it be to discover a real separating line in a small branch of any one Reign. I am therefore convinced, that if the whole vegetable creation lay before us, the gradations from one plant to another must be so insensible, that our boasted generical characters would vanish, and specific distinctions prove our only guide.

On the whole, therefore, I not only think these attempts to a natural method nugatory, but hold them to be subversive of the sole and proper use of systematical arrangements – the bringing us acquainted with an unknown plant.[63]

Thus, Bute argued as follows. There exists a great chain of being such that all the products of nature shade imperceptibly into each other both within and between the great kingdoms of nature. Given this, the creation of groupings (classes, orders, genera) must necessarily abstract from and distort reality, and it is illusory to believe that any system so constructed can be natural. Instead of pursuing the 'aerial scheme' of trying to arrange the vegetable kingdom into supposedly natural classes, orders and genera, we should pursue two paths. First, Bute advocates what we might call a 'holistic' approach to constituting orders, avoiding the use of partial characters and instead examining carefully 'every circumstance relative to a plant ... root, stem, branches, buds, flowers, &c. not omitting the habit, virtues, uses, &c placing those nearest to each other that in most things bear the strongest resemblance'. This is the highest task to which the botanist can aspire, and forms the 'solid basis of Natural History'. Second, and this is Bute's immediate purpose, we must produce artificial systems. Strictly conceived, these should be nothing more than an 'inverted dictionary', which his *Tables* were intended to be. Their lack of pretence to any features of a natural system he saw as a virtue. To use a modern term, they were to be a heuristic device and nothing more.[64]

Finally we must note that in his outline of the intended larger work Bute concluded with a brief discussion of the 'Natural History of the Vegetable Race'.[65] Here we leave behind what he calls the tiresome, but necessary, subject of methodical distributions and move on to the 'whole economy of nature'. He announces that because of the many new and interesting discoveries being made in this area 'this capital part of my intended plan must gain considerably by being deferred'. But he does give an outline of what he would deal with here: the growth of plants and their reproduction; the uses of plants for food, medicine in arts and manufactures; 'the hidden scenes, where Natural History, Philosophy and Chymistry united, teach us the amazing part vegetables are found to act in the most awful phenomena attending our Globe'. But here, as in his discussion of natural systems of plants, Bute expresses a caution. We must be humble in our ignorance of the powers of Nature and refrain from any overarching 'Hypothesis on the Natural History of our Globe':

> a plain and careful narration of facts, prov'd by various repeated Experiments is the only method of discovering the hidden springs of Nature, whereas the forming of an Hypothesis on the imperfect knowledge hitherto attain'd leads us out of the true road, and that path once lost becomes very difficult to recover; besides we already know enough with certainty, of Nature's works, to astonish and amuse the most curious Person, without the trivial ornaments of Fiction and Romance.[66]

Having outlined Bute's aims and views we must try to place them in relation to those of his contemporaries. In his criticism of Linnaeus, from his remark of the early 1750s concerning the possibility of more confusion with order than there had previously been with disorder, to the more developed views of the 1780s, Bute was by no means unusual. Linnaeus found several critics on the Continent. Albrecht von Haller, whose work Bute greatly admired, criticized Linnaeus's system particularly for the indeterminate cases which it included, much in the same spirit as Bute.[67] For all his doubts about the possibilities of a natural system Bute valued the work of the French naturalist Adanson as an example of the 'holistic' approach mentioned above.[68] Buffon, too, was approved of for the same reason, but particularly for his arguments against Linnaeus's pretensions to a partially natural system.[69] However, Bute was suspicious of Buffon's flights of fancy and

'Philosophical Romances' which like all hypotheses he regarded, as we have seen, as leading men out of the true road. Though gratified to find support for his views, and also inspiration for them, in the work of foreign naturalists, not surprisingly he also lamented some of their philosophical tendencies.[70] In Britain, Linnaeus had also had his critics in the early days of the reception of his system there. But by the 1780s such critics as were left, increasingly struggled against a firmly entrenched Linnaean orthodoxy.[71] This was, I believe, the case with Bute.

There is considerable evidence that Bute was not highly thought of by many leading naturalists in Britain in the late eighteenth century. A number of explanations might be offered for this. I want to suggest three mutually reinforcing and interlocking ones. First, there is Bute's increasing marginality in scientific circles, something which was both cause and effect so far as his botanical reputation was concerned. Second, there was from the 1760s a 'spill-over' effect in which political passions and jealousies over patronage shaped perceptions of Bute's scientific persona. Finally, and closely related to the first point, we must note the development of an increasingly inflexible Linnaean orthodoxy in Britain in the late eighteenth century, against which Bute was judged, and indeed judged himself, as a heretic.

The closest that Bute came to being part of a community of naturalists was probably in the 1740s and 1750s, as part of the Collinson circle. Thereafter he maintained and gained numerous scientific acquaintances, some of the closest, like the Revd Stephen Hales and Dr William Watson, established in or aspiring to membership of Court circles.[72] Bute's role at Kew Gardens undoubtedly expanded his network further. But he was never truly part of the 'high' scientific circles of the metropolis. Curiously, he was never elected a Fellow of the Royal Society of London or of the Society of Antiquaries, something which his role as a patron alone ought to have virtually assured him. His closest scientific associates (Hill and Woulfe) were widely judged eccentrics or outsiders or both. Where they were not (John Strange, Louis Dutens) they were overseas most of the time and could keep in touch only by correspondence. Nor, despite his association with the Edinburgh Society for the Importation of Foreign Seeds and Plants, his membership of the Philosophical Society of Edinburgh and subsequently of the Royal Society of Edinburgh, was Bute well integrated into the Scottish scientific scene. His important patronage of the 'moderate literati' was effective over quite a short period in the 1760s.[73] Though shown due deference by Scottish naturalists such as John Walker and John Hope, whose efforts he was in turn happy to support, he was rather a distant figure.[74]

By the early 1770s Bute's loss of contact with the Court, the centres of political power, and his replacement as Director of Kew made him even more marginal. This, together with the continued hounding by the Press and political pamphleteers and satirists, resulted in a very strong tendency for Bute to become an isolate. In these later years he felt it necessary to travel incognito on his Continental journeys. On at least one occasion he also deemed it wise to put a collection of fossils and minerals under Woulfe's name as it passed through the custom-house, having 'reasons for seeking to avoid its being known they are mine'.[75] In 1774, in informing Strange that he need have no worries about the scientific ideas Strange was entrusting him with being imparted to others, Bute wrote: 'indeed if you knew the very few people I converse with, you would laugh at your own caution'.[76] A year later he amplified the point:

> I have now lived with my door lockd these 8 years past almost all acquaintance ... broken & at an end, I see no body, I no longer know those I was once intimate with nor they me; after losing my health & prime of my life in the service of a most ungrateful and ungenerous people, I keep no measures, but spend the poor remains in my own way, & the greater part of it, in the inexhaustible researches into the works of nature.[77]

The new house which Bute had built at Highcliffe, near Christchurch, in Hampshire became the chief retreat for his 'inexhaustible researches'. His plant collection was moved there from Luton Hoo, although the laboratory and gardens at the latter were maintained.

The extent of Bute's isolation can be exaggerated however. It did not mean that he was unaware of what was happening in the scientific world. On the contrary he appears fully aware, in his correspondence with Strange, of the latest interest in 'fix'd air', or electrical experiments, or the discoveries of Volta.[78] He followed with interest the exploits of Banks and Solander with a degree of concern for their success which might have surprised his critic John Ellis.[79] And yet the prospect of a visit from Banks and Solander to Luton Hoo brought forth a statement apologetic in tone:

> [Lord Bute] is sorry Mr. Banks thinks it necessary to ask a permission to see Luton Garden. Can there be a spot dedicated to vegetables, & shut up from the inspection of the first Patron of Botany. The truth is Ld Bute has long wishd for the pleasure of seeing Mr. Banks & Doctor Solander at that place, when he might profit by their superior knowledge in his favourite Science.[80]

This is the letter of a man sensing the botanical generations passing him by, increasingly a spectator rather than an active participant.

A mixture of diffidence and defiance seems to characterize the production of Bute's *Botanical Tables* and his prefiguring of the greater plan of which it was a part. The very act of producing only 12 copies of such a lavish work with its severe criticism of Linnaeus might have been calculated to anger the botanical world of late eighteenth-century Britain. Dryander, Banks's librarian, judged it succinctly: 'splendidi magis quam utilis'.[81] James Edward Smith, the purchaser of Linnaeus's collections and founder of the Linnean Society, commented: 'it is easier to make a rare book, than a good one'.[82] Bute was undoubtedly anticipating such responses when, having uttered his criticisms of Linnaeus, he continued: 'after such a blasphemous sentence, these sheets are infallibly devoted to the flames: but I have gone too far to stop, and shall therefore pursue my object, let the consequence be what it will'.[83] That feelings ran high is indicated by the fact that in a book published some 30 years after Bute's death, Smith felt justified in indulging in arch editorial comments on letters critical of Linnaeus written by Bute in the 1750s. Smith must have been to the fore when Bute was not invited to join the Linnean Society (founded in 1788) 'on account of his dubious politics'.[84] Although this is plausible, since Smith and a number of founders of the Society were identifiably Whig in their political sympathies, Bute's botanical heterodoxy must also have played its part.

Enough has been said to indicate that Lord Bute's scientific 'career' is of considerable interest both in itself and for the light it can throw on the development of eighteenth-century natural history more generally. There are a number of topics which have not been covered here, notably Bute's collection of philosophical instruments, his herbarium and his extensive botanical library.[85] These must be left to future research. But we can draw several conclusions.

The standard perception of Bute's scientific persona has greatly underestimated the extent to which, throughout his life, he transcended the roles of mere planter, patron and collector. In early life he was a much respected botanist contributing to the exchange of seeds, specimens and information, and himself lamenting that the passion for planting among the nobility and gentry was not accompanied by more serious attention to botanical science. His interest in minerals and fossils, too, was not just that of a collector. Observations made on his travels were in part inspired by a good working knowledge of the latest views on volcanoes and of theories of the Earth. Back in his laboratory at Luton Hoo, he sought to apply to his mineral collection the most up-to-date techniques of chemical analysis with a view to developing a mineral classification on that basis.

However, Bute left no public trace of this higher-level activity in mineralogy. And even in the private records it appears that chemical analysis was dropped in the classification which was produced, reputedly for the convenience of Lady Bute who knew no chemistry. Certainly he had embarked on what can be seen in retrospect as an unrealistically ambitious scheme. When Bute did go into print with the *Botanical Tables*, this too was 'composed solely for the amusement of the fair sex',[86] a diffident dedication wholly out of tune in that unliberated age with the serious pretensions of the text. The *Botanical Tables*, based on views formed in the 1750s and reinforced in the interim by Bute's reading of Continental philosophical naturalists such as Buffon, Bonnet and Adanson, was wholly out of place in Britain in the 1780s when it appeared. Reservations about the Linnaean system which had been quite prevalent in the 1750s had by the end of the century been glossed over in the name of a higher good – establishing a standard system to make possible a co-ordinated, co-operative inventory of the vast botanical treasures gathered in by Banks at Kew Gardens and by members of the Linnean Society. Against this background Bute was crying in the wind and he knew it. Hence, I believe, came his reticence, his diffidence, his defeatism.

For these reasons Bute, already suspect in the eyes of influential naturalists like Ellis as a patron of 'quacks and compilers in Natural History', was convicted of heresy. Though I would not wish to exaggerate Bute's importance in eighteenth-century natural history – for certainly he was not a major figure – it is important that we recognize the extent to which he was written out of the story by succeeding generations, and to lasting effect.

In November 1790 Bute slipped and fell on the cliffs at Highcliffe, reputedly as he reached for a plant, a fall which it is supposed ultimately contributed to his death two years later.[87] To this poetic and tragic image of the man as a martyr to his science we can add the view that Bute was a martyr to his 'favourite studdys' in a much deeper sense.

NOTES

The primary manuscript resource for this paper are the Bute MSS. Items referred to in the notes only by date are part of the main sequence of correspondence at Mount Stuart. This sequence is organized chronologically by year and date. An important exception is the correspondence between Bute and John Strange which is held at Mount Stuart as a separate bundle. Another set of correspondence now held at Mount Stuart but previously held at Cardiff Central Library, is organized alphabetically by correspondent. Items in this set are referred to as the Cardiff MSS. I would like to thank the present Marquess of Bute for permission to consult and quote from the papers of the 3rd Earl, Mr Alexander Hunter for his considerable assistance and the following who helped in various ways: Karl Schweizer, David Allen, Roger L. Emerson, Ian Inkster, Jack Morrell, David Oldroyd and Jeffrey Sturchio.

1. E. Fitzmaurice, *Life of William, Earl of Shelburne* (3 vols, 1875–6), I, 110.
2. A.M. Coats, *Lord Bute. An Illustrated Life of John Stuart, Third Earl of Bute 1713–1792* (1975), 39,45.
3. W.P. Jones, 'The vogue of natural history in England, 1750–1770', *Annals of Science*, II (1937), 345–52; D.E. Allen, *The Naturalist in Britain: A Social History* (1976), 26–51. For Allen's remarks on Bute see *ibid.*, 43–4.
4. In practice, of course, exhibition and depiction of natural history specimens were guided by classificatory schemes of varying degrees of sophistication.
5. Archibald Campbell (1682–1761), Earl and Viscount of [Ilay] from 1706, succeeded to the Dukedom of Argyll in 1743. See *DNB*, III, 793–4.
6. Collinson's memo is in L.W. Dillwyn, *Hortus Collinsonianus. An Account of the Plants Cultivated by . . . Peter Collinson* (1843), 32n., and quoted in B. Henry, *British Botanical and Horticultural Literature before 1800* (3 vols, 1975), II, 100–1. On Collinson see N.G. Brett-James, *The Life of Peter Collinson* (1925); and G.F. Frick, 'Collinson, Peter', *Dictionary of Scientific Biography* (16 vols, New York, 1970–80), III, 349–51.
7. There is evidence that Bute did spend his school vacations at the English estate of his uncles (see J. Home, ed., *Lady Louisa Stuart: Selections from her Manuscripts* (New York, 1899), 3). The paternal influence was also strong, despite Bute's tender age at his father's

death. The continuity of interest in planting is revealed by a manuscript volume held at Mount Stuart the first section of which is headed 'A Journal of Planting &c Done by my Father & During My Minority from the beginning of 1718 to 1734'. The journal, which refers to planting and other work done at Mount Stuart, was kept regularly, with the exception of a break between 1737 and 1739, until 1744.

8. E. Peacock (ed.), *Index to English Speaking Students who have Graduated at Leyden University* (1883), 16.
9. On Linnaeus at Leiden and the naturalists who supported him there see W. Blunt, *The Compleat Naturalist. A Life of Linnaeus* (1971), 97–102, 123–5. On Gronovius (1690–1760), see also J. Nordstrom, 'Linné och Gronovius', *Svenska Linnésällskapets Årsskrift* (1954–5), 7–22.
10. On Lawson see Blunt, *op. cit.*, 99–101, 123–5 and *DNB*, XI, 732. In a letter to Gronovius Bute stated: 'my worthy friend Dr Lawson has made me very happy in procuring me the amiable correspondence of one of your learning and communicative temper' (Bute to Gronovius, 11 July 1745).
11. Coats, *op. cit.*, 10.
12. On the interrelations mentioned here see Frick, *op. cit.*, 350. Coats, *op. cit.*, 10, suggests that Bute 'may have met Catesby during his earlier sojourn in London, and perhaps subscribed towards the publication of his book'.
13. Bute to Collinson, 7 March 1745, Add. MSS 28726, fos. 154–5. A year later Bute, now at Twickenham, was again thanking Collinson for seeds and reciprocating in kind. See Bute to Collinson, 4 March 1746, Add. MSS 28726, f. 159.
14. Bute to Gronovius, 11 July 1745
15. Bute to Gronovius, 2 Feb. 1751. The house and 'garden' was Caen Wood (now Kenwood) at the north of what is now Hampstead Heath. Bute described it thus: 'at very great expense I repair'd a great house my father had within five miles of London,

in a situation that yields to none ...
My house is betwixt [the villages of
Hampstead and Highgate] ...
defended from the North by a great
wood ... to the South an old wood of
30 Acres belonging to me, over which
the whole city, with 16 miles of the
River appears from every window. A
Garden of 8 acres betwixt me and the
wood I am filling with every exotick
our climate will protect, & considering
I have not had but one year, the
number is very great.'

16. Collinson to Linnaeus, 10 Apr. 1755,
in J.E. Smith, *A Selection from the
Correspondence of Linnaeus and Other
Naturalists* (2 vols, 1821), I, 32–3.

17. Bute to Collinson, n.d., in Smith, *op.
cit.*, I, 33–5.

18. See Collinson to Linnaeus, 20 Sep.
1753; Bute to Collinson, 4 Aug. 1753;
and Bute to Collinson, 10 Aug. 1753,
all in Smith, *op. cit.*, I, 25–31.
Collinson's own response to the *Species
Plantarum* was generally favourable but
he also complained about the
numerous changes of names and new
names which it contained: 'Thus
Botany, which was a pleasant study
and attainable by most men, is now
become, by alterations and new
names, the study of a man's life, and
none now but real professors can
pretend to attain it. As I love you, I tell
you our sentiments' (Collinson to
Linnaeus, 20 April 1754, in Smith, *op.
cit.*, I, 31).

19. See especially G.S. Rousseau (ed.), *The
Letters and Papers of Sir John Hill 1714–
1775* (New York, 1982); and *idem*, 'John
Hill, universal genius manqué:
remarks on his life and times, with a
checklist of his works', in *The
Renaissance Man in the Eighteenth Century.
Papers read at a Clark Library Seminar 9
October 1976*, ed. J.A. Leo Lamay and
G.S. Rousseau (Los Angeles, 1978),
45–129.

20. See J. Hill, *Review of the Works of the
Royal Society of London* (1751); C.
Emery, '"Sir" John Hill versus the
Royal Society', *Isis*, XXXIV (1942), 16–
20; W.H.G. Armytage, *The Rise of the*

Technocrats: A Social History (1965), 41–
2.

21. Hill to Bute [1757], reproduced in
Rousseau, *op. cit.*, 31.

22. Hill to Bute, 11 Aug. 1759 in
Rousseau, *op. cit.*, 116–17. Hill's wife
later recalled that Hill at first was
hesitant to undertake the publication
because of the great expense and the
uncertain chances of recouping it. But
Lord Bute had responded that Hill's
'circumstances should not be injured'.
See Lady Hill, *An Address to the Public,
Setting forth the Consequences of the late Sir
John Hill's Acquaintance with the Earl of
Bute* (1788), 10–11.

23. T.G. Hill, 'John Hill 1716–1775', in
Makers of British Botany, ed. F.W.
Oliver (1913), 92–3; J. Hill, *The
Construction of Timber, from its Early
Growth* (1770).

24. Bute to John Strange, 6 Jan. 1774.

25. Thus on Hill's death: 'It [*The Vegetable
System*] has cost me for 17 years a great
sum, which I should not regret if I was
not told that notwithstanding the great
Expense I was at, His vanity, poor
man, has left a wife & 6 children with
very little'; see Bute to Strange, 22
Dec. 1775.

26. See Smith, *op. cit.*, I, 255; W.L. Tjaden,
'Drawings at Kew by Simon Taylor
(1742–*c.*1796)', *Kew Notes*, V (1972),
169; W. Blunt, *The Art of Botanical
Illustration* (3rd edn, 1955), 143–51.

27. W. Curtis, *Flora Londinensis* (1771); S.
Pullein, *An Essay Towards a Method of
Preserving the Seeds of Plants in a State Fit
for Vegetation, during Long Voyages*
(1759); A. von Haller, *Bibliotheca
Botanica* (1771). In 1781 Curtis asked
Bute for a £300 loan to continue his
work. Pullein accused the naturalist
John Ellis of using his work without
acknowledgment. Ellis was a severe
critic of Bute, whilst Pullein certainly
sought Bute's patronage. (See Henry,
op. cit., II, 101–2, and III, 185–6; on
Pullein seeking patronage, see Pullein
to Bute, 28 June [1764?], Cardiff MSS,
Bundle 11; and Rev. S. Hales to Bute,
13 Oct. 1757.)

28. Henry, *op. cit.*, II, 241. On the early

years of Kew Gardens, see W.T. Thistleton-Dyer, 'Historical account of Kew to 1841', *Kew Bulletin* (Dec. 1891), 279–327; M. Bingham, *The Making of Kew* (1975).

29. Coats, *op. cit.*, 19.

30. On Aiton see G. Taylor, 'Aiton, William', *Dictionary of Scientific Biography*, I, 88–9.

31. Peter Collinson remarked: 'From his Lordship's great knowledge in the science of botany the gardens at Kew have been furnished with all the rare exotick trees and flowers that could be procured' (see Brett-James, *op. cit.*, 87). One excited gardener of the time enthused:'my Lord Bute has already seatled a correspondence in Asia, Africa, America, Europe and everywhere he can; as, to be shure, my Lord is much the most knowing of any in this Kingdome by much of any in it' (see D. Turner, *Extracts from the Literary and Scientific Correspondence of Richard Richardson, M.D., F.R.S.* (1835), 406–7). Among letters addressed to Bute and identified as relating to obtaining material for Kew are those from: William Watson, 18 Dec. 1760, 14 Aug. 1761; Dr John Campbell, 14 Jan. 1763[4?], 7 Sept. 1764; Hugh Graeme, 21 Feb. 1761; Colonel Campbell Dalrymple, 3 June 1761; Dalrymple to Bute 14 April 1761, Cardiff MSS, Bundle 2. It is often difficult to tell whether seeds and plants were intended for Bute's private gardens or for Kew.

32. Coats, *op. cit.*, 24. It is uncertain on what information this latter claim is based since John Hill's catalogue of the plants in cultivation by 1768 contained 3,400 species, more than half the number named by Aiton in 1789.

33. Bute to Sir James Wright, 21 Sep. 1767.

34. Horace Walpole to Henry Zouch, 3 Jan. 1761, in W.S. Lewis (ed.), *The Yale Edition of Horace Walpole's Correspondence*, XVI (1951), 41–2. For an attempt to sort out Hill's precise status *vis-à-vis* Kew and Kensington Palace, see Henry, *op. cit.*, II, 243–5.

35. 'Remarks on the principles of the British government. Addressed to the guardians of the Constitution', *The Political Register*, I (May 1767), 1–9. The engraving appears between pp. 8 and 9.

36. On Ellis (1714?–76), see R.A. Rauschenberg, 'John Ellis, F.R.S.: eighteenth century naturalist and Royal Agent to West Florida', *Notes and Records of the Royal Society of London*, XXXII (1978), 149–64. Ellis was a greatly respected naturalist, particularly for his studies of zoophytes, which formed part of the basis for the award of the Royal Society's Copley Medal for 1767. He was thus a force to be reckoned with.

37. John Ellis to Linnaeus, 7 May 1771 (draft), in Ellis Correspondence, Linnean Society of London, Note-Book no. 2, 104V, reproduced in part in S. Savage, *Catalogue of the Manuscripts in the Library of the Linnean Society of London. Part IV. Calendar of the Ellis Manuscripts* (1948), 79. The actual letter, dated 10 May 1771 and differing in part, was printed in Smith, *op. cit.*, I, 259–62. In a previous letter, before the *Endeavour* expedition had set out, Ellis lamented the fact that Solander had not been introduced to the King and attributed this to 'Dr. Hill's being so great a favourite with Lord Bute' (see Ellis to Linnaeus, 19 Aug. 1768, in Smith, *op. cit.*, I, 232).

38. On Banks's appointment at Kew and subsequent activism, see H.C. Cameron, *Sir Joseph Banks K.B., P.R.S.: the autocrat of the philosophers* (1952), 61–101; and also David L. Mackay, *In the Wake of Cook: Exploration, Science and Empire, 1780–1801* (1985).

39. Bute, writing to Sir James Wright, 21 Sept. 1767, reported: 'I am now taking enough of Hemlock every day to kill a horse if given him at once without perceiving any good effect of it'.

40. See the auction sale catalogues in the BL(1255.c.15). There are three relating to minerals and fossils. The three auctions were held over a total of 14 days in March and May 1793 and

March 1794, and included 1,606 lots which realized a total of approximately £1,225; see G.L.'E. Turner, 'The auction sales of the Earl of Bute's instruments, 1793', *Annals of Science*, XXIII (1967), 214, n.5. Turner also identifies a catalogue of a sale on 3 June 1793 of the contents of Bute's laboratory which was concerned largely with minerals; see *ibid.*, 217–18, 240–1.

41. See *DNB*, XIX, 23, and below. Strange and Bute may have met in Italy where they both were in 1771.

42. The diaries are preserved at Mount Stuart as 'Bundle G'.

43. Bute to Strange, 20 Aug. [1772?].

44. R. Porter, *The Making of Geology: Earth Science in Britain 1660–1815* (1977), 174; G.R. De Beer, 'The volcanoes of Auvergne', *Annals of Science*, XVIII (1962), 49–61.

45. See J. Strange, 'An account of Two Giant Causeways, or groups of prismatic basaltic columns, and other curious vulcanic concretions', *Philosophical Trans.*, LXV (1775), 5–47; *idem*, 'An account of a curious Giants Causeway, or group of angular columns, newly discovered in the Euganean Hills', *ibid.*, LXV (1775), 418–23. For related studies of Strange see G.R. De Beer, 'John Strange F.R.S., 1732–1799', *Notes and Records of the Royal Society of London*, IX (1951), 96–108; and C.F. Engel, 'John Strange et la Suisse', *Gesnerus*, VI (1949), 34–44.

46. See, for example, Bute to Strange, 27 Dec. 1771; 20 Aug. [1772?]; 15 May 1775; 12 Sep. 1780; 28 Dec. 1780.

47. Porter, *op. cit.*, 114–15, 231n.

48. Bute to Strange, 27 Dec. 1771.

49. Bute to Strange, 4 Feb. 1772. The Scottish naturalist John Walker (on whom see n. 74) described Bute as adhering to the principle that neither classification by external characters nor by chemical characters could proceed independently of the other. See Walker's 'Systema fossilium', manuscript of *c.* 1790 in GUL Special Collections. A useful account of mineral classification and the

assimilation of mineralogy to chemistry is provided by E.M. Melhado, *Jacob Berzelius: The Emergence of His Chemical System* (1981), esp. 102–11, 293–309.

50. Compare the comment on Sir Ashton Lever made by John Walker in a letter to Bute, 28 Jan. 1773, after a visit to Lever's magnificent private museum: 'I could not but regret, that such a man should be devoid of Science, in the Study he so eagerly pursues'.

51. Peter Woulfe, F.R.S. (1727?–1803) was an eminent, if eccentric, chemist and mineralogist. He is best known for the apparatus which he developed for passing gases through liquids ('Woulfe's Bottle'). He received the Copley Medal of the Royal Society in 1768 and delivered the first three Bakerian lectures in 1775, 1776 and 1777. Woulfe's work thus gained him a substantial reputation. Woulfe generally spent the winter in London and the summer in Paris or on travels on the Continent. His laboratory at Barnard's Inn in London was a curious place, where, as well as his reputable work, Woulfe pursued alchemical investigations, affixing prayers to his apparatus (see *DNB*, XXI, 978–9; J.R. Partington, *A History of Chemistry* (4 vols, 1961–64, 1970), III, 245, 286, 290, 300–1).

52. Bute to Strange, 4 Feb. 1772.

53. At Mount Stuart (in Bundles C,D,E) are numerous manuscript papers, some in Bute's hand others in that of Woulfe, including: 'How to analise Earths & Stones in general'; 'An Account of such substances as have a Sparry Appearance & how to distinguish them from one another'; 'Of Saline Substances'. Lady Louisa Stuart, Bute's daughter, writing of her father's interest in chemistry and mineralogy, says that he would often have 'Mr. Wolf [*sic*], an eminent chymist' in the house for weeks together (see J.A. Lovat-Fraser, *John Stuart, Earl of Bute* (1912), 89).

54. Hill to Linnaeus, 10 Sep. 1772, in Rousseau, *op. cit.*, 175–6.

55. Bute to Strange, 15 Sep. 1772.
56. Bute to Strange, 17 Mar. 1773. The work itself has not been found, but it probably built on J. Hill, *Fossils Arranged According to the Obvious Characters* (1771), in which he used external characters on the grounds that it required no chemical knowledge.
57. Bute to [Sir William Musgrave], 27 Apr. 1782. Woulfe did continue experimental work for Bute, for example in the repetition of the 'beautiful experiment of a Gentleman at Bexley' in producing crystals by means of fixed air (see Bute to Strange, 28 Nov. 1777).
58. Bute to Strange, 22 Dec. 1775.
59. John Stuart, 3rd Earl of Bute, *Botanical Tables Containing the Different Familys of British Plants Distinguish'd by a Few Obvious Parts of Fructification Rang'd in a Synoptical Method* (9 vols, privately printed, 1785), I, 20. The introduction to this work was a slightly modified, but heavily edited, version of the introduction to Bute's *A Tabular Distribution of British Plants* (privately printed, 1780).
60. At Mount Stuart there are several copies of two printed documents. The first is the Preface, consisting of only five printed pages of text under a title page reading: *A Tabular Distribution of the Vegetable Kingdom containing the most distinguishing characters of all the Genera Hitherto Established* (printed by J. Davis, Chancery Lane, 1787). The second is a 51-page printed document entitled 'Introduction to the General Tables of Plants with a further explanation of the tabular arrangement' (n.d.). For previous notice of this second item see J. Britten, 'Lord Bute and John Miller', *J. of Botany*, LIV (1916), 84–7, who states: 'It is clearly the Introduction to a proposed larger work ... definitely asserted in the MS. note by Bute in the Windsor copy'. In the copy of the *Botanical Tables* at Windsor in volume 1 are not only the 51-page 'Introduction to the General Tables' but also two

notes in Bute's hand on loose sheets of paper. One note reads: 'These Pages contain a fuller Explanation of the Tabular Method. They are an Introduction to the General History of Vegetables, a very extensive Plan great part of which is done, but there remains still too much for a man at the Extreme of life to finish' (see W.B. Hemsley, 'Earl of Bute's Botanical Tables', *Kew Bulletin* (1892), 307)
61. J.L. Larson, *Reason and Experience. The Representation of Natural Order in the Work of Carl von Linné* (Berkeley, CA, 1971).
62. Bute, *Botanical Tables*, I, 14.
63. *Ibid.*, 16.
64. *Ibid.*, 19–20.
65. Bute, 'Introduction to the General Tables', 46–9.
66. *Ibid.*, 50–1.
67. Albrecht von Haller (1708–77), Swiss naturalist, poet and novelist, on whom see F.A. Stafleu, *Linnaeus and the Linnaeans: The Spreading of their Ideas in Systematic Botany* (Utrecht, 1971), 245–9. Haller dedicated his *Bibliotheca Botanica* (1771) to Bute. For his part, Bute sent Haller Hill's *Vegetable System* and held Haller in 'the highest Esteem'. See Rousseau, *op. cit.*, 125–6; and Bute to Strange, 20 Aug. [1772?].
68. Michel Adanson (1727–1806). On Adanson's rejection of Linnaeus, especially in his *Familles des Plantes* (2 vols, Paris, 1763), see Stafleu, *op. cit.*, 210–20. See also Bute, *Botanical Tables*, I, 15.
69. See Bute, *Botanical Tables*, I, 17–18, where he quotes from the first volume of Buffon's *Histoire naturelle* (44 vols, Paris, 1749–1804). On Buffon's criticism of Linnaeus see Philip Sloan, 'The Buffon–Linnaeus Controversy', *Isis*, LXVII (1976), 356–75, and J.L. Larson, 'Linné's French critics', in *Linnaeus: Progress and Prospects in Linnaean Research*, ed. G. Broberg (Stockholm and Pittsburgh, PA, 1980), 67–79. We know that Bute and Buffon were in contact, but to what extent is unclear. Using the Frenchman Louis Dutens (a long-standing friend of Bute) as intermediary, Buffon wrote in

1773 that he had sent 17 volumes of the *Histoire naturelle* and 624 coloured plates: 'Je vous supplie de dire à My Lord Bute que c'est avec autant d'instances que de Respect qu'il est prié d'accepter ces foibles marques de ma Reconnoissance'. Buffon had not yet received the 22 magnificent volumes which Bute had sent (presumably *The Vegetable System*) but, having seen the work in the King's library, he commented: 'en General c'est le plus grand et le plus bel ouvrage qui ait jamais été entrepris dans ce genre' (see Louis Dutens to Bute, 14 July 1773).

70. See Bute to Strange, 20 Aug. [1772?] and 15 May 1775. In the latter Bute comments rather amusingly: 'I observe your ... friend [Charles] Bonnet leans extrem'ly to that Romantick Hypothesis of [illegible] who had left Buffon far behind Him in His wild unphilosophick system, but Buffon in his last work on vegetables has got up his ground again'.

71. On the 'solid victory' of the Linnaean system in England see Stafleu, *op. cit.*, 199–240.

72. Even Bute's undoubted scientific friendship with Watson was uneasily overlaid by hopes of patronage. See Watson to Bute, 14 Aug. 1761, in which, after offering a number of presents in the natural history line, Watson seeks Bute's 'mediation' in seeking an appointment as physician extraordinary to 'her intended Majesty'.

73. See R.L. Emerson, 'The Edinburgh Society for the Importation of Foreign Seeds and Plants, 1764–1773', *Eighteenth Century Life*, VII (1982), 73–95; *idem*, 'The Philosophical Society of Edinburgh, 1748–1768', *The British Journal for the History of Science*, XIV (1981), 133–76; *idem*, 'The Philosophical Society of Edinburgh 1768–1793', *The British Journal for the History of Science*, XVIII (1975), 255–303. On the 'Moderate literati' and Bute's patronage of them see R.B. Sher, *Church and University in the Scottish*

Enlightenment: The Moderate Literati of Edinburgh (1985), 75–6, 106–7, 110–17.

74. Bute was approached to supply duplicate specimens to the Museum being established 'under the care of the worthy & ingenious Doctor Walker of Moffat' (see D.S. Erskine to Bute, 23 Mar. 1767, Cardiff MSS, Bundle 2). Walker reported to Bute on his journeys in England and in the Highlands and Islands of Scotland during which he collected fossils for Bute (see Walker to Bute, 28 Jan. 1773). On Walker see John Walker, *Lectures on Geology*, ed. H.W. Scott (Chicago, 1966); and G. Taylor, 'John Walker, D.D., F.R.S.E., 1731–1803, a notable Scottish naturalist', *Trans. Botanical Society of Edinburgh*, XXXVIII (1959), 180–203. Dr John Hope was appointed to the chairs of botany and *materia medica* at the University of Edinburgh in 1760 and as superintendant of the Royal Botanic Garden in Edinburgh in 1761. By all accounts Bute was of great assistance in obtaining government money for Hope's scheme to establish a new and better garden. See H.R. Fletcher and W.H. Brown, *The Royal Botanic Garden Edinburgh 1670–1970* (1970); and the up to date account by A.G. Morton, *John Hope, 1725–1786 Scottish Botanist* (1986) esp. 10–13. John Hope to [?] for transmission to Bute, 18 Oct. 1762, outlines the plan; Dr Alexander Dick to Dr John Pringle, 3 Dec. 1763 (enclosure in Pringle to Bute, 24 Dec. 1763) reports on its success 'by Lord Bute's friendship, which endears his Lordship still more to his friends here'. Bute was elected as President of the Society of Antiquaries of Scotland in 1780, but was apparently a merely titular and inactive one in a Society founded largely as a Whig initiative. See S. Shapin, 'Property, patronage and the politics of science: the founding of the Royal Society of Edinburgh', *British J. for the History of Science*, VII (1974), 23n.69.

75. Bute to [Sir William Musgrave], 27 Apr. 1782.

76. Bute to Strange, 6 Jan. 1774.

77. Bute to Strange, 15 May 1775.

78. Bute to Strange, 26 Sept. 1774, 3 May 1778.

79. Bute to Strange, 4 Aug. 1771; 27 Dec. 1771; 20 Jan. 1772; 15 Sep. 1772.

80. MS. note in Bute's hand [Jan. 1777].

81. J. Dryander, *Catalogus Bibliothecae Historico-Naturalis Josephi Banks* (5 vols, 1796–1800), III, 133.

82. Quoted in Coats, *op. cit.*, 45.

83. Bute, 'Introduction to the General Tables', 4.

84. Smith, *op. cit.*, I, 36n.; Coats, *op. cit.*, 44.

85. On Bute's instrument collection see G.L'E. Turner, *op. cit.*; David Allen kindly supplied the information that Bute's herbarium was auctioned in May 1794 and April 1809 and was finally purchased by Kew in 1926. See D.H. Kent and D.E. Allen, *British and Irish Herbaria* (1984), 253.

86. Bute, *Botanical Tables*, Dedication. Only 12 copies of the *Tables* were printed for private distribution. A manuscript note in vol. IX of the copy of the *Tables* now in the BL (originally Sir Joseph Banks's copy) notes the following initial disposition of the 12 copies: 2 for Lord Bute, and 1 each to the Queen, the Empress of Russia, Sir Joseph Banks, M. de Buffon, Lady B[y] Mackenzie, Lady Ruthven, Lady Macartney, Duchess of Portland, Mrs Barrington, Mr Dutens. The note is printed in Henry, *op. cit.*, III, 124.

87. See Coats, *op. cit.*, 45.

10

Bute in retirement

Peter D. Brown

When on 8 April 1763 Bute relinquished the office of First Lord of the Treasury to George Grenville, he did not think of himself as founding a precedent. This departure would develop into the problem of the former First Lord of the Treasury, or in modern parlance, the ex-Prime Minister. The title itself was a source of confusion. That the position of First Lord of the Treasury carried the government of the country was not altogether recognized, even by the country's greatest statesman, William Pitt. Yet none doubted that, when in May 1762 George III had appointed Bute in succession to the Duke of Newcastle, the complete direction of the administration had been the intention. Every one of Bute's predecessors, with the exception of the Duke of Devonshire, had either died in harness or been old men on retirement. Devonshire's example hardly counted, because his ministry was virtually an interregnum between Newcastle's first and second administrations.

Bute was the first Prime Minister to survive his resignation by a generation. His 50th birthday was due on 25 May and he was of a constitution sound enough to carry him through to see the loss of the American colonies, the younger Pitt's ministry of national revival and the initial stages of the French Revolution. The enigma of the ex-Prime Minister has two aspects: the attitude of men still in public life towards the fallen statesman is bound to be coloured by a suspicion that the desire for power is not dead, which must give his successors apprehension; also attention is due to those perplexities that must assail a man who can recall the flush of success on taking office, and is then faced with the acute disenchantment of obscurity. As applied to Bute, these considerations quite dominated Grenville and the first Rockingham administration which followed on. The glowing terms of the King's letter of 9 April 1763, the day after his resignation, gave Bute every certainty that, though no longer First Lord of the Treasury, he must be 'Mayor of the Palace'.[1]

Apart from his situation as the King's favourite, Bute was in no way likely to retire to his island off the west coast of Scotland. He was by right of his wife a magnate of England. The death of his father-in-law,

Edward Wortley Montagu, in October 1761 had transformed the impecunious Scottish earl into one of the richest men in the land. The extraordinary conduct of Lady Bute's brother, also Edward Wortley, which culminated in a bigamous marriage, was punished by his virtual disinheritance. Lady Bute was left a life interest in the Wortley estates in West Yorkshire, based upon Wharncliffe, near Sheffield, worth £17,000 per annum, subject to an allowance for the ne'er-do-well to keep the wolf from the door but insufficient to meet his outstanding debts.[2]

The Wortley interests also comprised parliamentary influence at Bossiney, a Cornish borough. By an arrangement with Lord Mount Edgecumbe, the other proprietor, arrived at in 1752, each family returned one member to Parliament. Edward Wortley was elected at the general election of 1761, though his circumstances compelled him to live abroad.[3]

Lady Bute's father had been a notorious miser, and yet more dazzling than the landed estates was her personal fortune, of which estimates have varied between £800,000 and £1,300,000. The magnificence of the Bute mode added to the irritation caused by his intervention in politics. Whilst yet Prime Minister he commissioned Robert Adam to build a mansion between Berkeley Square and Piccadilly, to be known as Bute House. This would rival Devonshire House next door, and put Bute on a par with the few noblemen such as Bedford and Newcastle who maintained town establishments on the *palazzo* model. Accompanied by his small daughter Louisa, Bute watched the first sod turned for the foundations. For the time being he continued the use of his house in South Audley Street.[4] Bute had appointed Adam Surveyor of the King's Works, which with the pension accorded Dr Johnson was one of the creditable features of his administration.

Desirous of becoming a landowner within reach of London, Bute purchased Luton Hoo, a Bedfordshire estate which comprised the mansion, sometimes known simply as The Hoo, together with over 4,000 acres, traversed by the River Lea. The vendor was Francis Hearne, and the price stated as £94,700 or £111,000: the larger figure probably included side purchases. The principal industry of Luton was that of the strawmakers, who had been transported from Scotland by James I. As lord of the manor Bute obtained the right to hold view of frankpledge, court leet and court baron at Luton Corn Exchange. He was also patron of St Mary's, the parish church. Though the Luton property was not extensive by the standards of an eighteenth-century nobleman, Bute's acquisition was bound to attract notice.[5]

The brilliant situation of the Butes was borne out further by the marriage in 1761 of their eldest daughter Mary to Sir James Lowther, of Lowther, Westmorland. He was the greatest landowner in the north-west border country in respect of income as well as acreage, with valuable coal deposits becoming increasingly utilized as the demands of industry expanded. Avidly ambitious of wealth and power, Lowther had every intention of cultivating his already considerable parliamentary influence.[6]

At the moment of resigning, Bute probably gave little thought to the future, such was his relief at abandoning the day-by-day harassment of business. Further, he did not experience the sensation of relinquishing authority. Bute and the King had done their best to circumscribe Grenville, so that he might not feel himself too much the master. Grenville had frustrated their wish to replace his brother-in-law the Earl of Egremont, Secretary of State for the South, with Bute's protégé, the young Earl of Shelburne. But the Earl of Halifax, the other Secretary of State, was a known friend to Bute. And Shelburne was placed in a position of growing importance as President of the Board of Trade. The entire management of Scotland was expressly reserved to Bute's brother James Stuart Mackenzie.[7] Charles Jenkinson, who had been Bute's personal secretary, became Joint Secretary to the Treasury. Bute retained the confidential situation of Keeper of the Privy Purse. In securing for his eldest son John, Viscount Mountstuart, the reversion to the auditorship of the imprest, a valuable sinecure, Bute merely followed the practice of the day.

Before handing over to Grenville, Bute had announced his intention of retiring for a time to distant Harrogate, ostensibly for his health. But in the days following his resignation, he was inundated with letters from the King. The business of allocating Household offices, usual on the accession of a new ministry, had previously been handled by Bute. Now the King had to take the decisions, at which he felt much perplexed. Apart from a long weekend at Lord le Despencer's seat, West Wycombe Park, Bute was unable to leave London until 2 May.[8] By this time John Wilkes had been arrested as author and publisher of issue no. 45 of the *North Briton*.

From the outset the King was uneasy with Grenville, whose dictatorial manner in the Closet, so different to Bute's dulcet purring, was resented. Bute was rapidly summoned back to London. The King's initial intention was not to dismiss Grenville but dilute his authority further by inducing some of the Newcastle Whigs to join the ministry. Bute called on Lord Royston, the eldest son of Lord Hardwicke, the Lord Chancellor of old. At the King's command Egremont, much against his wishes, offered the Presidency of the Council to Hardwicke, who proved unwilling to entertain overtures from the Court, and could be taken as speaking for Newcastle as well. In June Bute saw Pitt, who was probably not particularly glad to see him, and made clear he would not act other than in concert with Newcastle and the Old Whigs.

By the end of July the King came to the conclusion that his only course must be the reinstatement of the old coalition between Pitt and Newcastle. When, on 2 August, Grenville found the royal demeanour awkwardly distant, he guessed Bute to be engaged in some negotiation. After his recent rebuff Bute employed as emissary an old acquaintance of Pitt, John Calcraft. On 14 August Pitt emphasized to Calcraft his commitment to Newcastle, and prescribed that every politician who had supported the Peace of Paris be excluded from office, naming particularly the Duke of Bedford. The sudden death of Egremont on 21 August gravely weakened Grenville's position.[9]

Bute was above all anxious to please the King, so that when, on 25 August, William Beckford guided him into Pitt's presence, he willingly conceded everything. Two days later Pitt had an audience of the King: his brother-in-law Temple was to take the Treasury, with Cabinet posts for the Old Whigs, and in respect of places Newcastle's following must be restored at every level. Then, on Sunday 28 August, Bute's old friends Gilbert Elliot and Jenkinson went to Kew and pointed out to him the disastrous consequences the proposed change of ministry must have for themselves and all his old associates involved with the Peace. Bute's influence over the King was still so immediate, that when that evening Grenville was received in audience, he realized to his amazement that the plan for his disgrace had been abandoned.[10]

For Bute the result of his maladroit intervention was catastrophic. For years he had been best friend to 'dear George', and the new reign secured for him the approbation of the King. The stab in the back of Bute's intrigue came as a shock inevitably matched by the deepest resentment. Furthermore, the proceedings against Wilkes had miscarried: the villain had been discharged on his parliamentary privilege; court actions concerning general warrants were pending. When, in November, Parliament met, Pitt and the Old Whigs were bound to take issue, and the responsibility would fall on Grenville. Seeking to anticipate the inevitable, Bute caused Elliot to write to Grenville on Wednesday 31 August intimating his intention to retire completely from business and quit the Privy Purse: 'He seems extremely desirous that you may be armed with every degree of power necessary at this juncture.'

Grenville seized the opportunity. His circular letter of 3 September to some senior Members of Parliament carried the sentence of exile:

'Lord Bute out of regard for what he thinks will be most for His Majesty's interest has declared that he is determined to retire and to absent himself not only from the Councils, but from the presence and place of residence of His Majesty, until the suspicion of his influence on public life shall be entirely removed.'[11]

The way was open for Grenville to negotiate a coalition with the Bedford Whigs. A new Secretary of State to succeed Egremont was found in Bedford's old friend the Earl of Sandwich. Shelburne resigned the Presidency of the Board of Trade and attached himself permanently to Pitt. Then on 12 September Bedford, out of resentment at Pitt's personalized attitude to himself, accepted office as Lord Privy Seal. Bute could expect no sympathy from Pitt and Newcastle, who had thought themselves about to enter the promised land, only to find that he could not be relied upon to enforce a bargain.

On Wednesday 28 September Bute took his sad leave of the King. The new Keeper of the Privy Purse had yet to be decided, and in a talk with Grenville of 30 September the King insisted that Sir William Breton be the choice. Breton had been a Groom of the Bedchamber at Leicester House in the days of the King's father, and subsequently received a knighthood in the Coronation honours of September 1761. Grenville objected to him as a friend to Bute but the King insisted.[12]

A week later Bute left for Luton, and from Grenville's point of view was too near London for comfort. From this time the King's correspondence with Bute would appear to have terminated for a considerable period. The strong probability is that the King felt himself bound in honour not to maintain any direct relationship with 'My D. Friend'. In that case his surprise at the ruction only a fortnight after Bute's departure was genuine. It happened that Beckford had an estate in Bedfordshire. On 14 October Halifax and Sandwich, in a state of great trepidation, told Grenville of a report that Beckford had called on Bute, who had informed him that only Pitt's extreme demands had defeated the recent negotiation, 'and that if Mr. Pitt could bring himself to be more reasonable, it was not yet too late . . .'.

The King did not believe a word but rumour got around that Bute was intriguing as heartily as ever, and had written to Shelburne twice in one week. On 19 October Mackenzie called on Grenville to assure him that Bute was on no kind of terms with Shelburne, which was true. Jenkinson was sent to Luton to confront Bute, who admitted that Beckford had been to dine but no private word about politics had been uttered: 'Mr. Grenville reported to the King Lord Bute's disavowal of Mr Beckford's negociation; the King said he was glad to hear it; that he never doubted the falsehood of it, knowing Lord Bute could not do so base a thing.'

Bute, accustomed to the bustle of Court, soon wearied of country life. When, on 29 November, the House of Lords debated parliamentary privilege in respect of Wilkes, he gave his proxy to le Despencer to vote for the administration. During the winter, using Jenkinson as go-between, Bute did his utmost to build a bridge with Grenville. As no encouragement was forthcoming, Lady Bute took matters in hand. On 16 January 1764, she cleverly approached Lord Gower, whose sister Gertrude was Duchess of Bedford. To him Lady Bute confided her supposition that, if her husband ever returned to London, Bedford would resign and throw the ministry into confusion. Gower naturally repeated this conversation to his brother-in-law, who denied having made any such declaration but added that Bute's presence in town, by giving the impression of political interference, must be prejudicial to the King's affairs. Grenville praised the moderation of Bedford's answer and the conclusion.

Grenville could not possibly encourage Bute whilst the House of Commons was debating the expulsion of Wilkes. When, on 28 January, Jenkinson pressed the point of whether Bedford might resign, Grenville with some acerbity stressed that just as he had not caused the events which led to Bute's departure, so he had no power to keep him away. Jenkinson warned that Bute might well come to London privately for a day or so. By Sunday 12 February Grenville was daily expecting Bute's arrival, of which Lady Bute was talking quite openly. As the House of Commons was occupied with the issue of general warrants, it was no surprise that this plan was not acted on.

After Jenkinson had encountered a further repulse on Sunday 11 March, Bute fell into a deep depression. It was probably Lady Bute who persuaded him to defy Grenville and travel to London on the Monday week. The following day, 20 March, Bute saw the King, their first meeting for five months, which may well have been an emotional occasion. Bedford believed the interview began at 7 a.m. and lasted four hours, but he was prone to exaggerate. That evening over dinner Grenville, Bedford, Sandwich and Halifax resolved each to call upon Bute but confine conversation to generalities. When Grenville paid his visit on 22 March, he was given Bute's assurance that the King had spoken of him 'with the highest praise and satisfaction'. The day following the King received Grenville in the most flattering manner, and emphasized the necessity of his affairs being entrusted to one person exclusively; Bute had every confidence in him as 'an affectionate and able servant'. Bute's visit to London turned out no more than an incident, which was laid to rest when, on Thursday 24 March, he returned Grenville's civilities, and nothing remarkable passed on either side. Within the week, Bute was back at Luton.[13]

That Grenville no longer feared Bute's influence, at least for the time being, was indicated by a curious transaction in the second week of April. The Prime Minister had a liking to borrow New Lodge, one of the royal houses in Richmond Park, and actually engaged Bute's good offices. Bute dutifully informed the King, who on 18 April wrote to him of an audience in which he refused Grenville's request; New Lodge suited his own convenience when out riding. The King's letter went on to relate his rejection of Grenville's submission that Lord Chancellor Henley might be made an earl. In a further letter to Bute about this time, the King wrote of his insistence that Mackenzie have his way over a nomination to a Scottish judgeship. These appear to have been the only written exchanges between Bute and the King since July 1763.[14] The King yielded in respect of Henley, who on 12 May became Earl of Northington.

The parliamentary session ended, Grenville took his leave of the King on 26 June and retired to Wotton, his Buckinghamshire home, for ten days. Pitt attended the levee to be but coldly received. The world was agog with rumours of conferences between Bute and Pitt but Grenville, on his return, found no evidence of trouble brewing.[15] In fact Bute was no longer regarded as a principal in making ministers, whilst Pitt was suffering from a prolonged attack of his gout.

Bute had an innocent excuse for staying in town, with the impending marriage of his fourth daughter, Anne, to Hugh Percy, Lord Warkworth. The ceremony took place on 2 July 1764, by special licence at Bute's house in South Audley Street. The material aspects of this match were as formidable as with the Lowther connection. The groom's father, who had begun life as Sir Hugh Smithson, Bart., had inherited the revived earldom of Northumberland, together with the enormous Percy properties in that county, Sion House in Middlesex, and Northumberland House at Charing Cross.[16] Skilful management of colliery interests in the North had increased the Percy income to £50,000 per annum. Robert Adam had for some years been employed on the transformation of the interiors of the Percy residences. Soon Bute was also engaged with Adam on a project for Luton, the earliest plans dating from this time.[17]

From the remainder of 1764 until well into the following year Grenville governed supreme. His Stamp Act was enacted almost without opposition in the Commons and *nem. con.* in the Lords. It was not until March 1765 that Pitt was fit to resume political activity. Soon he was called upon by the Marquess of Rockingham, who was rapidly succeeding the ageing Newcastle as leader of the Old Whigs. Then Grenville, by his maladroit handling of the Regency Act, gave the King a suitable pretext to change his ministers. Obsessed by his hatred for Bute, Grenville proposed the omission of the Princess Dowager from those the Act nominated to a Regency Council. Her name was inserted by a House of Commons amendment, which made public the King's humiliating situation.

The King entrusted the engineering of a new administration to his uncle the Duke of Cumberland, and he would never have sought Bute's views. Northumberland was, however, the choice for First Lord of the Treasury in a coalition envisaged between Pitt and the Old Whigs. The embarrassing failure of this project was due entirely to Pitt's intransigence but he attached responsibility to Bute, whose views on government were he maintained so totally at variance with his own. The upshot was highly painful to the King.

Grenville insisted upon the dismissal of Mackenzie as Lord Privy Seal for Scotland, which the King had promised him for life. Though Bute wrote to George III releasing him from that undertaking, the indignation at the King being forced to go back on his word was general. The King retired to Richmond nursing a feverish condition and on Sunday 26 May failed to take the Sacrament. That day he wrote to Bute: 'My D. Friend's letter I owne overcomes my natural temper; I wish sometimes I were a private man that I might with my own arm defend my honour and freedom, against men whose families have formerly acted with more duty to the Crown than these wretches their successors'.[18]

From this point, though the King might keep Bute at a distance from a motive of caution, he surely felt no longer bound in honour to Grenville. And Grenville must in the last resort prove powerless against the King's resolve to change his servants. In the second week of June a futile approach to Rockingham and Newcastle convinced Cumberland that no ministry could be formed without Pitt. On this third occasion Pitt was far more accommodating than formerly. He naturally wanted Temple at the Treasury and his own way in foreign policy, and otherwise was ready to include men who, having originally owed their places to Bute, must have voted for the Peace: Mackenzie would at least have an equivalent, though without the management of Scotland. But in the end Cumberland's efforts came to naught, because Temple was unwilling to oust Grenville and carried Pitt with him. Pitt blamed this disappointment upon Bute's influence, which the King thought completely unjust.

Cumberland therefore decided on a ministry made up principally of the Old Whigs, which he achieved in the first week of July, with Rockingham First Lord of the Treasury. When on 10 July Grenville had a final audience with the King, his lecture of considerable length on the subject of Bute was snubbed with the assurance that he had nothing to do with the changes.[19] Indeed he had not, for the Old Whigs, every whit as jealous of Bute, exacted a promise from the King not to consult him. The King and Bute therefore agreed not to see one another until the end of the winter parliamentary session, which could not be before March 1766.[20]

Cumberland would readily have strengthened the ministry in the House of Commons with places for some of Bute's friends, including an honourable office for Mackenzie. Instead Sir Fletcher Norton, the forceful Attorney-General, and le Despencer, who could be counted Bute men, were turned out. Revenge and reinstatement for their own people who had been dismissed after December 1762 appeared almost the sole purpose of the Old Whigs. Yet this obduracy was not evidence of strength and cohesion. Rockingham was anxious to defer to Pitt's views in policy. The Duke of Grafton, new to office and a Secretary of State, always considered himself a Pitt disciple. Lord Chancellor Northington and the Earl of Egmont, First Lord of the Admiralty in Grenville's administration, continued in office. The King shared the general misgivings about the inexperience of Rockingham and Grafton. Initially the formidable presence of Cumberland, who even supervised Cabinet proceedings, concealed these weaknesses. Towards the end of the summer news arrived of resistance in America to the Stamp Act.[21]

That October Bute completed the sale of his unfinished mansion in Berkeley Square to Shelburne, who contracted to spend over £20,000 on completion. Bute House therefore became known as Shelburne House. The eclipse of his political importance was an obvious reason for Bute's decision, though his increasingly ambitious plans for Luton may have been a further consideration. Bute kept on the modest residence in South Audley Street which had been his before the Wortley riches came his way.[22]

The sudden death of Cumberland on the last day of October changed the fortunes of the ministry, which Rockingham must now head in reality. The loss of his uncle left the King without a guide and counsellor. The King stood loyally by his ministers but Grafton especially favoured an appeal to Pitt as the only resource. Whereas Cumberland would have been most reluctant to condone the resistance to the King's writ in America, Rockingham fully understood the concern of the merchants of Liverpool and Bristol for the restoration of normal trade by the repeal of the Stamp Act. Though the King was also sympathetic to repeal, the Cabinet was far from united on this crucial issue.

Immediately into the new year, 1766, Rockingham, without the King's authority, sent Newcastle's great-nephew, Tommy Townshend, to sound out Pitt. The King was not surprised when Pitt, so far from proposing terms, simply demanded that Temple replace Rockingham at the Treasury. Bute, solicitous about the King's well-being, suggested a meeting. This the King declined, so as not to give ministers provocation. Instead on 10 January he wrote Bute a long letter, the survivor of an intricate correspondence that winter which otherwise they presumably destroyed.

The King's letter recounted in considerable detail the recent abortive approach to Pitt. The King went out of his way to praise Northington, who expressed himself most kindly towards Bute and strongly favoured the inclusion of his friends in the ministry. Though obliged to support the administration, so long as they felt themselves able to carry on, the King had no objection to Bute and his friends, whom he expressly termed his own, following their own consciences with respect to the repeal of the Stamp Act. At his conclusion the King emphasized he would not

> entreat Mr. Pitt, which I think would for ever stain my name, please believe me incapable of ever thinking of you but with the greatest love and friendship, and keep my friends from personal opposition and when they from opinion differ let them be as civil in their expression as occasion will permit; as to the Peace it is not mentioned in the Speech.

That reference to the Peace of Paris, in connection with the King's Speech at the reassembly of Parliament on 14 January 1766, was perhaps a joke. The ministers allowed Pitt to take the lead with proposals to repeal the Stamp Act. Four days later the King gave way to Rockingham over yet a further approach to Pitt, which met with the rebuff he no doubt expected. The next month Bute and his followers combined with Grenville and his, to oppose the repeal of the Stamp Act in both Houses, though here was a parallelism rather than a coalition. Then on 4 March Pitt, in the course of the third reading, criticized the administration for the continued proscription of Mackenzie and Bute's adherents, words the King noted. The repeal passed the House of Lords on 11 March by only 73 votes to 61, with Bute voting in the minority.

On 28 April Grafton, who had always regarded the administration as a caretaker for Pitt, talked to the King of his impending resignation. A

Cabinet crisis ensued and when, on 1 May, the ministers met at Northington's, he and Egmont strongly favoured appointments for Mackenzie and Bute's followers. Two days later therefore the King addressed a long epistle to Bute asking whether or not his friends were prepared to accede:

> I beg an answer, but if possible shall when I have received that avoid writing till everything is one way or other settled; for you must see how very material that caution is, besides I have reason to suspect that my sister watched whenever I deliver any letters to my mother, not from ill intention, I hope, but curiosity and she has also said that during the great confusion in the winter that De Marche us'd frequently at five o'clock in the evening to bring letters from you on the day I went to my mother which she suppos'd must be for me; all this I beg may be trusted to no living soul; shews how cautious we must be, pity your unhappy friend for indeed he deserves it . . .

After Grafton had resigned, Rockingham initially offered the vacant post of Secretary of State to Egmont, who declined on the ground that no understanding with Bute's friends was being attempted. The King's opinion of the Duke of Richmond, who succeeded Grafton, was on a par with his contempt for most of the administration. Lord Chancellor Northington sought to ascertain Pitt's views on forming a government. The day after Pitt's arrival on 11 July, the King wrote to Bute describing events:[23]

> My D. Friend will easily conceive that I am now in a state of great agitation, as my attempts have so often proved fruitless; my resolution is to try through Mr. Pitt to build an Administration on as general a basis as the times will permit, to see as many of those gentlemen who were contrary to my inclinations remov'd reinstated, particularly Mr. Mackenzie, in short to see you my Dear Friend once quit of the unmerited usage you have so long suffer'd and openly appearing as my private friend . . .

Unfortunately Bute misconstrued the King's intention, which was simply that in future he would be free to attend Court openly. The three years of confusion since Bute had resigned as Prime Minister were hopefully ended and the haven of a sound administration in sight. By this time the King was taking his own measure of men and things. He was not surprised when Temple refused the Treasury except on his own terms. Pitt, who did not feel strong enough to undertake a daily supervision, became Earl of Chatham and chose Grafton for the Treasury. The obligation to Mackenzie was honoured with his restoration as Lord Privy Seal for Scotland.

Bute was ruffled that Chatham did not refer to himself about his brother, and some of his friends, particularly Norton, who were not given office went complaining. A pamphlet which attributed Temple's conduct to Bute's influence was deeply upsetting. Altogether, Bute felt his situation as a former Prime Minister was not being accorded due recognition, and protested to the King by letter. The upshot was a stiff and utterly unexpected royal rebuke. Bute in a hasty epistle poured out his grief at the loss of the King's friendship, though unwisely he also pleaded his mortification at Chatham's lack of condescension.[24] The spell which had bound the King to Bute all these years was broken for ever.

The shock and pain to Bute at this abrupt conclusion must have been terrible. It was 20 years since he had been introduced to the royal circle, and his affection for his young master had been of a consistent sincerity, which was no longer reciprocated. He had to recognize the termination of that confidential access to his Sovereign which had been his unique privilege. Perhaps Bute's distress found some alleviation in the conferment of a dukedom upon Northumberland on 22 October. Lord Warkworth took the second title of Earl Percy and Anne appeared to have a brilliant future as his duchess.

Bute could also look forward to the very grand marriage Mountstuart was shortly to enter. After Harrow and Winchester Mountstuart had not proceeded to university but was sent on a prolonged Grand Tour. Serious studies in Holland and France were followed by a tour of Italy, with James Boswell a travelling companion. He came of age on 30 June 1765 and the following January entered the House of Commons for the second seat at Bossiney.[25] Lady Sarah Lennox, who had caught the King's eye until Bute had steered him into a royal marriage, described Mountstuart as 'tall, well made, and very handsome; he is sensible, and 'tis fashionable to cry him up; I think he is very conceited, and seems to me very proud and vain, but yet is very well bred and does vastly well for a beau.'[26]

Mountstuart's bride was Charlotte Jane, elder daughter and, with her sister Alice Elizabeth, co-heir of Herbert Hickman Windsor, 2nd Viscount Windsor in the peerage of Ireland and Lord Mountjoy of the Isle of Wight in that of Great Britain. The Windsor family, one of the few of genuine Anglo-Norman ancestry, had been ennobled as Barons Windsor by Henry VIII in 1529 and Earls of Plymouth by Charles II in 1682. These Windsor girls were of a younger branch, and their wealth derived from their grandmother, Lady Elizabeth Herbert, wife of the 1st Viscount Windsor. As the only child of Philip Herbert, 7th Earl of Pembroke, Cardiff Castle, together with a great estate in Glamorgan, was made her portion.

Though Mountstuart might ignore the consideration that his be-
trothed was generally esteemed to have more money than looks, he
must have known his future mother-in-law to be a thoroughly tiresome
prospect. Lady Windsor could not fix a date for the wedding, because
a 'lucky day' was an absolute condition. Three times she changed
her mind, and then at only a week's notice hit upon Wednesday 12
November as the most propitious. The ceremony took place at St
John's Chapel, within St George's Hanover Square. Lady Bute gave
her daughter-in-law a pair of diamond earrings. The following day
Bute's cousin, Lady Mary Coke, called and received an account from
Mountstuart's sister Jane:[27]

> She told me they were twenty at Dinner, and that upon the whole it had
> been a very formal business. They staid at Lord Bute's till ten ocl., and
> then Lord and Lady Mountstuart went home. Lady Windsor was at the
> time playing cards, but the moment she miss'd them she threw her cards
> down in order to follow. But Lady Bute begg'd she would take them up
> again and finish her game, which she did with difficulty, and then made
> great haste for fear they should have gone to supper without her. That
> ended I hear she was an hour and a half in undressing her poor girl, to put
> her to bed, and then I believe she was prevailed upon to go home.

After the wedding night in London, Mountstuart took his wife to Luton
for six days. Their eldest son, the third John, was born on 25 September
1767, the first of a large family.

Lady Mountstuart's sister, Alice Elizabeth, likewise entered a
grand marriage, on 4 February 1768, with Francis Seymour-Conway,
Viscount Beauchamp, the Earl of Hertford's eldest son. Four years
later Alice Elizabeth died, leaving a daughter who did not long survive.
The entire Cardiff estate of over 20,000 acres thus passed to the Bute
family.

Early in 1767, Bute must have become increasingly conscious of his
isolation. His situation was solitary to a degree neither Grenville nor
Rockingham had to endure. There was not the least prospect of Bute's
exerting an influence over government. He had owed his entry to the
scene solely to the favour of the King. The withdrawal of the royal
countenance meant that the many peers and MPs who had toadied to
him as the man of power turned away. Grenville, though excluded by
the King from ever again holding office, was the most respected man in
the House of Commons. Rockingham nurtured the hope of leading his
Old Whigs back to power. It was no use Bute's speculating on the
many difficulties and errors of the Chatham administration, for certainly he would not be the beneficiary.

Yet some trappings of his former greatness remained. As a Scots representative peer, Bute was entitled to sit in the House of Lords. His electoral patronage and many connections guaranteed the presence of members of his family in the House of Commons. Bute was a Knight of the Garter and also Ranger of Richmond Park. He still supervised the royal gardens at Kew. In June 1765 he had become a trustee of the British Museum. Bute enjoyed the inestimable asset of serious intellectual pursuits, especially mathematics and botany; his libraries were well chosen and by no means a matter of show. Bute was reputed to have retained the friendship of the Princess Dowager. He was said to visit her secretly and make his departure by the back stairs whenever the King was announced. There were many who believed their relationship to exceed the proper limits of courtly love. Bute's breach with George III was private and his complete withdrawal from Court not generally credited.

Bute's character came out best in the domestic virtues, and he had a family of five sons and six daughters. After Mountstuart came James (Archibald), born in 1747, who underwent his initial education at Graffiani's Academy in Kensington. Frederick, born in 1751, was at Winchester, and the fourth son Charles, born in 1753, destined for the army. William, the youngest, born in 1755, followed Frederick to Winchester: the only son to show an academic propensity, his career was to be the Church. The six daughters were Lady Lowther, Jane, Augusta, Countess Percy, Caroline, and Louisa.

The second son, James, might one day be a rich man, with the opportunities for importance the period offered. As James Stuart Mackenzie was childless, James was heir to his properties, Rosehaugh, in Ross-shire, and Belmont, in Forfar. Far more important, he might also succeed his mother in the Wortley estates in West Yorkshire and Cornwall. Edward Wortley Montagu's Will had made provision for the male issue of his son by any legal marriage other than his present; James was named in reversion after his mother. As the scape-grace uncle's first and legal wife was still living, James's future was probable, though not watertight.

Only a few weeks after the Mountstuart nuptials, Bute received a rude shock at the news that James, up at Edinburgh University, had taken part in a student riot which resulted in the burning of the Playhouse. Then, on 8 June 1767, James was secretly married to Margaret, the daughter of Sir David Conynghame, an Ayrshire baronet. Early in 1768 he admitted to his situation but declared his intention never to live with his wife, towards whom he felt the deepest dislike. Bute put his foot down and insisted that James set up a marital home, for which a settlement was provided.[28]

After James's escapades, Bute may have found a relief in the marriage on 1 February of his daughter Jane to Sir George Macartney of Lissanoure Castle, Co. Antrim. In some respects this Irishman was not quite up to the mark for life with the Butes, but his wit, knowledge, and sincere good companionship compensated for his lack of connection. His knighthood had been conferred in 1764 when he was sent as envoy to St Petersburg, which he resigned owing to a disagreement with Chatham.[29]

Parliament, having run the full statutory seven years since 1761, was dissolved. Grafton, to whom Chatham had entrusted the conduct of the administration, showed no jealousy of Bute and allowed his re-election as a Scots representative peer. So far as the Bute family was concerned, the general election of 1768 had to go according to plan. Mackenzie continued to sit for Ross-shire. Bute used his interest in the Ayr burghs to have James elected to Parliament, in the vain hope that public business might mature him. Lowther put Macartney into Parliament for Cockermouth. Mountstuart was duly returned at Bossiney. In respect of the other Bossiney seat, the Duke of Portland paid Lord Mount Edgecumbe to direct the return of Henry Lawes Luttrell.

The peace of mind which by this time Bute may have acquired since his rupture with the King was completely shattered by the progress of Wilkes's campaign for election as knight of the shire for Middlesex. Every memory of issue no. 45 of the *North Briton* was disinterred. Bands of ruffians roamed the country lanes and the streets of North-West London. Bute and his wife were one night besieged in South Audley Street, and a brick thrown into Lady Bute's bedroom. The King's aunt, Princess Amelia, implored Lady Mary Coke to tell the Butes to keep themselves out of the way. Bute withdrew to the comparative safety of Luton Hoo, and by June reached a decision to leave England for a considerable period, as Lady Mary discovered when she went for dinner at the Mackenzies': 'He is going to Brouages in France to drink those waters for the recovery of his health, and perhaps he thinks the nation will be quieter when he has left it.'[30]

Bute's family troubles were not ended. Towards the end of 1768 his third son, Frederick, who had been sent up to Christ Church, Oxford, ran away to Paris. Unlike James, he had no prospects of an inheritance such as might lessen the anger of his outraged father. Frederick was obtained a writership in the East India Company and packed off to Calcutta.[31] Bute embarked upon his Continental tour accompanied by his favourite son, Charles, an Ensign in the 37th Foot. Adam's plans for Luton, involving the total demolition of the old house and building anew were to proceed in his absence.

By the end of the year Bute was in Italy, where the numerous British residents and visitors paid their court to two remarkable personalities, the Ministers in Florence and Naples, namely Sir Horace Mann and William Hamilton. Charles was not mentioned as being in Bute's company, and presumably had returned home. Mann, in a letter to Horace Walpole of 24 March 1769, gave a pathetic description: 'Lord Bute has resided for some time in Rome in the strictest incognito. He never received visits and returned cards under the name of Murray, nor ever wore his Garter.' Bute could not possibly feel settled under these conditions and in February 1769 moved to Naples. There he complained at the climate, though Hamilton was astonished at his alacrity in climbing Vesuvius.[32]

Bute was wise to be out of the country during the contests over the Middlesex election that took place in 1769. It was a complete accident, and in truth had nothing to do with Bute, that Luttrell, Mountstuart's colleague at Bossiney, should be the villain who lent himself to the Court as opponent to Wilkes. The seat at Bossiney for which Luttrell had been returned the preceding year was at the nomination of Mount Edgecumbe and not Bute, but these details are apt to become confused in the popular imagination.[33] Bute left Naples on 1 March and returned to Rome. Mann charitably offered him an apartment in his *palazzo* but Bute did not stay in Florence long. He was in Venice when on 15 April the House of Commons unseated Wilkes and declared Luttrell member for Middlesex in his place, the acme of Butism and unconstitutional influence.[34]

At the time of Chatham's return to health towards the end of 1769 Bute was still in Venice. Chatham at once entered into a triumvirate with Temple and Grenville, and made haste to establish contact with Rockingham. His condemnation of the ministry over Wilkes and the Middlesex election forced Grafton to resign that January. The King simply promoted Lord North from Chancellor of the Exchequer to First Lord of the Treasury, and the ministry underwent little change. Mackenzie, sent for by North, promised the general support of the Bute family.

The death of George Grenville on 13 November 1770, a month after his 58th birthday, must have stirred some old and odd memories with Bute. Their situations had become curiously reversed. Bute, once the King's apparently omnipotent favourite, who had ousted Pitt and Newcastle to become himself Prime Minister, was in hapless exile. Grenville, high in the popular esteem for his defence of the rights of the Middlesex constituency, had earlier that year secured the passage of his laudable Elections Act. Even young Edmund Burke, always a staunch

opponent of American taxation, shared the general admiration for
Grenville as a parliamentary statesman.

In April 1771 Bute made his preparations to leave Venice for the
journey home. That June North resolved to strengthen his ministry by
the appointment of Grafton as Lord Privy Seal, which *Junius* promptly
attributed to Bute's arrival.[35] Though North knew this to be nonsense,
he was not minded to be seen in any way as a Bute puppet. The death
of the Princess of Wales in February 1772 was sincerely mourned by
Bute, and the last ground for the suspicion which had haunted his
retirement was removed. Yet North showed an open dislike for the
Bute family. Initially he refused Mountstuart the Lord Lieutenancy
of Glamorgan, though towards the end of 1772 he had to give way:
'I kissed the King's hand without having the least notification of my
appointment which is usually given.'[36]

Shortly after his return, Bute purchased some land near Christchurch
in Hampshire. His property, known as Highcliffe, overlooked the sea
with the entrance to the Solent to the east and opposite a fine view of
the Needles of the Isle of Wight. Westward lay Christchurch harbour,
Hengistbury Head, and in the far distance the hills of Dorset. Bute
chose this idyllic spot to build himself a villa, which became his
favourite retreat. The climate was equable and the isolation afforded
a complete shelter from the hostile world which had driven him
abroad.[37]

At the general election of 1774 Mountstuart was again returned for
Bossiney and Mackenzie for Ross-shire. James, transferred from Ayr
burghs to become member for Bute-shire, still consorted with his old
enemies, drink and gambling, whilst he and his wife each went their
own way. Macartney succeeded James at Ayr burghs.[38] Wilkes was
inevitably returned for Middlesex and North wisely left him to take his
seat. North saw no difficulty in Bute continuing a Scots representative
peer. As the Prime Minister somewhat contemptuously observed: 'A
dowager First Lord of the Treasury has a claim to this distinction
and we do not now want a *coup d'état* to persuade the most ordinary
newspaper politician that Lord Bute is nothing more.'[39]

By this time the work on the new mansion at Luton had taken shape.
Bute's youngest son William, who had taken his M.A. and been elected
a Fellow of St John's College, Cambridge, was installed as Rector of St
Mary's. The house was on the model of a double 'T', running from
north to south, and between the cross of each 'T' ran the main edifice.
The west, or portico front, had an elevation of 244 feet. The east front
corresponding was without windows but decorated with alcoves, each
containing a statue. Within this main block were the state reception

rooms and the guest suites, each provided with accommodation for personal servants. The north 'T' was 150 feet long from west to east and 40 feet broad. The entire ground floor was taken up with the library, an apartment 20 feet high and containing 30,000 volumes. The south 'T', of identical dimensions, housed the private apartments.[40] Mrs Delany, in the company of the Duchess of Portland, visited Luton on 5 September 1774, and described the library: 'It is, in effect, three or five rooms, one very large and well proportioned in the middle, each divided off by pillars, in which recesses are chimneys: and a large square room at each end, which when the doors are open, make it appear one large room or gallery.'[41]

Lancelot 'Capability' Brown was employed to landscape the park, which was extended to 1,200 acres. As at Blenheim, he dammed up the small river to create a lake. This ambitious, indeed grandiose, memorial to the Bute family was illustrative of wealth rather than greatness. The Butes had no historic connection with Bedfordshire and the palace was absurdly large in relation to the Luton acreage.

Bute and his family gave North general support in respect of the American war. Since July 1774 his son-in-law Percy, Colonel 5th Foot, had been in Massachusetts with his regiment. North had assured Parliament that the subjugation of Boston would be merely a matter of four or five frigates. Percy chose the path of duty and once in America took the view that firmness was a necessity: 'If Great Britain relaxes in the least, adieu to the colonies.'[42]

General Thomas Gage, Governor of Massachusetts, had warned the home government that only an army of 20,000 men could subdue New England.[43] He acted on orders from London when the fruitless attempt was made to secure the powder and arms stored at Concord and Lexington in April 1775: had it not been for the coverage afforded by a brigade under Percy's command, the British troops might have been killed to a man. The costly storming of Bunker Hill, part of the Charlestown Heights commanding Boston, followed on 17 June. The day after, the 35th Foot, in which Bute's son, Charles, was a captain, disembarked. In his letter home of 24 July he described the confusion:

it is impossible to describe the horror that on every side presented itself – wounded and dead officers in every street; the town, which is larger than New York, almost uninhabited in appearance, bells tolling, wounded soldiers lying in their tents and crying for assistance to remove some men who had just expired.

This was the opening of a lively correspondence Charles maintained with his father during five years of service. Charles inevitably joined in the chorus of criticism against Gage, but sensibly appreciated the difficulties he was under in not being able to conduct the army as though they were in enemy territory. On the broad issue Charles took the popular stance: a speedy victory followed by a judicious policy of conciliation would wean the New England colonies back to their allegiance.

That indeed was the view in London, where, however, no serious preparations for war had yet been contemplated. Sir William Howe, appointed Commander-in-Chief of the army from Nova Scotia to Florida, asked for powerful reinforcements. The man expected to provide the directing energy demanded of the crisis was Lord George Germain, who that November was made a Secretary of State. He set himself to supply Howe with the army Gage had been denied, with the object of finishing the war in one campaign, to open in the spring of 1776. The great miscalculation was to suppose that loyalist sentiment could easily be rallied into effective action.

Bute was in the anxious situation of any father with a son on active service. Early in the new year he received Charles's letter dated 8 October 1775. He had taken part in a couple of rather futile skirmishes and the real point of his writing was to announce his purchase for £2,600 of the rank of major in 43rd Foot. When Charles again wrote on 14 December, Boston was totally invested: 'Every circumstance seems to promise a most Bloody Civil War, and I hope to God they will send some Generals worth the command of a British Army from home.'[44]

Bute continued with his works at Luton: the house was equipped with the finest furnishings; the best pictures that came available were purchased; the largest mirrors of which the glass industries of Britain or France were capable, with their heavy gilt frames, set off walls lined with white and green satin. Yet the family never became acclimatized and much preferred Highcliffe, to the annoyance of Luton. Bute spent his days alone with his books, cut off from mankind apart from his family. Isabella Elliot, whose husband Hugh was younger son to Bute's old friend Gilbert Elliot, dwelt on the sadness of Luton when she visited him in November 1775: 'Luton is the finest and most expensive palace I ever saw, pictures and every other refinement of taste that can be collected, but it shows plainly that these things are no way conducive to cheerfulness or happiness, as it is a kind of melancholy grandeur that is inexpressible.'[45]

Perhaps Bute in his solitude was consoled by the moving tribute of Robert and William Adam when they published their *Works*. Even then, public compliments to Bute were taken to require courage: 'We are happy in having the opportunity of expressing to the world that gratitude which we never cease to feel, for the protection and friendship with which we have always been honoured by his lordship.'[46]

Charles spent Christmas in Boston, without knowing that an evacuation had already been decided on. Germain saw New York as the centre of gravity. Already he had the concept of armies moving north from New York and south from Canada along the Hudson, to cut New England away from the middle colonies. For the time being New York was in the hands of the rebels, who seized the winter initiative with an invasion of Canada.

When Charles next sent word to his father on 29 January 1776, it was of the complete victory of Sir Guy Carleton, the Governor of Canada, over the attempt upon Quebec led by Benedict Arnold and Richard Montgomery, the latter losing his life. Though Arnold was severely wounded, a report quoted by Charles that he had been made prisoner was not accurate. Charles's letter of 28 April described the abandonment of Boston, which he obviously did not realize had a strategic purpose. On 3 March the triumphant rebels had opened up a regular barrage: 'The bombardment continued for five nights, and a nobler scene it was impossible to behold: sheets of fire seem'd to come from our Batteries; some of the shells cross'd one another in the air, and then bursting, look'd beautiful.'

Howe's supply situation did not allow him to proceed directly to an attack on New York. Instead he announced his intention to withdraw by sea to Halifax, Nova Scotia, promising not to fire Boston, provided his disembarkation was not interfered with. From Halifax Charles wrote to Bute on a happy note: 'I every day get more fond of my profession, and a better state of health than usual makes my friends say that promotion agrees with me.'[47]

At home Mountstuart was patriotically occupied with a bill to authorize the raising of a Scottish militia, presenting a motion in the Commons on 2 November 1775. By this time Frederick, who hated life in India, had returned home, much to Bute's annoyance. In January 1776 Bute put him into Parliament as member for Ayr burghs. North gave Mountstuart's bill his personal support without adoption as an administration measure, so that its defeat on 20 March by 112 votes to 93 was not altogether surprising. This was practically the end of Mountstuart's political career. The death of Edward Wortley on 29 April, a little short of his 63rd birthday, rid the family of an embarrassment and James became sole heir to the Wortley estates. On 20 May 1776 Mountstuart achieved his cherished ambition by being created Baron Cardiff: that father and son should both be of the House of Lords was unusual, though a good many instances have occurred. It was, however, a hat-trick in that Lady Bute also should be a peeress in her own right, as Baroness Mountstuart of Wortley. Charles, aged 23, and absent in North America, was elected member for Bossiney.[48]

Charles wrote home half an hour before sailing with Howe's army from Halifax on 10 June 1776. By the beginning of July they were off Sandy Hook, a peninsula six miles from New York. On 2 July a disembarkation was effected upon Staten Island, which Charles described:

> The next morning we were cantooned, in the Villages, and the inhabitants received us with the greatest joy, seeing well the difference between anarchy and a regular mild government; it is supposed we shall stay here, making frequent excursions into the plains.
>
> Our situation is by no means despicable; we are in the most beautiful Island that nature could form or art improve, we have everything we want, and six or seven deserters come in every day from Long Island or the Jersies who bring intelligence that the rebel army are very discontented, but there is no believing these poor deluded wretches.
>
> They likewise say that General Carleton's army is at Fort Edward, which is only 50 miles away from New York.

The Declaration of Independence of 4 July, historically a classic statement of the rights of freedom against tyranny, was looked upon by Charles and those with him merely as a tactical move to attract support for the rebellion.

By the beginning of August the heavy reinforcements promised by Germain had arrived. Howe had 25,000 men, including a strong contingent of Hessians without whom the subjection of America could never have been contemplated. But the year was already too late to think in terms of a junction with an army from Canada. George Washington had guessed New York to be Howe's objective, but the Royal Navy rapidly established control of the waterways. Howe disembarked on Long Island on 22 August and within a week captured Brooklyn, with 1,400 of the enemy killed and a like number made prisoner. Charles just escaped a severe wound: 'a slight scratch upon my hip with a muskit ball, which for three or four days was inconvenient but at present is quite well.'

Howe was criticized for allowing 15,000 American soldiers on Long Island to escape but Charles was relieved the thickly wooded country was not used for an inch-by-inch combat. In his letter of 26 September Charles described the landing on New York Island:

> A more glorious scene I never beheld; the thunder of the ships, the appearance of the enemy, the ardor of our troops, the whole army drawn up on Long Island ready to support us, surpassed everything of

magnificence. So well did the army do their business that the enemy
evacuated their lines, and we landed without opposition.

At the end of November Charles sent home an account of Howe's
victorious campaign, culminating in the capture of Fort Washington
with 3,000 prisoners, the outstanding British victory of the war. Lord
Cornwallis crossed into New Jersey, whilst Charles accompanied an
expedition commanded by Sir Henry Clinton, with Percy his second,
which took Rhode Island. Then on Christmas morning Washington
surprised and defeated the Hessians at Trenton, New Jersey, with most
discouraging consequences for loyalist hopes.[49]

A further year of campaigning would clearly be necessary. Charles
saw no prospect of an end, and not only for logistical reasons. He
thought Howe politically inept, making no effort to acquaint himself
with leading persons in American civilian life. The Congress Charles
considered the tool of a faction, whom the country gentlemen would
disdain to accept as their representatives. Charles looked to men of real
calibre from home, who might undermine the Congress by a reasoned
and independent approach to notabilities in each colony. For the
present, matters were by no means forwarded by the serious indisci-
pline in the British army: 'These poor unhappy wretches who had
remained in their habitations through necessity or loyalty were immediately judged by the soldiers to be rebels, neither clothing nor
property spared, but in the most inhuman and barbarous manner torn
from them.'[50]

In London Germain expected the year 1777 to turn in favour of
the mother country. General John Burgoyne was chosen to command
the army intended to move south from Canada up the Hudson to
New York. Then the fatal mistake was made of not instructing
Howe to devote his entire energies to meeting Burgoyne. Instead
Germain approved Howe's plan to launch a campaign against
Philadelphia.[51]

Charles had spent the winter at Newport and his letter to Bute of 29
March 1777 showed him discouraged. Percy had obtained leave to go
to England to attend to his private affairs. By July Charles was back in
New York after a singularly pointless campaign in which only small
losses were incurred but to little purpose. Charles believed that, instead
of an easy march through the Jerseys, Howe should move northwards to
support Burgoyne. As he put it in his letter of 10 July:[52]

> We should first dispossess the enemy of their forts on the North River, and
> assist Burgoyne either to reduce to obedience or crush the northern
> colonies, which, when effected, if the southern colonies do not then ask for

terms, you have the autumn, the finest season of the year, in which to deal with them.

In fact Burgoyne was supremely confident of battling his way through to New York without assistance from Howe. Washington was happy to keep Howe engaged in the Jersies and leave Burgoyne to the mercies of the New England militia.

In a few days Charles sailed with Howe's army to Chesapeake Bay, and from a naval transport sent his letter to Bute of 21 August. In a successful campaign Washington was defeated at Brandywine, which opened the Delaware to the Navy. Charles distinguished himself at the 'Brandy-wine', a bullet passing through the crown of his hat. On 26 September Philadelphia was taken, which Charles realized could not have real consequence because the Americans had no capital in the European meaning. The turning point was Burgoyne's surrender at Saratoga on 17 October.

Charles's bravery was noted at the subsidiary action at Red Bank, where Count von Donop, the Hessian commander, inadvisably attack-ed a strong enemy position. Donop was mortally wounded; Charles, in his letter home, referred to 'a pretty severe scratch on the cheek'. As his immediate commander General James Robertson made clear in his letter of commendation to Bute of 13 November, a bullet had passed so close to Charles's ear as temporarily to deprive him of hearing. Robertson gladly announced Charles's promotion to Lieutenant-Colonel the Cameronians, and asked his father to forbid the unnecessary ex-posure of his valuable life.[53]

Charles was given some well-earned leave but just missed the mar-riage on New Year's Day 1778 of his sister Caroline to John Dawson, member for Queen's county in the Irish Parliament, whose father was shortly to be created Viscount Carlow. Her sister Augusta was already married to a Captain Corbett, and had a son. Only Louisa was left and her heart was given to William Medows, who was serving as a soldier in North America. Though no exception could be taken on grounds of character or family, Bute would not hear of an engagement and con-demned Louisa to be his Cordelia and her mother's companion.[54]

The three months spent with Charles at Highcliffe were among the happiest of Bute's life. The villa, when complete, was rather of the Roman than the more generally understood version, and included a library 40 feet long. This Bute intended as a future home for Charles, and the family was delighted when he announced his engagement to Louisa, the younger daughter and co-heir of the late Lord Vere Bertie, third son of the 1st Duke of Ancaster. The marriage was solemnized on 19 April 1778: less than a month later Charles travelled the short distance to Portsmouth, where lay in readiness his ship *Lyoness*, part of a large reinforcement for America. Bute addressed to him a touching letter of farewell:[55]

> I can't let you go, my dearest Charles, without sending thee a tender line. May the Almighty who has so often preserved thee watch over thee and bring thee back in health and safety to the lovely partner of thy life, and to thy fond father, if it please Heaven to preserve thy life so long. I send thee the Zingri of Peckler we so much admired together, the most beautiful piece of antiquity. In looking at it thou wilt remember me and the days when we were first companions. My most affectionate love will attend my daughter-in-law,
>
> Thine,
BUTE.

Charles must have realized the entire character of the war to have altered, with the alliance between Louis XVI and the American Congress concluded that February. A French fleet commanded by Count d'Estaing had sailed from Toulon in April, and though the destination might be uncertain, America had to be the assumption. Whilst the British fleet was forced by contrary winds to anchor in Torbay, a cutter *Alert* was taken by a French man-of-war only four miles off-shore, and, yet more ominous, a rebel privateer captured a brig. Charles got Jenkinson, who at this time was a Lord of Admiralty, to reserve a berth in the packet conveying the mails to America and he arrived at Rhode Island on 8 July.

By this time Howe's successor, Sir Henry Clinton, had evacuated Philadelphia and settled his headquarters in New York. There Charles spent the next three months and established a close personal relationship with Clinton. He had no faith in the peace commissioners: the Earl of Carlisle, William Eden and Governor Johnstone failed signally to build any relationship of confidence with the Congress. As Charles put it in his letter of 16 September:[56]

> The Civil Commissioners look upon a War of ravage or destruction to be the only means of effecting success in this Country; I doubt whether they have, on this point, either power or understanding to advise; I fancy private resentments has drove them to adopt quite contrary opinions to those they came here with, not only from a greater or more extensive knowledge of the Country, but from a deep sense of the insults they have received, and a determination to revenge them.

The hope was to save the southern colonies, and find compensation for the loss of New England in the French West Indies. An expedition commanded by General James Grant, of 5,000 men, was to proceed to the defence of British possessions in the West Indies and the capture of

St Lucia. Charles would dearly have loved to have gone, despite the climate, and felt quite envious of Medows who was among those chosen.

In the event Charles was planning a return home on an important mission for Clinton. His letter to Bute of 7 October was written from Valentine Hill Camp. By this time news of the fall of Dominica had reached New York. Macartney was Governor of Grenada and Charles felt great anxiety for 'my dear sister Jane'. When Charles at the end of October 1778 sailed for England, Admiral John Byron, in command of the British fleet, was attempting to blockade d'Estaing in Boston.

Charles's purpose was to impress upon Germain the extreme urgency of the situation in America. The ministry appeared more concerned with the popular agitation in Ireland for legislative autonomy, but Charles was admitted to the Secretary of State early in the New Year of 1779. Germain did not accept that the French fleet presented a threat to Clinton for the moment. Such incredulity irritated Charles into making a little speech which from a mere Colonel to the Minister bordered on the impertinent. According to his letter to Clinton:

> I took the liberty of differing with his Lorship, and affirmed that no authentic intelligence could have been received, and, tho' I knew before that he neglected information that did not coincide with his wishes, yet I was astonished and hurt to find that upon such shallow grounds he should be lulled into a blind security which might prove fatal to our affairs.[57]

In fact Germain was more or less in the right. D'Estaing had slipped out of Boston on 4 November, the very day that Grant's expedition sailed for the West Indies. Grant reduced St Lucia, an action in which Medows acquitted himself well. D'Estaing eluded Byron and his destination was not New York but the West Indies, where Grant and Admiral Samuel Barrington gave him a sound thrashing.[58]

Bute and his wife must have been preoccupied with the appalling affair of Anne Countess Percy being divorced for adultery, which was finalized by Act of Parliament on 16 March 1779. For years stories had circulated that she and Percy were not well together. Only her childless condition, hard for a woman to endure, particularly of her station, can account for her instability. The co-respondent was William Bird, described as 'a young gentleman from the University of Cambridge'. The sad lady blundered into a marriage with Baron von Poellnitz, a chamberlain at the Prussian Court. Having briefly settled with him in New York, she eloped with yet another lover, Stephen Sayre. Percy married Julia, daughter of Peter Burrell MP, a happy union blessed with a family.[59]

Charles chose to ignore the advice of his uncle, Mackenzie, that he attend the House of Commons in respect of the American enquiry towards the end of April. He supported entirely the war in principle but disapproved of Germain's methods. Give comfort to the Rockinghams and Chathamites he would never do. Instead of troubling himself further with fruitless attempts to influence administration, Charles resolved on a return to the scene of action. He informed Germain and received a not unfriendly reply of 4 May: 'I am not so old but that I expect to see you in high command, and happy should I be if I could contribute in placing you in such situation that your merit entitles you to claim.'[60]

By July Charles was back at Clinton's headquarters at New York on his third tour. He was dismayed at news of the fall of Grenada on 3 July: Macartney and Lady Jane were taken prisoner, conveyed to France and subsequently exchanged. Clinton was in the deepest distress, convinced by a sense of failure that he was the object of detestation throughout his army. Charles dissuaded him from resigning and his letter to Bute of 24 August stressed Germain's folly in not reinforcing Clinton to the utmost in view of Washington's dire straits. On 2 November 1779, his regiment due home for a refit, Charles sailed from Portsmouth, James River, never to see America again.

Having arrived home, Charles desired nothing more than a military employment which, however, the authorities were not inclined to allow. Bute thought him far too sensitive:[61]

> I protest in this situation of things, I don't comprehend your meaning, when you ask my advice. Tho' indeed one thing calls for advice, seriously, my dear Charles, and that is that you should cease to think your honour every minute concerned because this or that desire is not complied with; for this will not only affect your looks, words, and actions, subversive of the capital point you ought to have in mind, which is that of gaining another step in Rank before the war ends.

Bute concluded by telling his son to go to Lord Amherst but Charles went empty away.

By this time Mountstuart, having failed to achieve much in the House of Lords, decided diplomacy to be his *métier*. He secured the important post of Minister at Turin and on 4 August 1779 was sworn of the Privy Council.[62] He and Charles happened to be in London during the Gordon Riots of June 1780, when luckily Bute and his wife were safely at Luton. Bute expressed his deep concern for the safety of the monarchy, which he erroneously supposed to have been the target of the riots.[63]

At the general election of 1780 Bute decided to retire as a Scots representative peer, solely on the ground of age. As Bute-shire was not represented in this Parliament – it being the turn of Caithness – James took a seat at Plympton Earle in Devon, in the Mount Edgecumbe interest. Charles continued to represent Bossiney. Frederick was by this time in serious financial trouble, and as his presence in London was deemed inadvisable, no seat was provided.[64] William Pitt the younger, who failed to secure election for Cambridge University, was put into Parliament by Lowther for Appleby.

The unhappy Clinton missed Charles and wrote to him of his taking Charlestown, Virginia, on 5 May 1780, part of a long correspondence. The campaigns in the south were not unsuccessful, until a local French naval superiority caused the capitulation of Yorktown in October 1781. The King was undismayed but the will of the ministry and the nation to fight on was broken. That February Germain was obliged to throw in his hand and retire to the House of Lords.

After North's resignation of 27 March 1782 the King had to accept Rockingham as Prime Minister of a coalition with the followers of Chatham. Shelburne and Charles James Fox became Secretaries of State. Rockingham can fairly be described as the first Prime Minister to live to fight another day. The King would gladly have continued the war, reckoning on the reduction of France to bankruptcy, but had to accept that his entire Cabinet was pledged to an accommodation with the 13 colonies, and public opinion demanded a general peace. The principal achievements of the second Rockingham administration were the recognition of the legislative independence of the Irish Parliament and Burke's Economical Reform Act. Mountstuart lost his auditorship of the imprest but received a pension of £7,000 per annum.

The death of Rockingham in July 1782 resulted in Bute's quondam pupil, Shelburne, becoming Prime Minister. Fox, who disagreed with Shelburne over the approach to negotiating with North America, resigned and took Rockingham's following with him. That made room for William Pitt as Chancellor of the Exchequer. Shelburne's administration was oddly similar to Bute's, in that the main business was the conclusion of a war. This analogy may not be pressed further: Bute had presided over a military and naval situation so overwhelmingly victorious that he felt bound to modify the consequences; Shelburne had to save as much as possible of the old British Empire under the impact of disaster. Shelburne recognized American independence on generous terms in respect of the boundary with Canada, because he intended a union of trade to restore cordiality between the new nation and the old. The peace was disappointing to Versailles and Madrid. The only West Indian island France gained as a result of the war was Tobago. Though

Minorca was reunited with the Kingdom of Spain, and Florida to her empire, the prize of Gibraltar remained British.

When, in November 1782, Mountstuart left Turin 'on leave', gossip rumoured his departure to be occasioned by 'some fracas of gallantry', and, according to Mann's letter to Horace Walpole of 30 November, this was not his first adventure.[65] The Mountstuarts arrived in London on 6 January. Whatever the truth of the stories, Shelburne appointed Mountstuart to be the first Ambassador in Madrid once the peace was completed.

Shelburne, never personally popular, was far from enjoying the parliamentary position commanded by Bute in December 1762. He and Pitt were keen to adopt ideas of free trade, administrative and parliamentary reform which must have sounded strange to Bute's ear, as indeed they did to the King and to many in Parliament. In the middle of February 1783 Fox and North entered into a coalition to destroy Shelburne when the peace preliminaries were debated. After being defeated in the House of Commons by 224 votes to 208 and 207 votes to 190, Shelburne resigned on 24 February. Despite the promise of the Madrid embassy for Mountstuart, James voted with the coalition.

Bute's disgust at the conduct of Fox and North knew no bounds, and his letter the following day to Charles, who was in Italy, ended with a touching reference to the King:[66]

> Lord Shelburne has resigned and a new set kissed hands, as you will see in the Papers – the Coalition, as it is called. How long it will last, or what excursions they will pursue, I know as little as I do of China.
>
> It would take days to tell you the unheard of scenes which have passed these three weeks. My heart bleeds for my Dearest – but none of this is proper for a letter.

Bute was mistaken in supposing the King about to give office to Fox and North. Sooner than yield, the King left the country without a government for six weeks. Finally, on 2 April, the Duke of Portland was appointed to the Treasury, with Fox and North Secretaries of State.

Mountstuart and James departed completely from their father's lead in their support for the Coalition. Though Mountstuart's embassy was confirmed, he never proceeded to Madrid and was indeed suspected of aiming for the glittering prize of Ambassador to Paris. On 18 December the ministers were dismissed and the younger Pitt appointed Prime Minister. No more was to be heard about Mountstuart being an ambassador.

The dissolution of Parliament on 25 March heralded that decisive general election which confirmed Pitt in power. No longer in need of a patron, he secured his election for Cambridge University: Lowther had his reward in being created Earl of Lonsdale on 24 May. Pitt's triumph entailed the almost total destruction of North's parliamentary follow-ing, a comment upon the effectiveness of the regal power of which Bute may well have approved. Shelburne, whom Pitt did not include in his Cabinet, passed into obscurity, when in December 1784 he was fobbed off with an empty promotion as Marquess of Lansdowne. The town house Bute had started became known as Lansdowne House, which in the next century shone as a centre of the Liberal Party.

Bute was becoming a patriarchal figure: his three married boys had between them thirteen sons and five daughters. Caroline, whose husband Carlow had become Earl of Portalington, was mother to nine. Though the family naturally continued to represent the parliamentary seats in which they possessed an interest, their continued loyality to Fox perhaps indicated a failure to acknowledge that Pitt was there to stay. Charles was a mere lieutenant-colonel on half-pay and gave his time to Continental travel.

On 7 April 1786 Sir Joshua Reynolds recorded the payment of 150 guineas for his full-length portrait of Lady Bute, on which he had been working since 1777. She almost certainly allowed him only two sittings each year, shortly before Christmas, which may indicate her visits to London were infrequent. In her sixties, Lady Bute was depicted walk-ing outside, accompanied by her snappy spaniel and carrying an umbrella. A woman of firm features with a strong jaw, she is suit-ably attired for a stroll, her pink silk dress covered with a black hooded cloak, and hands protected by half-mittens. No doubt Lady Bute dictated this unusual composition and the picture was hung at Luton.[67]

Charles, realizing that if he desired employment he must curry favour, abandoned opposition to support the ministry during the winter parliamentary session of 1786–7. But his applications for some diplomatic post were not met. In 1788 his vote for Pitt over the Regency may have helped promote a reconciliation between the Butes and the royal family. After the King's recovery, they were invited to a ball at Windsor in the spring of 1789. Bute, despite having been unwell, found himself able to attend, with Lady Bute, Mountstuart and his eldest son John, Caroline Macartney and Louisa. As Louisa remarked in her letter to Lady Portalington of 30 April: 'The King looked better than I had expected to see him – rather thin and older than he was, but on the whole very well.'

Louisa was not elevated at her next encounter with a member of the royal family that May, at the Duchess of Ancaster's masque: 'The Prince of Wales laid hold of me two or three times, and had a vast mind to be better acquainted, taking me, I believe, for a lady of a certain sort, so I was obliged to steal off quietly and hold my tongue.'[68]

Bute spent his declining years at Highcliffe. The outbreak of the French Revolution heralded the end of monarchy as he had known and revered the institution. In November 1790 Bute slipped while out walking and the sprained ankle did not clear up. He wrote to Charles on 6 April 1791: 'I grow stronger in the use of my leg, and can creep on crutches from room to room, tho' I fear it will be a long time before I have the full use of it.'

Early in 1792, the end was plainly approaching. Lady Bute, Lady Macartney and Louisa were with Bute when he died on 11 March at his house in South Audley Street. He was buried at Rothesay on the Isle of Bute:[69]

> Back to Scotland, whence he came, back to the lonely lochs and wooded hill-sides of the Western Isles, to lie for ever in the shadow of Rothesay's ruined walls among wiser generations of his forefathers, Lord of their littler World, and untouched by the bitterness of public life.
>
> There they lie, not heeding the mournful note of the pipes as another of the Clan comes for burial beside them. Comes he with glory or humiliation matters not to them; success or failure has no more substance than the mist that rolls in from the Atlantic, and now blots out, now reveals, the mountain summits.

Mountstuart succeeded as 4th Earl of Bute, and the Cardiff inheritance became united with the ancestral Isle of Bute, whilst his English seat was Luton Hoo. That October his eldest son, newly become Mountstuart, married a great heiress, Lady Penelope Elizabeth Crichton, only child of the 6th Earl of Dumfries. Three generations of the Bute family had won matrimonial fortunes. The future was assured by the birth of a son to the young couple, the fourth John, on 12 October 1792. She who was the Dowager Countess of Bute became a great-grandmother. Then followed the tragedy of Mountstuart's death, in consequence of a fall from his horse, on 22 January 1794. His wife did not long survive the blow.

When old Lady Bute died on 6 November 1794, James came into the Wortley estates in West Yorkshire and the parliamentary interest at Bossiney. Middle age and the loss of a favourite daughter had softened his disposition, and he settled down a model landlord. Frederick, who since 1783 had quite disappeared, was rumoured to be the inmate of some Continental monastery and even to have become the cashier. Charles, less fortunate than his eldest brothers, could not afford to maintain Highcliffe, which he sold and settled at Bure Homage, a small property nearby.

The outbreak of the French wars in January 1793 led to a broadening of the Pitt ministry in the following year. After a further brief spell as Ambassador to Madrid in 1795–6, the 4th Earl of Bute achieved a distinction which suited him better: on 21 March 1796 he was raised in the peerage as Marquess of Bute, with secondary titles Earl of Windsor and Viscount Mountjoy in compliment to his wife. That year Frederick came back not only to life but also as Member of Parliament for Buteshire. The war restored Charles to military employment. He commanded at the capture of Corsica and then Minorca, whilst his defence of Sicily from invasion was an important contribution to the British war in the Mediterranean, which culminated in Nelson's triumph at Aboukir Bay in 1798. Lieutenant-General Sir Charles Stuart, K.B. died on 25 March 1801.

When the Marquess of Bute died in 1814 his orphaned grandson succeeded. The 2nd Marquess was famous for the development of Cardiff as a major seaport, upon which he reputedly spent £400,000. This enterprise, and a serious fire at Luton Hoo, may have led to the sale of almost the entire Luton estate in 1844: of that forlorn extravagance only the gatehouse bearing the Stuart arms survives. Members of the family achieved distinction in public life. James's son, also James, continued a tradition as Member of Parliament for Bossiney until, in 1826, he joined the peerage as Lord Wharncliffe, and led the Tory 'waverers' in the direction of acquiescence over the Great Reform Bill. Charles's son, named after him, was Ambassador in Paris, became Lord Stuart de Rothesay, and bought back Highcliffe, where his Gothic castle replaced the villa. Lord Dudley Stuart devoted his life in Parliament and abroad to the cause of Polish freedom. When the 3rd Marquess of Bute, fourth in descent from the Prime Minister Earl, died in 1900 his estates of 116,000 acres were valued at over £5 million, supported by a seven-figure personalty. The lasting achievement of George III's favourite was not a political system but a British landowning dynasty.

Bute's contemporaries dilated upon his folly in allowing a young King to cast him in the role of hero and Prime Minister. There is no reason to suppose he suffered remorse over those brilliant two-and-a-half years which followed the accession of George III. He could congratulate himself, as indeed did others, as the statesman who, despite Pitt and the Old Whigs, achieved a peace founded upon victory tempered with good sense. Bute had done his best to protect his young King from the politicians: the Old Whigs no longer held the Crown to ransom, and because his own intentions had always been high-minded, he doubtless attributed the breach of 1766 to a misunderstanding.

Bute's death left four former Prime Ministers yet living, North,

272 Peter D. Brown

Grafton, Portland and Lansdowne. North, stricken with blindness, succeeded his father as 2nd Earl of Guilford and died in August 1792, five months after Bute. Grafton, who survived 41 years after his resignation in 1770, found a congenial recreation as Chancellor of Cambridge University. Portland, as leader of the Old Whigs, remained a political figure of importance and, a true successor to Rockingham, would one day have a second innings. Lansdowne, a lonely and to some a sinister person, opposed the war against revolutionary France, and, as the friend of young Jeremy Bentham, was a founder of philosophic radicalism: he lived until 1805. The generalization must be that prime ministers of a politically ineffective longevity failed in their day to grasp the opportunity. The reasons may be circumstantial as well as personal: Henry Addington was unavoidably overshadowed by Pitt; William Wyndham Grenville could not have surmounted the hurdle of Catholic relief where Pitt had failed. The Earl of Rosebery, who resigned in 1895 over a technical defeat in the House of Commons, was happier as a historian during his concluding 32 years. None compare with the eclipsed grandeur of Lloyd George, the victor of the First World War and arbiter of Versailles, who after his fall from power in October 1922 remained a private Member of Parliament until 1945. The Lloyd George earldom was one of Winston Churchill's more remarkable acts of state before he lost the general election to Labour.

NOTES

1. R. Sedgwick (ed.), *Letters from George III to Lord Bute 1756–1766* (1939), no. 298.

2. Sir Lewis Namier and John Brooke, *The House of Commons 1754–1790* (1964), III, 662.

3. *ibid.*, I, 223–4.

4. Arthur T. Bolton, *The Architecture of Robert and James Adam (1756–1794)* (1922), II, 1–17.

5. Victoria County History, *Bedfordshire*, II, 349–55.

6. Namier and Brooke, *op. cit.*, III, 56.

7. Philip Lawson, *George Grenville* (1984), chs. 5–6.

8. Sedgwick, *op. cit.*, nos. 299–330.

9. W.J. Smith (ed.), *The Grenville Papers*, (1852), II, 83–8, 93.

10. The Hon. George F.S. Elliot, *The Border Elliots and the Family of Minto* (1897), 376–81.

11. Smith, *op. cit.*, II, 101–7.

12. *Ibid.*, II, 209–10.

13. *Ibid*, II, 214–18, 230, 483–4, 493–501.

14. Sedgwick, *op. cit.*, nos. 333–4.

15. Smith, *op. cit.*, II, 504.

16. G.E. Cokayne (ed) *The Complete Peerage* (1910–59), IX, 745–6.

17. Bolton, *op. cit.*, I, 68.

18. Sedgwick, *op. cit.*, no. 336.

19. Smith, *op. cit.*, III, 127–62, 185–90.

20. Sedgwick, *op. cit.*, no. 337.

21. See Paul Langford, *The Rockingham Administration* (1973), for a general account.

22. Bolton, *op. cit.*, II, 1–17.

23. Sedgwick, *op. cit.*, nos. 337–9.

24. *Ibid.*, Appendix I.

25. Namier and Brooke, *op. cit.*, II, 502.

26. Cokayne, *Complete Peerage*, II, 443.

27. The Hon. Mrs. E. Stuart Wortley,

CBE (ed.), *A Prime Minister and His Son* (1925), 228–9.

28. Namier and Brooke, *op. cit.*, III, 501.
29. Peter Roebuck, *Macartney of Lissanoure* (1983).
30. Wortley, *op. cit.*, 231–3.
31. Namier and Brooke, *op. cit.*, III, 500.
32. W.S. Lewis (ed.), *The Correspondence of Horace Walpole*, (New Haven, CT, 1937–83), XXIII, 91.
33. Namier and Brooke, *op. cit.*, III, 65–6.
34. Lewis, *op. cit.*, XXIII, 96.
35. John Cannon (ed.), *The Letters of Junius* (1978), 252.
36. Namier and Brooke, *op. cit.*, iii. 502.
37. Wortley, *op. cit.*, 5–6.
38. Namier and Brooke, *op. cit.*, III, 500–2.
39. R. Hist, MSS. Comm. 5th Rep., Appendix 209; *DNB*, LV, 960.
40. Bolton, *op. cit.*, 70.
41. Lady Llanover (ed.), *The Autobiography of Mrs Delany* (1862), IV, 542.
42. Namier and Brooke, *op. cit.*, II, 270.
43. Piers Mackesy, *The War for America 1775–83* (1964), 54–60.
44. Wortley, *op. cit.*, 73–4.
45. The Countess of Minto, *A Memoir of the Right Hon. Hugh Elliot* (1868), 84.
46. *The Works of Robert and James Adam* (1773).
47. Wortley, *op. cit.*, 75–6.
48. Namier and Brooke, *op. cit.*, I, 223–4; III, 498, 503, 662.
49. Wortley, *op. cit.*, 80–90.
50. *Ibid.*, 99.
51. Mackesy, *op. cit.*, 112–18.
52. Wortley, *op. cit.*, 110–14; Mackesy, *op. cit.*, 123.
53. Wortley, *op. cit.*, 116–17.
54. Cokayne, *Complete Peerage*, X, 579; Wortley, *op. cit.*, 127.
55. Wortley, *op. cit.*, 123.
56. *Ibid.*, 130–6; Namier and Brooke, *op. cit.*, III, 498.
57. Wortley, *op. cit.*, 146.
58. Mackesy, *op. cit.*, 229–31.
59. Cokayne, *Complete Peerage*, IX, 745–6.
60. Wortley, *op. cit.*, 147–8.
61. *Ibid.*, 180; Namier and Brooke, *op. cit.*, III, 499.
62. Namier and Brooke, *op. cit.*, III, 502; G.E.C. Complete Peerage, II, 443–4.
63. Wortley, *op. cit.*, 182–9.
64. Namier and Brooke, *op. cit.*, III, 79, 498–506.
65. Lewis, *op. cit.*, XXV, 336, 346.
66. Wortley, *op. cit.*, 198.
67. Nicholas Penny (ed.), *Reynolds* (1986), 145, 292.
68. Wortley, *op. cit.*, 218–20.
69. *Ibid.*, 210.

Index